This work: "United Nations Peace Operations in a Changing Global Order", was originally published by Springer Nature and is being sold pursuant to a Creative Commons license permitting commercial use. All rights not granted by the work's license are retained by the author or authors.

AF703337

Cover Image Credit/Copyright Attribution: IIIerlok_Xolms/Shutterstock

Cedric de Coning · Mateja Peter
Editors

United Nations Peace Operations in a Changing Global Order

Editors
Cedric de Coning
Norwegian Institute of International Affairs
Oslo, Norway

Mateja Peter
School of International Relations
University of St Andrews
St Andrews, Fife, UK

https://doi.org/10.1007/978-3-319-99106-1

© The Editor(s) (if applicable) and The Author(s) 2019. This book is an open access publication.
Open Access This book is licensed under the terms of the Creative Commons Attribution 4.0 International License (http://creativecommons.org/licenses/by/4.0/), which permits use, sharing, adaptation, distribution and reproduction in any medium or format, as long as you give appropriate credit to the original author(s) and the source, provide a link to the Creative Commons license and indicate if changes were made.
The images or other third party material in this book are included in the book's Creative Commons license, unless indicated otherwise in a credit line to the material. If material is not included in the book's Creative Commons license and your intended use is not permitted by statutory regulation or exceeds the permitted use, you will need to obtain permission directly from the copyright holder.
The use of general descriptive names, registered names, trademarks, service marks, etc. in this publication does not imply, even in the absence of a specific statement, that such names are exempt from the relevant protective laws and regulations and therefore free for general use.
The publisher, the authors and the editors are safe to assume that the advice and information in this book are believed to be true and accurate at the date of publication. Neither the publisher nor the authors or the editors give a warranty, express or implied, with respect to the material contained herein or for any errors or omissions that may have been made. The publisher remains neutral with regard to jurisdictional claims in published maps and institutional affiliations.

Foreword

It is amazing now to recall that when Secretary-General Ban Ki-moon announced in June 2014 that he intended to commission a review of peace operations, it came as a surprise—indeed, so far as the Secretariat's Departments of Peacekeeping Operations and Political Affairs were concerned, as an unwelcome shock. In retrospect, as this book shows, it is clear that the radical changes in context that had taken place in the fourteen years since the Brahimi report made a further review if anything overdue.

Yet the timing of the review by the High-Level Independent Panel on Peace Operations (HIPPO) posed a problem. (When its Chairperson, José Ramos-Horta, said that he did not want our report to follow the Brahimi report in being named after him, he did not envisage that it would forever be dubbed HIPPO.) By the time the report was published, the end of Ban's term would be fast approaching; while some changes could be hoped for, major reform would inevitably have to await the leadership of the next Secretary-General and new department heads. Yet a new Secretary-General might not want to be associated with a predecessor's initiative, and the initial impact of a review on member states is not easily sustained.

Nearly four years on, however, the analysis and recommendations of the HIPPO report have continued to be valued as the framework for developments and debate regarding UN peace operations. Its recommendations having been largely accepted by Ban, modest reforms were set in motion in 2015–2016 before his term came to an end. Member state reactions to the report were generally positive, inevitably with some cherry-picking; and its analysis narrowed—while it did not resolve—the tension between traditional peacekeeping espoused by many troop-contributing countries and the trend towards more robust mandates adopted by the Security Council. The HIPPO's thinking, along with that of the other two major reviews published in 2015—regarding peacebuilding architecture, and women, peace and security—featured prominently in the public exchanges between member states and candidates to be the next Secretary-General. The early initiatives of Secretary-General António Guterres manifested his intention to improve strategic analysis and planning by the Secretariat, and to restructure its peace and security departments—described by the HIPPO as "hampering the effective assessment, design and conduct of peace operations"—as well as to further strengthen measures to address sexual exploitation and abuse, which have so damaged the reputation of UN peacekeeping.

The HIPPO's insistence on the primacy of politics—that "lasting peace is achieved not through military and technical engagements, but through political solutions", and therefore "politics must drive the design and implementation of peace operations"—is now widely emphasised, including in the Security Council itself. In this, the HIPPO was giving necessary reinforcement to the Brahimi report's critique of the strategic weaknesses of the Secretariat and the Security Council. But it is not always noted that in another respect, the HIPPO report went in the opposite direction from the Brahimi report: while the latter gave strong endorsement to the model of the large multidimensional peacekeeping operation with extensive peacebuilding functions, HIPPO's keywords are prioritisation and sequencing, which together with its emphasis on conflict prevention may point to smaller missions.

When Ban decided to launch the review, the most recent new missions were MINUSMA in Mali (April 2013) and MINUSCA in the Central African Republic (April 2014)—and Mali in particular had displayed the failures of UN planning, mandating and deployment at their most acute, for which peacekeepers have paid with their lives. Worsening conflicts in South Sudan and the Democratic Republic of Congo have shown how difficult it is to adapt the established configuration of large peace operations to changed circumstances, as the Secretariat and the Security Council are now trying to do more systematically through a series of strategic reviews. The HIPPO's emphasis on context-specific mission design, avoiding templates and its recommendation for a two-stage mandating process at the outset of a mission, have been widely supported in principle; but the ability to plan better in the future remains untested, as no new peacekeeping operation has been mandated since 2014.

The one new peace operation, launched in the positive context of a peace agreement at the request of both parties, has been the special political mission in Colombia, the design of which was most strongly influenced by its predecessor in Nepal. The HIPPO urged the abandonment of a binary distinction between peacekeeping operations and special political missions—it has become a cliché to note that peacekeeping operations often now have "no peace to keep", and (as I once entitled an article) "all missions are political". We advocated thinking instead in terms of a flexible spectrum of peace operations, the logic of which was accepted by Ban and is reflected in Guterres' proposals for a restructured Department of Peace Operations. But resistance to this terminological and conceptual shift remains strong in the Security Council and the Special Committee on Peacekeeping Operations; and the permanent members of the Council cling to the irrational funding of large special political missions from the UN's regular budget, rather than moving to a single assessment for all UN peace operations, open too to the funding of peace operations of regional organisations authorised by the Security Council.

The HIPPO's strong emphasis on partnerships with regional organisations was an endorsement of a trend already under way, and has found overwhelming acceptance—except when it comes to funding arrangements. It is now enshrined in the Joint United Nations-African Union Framework for Enhancing Partnership in Peace and Security, but the warm collaboration at the top of the organisations has yet to be consistently reflected in country contexts. It is at the country level, too, that the rhetorical embrace of the call for a people-centred approach in peace operations must be implemented and assessed.

The first year of new leadership in the Secretariat and a new administration in Washington saw a welcome thrust for strategic reviews of individual operations—but a completely non-strategic approach to the peacekeeping budget. The deep difficulties of the UN's largest missions, in Mali, the Democratic Republic of the Congo, the Central African Republic and South Sudan, compelled further introspection. Thus, in early 2018, the Department of Peace Operations drew up an action plan on improving the security of peacekeepers, and Secretary-General

Guterres announced a new initiative he dubbed "Action for Peacekeeping". His call for streamlined mandates, political solutions, partnership with regional organisations, improved training and preparedness of peacekeepers, alignment of human and financial resources with mandates, and member state influence to sustain the consent of host countries, should see further momentum for implementation of key HIPPO recommendations.

The Secretary-General's ambition to bring together all partners and stakeholders to develop a new set of mutually agreed principles and commitments requires recognition of trends well analysed in these chapters, both as regards conflict challenges and the geopolitics of multilateralism. The rise of China as an increasingly important peacekeeping actor and funder, and (in the words of the editors), "the rebalancing of relations between states of the global North and the global South", mean that the latter will not meekly accept decisions dominated by the former. In the Security Council, what Guterres has called the return of the Cold War is making consensus on issues of intervention and sovereignty harder to find. Yet if there is one common interest which cuts across these divides, it is surely how to be effective in a world of violent extremism and fundamentalist non-state actors.

The process of consultation carried out in 2014–2015 by the HIPPO was notable for the way in which it brought closer together peace operation practitioners and researchers, including the authors in this volume, and this valuable interaction has continued through subsequent debate and implementation. It is a landmark feature of this book, which is thus a major contribution to continuing efforts to adapt the UN's peace operations to a changing and increasingly challenging context.

London, UK Ian Martin

Acknowledgements

This edited volume has been long in the making and we have incurred many debts. The conversations with friends and colleagues in both academia and policy that have shaped its contours are too many to acknowledge individually. We nonetheless want to single out a few with important contributions. The idea for this project developed while we were providing research support to the High-Level Independent Panel on Peace Operations in 2015. We want to thank the Norwegian Ministry of Foreign Affairs for financially supporting us in this endeavour. The project would not have been possible without this early backing. We also want to thank José Ramos-Horta, the chair, and all the Panel members for generously involving us in their deliberations and regional consultations. A special recognition needs to be extended to Bela Kapur and the rest of the Panel Secretariat. They made sure our work with the Panel was not only productive, but also enjoyable. We have also benefited greatly from our continued conversations with the Friends of the HIPPO, a network of think tanks interested in UN peace operations. Its chair, Ian Martin, has been an invaluable resource in our research. Our colleagues at the Norwegian Institute of International Affairs (NUPI), in particular Kari Osland and the rest of the Peace, Conflict and Development research group, have supported us from the beginning. As we were finalising the volume, Mateja also greatly benefited from the research leave provided by the School of International Relations at University of St. Andrews. We also want to recognise Bård Drange, our editorial assistant, who helped us with copy-editing and other thankless editorial tasks. Sarah Roughley and her team at Palgrave Macmillan were more than helpful in ushering the project to the completion. Lastly, and most importantly, we want to thank the contributors to this volume. You are an infinitely patient group of people and we learned from each and every one of you. Thank you for being a part of this volume!

Cedric de Coning
Mateja Peter

Contents

Notes on Contributors

Adriana Erthal Abdenur is Fellow at Instituto Igarapé, a think and do tank based in Rio de Janeiro. Her research focuses on the role of rising powers, especially the BRICS countries, in international security and development cooperation. At Igarapé, she currently leads the Innovation in Conflict Prevention (ICP) initiative, which seeks to identify and analyse promising practices and approaches in conflict mediation, peacekeeping and peacebuilding in three regions of Africa. She co-edited, with Thomas G. Weiss, the volume *Emerging Powers and the UN* (Routledge, 2015) and is the co-author of the book *India China: Reimagining Borders* (University of Michigan, 2016). Recent peer-reviewed publications include articles in *Global Governance, Cambridge Review of International Affairs, Journal of Peacebuilding and Development, Africa Review* and *Revista Brasileira de Política Internacional.* Abdenur has also worked as a consultant for numerous international organisations, including the World Bank and the Inter-American Development Bank, and for several divisions of the UN, including the Department of Political Affairs (DPA) and the UN Office for South-South Cooperation (UNOSSC). She has a Ph.D. from Princeton and a B.A. from Harvard and is a National Productivity Scholar through the Brazilian National Council for Research (CNPq). She lives in Rio de Janeiro with her two children.

Jonathan C. Agensky is Assistant Professor of Political Science at Ohio University. He earned his doctorate at the University of Cambridge and specialises in the study of religion and international relations, with a focus on humanitarianism, global governance and postcolonial Africa. He works largely within the framework of interpretive IR, drawing on international historical sociology, postcolonial and African studies, and social and political theory. Agensky has been published in journals like the *European Journal of International Relations*, *Global Society* and *Globalizations* and is currently working on a research manuscript examining evangelical humanitarianism in South Sudan.

Mats Berdal is Professor of Security and Development in the Department of War Studies and Director of the Conflict, Security and Development Research Group (CSDRG) at King's College London. Between 2000 and 2003 he was Director of Studies at the International Institute for Strategic Studies (IISS). From 2015 to 2016, Berdal served on the Norwegian Commission of Inquiry on Afghanistan set up to evaluate Norway's military, humanitarian and civilian involvement in Afghanistan between 2001 and 2014. His publications include: *Realism as an Unsentimental Intellectual Temper: Lawrence Freedman and the New Interventionism* (in: Benedict Wilkinson and James Gow (eds.) *The Art of Creating Power—Freedman on Strategy*, Hurst & Co, 2017), *The State of UN Peacekeeping—Lessons from Congo* (Journal of Strategic Studies 39, 2016), *UN Peacekeeping and the Responsibility to Protect* (in William Maley and Ramesh Thakur (eds.) *Theorising the Responsibility to Protect*, CUP, 2015), *Building Peace After War* (Routledge, 2009), *United Nations Interventionism, 1991–2004* (co-edited with Spyros Economides, CUP, 2007), *The UN Security Council and Peacekeeping* (in Vaughan Lowe et al. (eds.) The Security Council and War, OUP, 2008), *Greed and Grievance: Economic Agendas in Civil Wars* (co-edited with David Malone, Lynne Rienner, 2000), *Disarmament and Demobilisation after Civil Wars* (OUP/IISS, 1996).

Arthur Boutellis is Non-resident Senior Adviser at the International Peace Institute (IPI), where he was Director of the Brian Urquhart Center for Peace Operations, responsible for developing and managing IPI's programs and research agenda in the area of peace and security from September 2015 to November 2017. In addition to IPI, Boutellis has worked with the UN missions in Burundi (BINUB), Chad and the Central African Republic (MINURCAT), Haiti (MINUSTAH) and Mali (MINUSMA) where he supported the 2014–2015 Mali peace negotiations as part of the UN Mediation Team. His prior work with humanitarian NGOs and think tanks focused on the Middle East and Africa.

He has published widely, regularly speaks at conferences and in the media, and teaches a graduate-level seminar at Columbia University. He holds a master's degree in public affairs from the Woodrow Wilson School at Princeton University and is a graduate of the Institut d'Etudes Politiques.

Adam Day is Senior Policy Adviser in the Centre for Policy Research at the United Nations University. Previously, he served for a decade in the UN, focused on peace operations, conflict prevention, mediation and protection of civilians. He served as Senior Political Adviser to MONUSCO (DRC), in the UN Special Coordinator's Office for Lebanon, in the front offices of both UNMIS (Khartoum) and UNAMID (Darfur), and was a political officer in the Department of Political Affairs and the Department of Peacekeeping Operations in New York. Prior to the UN, Day worked in Human Rights Watch's Justice Program; for the Open Society Justice Initiative in Cambodia; and supported the International Criminal Tribunal for the former Yugoslavia. An attorney and former member of the New York Bar Association, Day was an international litigator in New York, where he also worked pro bono for the Center for Constitutional Rights on behalf of Guantanamo detainees in their suits against former US officials for torture. He holds a Juris Doctorate from UC Berkeley School of Law, a Masters in Law and Diplomacy from the Fletcher School of Law and Diplomacy and a Masters in Comparative Literature from Brown University. He has several publications in the areas of international criminal law, head of state immunity for international crimes and peacekeeping. He is married and has two children.

Cedric de Coning is Senior Research Fellow with the Peace, Conflict and Development Research Group at the Norwegian Institute of International Affairs (NUPI) and a Senior Advisor for the African Centre for the Constructive Resolution of Disputes (ACCORD). De Coning served as an advisor to the High Representative of the African Union Peace Fund (2016), and as an advisor to the head of the Peace Support Operations Division of the African Union Commission (2010–2015). He has served on African Union panels to review the African Standby Force (ASF) and AMISOM (2013). He was a member of the UN Secretary-General's Peacebuilding Fund Advisory Group (2012–2014), and worked with the Department of Peacekeeping Operations (DPKO) in New York (2002) and with UNTAET in Timor Leste (2001). He started his career as a South African diplomat in Washington D.C. (1992–1994) and Addis Ababa (1994–1997). He holds a Ph.D. in Applied Ethics from the Department of Philosophy at the University of Stellenbosch in South Africa. His main research focus is on the theory, coherence and effectiveness of African Union and United Nations peace operations.

Hilde Frafjord Johnson former Minister and UN Special Representative, served as Member of the UN Secretary-General's High-Level Independent Panel on UN Peace Operations (HIPPO). In 2014, she completed her three-year tenure as Special Representative of the Secretary-General and Head of the UN Mission in South Sudan. In both these contexts she engaged in security sector reform, rule of law, and police reform issues. Following both engagements, she was co-chair of the UN Police Review process and at the same time served as Senior Visiting Fellow at the Norwegian Institute of International Affairs (NUPI) (2015–2016). From 2007 to 2011 Frafjord Johnson was Deputy Executive Director of UNICEF, where she oversaw the organisation's humanitarian operations, crisis response and security issues. Prior to her UN assignments, Frafjord Johnson was Minister of International Development of Norway for almost 7 years (1997–2000 and 2001–2005). During this time, she played a key role in the negotiations that ended Africa's longest civil war, the Sudan conflict, through the Comprehensive Peace Agreement in 2005. She was also a Member of Parliament for the centrist Christian Democratic Party of Norway (1993–2001) and is currently the Secretary-General of the party. Frafjord Johnson is the author of three books, *Waging Peace in Sudan* (Sussex Ac Press, 2011), *South Sudan: The Untold Story—From Independence to Civil War* (IB Tauris, 2016), and *Den vanskelige freden, Når fred ender i ny krig* (Cappelen-Damm, 2016, in Norwegian, translation: Fragile peace, when peace ends in new war).

John Karlsrud is Senior Research Fellow at the Norwegian Institute of International Affairs (NUPI). He earned his Ph.D. at the University of Warwick and has been Visiting Fulbright Fellow at the Center on International Cooperation, New York University, and Visiting Fellow at the International Peace Institute in New York. Topics of particular interest are peace operations, peacebuilding, and humanitarian action. He has served as Special Assistant to the United Nations Special Representative in Chad, and was part of the UN Development Programme's leadership program LEAD. He has published articles in *Disasters*, *Global*

Governance, *International Review of the Red Cross* and *Third World Quarterly*, among others, and the books *The UN at War: Peace Operations in a New Era* (Palgrave, 2018); *UN Peacekeeping Doctrine in a New Era* (co-edited with Cedric de Coning and Chiyuki Aoi, Routledge 2017); *Norm Change in International Relations* (Routledge, 2016); and *The Future of African Peace Operations: From the Janjaweed to Boko Haram* (co-edited with Cedric de Coning and Linnea Gelot, Zed Books, 2016). Karlsrud has worked in Bosnia and Hercegovina, Chad, Palestine, Norway and the USA, and conducted field research and shorter missions to Haiti, Liberia, Mali, Mozambique, Serbia, Sierra Leone, South Sudan and Ukraine.

Youssef Mahmoud is Senior Adviser at the International Peace Institute (IPI) supporting the Africa, Middle East and peace operations programs and serving as focal point on prevention mediation policies and practices. Before retiring from the United Nations in January 2011, Dr. Mahmoud was the Secretary-General's Special Representative and Head of the UN Peacekeeping Mission in the Central African Republic and Chad (MINURCAT). From 2007 to 2009 he served as Executive Representative of the Secretary-General and Head of the UN Integrated Peacebuilding Office in Burundi (BINUB). Prior to these assignments, he held several other UN senior positions, notably as United Nations Resident Coordinator in Guyana, Director in the UN Department of Political Affairs and Head of the Office of the Undersecretary-Secretary-General for Political Affairs. He periodically writes on the evolving concepts and practices in the areas of peacebuilding and sustaining peace and on political transitions in Africa with a focus on Tunisia. He is currently Visiting Professor at the African Leadership Centre, King's College, London and serves on the boards of several national and international non-profit organisations, including Al-Bawsala, a Tunisian NGO that aims to put citizens at the core of political action. Dr. Mahmoud has a Ph.D. in Linguistics from Georgetown University, Washington, DC, USA.

Kari M. Osland is Senior Research Fellow and Head of the Research Group on Peace, Conflict and Development, at the Norwegian Institute of International Affairs (NUPI). Her main fields of specialisation are peace- and state-building, in particular, international police reform, war crimes, comparative methodology, political analysis of the Balkans, insurgents and the changing character of war. Osland holds a Ph.D. from the University of Oslo, where she looked at international police intervention in five post-conflict countries over five years. She was co-editor of the Scandinavian journal *Internasjonal Politikk* and has done extensive fieldwork in Afghanistan, Albania, Bosnia and Herzegovina, FYR Macedonia, Kosovo, Montenegro, Serbia, South Sudan and the Sudan.

Mateja Peter is Lecturer (Assistant Professor) at St. Andrews University, where she co-directs the Centre for Global Constitutionalism. She is also Senior Research Fellow at the Norwegian Institute of International Affairs (NUPI). Peter obtained her Ph.D. from Cambridge University and subsequently held post-doctoral positions at research institutes in Washington, Berlin and Oslo. Her recent peer-reviewed articles appear in *Third World Quarterly*, *Global Governance* and *Cambridge Review of International Affairs.* Peter works at the intersection of international relations and law, researching on global governance and international organisations, peace operations and peacebuilding. Previously, she led a project providing research support to the UN High-Level Independent Panel on Peace Operations. She has extensive field experience and has recently done work in Bosnia and Herzegovina, Kosovo and Darfur. She is currently finalising a book on international authority in state-building.

Thierry Tardy is Senior Analyst at the European Union Institute for Security Studies (EUISS). He has researched and published extensively on military and civilian crisis management with a focus on the United Nations and the European Union, inter-institutional cooperation in security governance, security regionalism and the EU Common Security and Defence Policy. His latest publications include *The Oxford Handbook on United Nations Peacekeeping Operations* (co-edited with Joachim Koops, Norrie MacQueen and Paul Williams, OUP, 2015); *CSDP in Action. What Contribution to International Security?* (Chaillot Papers 134, EUISS, May 2015), *Recasting EU Civilian Crisis Management* (Report n°32, EUISS, February 2017) and *Permanent Structured Cooperation: What's in a Name?* (co-authored with Daniel Fiott and Antonio Missiroli, Chaillot Papers 142, EUISS, Nov. 2017). He is a member of the editorial board of International Peacekeeping. He teaches European Security and Crisis Management at the Institut d'Etudes Politiques (Paris), La Sorbonne and the National Institute of Oriental Languages and Civilisations (INALCO). Tardy also regularly lectures at the NATO Defense College and at the European Security and Defense College (ESDC), and sits at the ESDC's Executive Academic Board.

Stephanie Tiélès is transnational organised crime expert, currently working at the United Nations—DPKO Police Division Standing Police Capacity (SPC). In 18 years as Police officer with the French National Police, she served the European Union in Bosnia Herzegovina and was seconded to EUROPOL as specialist on criminal networks originating from the Western Balkans. She was recently seconded as one of the first members of the Serious and Organised Crime team created within the United Nations Police Division in 2015. Stephanie contributed in structuring and deploying teams specialised on transnational organised crime in Mali (MINUSMA), DRC (MONUSCO) and Central Africa (MINUSCA), and supported several peace operations in enhancing criminal investigation and intelligence capacities of post-conflict states. She holds a master's degree in law and criminal sciences.

Yin He is Associate Professor at the China Peacekeeping Police Training Center of the Chinese People's Armed Police Academy, where he has been teaching peacekeeping training courses for fifteen years. From October 2001 to October 2002, he worked in UNPOL in the peacekeeping missions in East Timor. From September 2006 to June 2007, he was Visiting scholar at Uppsala University, Sweden. From February to June 2015, he was Fellow at the Harvard Weatherhead Center for International Affairs. His recent publications include *Rising Power and International Peace: Essays on United Nations Peacekeeping and Peacebuilding* (Beijing: Current Affairs Press, 2017, in Chinese), *Developmental Peace: Chinese Approach to UN Peacekeeping and Peacebuilding* (Journal of International Studies, September 2017, in Chinese) and *United Nations Peacekeeping Affairs and Construction of China's Discursive Power* (Journal of World Economics and Politics, November 2016, in Chinese).

List of Models and Charts

List of Tables

Check for updates

CHAPTER 1

UN Peace Operations: Adapting to a New Global Order?

Mateja Peter

A New Global Order?

In early March 2015, the United Nations (UN) Secretary-General's High-Level Independent Panel on UN Peace Operations (HIPPO) made a stop in Cairo, Egypt as part of its regional consultations on reform of UN peace operations. One of the discussion questions for the first session asked, whether current UN peace operations in the Middle East are the right fit for today's security environment and, if not, what kind of UN presence makes the most sense now and in the future. Very soon into the session a young diplomat from one of the regional states challenged the premise of this question, arguing that the only role for the UN is in supporting regional approaches. His passionate intervention opened a floodgate, with speaker after speaker depicting the UN with deep suspicion. The message was clear: UN peace operations were seen to be a Western intervention into regional matters; the League of Arab States (LAS) should deal with Arab problems, same as the African Union

M. Peter (✉)
School of International Relations, University of St Andrews, St Andrews, UK
e-mail: mp240@st-andrews.ac.uk

© The Author(s) 2019

C. de Coning and M. Peter (eds.), *United Nations Peace Operations in a Changing Global Order*,
https://doi.org/10.1007/978-3-319-99106-1_1

(AU) should deal with African ones. The primacy of the UN was under challenge. Two years later, with the number of crises in the world not subsiding, the United States (US), as not only the leader of the Western world but also the biggest funder of UN peacekeeping, sought to cut $1 billion from the UN peacekeeping budget (Lynch 2017). Moments after the budget was adopted, the US ambassador to the UN exclaimed on twitter: "Just 5 months into our time here, we've cut over half a billion $$$ from the UN peacekeeping budget & we're only getting started" (Green 2017). All this is happening at a time, when UN peace operations are marred in sexual abuse scandals (UN 2015a; Essa 2017; Naraghi Anderlini 2017), hence losing legitimacy in the eyes of the global public and, more consequentially, the local population, which they are supposed to be serving. Local and global non-state actors are demanding accountability and the UN is increasingly forced to react. For example, in June 2017, after a non-governmental organisation (NGO) Aids Free World leaked internal UN documents detailing alleged sexual abuse and misconduct, the UN announced the withdrawal of 600 Congo-Brazzaville peacekeepers from the UN Mission in the Central African Republic (CAR) (UN 2017). Challenges are coming from all sides and the core dilemma addressed by this volume is whether and how UN peace operations are adapting to this new global order.

Since the turn of the century both conflicts and interventions have changed dramatically. Self-perpetuating cross-border conflicts fuelled by both greed and grievances (Berdal and Malone 2000; Collier and Hoffler 2004)—a key feature of the post-Cold War security environment—, have gained new dimensions with *the rise of illegitimate non-state actors*. Groups such as ISIS in Iraq and Syria, Al-Shabaab in Somalia, al-Qaeda–affiliated groups in northern Mali, Boko Haram from Nigeria, the Lord's Resistance Army from Uganda or the M23 militia in the eastern Democratic Republic of Congo (DRC) are rewriting the rules of war. These groups are not just spoilers of peace agreements (Stedman 1997), they are seen as *antithetical to peace agreements*: neither they nor the broader international community are interested in peace agreements that would include them (Peter 2015, p. 358). The scale and nature of their atrocities in their regions of origin and the fact that many of them have a global reach through terrorist activities, makes the international community, as a whole, and members of the UN Security Council (UNSC), more specifically, unlikely to allow them any legitimate claims. Despite this wide agreement, the UNSC is often at odds about the kind of action that should be taken to address their rise, something we have best seen in Syria. In other regions, where the permanent members of the UNSC have less polarising positions, UNSC responses indicate a new trend in interventions. Whether conducted through UN peacekeeping operations, such as in Mali, the DRC and the CAR, or through regional organisations, such as in Somalia or through the Multinational Joint Task Force against Boko Haram (de Coning et al. 2016), international responses are increasingly robust.

These new types of conflicts and interventions are happening at a time of dramatic shifts in the global order. For much of the twentieth century, the discourse on peace and security took place between the East and the West, tempering the UN's ability to get involved in intra-state conflicts. With the end of the Cold War and the newly found agreement in the UNSC, peacekeepers began addressing fallouts from civil wars and assisting post-conflict states in their reconstruction. But the much-hailed 'end of history' (Fukuyama 1992) resulting in the liberal 'peacebuilding consensus' (Richmond 2004), did not transpire in ways anticipated. This new century is one of *North–South rebalancing*. From bipolar, via unipolar, we have now entered a truly multipolar world (de Coning et al. 2014; Narlikar 2010). States from the global South have long been active participants in peacekeeping as troop and police contributors. This has not changed. At the time of writing, the top ten troop and police contributing countries are all from the global South, with Ethiopia, Bangladesh, India, Rwanda and Pakistan topping the list.[1] Throughout the history of UN peace operations, the role of these states in the field has not been matched by their participation in decision and policy making, with experts calling this division of work between the North and the South "a blue helmet caste system," (Lynch 2013) "apartheid," (Chesterman 2004, p. 11), and "imperial multilateralism" (Cunliffe 2013, p. 20). This is changing. States of the global South are not mere recipients and implementers of international interventions anymore, but are increasingly vocal about how these should take shape.

This rise of the global South is accompanied through and aided by the emergence of *regional organisations as providers of security*. During the second half of the twentieth century, the UN peacekeeping missions were often considered as the only viable and legitimate actor in

[1]The only OECD country among the top 20 contributors in February 2018 was Italy in the 20th place (UN 2018).

managing conflicts. This idea of an objective and unbiased respondent is enshrined in one of the key principles of UN peacekeeping: impartiality (UN 2008). Over the last two decades, due to both stalemates in the UN Security Council and the changing nature of conflicts, regional organisations, both from the global North and South, frequently became the first responders. The most striking of these is still the 1999 intervention in Kosovo, where the North Atlantic Treaty Organisation (NATO) responded to an escalating humanitarian crisis despite objections from Russia and China (Holzgrefe and Keohane 2008). Unlike the Kosovo intervention, other regional organisations' missions, from Somalia to the CAR and Mali, as a rule, received prior authorisation from the UNSC. With a notable exception of Libya, the UNSC authorisation now tends to follow a host state invitation to a regional organisation. The host states are often not seeking an impartial actor, but one that can deal with their internal problems efficiently. Responses to contemporary conflicts are increasingly robust and regional organisations are better equipped than the UN to execute them. But more and more it is not just *the efficiency* but also *the legitimacy* of the regional organisation over the UN that plays the role in the determination of an intervening actor. Sudan, for example, refused a deployment of a pure UN peacekeeping operation to Darfur and instead asked for a joint United Nations–African Union Mission in Darfur (UNAMID) (Burkeman and Rice 2006). In other cases, the fact that regional organisations responded first as peace enforcers brought them the legitimacy in the peacekeeping phase. Even when the UN deploys to the same area, regional organisations remain important players on the ground. In Mali and the CAR, Economic Community of West African States (ECOWAS) and AU troops, respectively, who were on the ground first, simply got re-hatted into UN troops (Williams and Boutellis 2014). Responses to conflicts today are more multifaceted than they were two decades ago. What this means for the primacy of the UN, as enshrined in the UN Charter, remains to be seen.

This rebalancing of relations is not only happening between the member states or the inter-governmental organisations, increasingly it is *the non-state actors* that put pressures on the international community to respond to atrocities. The plight of human populations half across the world and the inaction or inappropriate responses of states are not merely televised as they were directly after the Cold War, but are shared immediately and unfiltered on social media. These technological advances, combined with the post-Cold War spread of human rights ideas, mean that—at least in the eyes of non-state actors—the standards for what peace operations are supposed to achieve are higher than ever. The message from global and local non-state actors is clear: the main objective of peace operations should be improving security and well-being of people affected by conflicts. Interventions should not focus only on state security, but also improve *human security* (Suhrke 1999; Stoett 1999; Paris 2001). When peacekeepers get embroiled in abuse and misconduct scandals, their legitimacy is tainted from the start. While new technology has changed how the UN is responding to conflicts, it has also facilitated greater transparency over what peace operations are achieving and when they are failing.

In sum, global order is facing four key transformations, collectively presenting unique challenges to UN peace operations: (1) the rebalancing of relations between states of the global North and the global South; (2) the rise of regional organisations as providers of peace; (3) the rise of violent extremism and fundamentalist non-state actors; and (4) increasing demands from non-state actors for greater emphasis on human security.

United Nations Responses

The challenges the above transformations present are in many ways new for the UN, demanding a rethinking of some of the core assumptions of what peace operations can achieve and what they should be aiming to do. However, this is not the first time that the UN and the international community have had to rethink their approaches to peace and security. Throughout the 1990s and in the early 2000s, the UN was rethinking what role its peace operations should serve in the post-Cold War environment, culminating in the debates around *the Brahimi report* (UN 2000). The findings in the Brahimi report have shaped our understanding of modern multidimensional peace operations and led to institutional changes within the UN that continue today. Arguing for clear, credible and achievable peacekeeping mandates, the report also cemented the idea of longer-term peacebuilding approaches as part of effective peacekeeping. But the Brahimi report and debates around it were to a large extent a response to the challenges the UN was experiencing in the 1990s—from the disastrous international intervention in Somalia and the failure to prevent genocides in Bosnia and Herzegovina and Rwanda, to the then relatively novel emphasis on institution- and state-building as a method to build peace. Brahimi precedes the 9/11 terrorist attacks in the US, the intervention in Afghanistan, and the international rift over Iraq; it also precedes the idea of the BRICS[2] and even the formation of the AU, as well as the global financial crisis of 2008 and the emergence of fundamentalist non-state actors and violent extremism as one of the biggest perceived threats to the international peace and security. It is evident that much has changed in both the nature of conflict and international responses to it since the turn of the century.

Contemporary peace operations and the UN are faced with a challenging task of having to reconcile the post-Brahimi development of policies and thinking about human security, protection of civilians, local ownership, gender inclusivity, and longer-term institution-building, with the new realities of conflict and intervention. There are pressures to achieve more to assist states and people embroiled in or emerging from conflicts. At the same time, the UN is under pressure to include an increasing array of voices from within its membership. Each of these voices is advancing their own vision of interventions and with that also their own vision of UN peace operations. How do peace operations ensure legitimacy in the eyes of the local populations and the global public, while at the same time serving the interests of member states? Are the interests of member states compatible with the interests of the international community as a whole? How to balance between state and human security; between short-term solutions and long-term approaches? These questions arise in an era where regional organisations are emerging as possible alternatives to the UN, further pushing the UN to justify the relevance of its own peace operations. That previously advanced approaches linking peacekeeping with peace- and state- building have not had the desired effects on peace consolidation, is putting an additional pressure on the UN to reform (Heathershaw 2008; Campbell et al. 2011; Mac Ginty 2012).

In October 2014, aware of the implications all these developments are having on UN peace operations, the former Secretary-General Ban Ki-moon appointed the High-Level Independent Panel on UN Peace Operations (HIPPO) (UN 2014). The expert panel was to produce a report akin to the Brahimi report and was encouraged by the Secretary-General and other senior figures in the UN to be bold and creative in

[2] BRICS acronym is used for emerging powers Brazil, Russia, India, China and South Africa and was coined by the chief economist for Goldman Sachs (O'Neill 2001).

its recommendations. While members of the panel were appointed in their personal capacity, the composition of the panel showed that the Secretary-General had regional balance and the changing global order in mind. All five permanent members of the Security Council were represented. In addition, there were three representatives from Africa (Tunisia, Ghana, Burundi), three South Asian members (India, Bangladesh, Sri Lanka), three key financial contributors (Norway, Canada, Australia), as well as representatives from Latin America (Brazil) and the Middle East (Jordan). The panel—working under the leadership of the Nobel Laureate and former President of Timor-Leste Jose Ramos-Horta— delivered its report in June 2015 (UN 2015b).

The HIPPO report reviews past engagements and maps out future directions for UN peace operations by proposing four "fundamental shifts" that the UN needs to undertake to remain relevant: (1) primacy of politics: peace operations should be underpinned by political solutions, and not military and technical engagements; (2) a spectrum of peace operations: the UN should deliver more tailored 'right fit' and not 'template' missions that better take into account specificities of the situation; (3) a global and regional partnership for peace and security: the UN should embrace the era of partnership with regional organisations and national capacities and use their comparative advantages; and (4) more field-focused UN Secretariat and more people-centred UN peace operations (UN 2015b).

These four core recommendations reflect the changing nature of conflict as well as a global re-ordering. The first two recommendations can to a large extent be interpreted as a response to the rise of violent extremism; they reflect the reality that peace operations are now often deployed to areas where there is no peace to keep. Technical solutions and bureaucratic approaches have a limited scope in such situations. These two recommendations are undoubtedly also a reaction to the critiques in both scholarly and policy literature, which have long argued against one-size-fits-all approaches and encouraged conflict sensitivity. The third fundamental shift proposed by the HIPPO panel reflects the changing role of the UN in the world. Calling for an era of partnership with regional organisation—and singling out Africa in the remainder of the report—is a good indication that the panel was aware that the UN is not necessarily the most effective or legitimate actor in many areas of the world. The last and in many ways the most ambitious shift reminds both the UN and member states that in the end, the UN and its peace operations will only remain relevant to the extent that they successfully respond to the expectations of people. The preface of the document is couched in the language of peace operations serving people, not just states, showing that the panel tried to reconcile the aspirational with what is feasible. As the panel was carefully selected to reflect the current global order, its report and responses to it are a good indication of what the international community could agree upon at the aspirational end of the spectrum. Whether that is enough for the UN to respond to the pressures emanating from changes in the global order to retain its relevance for the twenty-first century is another question altogether.

Four Transformations in Global Order and Their Implications on UN Peace Operations

This edited volume generates a discussion about UN approaches to peace by studying challenges and opportunities that the organisation is facing in the twenty-first century. We use some of the findings from the HIPPO report as an inspiration and put both its recommendations and broader UN actions in a wider context. We identify four transformations in the global order and study what implications these have on UN peace operations. The first two transformations emanate from the changing relations between states and reflect the increasingly multipolar character of contemporary global governance. The latter two transformations reflect the changing relations between state and non-state actors. These two broad groups of non-state actors are fundamentally incompatible in their outlook on how and whether the international community should be intervening. That notwithstanding, both groups of non-state actors also force the UN and its member states to rethink the centrality of state-based approaches to security and intervention.

In this volume, we identify four transformations in the global order and study their implications on the United Nations peace operations. We ask:

- How is the *rebalancing of relations between states of the global North and the global South* impacting the UN's decision-making, financing and ability to design operations that go beyond the minimum common denominator;
- How is *the rise of regional organisations* as providers of peace impacting the primacy of UN peace operations and how and whether the UN can remain relevant in this era of partnership and competition;

- How have *violent extremism and fundamentalist non-state actors* changed the nature of international responses and what does this mean for previously advanced longer-term approaches to conflict resolution;
- How are *demands from non-state actors for greater emphasis on human security* impacting the UN's credibility, and whether, in light of the first three transformations, the UN is even able to prioritise people-centred approaches over state-centred ones.

Our core finding is that with the entry of new actors from the global South as important players in the peace arena, we seem to be entering *a more pragmatic era of UN peace operations.* As contributions to this volume show, there is a greater willingness to innovate and experiment with new forms of conflict management, including more robust interpretations of UN peacekeeping and an increasing reliance on regional actors as providers of peace. At the same time, the UN is facing *a classic struggle between the promotion of liberal international norms and realist security concerns.* The resolution of this struggle is less clear. The contributors to this volume emphasise the importance of people-centred approaches, conflict sensitivity and longer-term thinking as key aspects to continued relevance of the UN, but their conclusions as to how achievable these are by the UN are not as clear cut.

New Vocabulary for a New Era

The terminology of (post-)conflict intervention is confusing and confused. Even experts in international relations would be hard pressed to explain the difference or the similarity between peacekeeping and peacebuilding and often equate the two without much thought.[3] Similarly, in UN hallways, many would find it difficult to articulate any difference between peace operations and peacekeeping. As international interventions diversify, new terms emerge. The following paragraphs won't resolve this confusion; their intention is to operationalise terms used in this volume as well as to indicate why the UN vocabulary is changing.

[3]As a rule, the more problem-solving approaches will tend to refer to an activity as peacekeeping to focus on the more time-defined engagement and on the missions, themselves, with critical approaches referring to the same activity as peacebuilding to capture the broader context (Cox 1981; Pugh 2004).

In line with the broader argument of the book, we see these adaptations in UN language as a manifestation of the more pragmatic approach the UN has taken in recent years. This pragmatism is paradoxically addressing many of the critiques about rigidity of UN peacekeeping coming both from policy circles and critical literature.

Contemporary lexicon of UN operations can be found in the Capstone doctrine (UN 2008). This document situates peacekeeping—an activity it aims to operationalise—on the spectrum of peace and security activities. *Peacekeeping* is defined as "a technique designed to preserve the peace, however fragile, where fighting has been halted, and to assist in implementing agreements achieved by the peacemakers" (ibid., p. 18). Peacekeeping is to follow and to some extent overlap any peacemaking and peace enforcement activities. *Peacemaking* involves diplomatic activities to bring hostile parties to the negotiated agreement and can be conducted by either the UN itself, regional organisations, states or non-governmental actors. Such activities would fall under Chapter VI of the UN Charter. *Peace enforcement* involves the use of a range of coercive measures, such as sanctions or the military force, intended to halt the conflict and bring warring parties to the negotiating table. These are the so-called Chapter VII actions authorised by the UN Security Council. Both peacemaking and peace enforcement are striving for the same outcome: a ceasefire. As peacekeeping sits in-between and succeeds both peacemaking and peace enforcement, it is often referred to as a 'Chapter VI and a half' tool. The UN sees peacekeeping as one element of post-conflict *peacebuilding* activities, which constitute "a complex, long-term process of creating the necessary conditions for sustainable peace" (ibid.). These peace and security activities seldom occur in a linear or sequential manner, showing linkages not only between different international actors but also between different parts of the UN.

In addition to peacekeeping operations, *special political missions* (SPM) have come to play an important role in how the UN engages in its peace activities. In February 2018, the UN had 25 SPM operations deployed across Africa, Central Asia, and the Middle East.[4] This was in addition to the 15 peacekeeping ones.[5] The Capstone doctrine doesn't list special

[4]For a full list of current SPMs see http://www.un.org/undpa/en/in-the-field/overview.

[5]For a full list of current peacekeeping operations see https://peacekeeping.un.org/en/where-we-operate.

political missions as part of UN peace and security activities, but considers them as a type of operation that may precede or be deployed alongside a peacekeeping operation (ibid., p. 87). These missions engage in conflict prevention, peacemaking, and peacebuilding and therefore do not fit neatly on the spectrum of peace and security activities. Unlike peacekeeping operations, which necessarily include a military component, SPM operations are smaller. Some of them have regional mandates—for example, the UN Office for West Africa and the Sahel (UNOWAS) or the UN Regional Centre for Preventive Diplomacy for Central Asia (UNRCCA). Others may be deployed to conflict-ridden countries, where it would be difficult to obtain consent of the host state or the UN Security Council for a deployment of a UN military mission. The clearest examples of these today are the missions to Yemen and Syria.

While often taking on many of the same tasks, peacekeeping operations and special political missions are managed by two separate departments within the UN Secretariat, the Department for Peacekeeping Operations (DPKO) and the Department of Political Affairs (DPA), respectively. Peacekeeping operations have their own separate budget (the so-called assessed contributions) and have therefore somewhat more predictable funding and planning cycles (Diehl and PharaohKhan 2000). In contrast, SPMs are funded through the regular UN budget. To rapidly respond to crises unanticipated in the regular budget, SPMs are increasingly reliant on extra-budgetary resources. These voluntary contributions fund about 40% of DPA's work today.[6] Funding and management disparities were one of the main reasons why the most recent review of peace operations recommended to make away with the sharp distinction between peacekeeping operations and special political missions. The HIPPO report strongly urges the UN to embrace the term *peace operations* to signify the full spectrum of responses required (UN 2015b, p. viii). Such change in thinking would bring peacekeeping and SPMs under one label, a move that could eventually pave the way for the reform in financing and management of UN responses. It would also allow for more fundamental changes to the structure of individual missions over time, including more clearly sequenced mandates.

More importantly for the argument of this book, the term peace operations also better denotes changes that UN responses to conflicts

[6]For an overview of voluntary contributions see http://www.un.org/undpa/en/funding.

have undergone, as well as changes the UN would need to implement if it wants to remain relevant in responding to contemporary conflicts. Both policy and scholarship have long been critical of the rigidity of UN peacekeeping, calling for a greater local sensitivity and development of tailor-made approaches. Not all conflict responses require a large military component to keep peace. Others might be best addressed through a deployment of a military component to a whole region, not just a single state. Some peace operations are closer in their activities to peace enforcement, others to peacebuilding. Their mandates and composition need to reflect this reality and not follow bureaucratic templates. A comprehensive reform of UN financing is highly unlikely in the current political climate. As a result, the UN Security Council will almost certainly continue privileging peacekeeping operations, when it wants to provide a comprehensive UN response. Recognising this political reality, authors in this volume nonetheless emphasise the increasing diversity of existing approaches and the need for a greater context-sensitivity of international responses to conflicts. Both critical and policy-oriented contributions share this sentiment. Terms and categories used by both policymakers and scientists serve as political tools. Although individual authors highlight particular processes through their own terminology, the volume as a whole embraces the broader analytical category of peace operations. We chose to use it in the title of the volume to highlight the diversity of international approaches to conflicts and the need to go beyond technocratic solutions.

Aims of the Book

This edited volume offers a comprehensive review of challenges and opportunities the UN peace operations are facing in the twenty-first century. It serves as a conversation between scholars and practitioners, with an intent to capture experiences of both. Despite an increasingly active interest in UN peace operations and third-party interventions in public and scholarly discourse, much of these discussions operate in parallel to policy discussions. Public debates focus on sensational stories and failures of the UN, ascribing these to organisational inadequacies. On the other hand, much of the scholarly literature operates with an insufficient understanding of the dramatic changes in the global context, nature of conflicts, and international responses that have occurred over the past decade. Many of the policy developments and debates do not reach the ivory towers. This volume uniquely tries to bring recent developments in policy as well as practitioners' debates on the future of the UN peace tools to the scholarly community. We have invited two former Special Representatives of the Secretary-General and members of the HIPPO panel to reflect on areas of peace operations they are passionate about—people-centred approaches and protection of civilians. At the same time, the volume provides for a reflexive engagement on recent policy developments from academic authorities from both the global North and South. It situates policy debates in the global reordering and provides an idea of where the UN and the broader international responses to conflicts are heading in the medium-term future. Through this conversation, the edited volume will be of interest to both practitioners and scholars.

Stressing different aspects of peace operations and partnerships, contributors to this volume collectively query the relevance and ambition of the UN and its peace operations. By examining the four shifts in the global order, the volume's ambition is to:

- Map recent developments in UN peace operations and assess where UN approaches to peace are heading;
- Analyse what kind of pressures the changing nature of conflicts is putting on UN peace operations and what alternatives to UN responses are emerging;
- Assess how changes in the global order are affecting UN peace operations and the role of the United Nations as a whole;
- Examine how the state of the art understanding about protection of civilians, local ownership, gender inclusivity and institution-building, can be accommodated in increasingly robust UN peace operations;
- Inform future debates in both scholarship and practice by providing innovative ideas for rethinking of UN approaches to peace.

Structure of the Book

This volume is divided into three parts, each combining voices of practitioners and scholars. The first part of the volume looks at the political and strategic context, situating current debates within a longer trajectory of UN interventions. It highlights major shifts in UN approaches to peace, emphasising pressures on peace operations coming from both state (emerging powers and regional organisations) and non-state actors. In the second part, authors examine mandates and strategy, highlighting some of the key changes UN peace operations have undergone in recent years as well as weighing in on the challenges that remain. While other equally important issues have been introduced to the agenda of UN peace operations in recent years (for example, women, peace and security or disarmament, demobilisation and reintegration), we prioritised developments that are putting major strain on the functioning of peace operations and are potentially changing the nature of UN approaches to peace. In the third part, contributors explore new and old partners to UN peace operations, querying how the UN relates to some other key players in contemporary interventions. While necessarily selective, this section's choice of UN partners (China, African Union, European Union and religious humanitarians) aims to underscore the complexity of UN partnerships with both state and non-state actors in the twenty-first century.

Part 1—Political and Strategic Context: Past, Present, Future—consists of four contributions. In Chapter 2, *Mateja Peter* examines the evolution of the idea of UN peacekeeping, asking how an instrument developed in the late 1940s managed to not only survive but also respond to the changing geopolitical and conflict landscape over the last seventy years. Through an overview of major doctrinal developments and institutional adaptations, she analyses how the peacekeeping tool was adapted from a bipolar world, via a unipolar one to today's multipolar world. The label of peacekeeping has encompassed very different activities over this period and peacekeeping today bears only casual resemblance to peacekeeping from decades ago. In her contribution, Peter argues that peacekeeping started as a conflict management instrument, which was adapted to a conflict resolution mechanism after the end of the Cold War, but has now come full circle and is again increasingly used to manage and contain, not resolve conflicts. And in this ability to adapt to the needs of the states and the changing global relations lies the resilience of the idea of peacekeeping itself.

In Chapter 3, *Adriana Erthal Abdenur* asks how the changing global order is impacting UN peace operations. She contends that the multipolarisation of the world order is accelerating, due to both the decline of Western powers and the increasing contestation of Western dominance by several rising powers. Throughout the chapter, Abdenur examines two inter-related implications of multipolarisation for UN peace operations: norms-setting and role expectations. Uncertainties about global leadership and constraints on resources prompt changing expectations of, and concern about, rising powers, especially those viewed as playing a pivotal role in UN security governance. She highlights China as a potential leader in UN peacekeeping, but contends that Beijing's willingness and ability to quickly expand its influence should not be taken for granted.

In Chapter 4, *Adam Day* turns his attention to UN's conflict prevention work, where politically-driven solutions have become more elusive. He traces how good offices have evolved from early Secretaries-General through the expansion of UN peace operations in recent decades. This lays the groundwork for a comparative analysis of modern applications of good offices in more recent conflicts, examining how the UN has attempted to reshape its political engagement to accommodate the changing nature of armed conflict. Based on a comparative assessment of the UN's political engagement across different settings and eras, Day lists four key elements for successful use of good offices: (1) in-depth understanding of the conflict based on sustained contact and relationships on the ground; (2) timing of the intervention; (3) leverage over the key conflict actors; and (4) credibility of the mediator. He contends that a light, nimble presence on the ground—rather than multidimensional peace operations—appear best placed to achieve these elements of success.

In Chapter 5, *Youssef Mahmoud* provides an impassionate argument for why UN peace operations should shift towards and prioritise people-centred approaches. Drawing on his experience as a former Special Representative of the Secretary-General and a HIPPO panel member, he contends there is a growing and wide recognition that peace, like a tree, grows from the bottom up, but that many challenges still stand in the way of realising this shift on the ground. In his contribution, Mahmoud provides a cursory review of the factors underpinning these challenges and explains the rationale of the Panel's renewed focus on people-centred approaches. He continues by reflecting on the conundrums faced by the UN Security Council in its attempts to embrace such an approach in a changing security landscape, providing concrete recommendations to the Security Council and member states.

Part 2—Mandates and Strategy—is composed of five chapters exploring recent developments in UN peace operations, all potentially changing the nature of UN approaches to peace. In Chapter 6, *Mats Berdal* explores the outer limits of the use of force by UN peacekeepers. He traces the thinking and the practices surrounding the use of force from the conceptual foundations laid in the era of classical peacekeeping to the contemporary focus on the protection of civilians and more "robust" operations. He contends that at the tactical level, a properly equipped and properly commanded force has on occasion been used with decisive effect in response to immediate crises or emergencies. In contrast to that, Berdal sees the larger and more critical strategic lesson from the history of robust peacekeeping since 1999 as a cautionary one; one that highlights the need for the activities of UN "blue helmets" to be much more closely aligned than they have become over the past decade and a half, to the search for viable political solutions to conflict.

In Chapter 7, *Hilde Frafjord Johnson*, a former Special Representative of the Secretary-General and a HIPPO panel member, shares her experience on a topic at the centre of UN peace operations: protection of civilians. Reflecting on the fact that today a vast majority of UN military and police personnel have a mandate to protect civilians, she queries whether UN operations are provided with the necessary means to fulfil this mandate. Drawing on her experience from the UN Mission in South Sudan (UNMISS), Frafjord Johnson reveals systemic weaknesses in the way the UN deploys, resources, and supports missions. A major problem is lack of guidance in cases where host governments prove to be the main perpetrator. Frafjord Johnson maintains that the primary responsibility to protect civilians rests with host governments, but that the UN system also needs to train its forces in protection of civilians operations and security reform, which has not been a priority so far. She concludes that protection will remain an illusion for many civilians at risk unless these challenges are addressed.

In Chapter 8, *John Karlsrud* looks at how UN peace operations have been responding to violent extremism and terrorism. He argues that there are practical and financial reasons to give UN peace operations more robust mandates to mitigate and respond to new threats. But the idea of UN peacekeepers conducting counter-terrorism operations is not without challenges. Karlsrud contends that UN peace operations neither are, nor will be ready operationally, doctrinally or politically to take on counter-terrorism tasks. Such a development could jeopardize the legal protection of UN staff; remove the ability of the UN to be an impartial arbiter of the conflict; and strongly undermine the ability for other parts of the UN family to carry out humanitarian work. However, UN peace operations should, in cooperation with the UN Country Team, strengthen their conflict prevention and early peacebuilding agenda, to remove root causes for radicalisation.

Chapter 9, co-authored by *Arthur Boutellis and Stephanie Tiélès*, examines how peace operations have responded to organised crime. While scholars have increasingly recognised the importance of criminal agendas in post-conflict politics, organised crime is still a relatively understudied and misunderstood issue in the field of peace operations. With their contribution, Boutellis and Tiélès examine how transnational organised crime has increasingly become recognised by the UN Security Council as a threat to international peace and security. They provide a thorough analysis of the limitations of the dominant law enforcement and capacity building approaches adopted by UN missions to date. Building on recent examples, they provide lessons on how UN peace operations could deal more effectively with the issue of organised crime, contending that missions need to engage more strategically with both the host state and local communities as well as identify strategic partners to take longer-term preventive approaches.

In Chapter 10, *Kari M. Osland* examines the role of police in UN peace operations. She observes that the increasing demand for UN police comes from the recognition that functioning local police is a central element of the UN exit strategy. However, reaching that point is very challenging. In her contribution, Osland contends that UN policing was never easy, but that the combination of an increasing deployment of UN operations in the midst of on-going wars and the steady increase of UN police tasks without adequate increases in resources or training, has made UN policing even more complicated in recent years. Examining both the security and trust role of police in society, she argues that the main challenge for UN police in post-conflict situations is to close the security–trust gap. So far, most of the focus of UN operations has been on the security part of the equation. In this chapter, Osland asks whether the UN is even set up to achieve both.

Part 3—New and Old Partnerships—is composed of four chapters reflecting on the role of other actors in peace operations and the impact they have on the UN. In Chapter 11, *Cedric de Coning* examines Africa's increasing peace operations capacity. African states have deployed operations of their own and they now contribute half of all UN peacekeepers. De Coning argues that the AU and the UN have developed a strategic partnership that plays out at the political, policy, and operational levels, and reflects the reality that neither will deploy peace operations in Africa without close consultations and some form of cooperation with the other. While the UN peacekeeping model is not found to be well-suited to enforcement, counter-terrorism or trans-national operations, de Coning argues that, the AU, sub-regional organisations and ad hoc regional coalitions have developed capabilities designed to address these challenges. These African capabilities help relieve the pressure on the UN to conduct such operations.

Chapter 12, authored by *Thierry Tardy*, looks at the evolving relationship between the European Union (EU) and UN peace operations. Tardy argues that over the last twenty years, the EU has become a prominent crisis management actor alongside and sometimes together with the UN within the field of peacekeeping. He locates the EU's crisis management role in the UN's general mandate of "maintaining international peace and security". Throughout the chapter, he grapples with questions such as: What is the EU's approach to managing crises? To what extent does the EU's approach converge with and support the UN peacekeeping agenda? And what do EU member states' own institutional choices tell us about the UN–EU global–regional peace and security partnerships? Tardy provides a comprehensive overview of EU crisis management operations, compares EU and UN operations, and sheds light on the causes of this cooperation and its consequences for their relationship. Finally, he assesses the European participation in the UN operation in Mali and suggests how EU member states' institutional preferences may evolve in the coming years.

In Chapter 13, *Yin He* turns attention to China's rising prominence in UN peace operations. He contends that China's UN peacekeeping policy can to a large extent be explained by changes in China's national identity. Since China's return to the UN in 1971, China's national identity has undergone a considerable transformation, from a semi-revolutionary state in the 1970s and an integrated member of the international community in the 1980s and 1990s, to a rising power in the twenty-first century. The country's policy on UN peacekeeping has reflected these transformations. The Chinese position on UN peace operations has changed from opposition in the 1970s, to gradually expanded and reactive participation in the 1980s and 1990s, and finally to an increasingly active involvement in the new millennium. Yin argues that China's ambition is to contribute more than personnel and finances to UN peace operations, with this rising power also wanting to shape governance of UN operations.

In Chapter 14, *Jonathan C. Agensky* turns to non-state actors and their relation to UN peace operations. He highlights practices that seek similar outcomes as UN peace operations or otherwise affect the background conditions necessary for their success. Treating South Sudan as an illustrative case study, Agensky demonstrates how the incorporation of religious institutions into global and regional aid-based governance networks enables church-based actors to pursue political, social, and structural interventions critical to UN peace operations. In doing so, he emphasises the impact of religion, aid, and governance on longer-term peacebuilding in Africa, with a view toward contributing to discussions about holistic, integrated, and people-centred approaches to sustainable peace.

In the concluding chapter, *Cedric de Coning* synthesises several major findings of the volume and advances the argument that we are now entering a more pragmatic era of UN peace operations. He sees peace operations as likely becoming less intrusive and more supportive of locally-led solutions. Looking forward, de Coning identifies three overarching themes. First, the degree to which a peace operation contributes to the strategic political coherence of the larger national and international effort is likely to become a key measure of its effectiveness. Second, the principle of minimum use of force is likely to remain a defining feature of peace operations. And third, the scope of peace operations mandates may be trimmed down to focus on protection, stability, and politics. He argues that peace operations have shown a remarkable capacity to continuously adapt to new challenges, but at the same time remained resiliently identifiable by the enduring principles of peacekeeping.

References

Berdal, Mats, and David Malone (eds.). 2000. *Greed & Grievance: Economic Agendas in Civil Wars.* Boulder: Lynne Rienner.

Burkeman, Oliver, and Xan Rice. 2006. Sudan Rejects UN Peacekeeping Plan. *The Guardian*, September 1. https://www.theguardian.com/world/2006/sep/01/sudan.oliverburkeman. Accessed 14 Mar 2018.

Campbell, Susanna, David Chandler, and Meera Sabaratnam (eds.). 2011. *A Liberal Peace? The Problems and Practices of Peacebuilding.* London: Zed Books.

Chesterman, Simon. 2004. The Use of Force in UN Peace Operations, Peacekeeping Best Practices Unit (External Study). http://www.operationspaix.net/DATA/DOCUMENT/5808~v~The_Use_of_Force_in_UN_Peace_Operations.pdf. Accessed 14 Mar 2018.

Collier, Paul, and Anke Hoeffler. 2004. Greed and Grievance in Civil War. *Oxford Economic Papers* 56: 563–595.

Cox, Robert W. 1981. Social Forces, States and World Orders: Beyond International Relations Theory. *Millennium—Journal of International Studies* 10 (2): 126–155.

Cunliffe, Philip. 2013. *Legions of Peace: UN Peacekeepers from the Global South*. London: Hurst.

de Coning, Cedric, Linnéa Gelot, and John Karlsrud (eds.). 2016. *The Future of African Peace Operations: From the Janjaweed to Boko Haram*. London: Zed Books.

de Coning, Cedric, Thomas Mandrup, and Liselotte Odgaard. 2014. *The BRICS and Coexistence: An Alternative Vision of World Order*. London: Routledge.

Diehl, Paul F., and Elijah PharaohKhan. 2000. Financing UN Peacekeeping: A Review and Assessment of Proposals. *Review of Policy Research* 17 (1): 71–104.

Essa, Azad. 2017. UN Peacekeepers Hit by New Allegations of Sex Abuse. Aljazeera, July 10. http://www.aljazeera.com/news/2017/07/peacekeepers-hit-allegations-sex-abuse-170701133655238.html. Accessed 14 Mar 2018.

Fukuyama, Francis. 1992. *The End of History and the Last Man*. New York: Free Press.

Green, Miranda. 2017. Haley Cheers Cuts to UN Peacekeeping: 'We're only Getting Started'. *CNN Politics*. http://edition.cnn.com/2017/06/29/politics/haley-on-un-cuts/index.html. Accessed 14 Mar 2018.

Heathershaw, John. 2008. Unpacking the Liberal Peace: The Dividing and Merging of Peacebuilding Discourses. *Millennium: Journal of International Studies* 35 (3): 597–621.

Holzgrefe, J.L., and Robert J. Keohane (eds.). 2008. *Humanitarian Intervention: Ethical, Legal and Political Dilemmas*. Cambridge: Cambridge University Press.

Lynch, Colum. 2013. The Blue Helmet Caste System. *Foreign Policy*, April 11. http://blog.foreignpolicy.com/posts/2013/04/11/the_blue_helmet_caste_system. Accessed 14 Mar 2018.

Lynch, Colum. 2017. Trump Administration Eyes $1 Billion in Cuts to U.N. Peacekeeping. *Foreign Policy*, March 23. http://foreignpolicy.com/2017/03/23/trump-administration-eyes-1-billion-in-cuts-to-u-n-peacekeeping. Accessed 14 Mar 2018.

Mac Ginty, Roger. 2012. *International Peacebuilding and Local Resistance: Hybrid Forms of Peace*. Basingstoke: Palgrave Macmillan.

Naraghi Anderlini, Sanam. 2017. UN Peacekeepers' Sexual Assault Problem. *Foreign Affairs*, June 9. https://www.foreignaffairs.com/articles/world/2017-06-09/un-peacekeepers-sexual-assault-problem. Accessed 14 Mar 2018.

Narlikar, Amrita. 2010. *New Powers: How to Become One and How to Manage Them*. London: Hurst.

O'Neill, Jim. 2001. Building Better Global Economic BRICs. Global Economics Paper No. 66, Goldman Sachs, New York.

Paris, Roland. 2001. Human Security: Paradigm Shift or Hot Air? *International Security* 26 (2): 87–102.

Peter, Mateja. 2015. Between Doctrine and Practice: The United Nations Peacekeeping Dilemma. *Global Governance: A Review of Multilateralism and International Organizations* 21 (3): 351–370.

Pugh, Michael. 2004. Peacekeeping and Critical Theory. *International Peacekeeping* 11 (1): 39–58.

Richmond, Oliver P. 2004. UN Peace Operations and the Dilemmas of the Peacebuilding Consensus. *International Peacekeeping* 11 (1): 83–101.

Stedman, Stephen John. 1997. Spoiler Problems in Peace Processes. *International Security* 22 (2): 5–53.

Stoett, Peter J. 1999. *Human and Global Security: An Exploration of Terms.* Toronto: Toronto University Press.

Suhrke, Astri. 1999. Human Security and the Interests of States. *Security Dialogue* 30 (3): 265–276.

United Nations. 2000. *Report of the Panel on United Nations Peace Operations.* New York: United Nations.

United Nations. 2008. *United Nations Peacekeeping: Principles and Guidelines, Department of Peacekeeping*. New York: DPKO.

United Nations. 2014. Press Release: Secretary-General Appoints High-Level Independent Panel on Peace Operations, October 31. New York: United Nations.

United Nations. 2015a. *Evaluation of the Enforcement and Remedial Assistance Efforts for Sexual Exploitation and Abuse by the United Nations and Related Personnel in Peacekeeping Operations*, May 15. New York: UN Office of Internal Oversight.

United Nations. 2015b. *Report of the High-Level Independent Panel on Peace Operations on Uniting Our Strengths for Peace: Politics, Partnership and People*. New York: United Nations.

United Nations. 2017. *UN Secretary-General Statement: Note to Correspondents on MINUSCA*, June 21. New York: United Nations.

United Nations. 2018. Troop and Police Contributors. United Nations Peacekeeping. https://peacekeeping.un.org/en/troop-and-police-contributors. Accessed 14 Mar 2018.

Williams, Paul D., and Arthur Boutellis. 2014. Partnership Peacekeeping: Challenges and Opportunities in the United Nations-African Union Relationship. *African Affairs* 113 (451): 254–278.

Open Access This chapter is licensed under the terms of the Creative Commons Attribution 4.0 International License (http://creativecommons.org/licenses/by/4.0/), which permits use, sharing, adaptation, distribution and reproduction in any medium or format, as long as you give appropriate credit to the original author(s) and the source, provide a link to the Creative Commons license and indicate if changes were made.

The images or other third party material in this chapter are included in the chapter's Creative Commons license, unless indicated otherwise in a credit line to the material. If material is not included in the chapter's Creative Commons license and your intended use is not permitted by statutory regulation or exceeds the permitted use, you will need to obtain permission directly from the copyright holder.

PART I

Political and Strategic Context: Past, Present, Future

CHAPTER 2

Peacekeeping: Resilience of an Idea

Mateja Peter

Introduction

Peacekeeping is not only one of the activities that the United Nations (UN) does, it is in many ways what the UN is. In countries emerging from the scourge of war, the acronym UN is customarily used as a synonym for the deployed peacekeeping operation. When member states, the public or the academics criticise *the UN* for not resolving conflicts, they not only talk of the political stalemates in the UN Security Council (UNSC, Council), but also invoke the failures of its peacekeeping missions. The significance of peacekeeping to member states is evident in financial terms: while the UN General Assembly agreed on a $5.4 billion for the regular budget for the 2016–2017 biennium,[1] the approved budget for UN peacekeeping operations for the fiscal year 1 July 2016–30 June 2017 was $7.87 billion (UN 2016). Although UN peacekeeping still constitutes less than 0.5% of world military expenditures,[2] it is the activity that the UN is most visibly associated with.

[1] The UN regular budget comes in two-year cycles (UN 2015a).
[2] http://www.un.org/en/peacekeeping/documents/factsheet.pdf.

M. Peter (✉)
School of International Relations, University of St Andrews, St Andrews, UK
e-mail: mp240@st-andrews.ac.uk

© The Author(s) 2019

C. de Coning and M. Peter (eds.), *United Nations Peace Operations in a Changing Global Order*,
https://doi.org/10.1007/978-3-319-99106-1_2

UN peacekeeping is almost as old as the organisation itself. This chapter looks at the evolution of the idea of peacekeeping, asking how an instrument developed in the late 1940s managed to not only survive but also respond to the changing geopolitical and conflict landscape over the last seventy years. I do not plan to examine whether UN peacekeeping is the most appropriate response to conflicts emerging out of global fault lines. This would not only require an in-depth analysis of different conflicts, but I would even argue that in many respect the persistent reliance on UN peacekeeping is a result of a cognitive bias known as the law of the instrument: 'if the only tool you have is a hammer, you will treat everything as if it were a nail.' The UN Security Council has used this tool in 71 conflict situations, with 16 peacekeeping operations deployed at the time of writing. Evidently, member states have found peacekeeping useful. What I am primarily interested in here is the adaptation of the tool, examining for what purposes it has been used and why. I argue that peacekeeping started as a conflict management instrument, which was adapted to a conflict resolution mechanism after the end of the Cold War, but has now come full circle and is again increasingly used to manage and contain, not resolve conflicts. The strength of the idea comes from this resilience.

Peacekeeping and the Cold War

Despite their rapid importance for the identity of the organisation, the UN founders did not envisage peacekeeping operations as a tool for addressing conflicts. Peacekeeping is therefore not mentioned in the UN Charter (1945). According to the organisation's constitutive document, the UN Security Council, as the organ primarily responsible for the maintenance of international peace and security, could either take note of the threat to peace and security and recommend to conflict parties to resolve their dispute peacefully (Chapter VI) or it could take binding action to enforce measures to address the conflict by itself (Chapter VII). The Charter was devised to prevent the eruption of another world war. It ensured that great powers had a vested interest in the system designed to collectively punish a wrongdoer and set it on the right path (Kelsen 1948). In stark contrast to this, most conflicts in the subsequent years were tied to the processes of decolonialisation, where identifying the wrongdoer was not as clear cut. Throughout the Cold War, decolonialisation-related conflicts were also the only ones that the UNSC was willing to take up. As the Council was gridlocked, the only measures that could be adopted were in areas of secondary significance to the Union of Soviet Socialist Republics (USSR) and the United States (US). But even in these conflicts, enforcement measures were off the table. This was partly as these conflicts were mostly not as unambiguous to warrant clear enforcement measures, but primarily because great powers did not want to sanction an actor they could not entirely control—the UN—to use force. When coercive measures were deemed to be needed in their allied or client states, the two blocks employed them unilaterally. The core characteristics and principles of UN peacekeeping developed as a direct result of this Cold War schism. Peacekeeping emerged as a tool of necessity, sitting between Chapter VI and Chapter VII mandates.

The first UN peacekeeping missions were established already in 1948 and 1949. They signalled what kind of conflicts the UN would be preoccupied with in its first decades. The 1948 mission, *the United Nations Truce Supervision Organization* (UNTSO), was established following the conclusion of the first Arab-Israeli War (UN 1948). With it the UNSC sent a small number of unarmed military observers to monitor the ceasefire and report to the Council any violations. The mission had a similar mandate to *the United Nations Military Observer Group in India and Pakistan* (UNMOGIP) established a year later and tasked with monitoring the ceasefire of the Indo-Pakistani War of 1947–1948 (UN 1949). Both missions and conflicts share several characteristics. The conflicts erupted following recent declarations of independence. Israel declared statehood in 1947, as did both India and Pakistan. In the case of Israel, Arab states contested its statehood. India and Pakistan fought over a large border area of Kashmir and Jammu, both claiming it belonged to them. In both conflicts, the two Cold War rivals supported the opposing sides.[3] To ensure that the clash would not escalate and involve the US and the Soviet Union directly, a mechanism was devised to keep the sides separated. UN peacekeeping troops were tasked to monitor whether all sides were complying with the ceasefire and thus created a buffer zone between them. Peacekeepers had clear instructions not to get involved in internal affairs of the states and not to attempt to resolve conflicts. They were sent to manage these conflicts, not resolve them. Attempts

[3] India started openly cultivating strategic and military relations with the Soviet Union in the mid-1950s, after the US made Pakistan a Central Treaty Organisation ally. However, the split could be anticipated already in the late 1940s.

at their resolution were taken up in other fora, both within and outside the UN. Indicating the intractability of both the Middle East and the Indo-Pakistani conflict, both missions are still in existence seven decades after. Compared to the post-Cold War operations, these are small enterprises (UNTSO is staffed by around 400 peacekeepers, including local staff; around 100 peacekeepers serve in UNMOGIP). Their continued presence speaks to the variety of conflicts that UN peacekeepers play a role in, as well as the coexistence of various peacekeeping models in the twenty-first century.

The first 'real' UN peacekeeping operation, which included armed military personnel, was sent to Egypt in 1956 following the Suez Crisis. The crisis erupted as Egypt was getting increasingly closer to the Soviet Union, which led to the withdrawal of US and UK support for the construction of the Aswan Dam. In turn, Egypt nationalised the Suez Canal. To regain Western control of this strategic trade route, Israeli, British, and French forces invaded Egypt. While the crisis was linked both to the decolonialisation and the Cold War power politics, it was also a clear act of aggression against a sovereign state. UK and French occupancy of the UNSC permanent seats meant that any proposed enforcement measures would have been immediately vetoed. But this time, the US and the Soviet Union had an interest in quickly resolving the crisis and through that also protect the collective security arrangements of the UN Charter. As political pressure from the two superpowers grew, all parties agreed that foreign forces should withdraw from the Egyptian territory and that their withdrawal should be overseen by a neutral force. This peacekeeping mission would then also serve as a buffer between the Egyptian and Israeli forces and provide impartial supervision of the ceasefire. The *First United Nations Emergency Force* (UNEF I) was in large measure a result of efforts by the UN Secretary-General Dag Hammarskjöld, who cobbled the mission together and obtained Egypt's consent for deployment of military personnel in its territory. The mission mandate was approved, not by the UNSC, but by the UN General Assembly (UN 1956). Importantly, peacekeepers were explicitly forbidden to interfere in internal matters of Egypt or undertake any activities that could influence the balance of power between conflicting parties.[4] Again, the mission was to manage, not resolve, the conflict.

[4]For more on the mission, see Rosner (1964).

Two years after the deployment of UNEF I, the Secretary-General published an extensive report summarising lessons learned from this first proper experience with UN peacekeeping, recommending a set of basic principles that should guide any future deployments. This was the first of the many times that initiatives in peacekeeping were developed and proposed by the central organ of the UN and not by the member states. The key principles of UN peacekeeping became consent, limited use of force, and non-interference in internal affairs of host states (UN 1958, pp. 154–193). The report stressed that for these missions to comply with international law and the UN Charter, "the United Nations cannot undertake to implement them by stationing units on the territory of a Member State without the consent of the Government concerned" (ibid., p. 155). Not limiting the authority of the UN to decide on the composition of the mission, the host government should also consent to the nationality of military troops deployed. Hammarskjöld envisaged this would not include contingents from permanent members of the UNSC or regional countries that might have a special interest in the situation, thus ensuring impartiality of the operation (ibid., p. 160).[5] The report also underlined that authority granted to a UN mission could not be exercised in competition with the host government or in cooperation with it through a joint deployment. It concluded that "a United Nations operation must be separate and distinct from activities by national authorities" (ibid., p. 165) and "cannot be permitted in any sense to be a party to internal conflicts" (ibid., p. 166). Any intervention in internal affairs of a host state would not only make the peacekeeping mandate more difficult to achieve but could also negatively impact relations between the UN and its member state.

Consent, limited use of force, and non-interference in internal affairs of host states became the bedrock for UN peacekeeping interventions throughout the Cold War. While proposed by the UN Secretary-General, his ambition was limited by what the two great powers allowed the UN to develop. For the first forty years, UN peacekeeping essentially meant observation of ceasefires in inter-state disputes. That notwithstanding, the organisation launched two operations that signalled where UN peacekeeping would develop after the bipolar order had

[5] In the case of UNEF I, contingents came from ten countries: Brazil, Canada, Colombia, Denmark, Finland, India, Indonesia, Norway, Sweden, and Yugoslavia.

collapsed. These missions also indicate that the type of conflicts we tend to associate with the post-Cold War order, predate its collapse.

The first operation to stray from the typical Cold War peacekeeping model was deployed in 1960 to the former Belgian colony of Congo, the modern day Democratic Republic of the Congo (Congo).[6] *The United Nations Operation in Congo* (Opération des Nations Unies au Congo, ONUC) is to this day one of the largest UN peacekeeping operations to be deployed and at its height counted almost 20,000 armed troops.[7] It is also the first peacekeeping mission, which due to developments on the ground, ended up intervening into a civil war. The original mandate of the operation was in line with Hammarskjöld's vision as the mission was supposed to supervise the withdrawal of Belgian colonial forces from the Congolese territory (UN 1960). ONUC was set up to help the newly independent country stabilise the situation on the ground and pave the way for the new government. Instead, peacekeepers became caught up in an armed conflict between two groups of warring factions supported by the USSR and the US. While the UNSC agreed to a strengthened mandate in 1961 (UN 1961), ONUC could not resolve the crisis which grew into a series of civil wars. But the mission was influential for the development of UN peacekeeping. Besides being the first operation to intervene in an intra-state conflict, it was also the first mission where the UNSC authorised the use of force for purposes beyond self-defence. At the time, there were disagreements over what that meant in practice. The issue was far from resolved, but the debate itself foreshadowed the difficulties with strict adherence to the peacekeeping principles that peacekeeping missions face today in intra-state conflicts (Gibbs 2000; Spooner 2010).

The second atypical peacekeeping operation during the Cold War was *the United Nations Security Force in West New Guinea* (UNSF). UNSF was authorised by the UN General Assembly to administer the territory of West New Guinea between October 1962 and April 1963 (UN 1962). After that period this former Dutch colony became part of Indonesia.

[6]In 1960, the former colony declared independence as the Republic of Congo. The country changed its name to the Democratic Republic of Congo in 1964.

[7]The current operation in the DRC (MONUSCO) is also the largest peacekeeping operation at the time of writing. Its strength in October 2017 was over 21,000 uniformed and civilian personnel. See: https://peacekeeping.un.org/en/peacekeeping-fact-sheet-oct-2017. More on MONUSCO below.

In the context of the Cold War any administration of the territory by a peacekeeping force was almost unimaginable, but UNSF represented a viable compromise for a resolution of a long-standing dispute between Indonesia and the Netherlands. As Indonesia grew increasingly close to the USSR, the US obtained the Dutch agreement to the Indonesian claim in exchange for Indonesian support of the Western bloc. To preserve the Dutch dignity, the territory was not to be handed over to the Indonesians directly, but to the UN peacekeepers, who ended up managing it for over half a year.[8] While both ONUC and UNSF sowed the seeds for what UN peacekeeping would look like after the end of the Cold War, for the first forty years peacekeeping was largely contained to supervising ceasefires. It was only with dramatic global changes that these missions could develop into what they are known for today.

End of the Cold War and the New UN Peacekeeping

The fall of the Berlin Wall presented a tectonic change in how the UNSC and member states of the UN responded to conflicts. Not only was there more cooperation between the Cold War rivals on the Security Council, but many states came under increasing pressure from their constituencies to address human plight in far-flung places. Globalisation and the 24-hour news cycles brought these conflicts to the attention of audiences in the global North. During the last years of the Cold War, the two superpowers also showed much less interest in directly addressing problems of and within their allied and client states. They relinquished a bulk of this task to international organisations, most notably the United Nations. This lead to a boom in international peacekeeping, with 58 out of a total of 71 UN missions established after 1988.[9] But the change was not only quantitative. These new missions, often referred to as second generation peacekeeping (Mackinlay and Chopra 1993), also changed qualitatively. A small number of post-1988 missions—for example, *the United Nations Good Offices Mission in Afghanistan and Pakistan* (UNGOMAP), which supervised the withdrawal of Soviet troops from Afghanistan and Pakistan (UN 1988)—retained their traditional mandates, but most operations substantially gained in complexity receiving

[8] More on the background of the mission at https://peacekeeping.un.org/mission/past/unsf.htm.

[9] https://peacekeeping.un.org/en/past-peacekeeping-operations.

mandates addressing internal matters of sovereign states. This was a brand-new experience for the UN.

The first group of these multi-dimensional missions, established between 1988 and 1992, preserved some of the characteristics of the Cold War monitoring missions. The main difference was that these new missions were primarily tasked with monitoring non-military activities. *The United Nations Transition Assistance Group* (UNTAG) was mandated to ensure the early independence of Namibia through free and fair elections (UN 1989). Its police component was tasked with monitoring and reporting on the actions of local police and security forces. UNTAG also helped with monitoring and assisting in the return of refugees. UN peacekeeping operations in El Salvador, Angola, Western Sahara, Cambodia, and Mozambique were similarly tasked with observing elections, reporting on human rights violations and the establishment of a basic post-war rule of law. While these tasks are a common feature of any UN mission deployed in the twenty-first century, at the time, they were nothing less but revolutionary. Peacekeepers were no longer being sent into troubled territories to monitor inter-state disputes, but primarily dealt with intra-state conflicts. Moreover, peacekeeping now meant not only the deployment of military troops, but also of a civilian and a police component, leading eventually to the establishment of the United Nations Office of Rule of Law and Security Institutions (OROLSI).

These early multidimensional peacekeeping attempts have been judged as largely successful by both the UN and outside experts (Howard 2007). They did nonetheless present a challenge for the peacekeeping principles proposed by Hammarskjöld as the UN had to adapt to the new geopolitical and conflict environment. The 1992 document *An Agenda for Peace*, prepared by the UN Secretary-General Boutros Boutros-Ghali, foreshadowed some of these challenges but maintained that "the established principles and practices of peace-keeping have responded flexibly to new demands of recent years" and that "the basic conditions for success remain unchanged" (UN 1992, para. 50). Highlighting the increasing number of tasks given to UN peacekeepers by the Security Council, the report nonetheless drew sharp lines between peacekeeping, peace enforcement, and peacebuilding.[10] As early as 1992, the Secretary-General and his advisers were acutely aware of complications that could emerge if the concept

[10] See the introduction of this volume for distinctions between the three.

of peacekeeping was stretched into peace enforcement. The document therefore urged the UNSC that when fighting resumed and ceasefires were broken, peace enforcement units should be utilised. Such units would be more heavily armed than peacekeepers and would be mandated to use force beyond self-defence (UN 1992, para. 44).

While distinctions between peacekeeping and peace enforcement were drawn sharp on paper, in practice, the UNSC increasingly deployed peacekeeping missions into situations where peace was extremely fragile. The two most notorious of these missions were based in Rwanda (*United Nations Assistance Mission for Rwanda*, UNAMIR) and Bosnia and Herzegovina (*United Nations Protection Force*, UNPROFOR), where peacekeepers were deployed amid genocidal wars. The ongoing fighting and ethnic cleansing created substantial confusion among UN troops, who were worried not just about overstepping their mandates but also about getting involved in civil wars. They interpreted peacekeeping principles narrowly and as a result failed to use force to protect civilian population. Srebrenica and Rwanda to this day serve as poignant reminders of the failures of UN peacekeeping and the UN system to act on evolving genocides. The UNSC became more willing to deploy peacekeepers to civil wars, but these early post-Cold War mistakes highlighted that willingness to deploy is not enough; peacekeeping would need to adapt if it was to remain a useful tool.

Rethinking UN Peacekeeping for the Post-Cold War Era

The gravity of these failures created an opportunity for a deeper reflection on the role of the organisation in the post-Cold War order (Barnett 2002; Malone and Thakur 2001; Western 2002). In 1999, the Secretary-General Kofi Annan appointed an independent Panel on United Nations Peace Operations, asking it to address the shortcomings of existing peace operations system and to make realistic recommendations for their future. Notwithstanding the recent crises, the Brahimi report (UN 2000), named after the chair of the panel, called for a renewed political commitment to UN peace operations. Most of the report deals with the increasing complexity of conflicts that peacekeeping operations have been mandated to address since the end of the Cold War. Many of its core findings remain relevant to this day, despite it being created at the time of undisputed Western hegemony.

UN peacekeeping operations had only a limited experience in peacebuilding when the report was written, but the trend towards longer-term peacebuilding mandates was already visible. The Brahimi report therefore aptly noted that as peacekeeping operations took on more peace-building tasks, their mandates would become more difficult to accomplish (UN 2000, paras. 19–20). Unlike early experiences of peacekeeping, where operations had been deployed to manage conflicts, the post-1995 operations were being deployed with an objective to help countries resolve their conflicts. Mandates of missions from Bosnia and Herzegovina to Haiti and Sierra Leone asked peacekeepers to help with reforms of the rule of law and security sector in addition to the more traditional monitoring tasks of earlier missions. Such peacekeeping missions were becoming pieces of a broader (liberal) statebuilding agenda (Fukuyama 2004; Paris 2004; Richmond 2004). UN peacekeepers, together with regional organisations and international financial institutions, which focused more on the economic aspects, were asked to build basic institutional structures and assist states in establishing post-conflict functionality and legitimacy. More stable institutions were seen as a precondition for peace. In the most extreme cases—in Kosovo and in Timor-Leste—UN peacekeepers were even given a temporary executive law enforcement and administrative authority over a territory (UN 1999a, b; Caplan 2005; Chesterman 2005). Such conflict resolution mandates were undeniably a more ambitious task than conflict management undertakings of earlier missions.

Peacekeeping operations started growing, and complexity necessitated a discussion on the coherence of international approaches to conflicts. If different parts were acting at cross-purposes, less could be achieved. The Brahimi report asked for establishment of Integrated Mission Task Forces at the level of UN headquarters. These entities would substitute the *ad hoc* coordination activities and would mirror the various functions of the missions themselves. They would be responsible for mission-specific planning and would act as a coordination group for all UN departments involved (UN 2000, paras. 198–217). Over the next decade, the UN launched a series of initiatives expanding on this thinking. These initiatives aimed to ensure more coherence of UN action. Most notable of these were the introduction of UN Integrated Missions in 2006 (UN 2006), which then developed into a broader UN Integrated Approach in 2008, which is still in place today (UN 2008a). Yet despite these innovations, many of these new multi-dimensional operations saw less success in the implementation of their mandates than the early-era peacekeeping.

The Brahimi report also reiterated the stark distinction between peace enforcement and peacekeeping found in earlier documents. The panel recognised that "the United Nations does not wage war" (UN 2000, para. 53) and urged the UNSC to entrust enforcement actions to coalitions of willing states. It maintained that "consent of the local parties, impartiality and use of force only in self-defence should remain the bedrock principles of peacekeeping" (UN 2000, para. 48). But despite this strong and unambiguous language, strict adherence to these principles was virtually impossible to maintain (de Coning et al. 2017). This became even more pronounced from mid-2000s on, when the UNSC started deploying operations with explicit mandates to protect civilians (Holt and Taylor 2009). The Capstone doctrine from 2008, which to this day provides guidance for modern UN-led peacekeeping operations, tried to clarify some of the ambiguity over how peacekeeping principles should be interpreted. Its guidance explained that "impartiality … should not be confused with neutrality or inactivity," and that "a peacekeeping operation should not condone actions by the parties that violate the undertakings of the peace process or the international norms and principles" (UN 2008b, p. 33). But in practice things were murkier as troop contributing countries and mission leadership were often reluctant to use force robustly, worrying about casualties and about getting involved in civil wars.[11]

The experience with *the United Nations Mission in the Republic of South Sudan* (UNMISS) demonstrates how swiftly missions need to adapt in contemporary conflicts and what challenges they face when protecting civilians. UNMISS was established in 2011 (UN 2011) and was simultaneously mandated to support the government of South Sudan in establishing the institutions necessary to govern a new country and to hold it accountable to international norms and standards (da Costa and Peter 2017). Reconciling the two was difficult from the beginning, but as political wrangling between President Kiir and Vice-President Machar escalated, the newly independent country descendent into a civil war. UNMISS was now caught between a rock and a hard place, mandated to help the government which was swiftly becoming the biggest threat to its own population. While the UNSC changed the mandate to a protection of civilians one (UN 2014a), and the mission became more proactive in

[11] For more on the use of force in UN peacekeeping see Mats Berdal in this volume.

protecting civilians, including by opening the gates of its compounds,[12] problems remained. The mission was not perceived as impartial by the warring parties, which repeatedly threatened to withdraw their consent to UN presence. At the same time "a de facto dual line of command involving mission leadership and troop-contributing countries that regulates the use of force by missions" (UN 2014b), meant that peacekeeping contingents were not intervening when civilians were under attack.

The High-Level Independent Panel on Peace Operations Report (HIPPO report) identified protection of civilians as "a core obligation of the United Nations" (UN 2015b, p. ix). This requirement is also explicitly included in the great majority of mandates of current missions. While this emphasis is not revolutionary—UN reports dating back to the early 2000s have been stressing protection of civilians as a core function of UN peacekeeping—the need for protecting vulnerable populations has never been so high. Protecting civilians, as imperfectly as it is implemented, is what both the local population and the international community expect of UN peacekeeping today. But while this normative change is essential for the credibility of the UN, it also means that the nature of peacekeeping is changing. As more mandates switch from peacebuilding/statebuilding ones to what is essentially an emergency humanitarian peacekeeping, newly deployed peacekeeping operations are increasingly moving away from a conflict resolution to a conflict management tool.

A New Era of Enforcement Peacekeeping?

Peacekeeping has undergone substantial changes over the last decade and these operations are now firmly moving away from conflict resolution to conflict management. Protection of civilians is and will remain the core challenge if the UN as an institution wants to retain its credibility in the twenty-first century. At the same time, we are seeing a new trend in the kind of operations the Council is mandating. After a short period of seeming decline in large-scale operations, the UNSC has since 2013 become more comfortable authorising larger operations. In addition to the Democratic Republic of the Congo (DRC) mission, which was strengthened with additional forces and amounts to over 22,000 troops, the Council authorised a deployment of 12,000 troops and police to

[12] See Hilde Frafjord Johnson in this volume for more on how the mission was adapting to include the protection of civilians mandate.

Mali and 10,000 to the Central African Republic (CAR) (UN 2013a, 2014c). More importantly for the idea of peacekeeping itself, the types of activities that these new missions and the newly enhanced missions are mandated to perform substantially expand and change the nature of UN peacekeeping. Peacekeeping operations deployed to the DRC, Mali, and the CAR operate in midst of open conflicts, in the first two cases no comprehensive peace agreement had been negotiated before missions were deployed. In the past, both the Secretariat and the UNSC were reluctant to deploy under such circumstances, but that seems to be changing. As a result, these operations actively borrow elements from peace enforcement missions, walking the line between peacekeeping and peace enforcement. After traditional and multidimensional peacekeeping, we are on the cusp of a new era of enforcement peacekeeping. This introduces a possible new type of peacekeeping operations, which will end up coexisting with previous types of peacekeeping.

Enforcement peacekeeping manifests itself through two inter-related developments: (a) in enforcement of political solutions through support of a government's state-building ambitions in its attempts to extend state authority amid an ongoing conflict, and (b) in enforcement of military victories through offensive use of force.[13] As targets of peacekeeping actions are non-state actors that enjoy little international legitimacy due to their appalling human rights and war crimes records, no comprehensive peace agreements with them are sought before peacekeepers are deployed, something that is in stark contrast with multidimensional peacekeeping developed after the end of the Cold War.

The most noticeable and talked about mission in this regard has been the *UN Organization Stabilization Mission in the Democratic Republic of the Congo (MONUSCO)*. To MONUSCO, the Security Council authorised the inclusion of a force intervention brigade (FIB) within an existing mission structure (UN 2013b). This is the "first-ever 'offensive' combat force" in UN peacekeeping (UN 2013c), which was set-up to "neutralize and disarm"—a euphemism used by the military when engaging in offensive operations—the Tutsi March 23 (M23) militia in the eastern parts of the DRC. FIB is mandated to assist Congolese forces in fighting all armed groups in the Eastern Congo, with a few of them explicitly listed in the UNSC resolution. This was the first time in the history

[13]For more details on enforcement peacekeeping discussed in this section, see Peter (2015).

of UN peacekeeping that the Council created a list of enemies that UN peacekeepers were supposed to engage with, making some researchers wonder whether the UN now wages war (Karlsrud 2015).

Although the Congolese experience has not been entirely replicated in other missions so far, it does indicate a wider trend towards more robust UN operations, opening doors for offensive use of force. For example, *the United Nations Multidimensional Integrated Stabilization Mission in Mali* (MINUSMA) (UN 2013a) assimilated an extant Economic Community of West African States (ECOWAS) mission named AFISMA, which was previously mandated to support the government of Mali, an ECOWAS member nation, in its fight against Islamist rebels in the northern Mali conflict. The resolution establishing MINUSMA also authorised French troops conducting Operation Serval to use all necessary means to intervene within the limits of their capacities and areas of deployment in support of elements of MINUSMA, essentially mandating an intervention brigade just outside the UN command structures. UN missions are, as these examples indicate, increasingly more robust.

One good indication of increasing involvement of UN peacekeepers in enforcement of political and military solutions can be found in the types of capabilities that these missions are relying on. The UN has advocated for the use of surveillance drones in the eastern DRC, on the border between Côte d'Ivoire and Liberia, in South Sudan, and in Mali. In Somalia, the UN is engaged in strategic communication campaigning and has hired a consultancy firm that, according to its statements, "runs a fully integrated campaign to counter the radicalising effect of Al-Shabaab and engage Somalis in building a positive future for their country" (Albany Associates 2017). In Mali, peacekeepers have been openly relying on strategic intelligence in their engagement with Islamic rebels. In 2000, when the Brahimi report suggested incorporation of field intelligence in peace operations so that they could better respond to complex situations (UN 2000, para. 51), member states flat out rejected the proposals. A good decade later their outlooks have changed. Drones, intelligence, and strategic communication all evoke ideas of stabilisation missions in Iraq and Afghanistan. The major difference is that the UN peacekeeping activities are conducted on request of governments in target states.

As mandates change, we are also seeing a change in the composition of troops in UN peacekeeping. UN operations increasingly rely on regional contributions, as only highly interested states are willing to risk the lives of their citizens in increasingly robust operations. When Hammarskjöld penned the peacekeeping principles in the 1950s, this would have been unheard of. A prime example of this development is MINUSMA, which by incorporating AFISMA became ostensibly a mission composed of regional troops. Among the top five troop contributors to the Mali mission in October 2017 were Burkina Faso, Chad, Senegal, and Togo, all regional states.[14] In the DRC, the primary contributors to the intervention brigade are South Africa, Tanzania, and Malawi, while the rest of the MONUSCO mission is composed mainly of South Asian troops. Inclusion of regional forces has already flagged up some problems in the CAR, where Chadian forces needed to be redeployed due to Chad's perceived backing of the Muslim rebel group Séléka, which led the coup against the CAR government (Al Jazeera 2013).

The switch towards more robust operations has several implications on peacekeeping principles and broader UN peacebuilding attempts (Peter 2015; Hunt 2017; de Coning et al. 2017). Most important for the argument in this chapter, is that these missions are abandoning their conflict resolution ambitions, focusing only on the management and containment of these conflicts. But unlike the Cold War peacekeeping operations, which similarly focused on conflict management, the new missions are actively siding with the often-contested governments. When UN peacekeepers side with one party in a conflict, whether by helping it extend state authority or defeat enemy combatants, this substantially affects the conflict and political dynamics at that time. As political reincarnations of these same armed groups will in many cases need to be included in peace settlements for these to become sustainable, this will have far-reaching consequences for the UN's ability to act as an impartial broker in peace processes.

These new UN attempts to manage conflicts could have negative implications on UN's ability to contribute to conflict resolution. It is therefore unsurprising that UN reports, including the report of the HIPPO panel, convey discomfort with the idea of robust enforcement peacekeeping. The big question for the future is whether the UN as an institution will be able to resist the pressures from member states to morph peacekeeping with peace enforcement.

[14] See: https://peacekeeping.un.org/en/mission/minusma.

Conclusions

The history of UN peacekeeping almost serves as a history of the types of conflicts that the international community has been dealing with since the end of the Second World War. It also reminds us how the peacekeeping tool was adapted from a bipolar world, via a unipolar one to today's multipolar world. In many ways, it is remarkable that an instrument developed in the immediate aftermath of the Second World War managed to survive so long. Blue helmets are a poignant symbol of conflict interventions over the last seventy years. But we should also be cognisant that the label of peacekeeping has encompassed very different activities over this period. While the UN maintains that the core principles—consent, impartiality, and the non-use of force—developed in the 1950s remain relevant today, these principles have changed substantially as missions evolved. Peacekeeping today bears only casual resemblance to peacekeeping from decades ago.

In one respect, however, the UN is returning to its roots. Peacekeeping started as a conflict management tool, aiming to keep warring states at bay. It was an instrument designed to facilitate de-escalation of conflicts, or at minimum to curb their escalation. With the end of the Cold War, the UN and its member states adapted this tool for conflict resolution purposes, aiming to help states deal with their internal struggles. This was primarily a reflection of the newly found consensus within the UNSC that came with the Western hegemony in global institutions. Peacebuilding through statebuilding became the agenda. The scholarly community is split over how successful these attempts have been and whether it is even desirable for the UN to get involved in the domestic affairs of post-conflict states. But these debates seem somehow outdated at the time when most new UN missions are either tasked with the protection of civilians or are adopting peace enforcement elements. While such operations are designed to respond to contemporary conflicts, they have all but abandoned any conflict resolution ambitions. Contemporary operations are deployed to manage and contain the conflicts they are addressing, countering pressures from non-state actors on the state system. With that, UN peacekeeping has come full circle as it is again used as a tool to curb escalation of local and regional conflicts into bigger problems for the international system. And in this ability to adapt to the needs of the states lies the resilience of the idea of peacekeeping itself.

References

Al Jazeera. 2013. Chad Troops in CAR Accused of Pro-Seleka Bias. Al Jazeera, December 26. http://www.aljazeera.com/news/africa/2013/12/chad-troops-car-accused-pro-seleka-bias-201312261218569193.html. Accessed 19 Dec 2017.

Albany Associates. 2017. Somalia: AU/UN Information Support. www.albanyassociates.com/projects/somalia. Accessed 19 Dec 2017.

Barnett, Michael. 2002. *Eyewitness to a Genocide*. Ithaca and London: Cornell University Press.

Caplan, Richard. 2005. *International Governance of War-Torn Territories: Rule and Reconstruction*. Oxford: Oxford University Press.

Chesterman, Simon. 2005. *You, the People: The United Nations, Transitional Administration, and State-Building*. Oxford: Oxford University Press.

da Costa, Diana Felix, and Mateja Peter. 2017. UN Support in the Formation of New States: South Sudan, Kosovo and Timor-Leste. In *UN Peacekeeping Doctrine Towards in a New Era: Adapting to Stabilisation, Protection and New Threats*, ed. Cedric de Coning, Chiyuki Aoi, and John Karlsrud, 189–210. Abingdon, Oxon: Routledge.

de Coning, Cedric, Chiyuki Aoi, and John Karlsrud (eds.). 2017. *UN Peacekeeping Doctrine Towards in a New Era: Adapting to Stabilisation, Protection and New Threats*. Abingdon, Oxon: Routledge.

Fukuyama, Francis. 2004. *State-Building: Governance and World Order in the 21st Century*. Ithaca: Cornell University Press.

Gibbs, David N. 2000. The United Nations, International Peacekeeping and the Question of 'Impartiality': Revisiting the Congo Operation of 1960. *The Journal of Modern African Studies* 38 (3): 359–382.

Holt, Victoria, and Glyn Taylor. 2009. *Protecting Civilians in the Context of UN Peacekeeping Operations. Successes, Setbacks and Remaining Challenges. Independent Study*. New York: UN Department of Peacekeeping Operations and Office for the Coordination of Humanitarian Affairs.

Howard, Lise Morje. 2007. *UN Peacekeeping in Civil Wars*. Cambridge: Cambridge University Press.

Hunt, Charles T. 2017. All Necessary Means to What Ends? The Unintended Consequences of the 'Robust Turn' in UN Peace Operations. *International Peacekeeping* 24 (1): 108–131.

Karlsrud, John. 2015. The UN at War: Examining the Consequences of Peace-Enforcement Mandates for the UN Peacekeeping Operations in the CAR, the DRC and Mali. *Third World Quarterly* 36 (1): 40–54.

Kelsen, Hans. 1948. Collective Security and Collective Self-Defence Under the Charter of the United Nations. *American Journal of International Law* 42 (4): 783–796.

Mackinlay, John, and Jarat Chopra. 1993. *A Draft Concept of Second Generation Multinational Operations*. Providence: Watson Institute.

Malone, David M., and Ramesh Thakur. 2001. UN Peacekeeping: Lessons Learned? *Global Governance* 7 (1): 11–17.

Paris, Roland. 2004. *At War's End: Building Peace after Civil Conflict.* Cambridge: Cambridge University Press.

Peter, Mateja. 2015. Between Doctrine and Practice: The United Nations Peacekeeping Dilemma. *Global Governance* 21 (3): 351–370.

Richmond, Oliver P. 2004. UN Peace Operations and the Dilemmas of the Peacebuilding Consensus. *International Peacekeeping* 11 (1): 83–101.

Rosner, Gabriella. 1964. *The United Nations Emergency Force.* New York: Columbia University Press.

Spooner, Kevin A. 2010. *Canada, the Congo Crisis, and UN Peacekeeping, 1960–64.* Vancouver: UBC Press.

The Charter of the United Nations, signed in San Francisco on 26 June 1945, came into force on 24 October 1945.

United Nations. 1948. *United Nations Security Council Resolution 50.* New York: United Nations.

United Nations. 1949. *United Nations Security Council Resolution 90.* New York: United Nations.

United Nations. 1956. *United Nations General Assembly Resolution 1001 (ES-I).* New York: United Nations.

United Nations. 1958. *Report of the Secretary General: Summary Study of the Experience Derived from the Establishment and Operation of the Force, October 9.* New York: United Nations.

United Nations. 1960. *United Nations Security Council Resolution 143.* New York: United Nations.

United Nations. 1961. *United Nations Security Council Resolution 161.* New York: United Nations.

United Nations. 1962. *United Nations General Assembly Resolution 1752.* New York: United Nations.

United Nations. 1988. *United Nations Security Council Resolution 622.* New York: United Nations.

United Nations. 1989. *United Nations Security Council Resolution 632.* New York: United Nations.

United Nations. 1992. *An Agenda for Peace, Preventive Diplomacy, Peacemaking and Peace-Keeping: Report of the Secretary-General pursuant to the statement adopted by the Summit Meeting of the Security Council on 31 January.* New York: United Nations.

United Nations. 1999a. *United Nations Security Council Resolution 1244.* New York: United Nations.

United Nations. 1999b. *United Nations Security Council Resolution 1272.* New York: United Nations.

United Nations. 2000. *Report of the Panel on United Nations Peace Operations.* New York: United Nations.

United Nations. 2006. *Integrated Missions Planning Process (IMPP), Guidelines Endorsed by the Secretary-General 13 June 2006.* New York: United Nations.

United Nations. 2008a. *Decision Number 2008/24—Integration, Decisions of the Secretary-General, 25 June 2008, Policy Committee.* New York: United Nations.

United Nations. 2008b. United Nations Peacekeeping: Principles and Guidelines (Capstone Doctrine). New York: UN Department of Peacekeeping Operations.

United Nations. 2011. *United Nations Security Council Resolution 1996.* New York: United Nations.

United Nations. 2013a. *United Nations Security Council Resolution 2100.* New York: United Nations.

United Nations. 2013b. *United Nations Security Council Resolution 2098.* New York: United Nations.

United Nations. 2013c. 'Intervention Brigade' Authorized as Security Council Grants Mandate Renewal for United Nations Mission in Democratic Republic of Congo. UN News, press release, March 28, New York.

United Nations. 2014a. *United Nations Security Council Resolution 2155.* New York: United Nations.

United Nations. 2014b. *Report of the Office of Internal Oversight Services. Evaluation of the Implementation and Results of Protection of Civilians Mandates in United Nations Peacekeeping Operations.* New York: United Nations Office of Internal Oversight Services.

United Nations. 2014c. *United Nations Security Council Resolution 2149.* New York: United Nations.

United Nations. 2015a. Fifth Committee Recommends $5.4 Billion Budget for 2016–2017 Biennium as It Concludes Main Part of Seventieth Session. https://www.un.org/press/en/2015/gaab4185.doc.htm.

United Nations. 2015b. *Report of the High-Level Independent Panel on Peace Operations on Uniting Our Strengths for Peace: Politics, Partnership and People.* New York: United Nations.

United Nations. 2016. UN General Assembly, Approved Resources for Peacekeeping Operations for the Period from 1 July 2016 to 30 June 2017, June 22, A/C.5/70/24.

Western, Jon. 2002. Sources of Humanitarian Intervention: Beliefs, Information, and Advocacy in the U.S. Decisions on Somalia and Bosnia. *International Security* 26 (4): 112–142.

Open Access This chapter is licensed under the terms of the Creative Commons Attribution 4.0 International License (http://creativecommons.org/licenses/by/4.0/), which permits use, sharing, adaptation, distribution and reproduction in any medium or format, as long as you give appropriate credit to the original author(s) and the source, provide a link to the Creative Commons license and indicate if changes were made.

The images or other third party material in this chapter are included in the chapter's Creative Commons license, unless indicated otherwise in a credit line to the material. If material is not included in the chapter's Creative Commons license and your intended use is not permitted by statutory regulation or exceeds the permitted use, you will need to obtain permission directly from the copyright holder.

CHAPTER 3

UN Peacekeeping in a Multipolar World Order: Norms, Role Expectations, and Leadership

Adriana Erthal Abdenur

Introduction

Shortly after Donald Trump was elected President, in November 2016, US government representatives announced that the US would significantly cut back on its financial contributions to the UN. In addition, the new administration pledged to pressure the UN to reduce its peacekeeping budget, for instance by closing a number of missions and undertaking a comprehensive review of peace operations (Lynch 2017). The announcements provoked alarm due not only to the financial and political implications, but also because of the repercussions to the internal politics of the US. In mid-2017, this foreshadowing became concrete when, under pressure from the US, the General Assembly agreed to significant cuts to the peacekeeping budget. American Ambassador Nikki Haley gloated that the US, in seeking "more bang for its buck," was trimming the "fat around the edges" of the UN security budget (Haynes 2017).

A. E. Abdenur (✉)
Instituto Igarapé, Rio de Janeiro, Brazil

© The Author(s) 2019

C. de Coning and M. Peter (eds.), *United Nations Peace Operations in a Changing Global Order*,
https://doi.org/10.1007/978-3-319-99106-1_3

Although the cuts remained below what the Trump administration had sought, the reduction in both resources and US interest have created more pressure to scrutinise and improve peacekeeping effectiveness.

Yet the perception of tectonic shifts within the world's most important global governance body predated these budget cuts and even Trump's election. US hegemonic power has not only been cast into doubt, but in fact has been actively contested, especially by "rising powers" whose leaders decry the injustices and resulting challenges of key mechanisms—including the asymmetries built into UN peace operations. Moreover, the US is not the only Western power in apparent decline. The European Union (EU) has delved into an identity crisis since the June 2016 Brexit referendum, and other member states have seen the rise of Euroscepticism. Against this backdrop, Trump's cavalier detachment from UN security issues has added further urgency for structural changes in global governance.

The UN itself has long acknowledged the need to revamp its peacekeeping norms and practices. The UN High-Level Independent Panel on Peace Operations (HIPPO), launched in 2014 by Secretary-General Ban Ki-moon, deepened this discussion and produced concrete recommendation for enhancing effectiveness. Although the panel report concentrated on the nuts and bolts (and norms) of UN peacekeeping rather than the geopolitical underpinnings of those challenges, the effort was undertaken within broader debates about systemic change in global governance. As the first major external review of UN peacekeeping since the Report of the Panel on UN Peace Operations chaired by Lakhdar Brahimi in 2000 (UN 2000), the HIPPO (henceforth the Panel) opened up a window of opportunity to reflect not only upon the reforms implemented over the past fifteen years, but also upon the unmet and emerging demands. Change in top leadership seemed to further expand this perceived window. At the end of 2016, António Guterres became UN Secretary-General. Guterres has held up the banner of conflict prevention since his campaign, also indicating that more effort would be placed on political strategies to avoid and resolve conflict. Discussion of conflict prevention, however, remains thus far rather abstract, disperse, and all-encompassing, especially since Guterres has had to devote considerable energy to addressing the tensions and uncertainties triggered by the Trump administration.

These tectonic shifts, emerging uncertainties, and shifting leaderships are not the only source of change in the peacekeeping field. Scholars of armed conflict have long noted structural changes in the nature of conflicts, such as the proliferation of so-called "new" or "hybrid" wars—the growing incidence of intra-state violence associated with fundamentalist non-state groups, ethno-political tensions, rebel separatism, armed resistance to authoritarian regimes, and non-state criminal groups, all of which are often associated with new dynamics in the conduct of war as well as increasingly fragmented battlefields. In the post-Cold War, as Kaldor (2013) has noted, there is increasingly a "blurring of war and crime." Combined, these factors point to serious challenges ahead for a peacekeeping system that originated in the rigid and predominantly state-centric order of the Cold War and that remains generally ill-prepared to deal with the particularities of post-Clausewitzean conflicts.

Given this changing context, what are the main implications of the multipolarisation of the world order for UN peacekeeping? This chapter explores two interrelated dimensions of security global governance and conflict management: norms-setting and role expectations. New uncertainties about leadership and emerging resources on constraints prompt changing expectations of, and concern about, rising powers. China, in particular, emerges as a potential leader, but Beijing's willingness and ability to quickly expand its influence over UN security architecture should not be taken for granted.

The chapter is structured as follows. The first part briefly explores the concept of multipolarity and the new (if highly variable) salience of rising powers in international affairs. Next, the paper looks at how these phenomena have affected UN peacekeeping with reference to normative debates and role expectations. The conclusion highlights some of the key takeaway points and notes directions for future research.

Multipolarisation of the World Order

Working to decipher the interactions among world leaders in the 2017 G-20 meeting, held in Hamburg, political scientists and pundits grasped for new expressions to describe the apparent end of the US-dominated world order; one recurring term was "G-Zero world," where no single country or bloc is able to shape or direct global events. "The era of the cacophony is upon us," proclaimed the *Economist* (2017). Chaos became the leitmotif within the mainstream media coverage of the event.

Major summits like the G-20 underscored a trend that has been hotly debated in international relations discussions, both theoretical and empirical. Some international relations scholars argue that the system is already undergoing a transition towards a more multipolar system,[1] with new engines of economic growth and political agency challenging the presumed hegemony of global powers, especially the United States. Indeed, more than in any other period of modern history, rising powers have become more vocal in their revisionist stances and increasingly work together in pressing for change, including at the UN (Acharya 2014). In 2009, for instance, Brazilian President Luiz Inácio Lula da Silva titled his opening speech at the UN General Assembly "The Multipolar World and the Revitalisation of the United Nations" (da Silva 2009).

Here the expression "rising powers" refers to states that exert a considerable degree of influence within their respective regions, and whose leaderships nurture broader ambitions at a global level yet face constraints on their ability to project both soft and hard power. In some cases, this ambition to expand power is partially motivated by a desire to recover a perceived lost status of global power, as in the cases of Russia and China. It is also rooted in the idea that there are alternatives to "Western" ideals and principles. As a result, while China, India, and Brazil, among others, remained open to cooperation with Western powers, they also found themselves at odds with certain established governance systems and norms. In general, they also became more sceptical of the Western strategy of incorporating the rest of the world into a value system presented as being universal. Under Putin, for instance, Russia—particularly since the 2014 annexation of Crimea—has steadfastly refused to "follow the West" (Lukin 2016).

In addition to contesting the status quo individually, these countries began to pool together their voices and, to some extent, their resources in pressing for a more representative global governance system—one that would not only better reflect the current distribution of power, but that would also expand their own influence in international relations. The formation of the G20, in 1999, brought together major powers and rising ones and represented an attempt to expand the "inner circle" of global leadership (previously firmly entrenched in the G-7) while foment dialogue outside the confines of established institutions like the UN. The importance of these fora, however, have varied in the eyes of rising powers Their primary collective strategy has entailed loose,

[1] For an overview of the debate until the turn of the millennium, see Lynn-Jones (2008). For more recent discussions, see Haass (2008) and Laidi (2014).

transregional groupings of rising powers—not only the BRICS, but also the India, Brazil, South Africa (IBSA) Dialogue Forum and the Shanghai Cooperation Organisation, where the absence of Western powers allows member states to promote a contestation discourse far more openly.

These coalitions vary in both composition and agenda, but they have adopted openly revisionist (if often rather vague) official discourses. Although these coalitions bring together economically, politically, and geographically diverse countries, they share the perception of having stood outside the international core group of the West (and Japan) that has dominated the world system for the past decades (de Carvalho and de Coning 2013; Wiharta et al. 2012). In 2013, at the annual BRICS Summit, Russian President Vladimir Putin called the BRICS coalition formed by Brazil, Russia, India, China, and South Africa "a key element of the emerging multipolar world" (RT 2013).

The shift towards a more multipolar order has been highly variable, both across different arenas of international affairs and over time. In international security, the multipolarisation process has been more incremental and uncertain. Here the status quo in international security has rested on two pillars. The first pillar is the continuing military supremacy of the United States: despite the recent expansion of Chinese military power, US hard power outpaces that of any other state by a wide margin, along all key measures. The second pillar is the failure to reform the UN Security Council (UNSC), which means that major decisions regarding the use of force are still taken by the Permanent Five (P5).

Despite these elements of continuity, there are growing challenges to Western dominance. The number of states possessing nuclear weapons has expanded, especially among non-Western states. Although US hard power exceeds that of other states by a wide margin, the robustness of US military power is cast into doubt as the United States finds itself embroiled in complex conflicts in the Middle East, North Africa, and Central Asia—as well as rising inter-state tensions in the Pacific. In addition, attempts by previous administrations to expand US soft power through mega-agreements like the Trans-Pacific Partnership (TPP) have been reversed by the Trump administration and opened up windows of opportunity that China and Russia, in particular, have been quick to seize, including through multilateral initiatives like the Belt and Road Initiative.

Far from uniform, multipolarisation of the world order has also varied over time, even within the relatively short span of time since the turn of the millennium. For some rising powers, the bravado exhibited by rising power leaderships in the 2000s has given way to a more discreet participation in world affairs. This is especially the case for states undergoing significant economic slowdown or political turmoil, as in the cases of Brazil and South Africa. Others, such as Russia and Turkey, have become more combative of perceived Western pressures due to a combination of domestic politics and geopolitical interests. While the word "chaos" may overestimate the fragmentation of the current world order, rising powers certainly find more space in which to manoeuvre, certainly within their own regions and, in some cases, even beyond them. Although it remains to be seen what type of scenario will emerge out of these changes in world leadership and realignments among rising powers, the reconfiguration of the system has deep repercussions for the UN security architecture, including its peace operations.

Impact of Multipolarisation on UN Peace Operations

Multipolarisation has already generated new demands and changing expectations about UN peacekeeping. From the perspective of rising powers, although they have long been contributors (especially of troops and police) to UN peacekeeping operations, a systemic transition offers a chance to boost their normative influence as well as operational role in international security and governance. UN peacekeeping has thus become part of a broader "rising power strategy" that combines intensifying engagement even as those states remain dissatisfied with the concentration of decision-making at the hands of Western states. However, not all rising powers are alike; those that are part of the P5 states (China and Russia) assume a more pivotal role than non-P5 rising powers. Broadly put, however, the resulting tension between engagement and contestation of the UN security architecture becomes apparent across both norms-setting and roles expectations.

Norms-Setting

UN peace operations are characterised by some glaring asymmetries in terms of which countries mandate, fund, and implement peacekeeping—an imbalance that has sharpened since the 1990s, when Western countries decreased uniformed personnel from UN operations and as UN peacekeeping underwent a dramatic surge in the 2000s (Bellamy and

Williams 2013). Industrialised states and P5 member states, bolstered by financial resources, political leadership, and accumulated institutional learning, lead the process of setting rules but do not all contribute significant numbers of troops and police to peace operations. There have been some efforts to redress this asymmetry. The "New Horizon" initiative, launched in 2009 by the UN Department of Peacekeeping Operations (DPKO) and Field Support (DFS), sought to expand the pool of Troop Contributing Countries (TCCs) and Police Contributing Countries (PCCs). The 2015 report issued by the HIPPO addresses the normative imbalances in peacekeeping timidly and indirectly, through general recommendations on partnerships and effectiveness yet without addressing the geopolitical underpinnings of this divide (UN 2015).

Thus far, however, this picture has not been reverted. In 2016, the top providers of assessed contributions to UN peacekeeping operations were the United States (28.57%), China (10.29%), Japan (9.68%), Germany (6.39%), France (6.31%), the United Kingdom (5.80%), Russia (4.01%), Italy (3.75%), Canada (2.92%), and Spain (2.44%) (UN 2017a). In other words, aside from China and Russia (both P5 countries and states that are sometimes classified as rising powers), all top contributors are Western states and Japan.

Developing countries, on the other hand, provide the bulk of military and police staff, who are deployed to the field often without proper equipment and training (especially when compared with their Western counterparts) and are exposed to direct risks and suffer the majority of casualties. In 2016, the top peacekeeper contributors (military and police combined) were all African and Asian: Ethiopia, India, Pakistan, Bangladesh, Rwanda, Nepal, Senegal, Burkina Faso, Ghana, and Egypt (UN 2016a). These states have little voice in the formulation and adoption of peacekeeping mandates. China—the top contributor among the members of the UNSC since 2004—has moved up the ranks consistently and will probably continue to do so, but it has not yet broken into the top ten (China was listed as number 12 in early 2017).

This uneven distribution of decision-making power and risk can directly influence the operations of a UN peacekeeping mission. For instance, Western powers can override the authority of commanding officers of peacekeeping forces, including where geopolitical interests are at stake (Khan 2006). The Indian representative to the UN has recently complained about the lack of consultation between the Council and Member States contributing troops to peacekeeping missions, adding that "the current structure and working methods of the 15-member body were divorced from reality and represented a bygone era …" and hoped that "a cataclysmic crisis would not be needed to foster such a fundamental change" (UN 2016b).

The imbalance also appears increasingly sharp in the changing division of labour between the UN and the African Union, as well as African Regional Economic Communities (RECs). Although African states and organisations stress the importance of local and regional agency in dealing with conflicts around the continent—to the extent permitted by its evolving capabilities—these partnerships face significant coordination challenges in terms of strategic, operational, and funding issues. Some African state complain that particularly the Security Council does not adequately take into consideration the region's views (Williams and Boutellis 2014). The asymmetries built into UN peace operations—some of which UN officials have referred to as "peacekeeping apartheid"[2]—thus undermine both the legitimacy and effectiveness of peace operations.

These asymmetries are a direct consequence not only of disparities in the ability to make financial contributions, but also of the anachronistic way in which the UN still reflects the distribution of power at the end of World War II.[3] Non-P5 rising powers have been more vocal about contesting global governance, including norms of peacekeeping, and are bound to continue to challenge them in two ways. First, rising powers seek to influence global governance mechanisms and to participate more directly in rules-making (rather than to be mere "rules-takers") in international security. As the Indonesian ambassador to the UN spelled out it in a 2016 Security Council debate, "Responsibility should be shared by giving emerging powers responsibilities commensurate to their respective capacity and competence to contribute to regional and global peace." (UN 2016c)

As such, rising powers have been critical of the power structures, both formal and informal, that underpin decision-making. Second, they contest more specific elements of the normative framework, including

[2]The phrase was used by Jean-Marie Guéhenno (2005), then Under-Secretary-General for Peacekeeping Operations, in a statement made to the Challenges Project on 2 March 2005 in London. See also Sidhu (2007).

[3]The only significant changes have been the replacement of Taiwan by the PRC and that of the Soviet Union by Russia.

aspects of peacekeeping. For instance, many such countries have contested the Responsibility to Protect (R2P) norm and, more recently, the intersection between peacekeeping and anti-terrorism initiatives. Rising powers, in other words, want a greater say in deciding under what circumstances to undertake such operations, when to allow the use of force, and what the rules of engagement should be. This helps to explain why reform of the UNSC is such a central element in these countries' multilateral agendas.

Three trends can be discerned in non-P5 rising powers' recent participation in normative debates about UN peacekeeping. First, reflecting their aspirations to influence conceptual developments more closely, these states have stressed that peacekeeping operations should only take place with the permission of, and/or in partnership with, the UN. While this may remain true, with multipolarisation, rising powers may find more manoeuvre space for pursuing their regional ambitions, as well as deepening rivalries in areas where regional cooperation fails to take off or is undertaken in a lopsided manner.

For instance, regional dynamics in Eurasia have already begun to change dramatically not only due to the rise of China, but also due to the implementation of the Beijing-led Belt and Road Initiative. Although it remains largely a vision rather than a concrete project, the platform has already begun to change geopolitical and geo-economic relations between major regional players in Asia, promoting new configurations in cooperation but also potentially triggering new tensions in an area where rising powers have already resisted the presence of the UN security mechanisms (The Indian government, for instance, has called for an end to the UN Military Observer Group in India and Pakistan (UNMOGIP), which supervises the ceasefire line between the two countries). In June 2017, for instance, just as India grew more resistant to participating in the OBOR, India and China experienced another border flare-up when Indian troops halted a Chinese road-building project in the Himalayas (Barry and Huang 2017). Multipolarisation of the world order may heighten the regional geopolitical concerns and interests of some rising powers, hence weakening the position of the UN as the leading conflict management actor.

Second, rising powers have upheld the principle of respect for national sovereignty, for instance questioning the Responsibility to Protect (R2P) on the grounds that it can lead to violations of national sovereignty, that the norm is invoked in a highly selective manner that serves narrow Western interests, and that it has tended to lead to (at best) highly uncertain outcomes (Laskaris and Kreutz 2015). This scepticism was in full view when the BRICS countries criticised the UNSC Resolution 1973 in 2011, which permitted the establishment of a no-fly zone over Libya. The resulting intervention was presented by critics as an abuse of the UN mandate; as de Carvalho and de Coning put it, "The representatives of the BRICS in the Security Council argued that they will not make the mistake again of trusting the West with the authority to undertake 'limited action,' which can then be used as a justification to launch an intervention that amounts to regime change" (de Carvalho and de Coning 2013). In a Security Council meeting in February 2016, the Egyptian ambassador stressed that "the Council must remain objective and it must adopt the 'natural path' to address issues according to the Charter, giving priority to peaceful means of conflict resolution and respecting the sovereignty of States" (UN 2016c).

The Russian annexation of Crimea and, more recently, its role in the Syrian conflict have cast doubt on Russia's commitment to the principle of non-intervention, at least as understood from a Western perspective. Although China has historically adopted a cautious stance in UN security discussions (most notably by exercising its veto power very infrequently), its economic and defence interests have rapidly globalised, not only in Asia but increasingly in Africa and Latin America. Some analysts argue that China is beginning to be flexible in its stance on non-interference in the internal affairs of other states, for instance by offering to carry out some mediation of international conflicts, by carrying out large-scale evacuations of Chinese citizens when conflict breaks out, or even through its increasingly bold peacekeeping engagement, for example deploying peacekeepers in South Sudan starting 2017 (The State Council of the People's Republic of China 2017). Within the UNSC, however, China has generally remained more engaged in tempering the use of force than in proposing new norms for peacekeeping altogether (International Crisis Group 2009, pp. 2–3).

Third, rising powers have often opposed what they consider to be the sometimes premature mobilisation of peacekeepers to address outbreaks of conflict, arguing that instances of escalating violence must be analysed on a case-by-case basis. The trend towards more robust peacekeeping mandates notwithstanding, in their view, UN mechanisms such as economic sanctions and especially the use of military force is to be used only as a last resort, when peaceful means to conflict resolution have been exhausted. In this perspective, despite the UN Charter's emphasis on early warning, preventive diplomacy, good offices, and mediation, the UN sometimes exhibits a knee-jerk reaction in deploying peacekeepers.

Within a more multipolar world order, there may be room for further convergence between rising powers and Western states as scepticism of nation- and state-building, based on the assumption that societies can be (re)engineered through a top-down approach to "fixing" "failed states," also spreads in Western countries and institutions. As more people recognise that, rather than invariably benevolent and objective, the liberal peace paradigm of democracy and market economy can lead to unexpected results, including exacerbated instability (Zambakari 2017), rising powers are bound to feel less isolated in their positions at the UN. This convergence, however, will depend heavily on Secretary General Guterres' ability to push forward an agenda for reform of peace operations that not only ensures the implementation of the HIPPO recommendations but, in fact, goes well beyond those.

Rising powers have at times been accused of acting more as norms-blockers—setting up obstacles to the implementation of proposed norms—than as norms-entrepreneurs who bring to the table new ideas and invest politically so as to back up innovative proposals (Abdenur 2016). Brazil's proposal of the Responsibility while Protecting (RwP) concept was an important contribution to the ongoing debate over the use of force and the protection of civilians, but the proposal was hampered in part by a lack of political commitment to advancing the discussion (Almeida 2013). South Africa's introduction of the concept of non-indifference has been influential in other states' foreign policies (including that of Brazil's) and within the discourse of the African Union, but the concept has remained rather vague and is applied in a highly uneven fashion. In a context of declining US leadership within the UN, rising powers (both those within and outside the Security Council) may find more space for proposing normative innovation, but gathering the political momentum required to enact change will require creating a critical mass around new proposals.

Role Expectations

Most discussions around role expectations and UN peacekeeping revolve around missions' ability to carry out their mandates, or the mandates themselves. Here I refer more specifically to expectations on the part of the international community, especially at the UN and partner organisations, regarding the official and unofficial division of labour that emerges in defining, structuring, and implementing peacekeeping. With multipolarisation, expectations have begun to shift, especially around "pivotal states"—countries that could help fill the space left behind by a declining US leadership.

This idea was reinforced during a June 2017 news conference in New York, when Secretary-General Guterres warned that an American retreat from the world meant serious risks: "When someone leaves space, that space is always occupied by others" (UN 2017b). In May, during a talk at New York University, Guterres had given concrete examples: "It's not only the Russias and the Chinas that are occupying the ground; if you look at Saudi Arabia, Turkey, Iran, the regional powers in many parts of the world—when the big powers leave some space, they will occupy it" (Nichols 2017). In addition to voicing concerns about the Trump administration's decision to withdraw from the Paris climate agreement, new US migration policies, and deep cuts to the UN budget, Guterres was raising the issue of what leadership at the UN will look like in a multipolar world order.

Many of these changing expectations concern the responsibilities that different sets of actors should assume within a world order in which conflict-related demands seem to grow more complex even as available resources shrink. As suggested by Guterres' comments, leadership roles are up for grabs, with expectations of the European Union (EU) stepping in dashed by the uncertainties and identity crisis unleashed by the UK Brexit referendum in 2016. The 2017 G-20 meeting, held in Hamburg, was widely interpreted as reflecting a divided world leadership and signalling a rapid decline in expectations of the US. Many G20 countries, including traditional partners like France and Canada, have opted to circumvent the Trump administration rather than bandwagon with the new foreign policy decisions implemented by the US; at the same time, Russia and Turkey have stepped up their defiant tones. In as much as UN politics mirror broad shifts in geopolitics, these shifting alignments generate further uncertainty for UN peacekeeping.

Another set of expectations subject to change involves the North/South split in UN peacekeeping decision-making and implementation. Budget cuts means there will be even fewer resources with which to level the playing field in terms of equipment, training, intelligence, and coordination, increasing risks to the TCCs and PCCs. These problems are of particular concern in robust peacekeeping operations like the United Nations Organization Stabilization Mission in the Democratic Republic of Congo (MONUSCO) and the United Nations Multidimensional Integrated Stabilization Mission in Mali (MINUSMA), in which troops, police, and other personnel are subject to complex conflicts. In Mali, for instance, MINUSMA peacekeepers are increasingly targeted by improvised explosive devices and car bombs; a total of 146 peacekeepers there have been killed since 2013 (UN 2017c). Although including counterterrorism operations in peacekeeping mandates is controversial, as the commander of the MINUSMA intelligence unit has put it, those risks are unlikely to abate in peacekeeping settings: "This is not the end of this type of mission. It's the beginning" (Sieff 2017). Coupled with growing scepticism of UN peacekeeping effectiveness, these risks, as well as more traditional ones from state and non-state armed groups, are likely to magnify the perception of unfair burdens assumed by Global South contributors to UN peacekeeping.

Regarding rising powers like the BRICS states, there are increasing expectations (by global powers as well as lower-income states) that they will expand and diversify their contributions to international security. This applies to both the Security Council permanent seat holders and to the other three countries, but unevenly. Among the P5, China in particular is called upon to expand its contributions, not only in terms of financing and personnel deployment, but also with respect to defining mandates and the appropriateness of the use of force. Even before Guterres was selected as Secretary General, China had been diversifying and intensifying its commitments to UN peacekeeping, contributing thousands more troops, making major investments in peacekeeper training, and placing 8000 troops at the disposal of a UN standby force. By 2016, China was the second-largest contributor to the UN peacekeeping budget and deployed more peacekeepers than the four other P5 countries combined (Lynch 2017).

China's increased interest in, and engagement with, UN peacekeeping—especially at a time when the Trump administration voiced open disdain for the United Nations—triggered alarm bells among some Western specialists. In October 2016, a *Foreign Policy* article warned that China had set "its sights on the United Nations' top peacekeeping job," adding that Chinese leadership in this area would have serious normative implications, especially for human rights. The article cited a senior UN official stating Russia was also "making a play for DPA" and an expert saying that

"We're seeing the first phase of a Chinese bid to, firstly, assert itself over UN peacekeeping and, secondly, to rewrite the rules of UN peacekeeping" (Lynch 2017). The *Diplomat* asked, "Is the UN About to Enter the Era of Chinese and Russian Dominance?" (Witthoeft 2016). New York-based think tanks viewed the bid as a potential turning point; the International Peace Institute (IPI) opined that "China heading up the United Nations Department for Peacekeeping Operations (DPKO) would represent one of its most significant overtures toward leading, rather than merely participating in, the post-1945 global order" (Bowen 2016). Although Guterres ended up appointing France's Jean-Pierre Lacroix as Under-Secretary for Peacekeeping Operations, the breathless tone of the debate about expanding non-Western influence at the UN—especially the concerns over an ambitious China and a revisionist Russia—reflects the changing expectations for rising powers in UN peacekeeping.

While the recent increases in China's contributions to UN peacekeeping signal a clear uptick in its commitment to peace operations, it is not yet clear whether Beijing would be willing to assume a clear-cut leading role—or, even if it is, whether it is capable of doing so in the near future. Xi Jinping is attempting to lead a difficult (albeit not insurmountable) structural transition, and the relative deceleration of the Chinese economy—down from double-digit rates to a "mere" 6.5% annual GDP growth per year—translates into fewer resources. Abroad, aside from the UN, China has many other areas of diplomacy and cooperation it is trying to build up, both regionally and globally. Alongside China's engagement with the UN, its multilateral diplomacy (and its engagement with international security) also encompasses a variety of non-UN initiatives, including emerging regional or trans-regional cooperation configurations such as the two-pronged OBOR, the Shanghai Cooperation Organization, and the new financial institutions it has helped to launch, especially the Asian Infrastructure Investment Bank (AIIB) and the BRICS New Development Bank (NDB). In addition, China deals with a large number of domestic security issues, including separatist groups, as well as territorial disputes and reawakened historical rivalries in the South China Sea and recurring instability in the Korean peninsula. Chinese scholars have warned that, even within the context of a rapidly changing world order and the emergence of new opportunities, "China mustn't spread too thin" (Yinhong 2016).

Thus far, even as China openly competes with the US for power, leading both countries to reappraise their positions vis-à-vis one another as well as in global governance, Beijing has generally opted for a cautious projection rather than brash power-grabbing. Deng Xiaoping's exhortation to "keep a low profile, never take the lead, and make a difference" may have been toned down, but it has not been altogether discarded.[4] A China-dominated UN peacekeeping field is possible, but unlikely to materialise in a just a few years.

To expand global peacekeeping engagement, the three rising power aspirants to a permanent seat at the Security Council—Brazil, India, and South Africa—have been called upon to assume greater responsibilities both within and beyond their immediate regions. The rationale is that, if these countries aspire to global power status, for instance as reflected in their bids for a permanent seat at the UNSC, then they should demonstrate deeper long-term commitment (political, financial, and otherwise) to hands-on engagement in UN peace operations, both at the normative and at the operational levels. However, particularly during economic downturns, these states resist committing further resources by invoking their status as developing countries, with important challenges to tackle internally that constrain their capacity to contribute (particularly financially) to UN peacekeeping. At the time of this writing, this is particularly true of Brazil and South Africa, both of which have experienced a combination of economic deceleration and political turmoil at home—in both cases, fuelled by allegations of extensive corruption. Just how "pivotal" these rising powers will be in a multipolar order will depend not only on their ability to restore stability and inclusive growth at home, but also in their capacity to take advantage of the rapidly changing international order.

Finally, multipolarisation also changes expectations regarding the role of regional organisations. The UN has retained primacy in peacekeeping, handling the largest number of peacekeeping operations (including robust missions) and serving as the main normative platform for debating and discussing when and how peacekeeping should be carried out. Nonetheless, in some places, regional organisations have assumed increasing protagonism, not only due to the limits of UN capacity but also because of the growing belief in the legitimacy and efficacy of more regional, sub-regional, or even localised solutions.

Because the bulk of peacekeeping takes place in Africa—it is estimated that 87% of uniformed UN personnel are deployed around the

[4] For more on this debate, see *People's Daily* (2012).

continent—this growing complexity is particularly relevant to the region (de Carvalho 2015). As de Coning explains in this volume, the AU's African Peace and Security Architecture (APSA) has expanded considerably in the past decade. Recent innovations, such as a mediation unit and gender-specific policies, have lent momentum to some areas. However, the organisation's capacity is still highly uneven, with considerable weaknesses due to financing and capabilities. As multipolarisation accelerates, so do pressures for the AU and other regional organisations to take on an even bigger role in tackling conflicts within its geographic space. In addition, as regional powers like Egypt, Nigeria, Ethiopia, and South Africa find more room for manoeuvring within a multipolar context, geopolitics will continue to shape AU politics as those countries jockey for influence at a regional level.

Conclusion

The multipolarisation of the world order is well under way. Some of the notable changes in leadership and alignments observed over the past decade include the emergence of new economic growth nodes, more vocal contestation of the current global governance system by rising powers, and emerging "parallel" institutions of the Global South. Since 2016 especially, these trends have dovetailed more clearly with the decline of Western powers, especially the retraction of US power under Trump and the identity crisis besetting the European Union since the Brexit vote. Yet some rising powers are bound to play a more pivotal role than others.

The shift towards a multipolar configuration has significant implications for UN peacekeeping, and some of the effects are already becoming apparent. At a political level, the perceived leadership vacuum creates pressure for new sources of leadership in global governance, and it raises concern among some circles with the possibility of non-Western states, namely China, occupying this space, with important normative repercussions. While China has shown growing interest in assuming a more proactive role at the UN, taking up leadership will require concerted effort, investment of resources and diplomacy, and time.

Russia stands to gain influence, but will likely retain its predominantly legalistic views at the UN, including with respect to peacekeeping. Unlike China, it has no intentions of making a leap in contributions so as to expand influence on peace operations from outside the UNSC. Its military attention is more focused on countering NATO in Eastern

Europe and in maintaining its footholds in Central Asia and the Middle east.

The role of other rising powers is more variable. Countries that experience considerable turbulence at home, Brazil and South Africa, may lack the resources of the pivotal states, but their long tradition of multilateral diplomacy will allow them to retain relevance in a multipolar world, including at the regional level. Rising powers that are directly embroiled in geopolitical hotspots, such as Turkey and Iran, may assume increasingly contestatory stances, at least with respect to their immediate vicinities.

At an operational level, the impending budget cuts provoked by US pressure lead to the closing of a number of missions and are bound to reinforce some of the asymmetries seen in the field. Although other Western states have begun signalling that they will not bandwagon with the US on major foreign policy decisions, the Trump administration's dismissive attitude towards the UN may promote a more hands-off approach to conflict management on the part of longstanding allies such as Canada, even if they diverge on other issues, such as the Paris climate agreement.

Multipolarity increases uncertainty and provokes realignments, but it is not equivalent to chaos. New nodes of decision-making emerge and upend normative engines of previous eras. At the same time, multipolarisation is not uniform or unidirectional; it may web and flow and manifest itself differently in different areas and spaces. Just as the fortunes of rising powers are subject to oscillations and even, in some cases, reversals, so is the decline of Western powers. It remains to be seen whether the world is experiencing a Tump Era or merely a Trump Interregnum, but analysis over time shows that the policies implemented by the US governments in 2017 are not the only driver of systemic change. This means that UN peacekeeping will undergo geopolitical pressures and changes not foreseen in organisational initiatives such as the HIPPO process.

Further research on the impact of multipolarisation on UN peacekeeping should thus ratchet down the level of analysis to look more specifically at how macro–level changes in inter-state and intra-state dynamics create new challenges for the UN architecture. Secondly, future research should investigate the ways that emerging regional cooperation arrangements like OBOR affect conflict prevention and management, whether within the realm of peacekeeping or in parallel to it. Finally, special attention should be paid to how multipolarisation affects the behaviour, choices, and expectations of other member states, whether individually or through groupings like the G7+.

References

Abdenur, Adriana Erthal. 2016. Rising Powers and International Security: The BRICS and the Syrian Conflict. *Rising Powers Quarterly* 1 (1): 109–133.

Acharya, Amitav. 2014. *The End of the American World Order*. London: Polity.

Almeida, Paula Wojcikiewicz. 2013. From Non-Indifference to Responsibility while Protecting: Brazil's Diplomacy and the Search for Global Norms. Occasional Papers No. 138, South African Institute of International Affairs, Johannesburg.

Barry, Ellen, and Yufan Huang. 2017. With Modi in Washington, China and India 'Jostle' on Their Border. *New York Times*, June 27.

Bellamy, Alex J., and Paul D. Williams. 2013. Introduction: The Politics and Challenges of Providing Peacekeepers. In *Providing Peacekeepers: The Politics, Challenges, and Future of United Nations Peacekeeping*, ed. Alex J. Bellamy and Paul D. Williams. Oxford: Oxford University Press.

Bowen, James. 2016. Peacekeeping with Chinese Characteristics? October 20. New York: IPI Global Observatory.

da Silva, Lula. 2009. O mundo multipolar e a revitalizacão da ONU, Opening Speech at the UN General Assembly, October 9. New York: United Nations.

de Carvalho, Benjamin, and Cedric de Coning. 2013. Rising Powers and the Future of Peacekeeping and Peacebuilding, November 14. Oslo: Norwegian Peacebuilding Resource Centre.

de Carvalho, Gustavo. 2015. What's the Future of UN Peacekeeping? World Economic Forum, February 26. https://www.weforum.org/agenda/2015/02/whats-the-future-of-un-peacekeeping/. Accessed 10 Nov 2017.

Guéhenno, Jean-Marie. 2005. Statement by Jean-Marie Guéhenno Under-Secretary General for Peacekeeping Operations to the Challenges Project, March 2. http://www.un.org/en/peacekeeping/articles/article020305.htm. Accessed 10 Nov 2017.

Haass, Richard N. 2008. The Age of Nonpolarity: What Will Follow U.S. Dominance. *Foreign Affairs* 87 (3): 44–56.

Haynes, Suyin. 2017. Nikki Haley Praises Cuts to the UN's Peacekeeping Budget, Sparking Online Backlash. *Time*, June 28. http://time.com/4838459/nikki-haley-tweet-un-peacekeepers-reaction/. Accessed 9 Nov 2017.

International Crisis Group. 2009. China's Growing Role in UN Peacekeeping. Asia Report No. 166, April 17, International Crisis Group, Beijing, New York and Brussels.

Kaldor, Mary. 2013. In Defence of New Wars. *Stability: International Journal of Security & Development* 2 (10): 1–16.

Khan, Adil Hasan. 2006. *Emerging Challenges in UN Peacekeeping Operations.* New Delhi: Institute of Peace and Conflict Studies, article # 1956, March 1.

Laidi, Z. 2014. Towards a Post-hegemonic World: The Multipolar Threat to the Multilateral Order. *International Politics* 51 (3): 350–365.

Laskaris, Stamatis, and Joakim Kreutz. 2015. Rising Powers and the Responsibility to Protect: Will the Norm Survive in the Age of BRICS? *Global Affairs* 1 (2): 149–158.

Lukin, Alexander. 2016. Russia in a Post-bipolar World. *Survival* 58 (1): 91–112.

Lynch, Colum. 2017. White House Seeks to Cut Billions in Funding for United Nations. *Foreign Policy*, March 13.

Lynn-Jones. 2008. Preface. In *Primacy and Its Discontents: American Power and International Stability*, ed. Michael E. Brown, Owen R. Coté, Sean M. Lynn-Jones, and Steven E. Miller. Cambridge: MIT Press.

Nichols, Michelle. 2017. UN Chief Warns If US Pulls Back, Others Will Fill Leadership Role. Reuters, May 31. http://www.reuters.com/article/us-usa-trump-un-idUSKBN18Q2MD. Accessed 10 Nov 2017.

People's Daily. 2012. Should China Continue to Keep a Low Profile Attitude? December 13. http://en.people.cn/90883/8057776.html. Accessed 10 Nov 2017.

RT. 2013. BRICS Key Element of Emerging Multipolar World—Putin. *Russia Today*, March 22.

Sidhu, Waheguru Pal Singh. 2007. Regional Groups and Alliances. In *The Oxford Handbook on the United Nations*, ed. Thomas Weiss and Sam Daws, 217–232. Oxford: Oxford University Press.

Sieff, Kevin. 2017. The World's Most Dangerous UN Mission. *The Washington Post*, February 17.

The Economist. 2017. Angela Merkel, the G-Zero Chancellor. *The Economist*, July 7.

The State Council of the People's Republic of China. 2017. Chinese Peacekeepers Depart for South Sudan, February 26. The State Council of the People's Republic of China. http://english.gov.cn/state_council/ministries/2017/02/26/content_281475578780906.htm. Accessed 10 Nov 2017.

United Nations. 2000. *Report of the Panel on United Nations Peace Operations.* New York: United Nations.

United Nations. 2015. *Uniting our Strengths for Peace—Politics, Partnerships, and People: Report of the High-Level Independent Panel on United Nations Peace Operations.* New York: United Nations.

United Nations. 2016a. Ranking of Military and Police Contributions to UN Operations. Monthly Report, August 31. http://www.un.org/en/peacekeeping/contributors/2016/aug16_2.pdf. Accessed 10 Nov 2017.

United Nations. 2016b. Speakers in Security Council Urge Balance Between UN Role in State Sovereignty, Human Rights Protection, But Differ Over

Interpretation of Charter Principles. United Nations General Assembly meeting, February 15. https://www.un.org/press/en/2016/sc12241.doc.htm. Accessed 4 Dec 2017.

United Nations. 2016c. Speakers in Security Council Urge Balance Between UN Role in State Sovereignty, Human Rights Protection, but Differ Over Interpretation of Charter Principles. Security Council Meeting, 15 February 2016. https://www.un.org/press/en/2016/sc12241.doc.htm. Accessed 10 Nov 2017.

United Nations. 2017a. How We Are Funded. www.peacekeeping.un.org, https://peacekeeping.un.org/en/how-we-are-funded. Accessed 4 Dec 2017.

United Nations. 2017b. Press Conference by Secretary-General António Guterres at United Nations Headquarters. SG/SM/18580, June 20. https://www.un.org/press/en/2017/sgsm18580.doc.htm. Accessed 10 Nov 2017.

United Nations. 2017c. Fatalities Geographic Map. United Nations Peacekeeping. https://peacekeeping.un.org/en/fatalities-geographic-map. Accessed 4 Dec 2017.

Wiharta, Sharon, Neil Melvin, and Xenia Avezov. 2012. *The New Geopolitics of Peace Operations: Mapping the Emerging Landscape*. Stockholm: Stockholm International Peace Research Institute.

Williams, Paul D., and Arthur Boutellis. 2014. Partnership Peacekeeping: Challenges and Opportunities in the United Nations–African Union Relationship. *African Affairs* 113 (451): 254–278.

Witthoeft, Andrew. 2016. Is the UN About to Enter the Era of Chinese and Russian Dominance? *The Diplomat*, October 12.

Yinhong, Shi. 2016. Amid Western Uncertainties, China Mustn't Spread Too Thin. *Global Times*, October 26.

Zambakari, Christopher. 2017. Challenges of Liberal Peace and Statebuilding in Divided Societies. ACCORD Conflict Trends 2016/4, February 16.

Open Access This chapter is licensed under the terms of the Creative Commons Attribution 4.0 International License (http://creativecommons.org/licenses/by/4.0/), which permits use, sharing, adaptation, distribution and reproduction in any medium or format, as long as you give appropriate credit to the original author(s) and the source, provide a link to the Creative Commons license and indicate if changes were made.

The images or other third party material in this chapter are included in the chapter's Creative Commons license, unless indicated otherwise in a credit line to the material. If material is not included in the chapter's Creative Commons license and your intended use is not permitted by statutory regulation or exceeds the permitted use, you will need to obtain permission directly from the copyright holder.

CHAPTER 4

Politics in the Driving Seat: Good Offices, UN Peace Operations, and Modern Conflict

Adam Day

Political Solutions to Intractable Conflicts

"Today's conflicts are more intractable and less conducive to political resolution" (UN 2015, p. 2). This finding of the High-Level Independent Panel on Peace Operations (HIPPO) recognises that modern conflict is increasingly complicated by the rising prominence of non-state actors, especially the growing influence of global terrorist groups and transnational criminal networks. Similarly, increasing involvement of regional players in intra-state wars and expanding illicit flows of money and materiel across national boundaries in places like the Sahel, the Great Lakes and the Middle East have contributed to an entrenchment of conflict and have complicated the search for sustainable peaceful outcomes (Bosetti and Einsiedel 2015). This evolution in conflict raises difficult questions about the traditionally state-centric approach of the UN, and how to effectively engage with a broader cast of characters at the local, national, regional, and international levels (Griffiths and Whitfield 2010).

A. Day (✉)
United Nations University, Tokyo, Japan

© The Author(s) 2019

C. de Coning and M. Peter (eds.), *United Nations Peace Operations in a Changing Global Order*,
https://doi.org/10.1007/978-3-319-99106-1_4

Modern conflict presents a particularly complicated terrain for the UN's political work, which the HIPPO places at the centre of conflict prevention and management. Today, the UN is called upon to engage politically in a far broader range of conflict settings and with a much more diverse set of interlocutors, with good offices mandates now specifically included special political missions in Afghanistan, Lebanon, Haiti, and Iraq, and peacekeeping operations in the Central African Republic, the Democratic Republic of the Congo (DRC), and Mali.[1] These cases have given rise to a new set of questions about the application of good offices in modern conflict. How can UN representatives—from the Secretary-General's level down to the deep field—employ good offices in situations where key players are resistant to traditional diplomatic tools of persuasion and pressure? How has the UN adapted good offices to address sub-national conflict dynamics and the lines of regional influence that cross state boundaries? To what extent is the UN well-placed to drive modern conflict situations towards sustainable peace, and what kinds of partnerships would help it meet new challenges?

The new Secretary General is calling for "surge in diplomacy for peace," (UN 2017) placing good offices centre stage. But have we learned our lines, and who is the audience?

In this chapter, I briefly trace how good offices has evolved from early Secretaries-General through the expansion of UN peace operations in the 1990s. This lays the groundwork for a comparative analysis of modern applications of good offices in more recent conflicts, examining how the UN has attempted to reshape its political engagement to accommodate the changing nature of armed conflict. I argue that the inherently vague definition of the term "good offices" has helpfully allowed for entrepreneurial approaches to political engagement, and that in many cases this has aided the UN in effectively preventing and de-escalating violent conflict.

From these cases, I identify some of the key elements for the success of good offices, including: a sustained political presence on the ground; the ability to respond quickly to changing circumstances; a broad set of relationships; the effective use of both local and regional leverage; and often the personal credibility of the UN representative. But these

[1]See Security Council resolutions 2277 (UN 2016a), 2299 (UN 2016b), 2274 (UN 2016c), 2039 (UN 2012). As discussed below, there is a school of thought which holds that all UN missions inherently possess a good offices mandate.

rarely come together, especially in large peace operations. In fact, I find a tendency for larger multi-dimensional missions to bifurcate their work into the operational and the political—often due to the enormous burdens of deploying and maintaining a large field presence—with the political work sometimes dropping in priority. This can result in incoherent, often contradictory approaches and missed opportunities to leverage the UN towards its political objectives. On this basis, I argue that the political shift encouraged by the HIPPO is best achieved by moving away from larger peace operations to focus on leaner, more nimble approaches for the future, with good offices more deeply embedded in regional and sub-national networks.

What Are Good Offices? An Old Question Worth Repeating

"Good offices" is a widely-used term outside of armed conflict, present in a variety of international bodies (World Trade Organization 1994, art. 5; Vienna Convention 1985, art. 11), and in multilateral treaties preceding the formation of the United Nations (Convention for the Pacific Settlement of International Disputes 1899, 1907). Traditionally, the term described the role played by a state in mediating international disputes, such as Switzerland in a range of inter-state crises from the Suez to Afghanistan (Fischer 2002), or the Security Council's establishment of a Good Offices Committee to help resolve a dispute between Dutch and nationalist forces in Indonesia in 1947 (Wainhouse 1966).

The Preparatory Commission for the UN Charter envisaged that the Secretary-General would have a "role to play as a mediator and as an informal advisor of many governments ... to take decisions which may be justly called political" (UN 1945, pp. 86–87). However, the UN Charter itself contains no direct reference to good offices or even this advisory role. The most relevant provision is Article 99, which allows the Secretary-General to bring to the attention of the Council any threats to international peace and security, and considered a basis for much of the Secretary-General's authority.[2] As Kofi Annan has pointed

[2]See Chesterman (2011); see also Johnstone (2003) arguing that Article 99 was expanded under Resolution 1366 to allow the SG to also act in cases of serious violations of international law.

out, Secretaries-General have invoked this article "very sparingly,"[3] but the provision does open the door for direct engagement with disputing parties. And the fact that the earliest General Assembly resolutions overtly called on the Secretary-General to employ his good offices to help Member States resolve disputes (UN 1988a, para. 20; UN 1982) affirms that they were seen from the outset as inherent to the job.[4]

The more difficult task is defining good offices. The UN Handbook offers a very restrictive and state-centric definition,[5] but that is rarely, if ever, invoked in practice. Javier Pérez De Cuéllar simply referred to good offices as "quiet diplomacy" (Adams and Kingsbury 1994, p. 133). Boutros Boutros-Ghali more pragmatically described the term as "any diplomatic action taken to prevent disputes from arising between parties, to prevent existing disputes from escalating into conflicts, and to limit the spread of the latter when they occur" (UN 1992a). In a similar vein, Teresa Whitfield (2010a) has noted that good offices can mean "almost anything – from a well-timed telephone call by the Secretary-General, to exploratory conversations, or a full-fledged mediation effort conducted in his or her name." In my view, Ian Johnstone's (2010) concise but expansive definition captures modern usage nicely: "everything the UN can do of a diplomatic nature to help prevent, manage or resolve conflicts." This is particularly convenient because it covers pre-conflict, conflict, and post-conflict settings, and includes mediation without being limited to it. However, good offices have not always been thought of so broadly, and a brief look at the evolution of the term from its early days is instructive in understanding how to implement the HIPPO's politics-first agenda.

[3] Annan (2001); see also Chesterman (2011) (noting that the Secretary-General has only invoked Article 99 explicitly twice).

[4] Furthermore, the so-called "implied powers doctrine" would strongly indicate that good offices are inherent to the office. This doctrine is articulated in the International Court of Justice: "under international law, the Organization must be deemed to have those powers which, though not expressly provided by the Charter, are conferred upon it by necessary implication as being essential to the performance of its duties" (International Court of Justice 1949).

[5] "When States party to a dispute are unable to settle it directly, a third party, may offer his [or her] good offices as a means of preventing further deterioration of the dispute and as a method of facilitating efforts towards a peaceful settlement of the dispute" (United Nations 1988b).

The Evolution and Expansion of Good Offices

The first recorded uses of the Secretary-General's good offices underscore two facets of the role: initiative and independence. In response to the 1946 Soviet invasion of the northern Azeri region of Iran, the Security Council tasked the parties to report to Secretary-General Trygve Lie on troop withdrawal, placing the UN at the centre of inter-state conflict resolution (UN 1946). Perhaps more notable, however, was the fact that Lie had already begun talks with the parties prior to the resolution, indicating his willingness to employ good offices on his own authority. When Lie was again asked to provide good offices and report on the North Korean invasion of South Korea in 1950, he took a personal line in his reports, often at significant variance with the parties and members of the Council (Franck 1995, pp. 360, 384). In these early uses of good offices, Lie began to carve out an important space for the Secretary-General to manoeuvre independently.

Under the dynamic Dag Hammarskjöld, good offices arguably expanded more quickly than at any other time in the history of the UN. In the 1956 Suez crisis, for example, he took on the role of guarantor, restoring the parties' confidence through direct talks with them, and working to ensure the armistice arrangements were effective.[6] Hammarskjöld was also willing to stretch his own terms of reference, as in 1960 when he invoked Article 99 of the Charter to recommend the deployment of peacekeepers to the DRC. The resulting Security Council resolution granted Hammarskjöld unprecedented breadth to engage with the parties and command UN assets in the DRC (O'Donoghue 2014).

Perhaps the most important element of Hammarskjöld's use of good offices was his willingness to contradict other UN organs. In the context of a crisis involving US aircrew hostages held in China, the General Assembly presented Hammarskjöld with a deeply biased resolution, condemning the Chinese action as the basis for the Secretary-General's good offices mandate (UN 1954). Hammarskjöld openly distanced himself from this resolution and reassured the Chinese government that he had an independent basis for negotiating the issue. This so-called "Peking Formula" rests on Hammarskjöld's vision that the Secretary-General

[6] See UNSC Resolution 118 (UN 1956a) on a complaint by France and the United Kingdom against Egypt, and Resolution 119 (UN 1956b) on a complaint by Egypt against France and the United Kingdom.

should foremost follow "the principles and purposes of the Charter which are fundamental law and accepted by and binding on all States" (Jacobson 1979, p. 137). Drawing authority directly from the Charter, the Secretary-General is able to act nimbly, to initiate political engagement and take positions at odds with other UN organs.[7]

The intractable Cyprus conflict—which has required a UN operation from 1964 to this day—captures key points along the trajectory of good offices over roughly the next 40-year period. U Thant's involvement with Cyprus in 1964 followed directly from a request by the Council, and was initially limited to his appointment of a mediator to work with the parties (UN 1964). In 1974, after the Turkish invasion of Cyprus, Kurt Waldheim adopted a more intrusive approach and proposed a common framework for negotiation between the parties (Waldheim 1980, pp. 70–71). Boutros-Ghali took it a step further, initiating intensive direct talks with the parties to generate proposals, rather than simply focusing on the forum and framework for negotiations (Michael 2009, p. 132). Annan went further still by proposing a final settlement to the parties, and attaching an ultimatum that failure to agree would put the plan to a referendum for Greek and Turkish Cypriot populations. As Annan (UN 2004) himself stated, this "enlarged the role foreseen for me, from completing any unfinished parts of the plan … to resolving any continuing and persistent deadlocks in the negotiation." It was also the first time the Secretary-General's plan for conflict resolution would directly involve affected populations, rather than solely state-level representatives.

Cyprus is but one example of a broader trend over the development of the UN's good offices role: Secretaries-General increasingly saw themselves as active participants in conflict resolution with the ability to proffer substantive proposals, push the parties with external tools, and even engage outside the state-to-state framework by communicating with populations.[8]

[7]This formula has been used since, including by Javier Pérez de Cuéllar to get around problematic General Assembly resolutions on Afghanistan in 1980, see UN (1980).

[8]The 1983 decision of Secretary-General Javier Pérez de Cuéllar to partner with the Secretary-General of the Organization of American States and a broader Contact Group to resolve several entrenched disputes in Latin America is another example of increasing use of points of leverage outside of the UN. See O'Donoghue (2014).

Key Shifts: Delegation, Regionalisation, Expansion

Immediately after the Cold War, the rates of negotiated settlements of international conflict increased, and by the end of the 1990s the number and intensity of armed conflicts globally had dropped significantly, continuing to do so into the early 2000s despite major exceptions like Afghanistan and Darfur (Griffiths and Whitfield 2010). Renowned experts might have been justified in assuming that the need for good offices would eventually dry up.[9]

However, while armed conflict dropped during this period, the use of good offices did not in fact dissipate. Instead, there was a rapid increase in the establishment of peace operations through the 1990s, with 21 UN operations established between 1991 and 1995 alone.[10] Unlike the Cold War period, where the Secretary-General tended to address conflicts personally with Member States, the good offices function quickly began to spread across operational contexts and various representatives of the Secretary-General, requiring engagement with a broader range of non-state actors.[11] This reflected the post-Cold War optimism that the UN

[9]Thomas Franck (1997, p. 180) predicted that the good offices function would "stagnate" in the light of these conflict trends.

[10]The United Nations Iraq-Kuwait Observation Mission (1991); United Nations Mission for the Referendum in Western Sahara (1991); United Nations Angola Verification Mission II (1991); United Nations Observer Mission in El Salvador (1991); United Nations Advance Mission in Cambodia (1991); United Nations Protection Force (1992); United Nations Transitional Authority in Cambodia (1992); United Nations Operation in Somalia I (1992); United Nations Operation in Mozambique (1992); United Nations Operation in Somalia II (1993); United Nations Observer Mission Uganda-Rwanda 1(1993); United Nations Observer Mission in Georgia (1993); United Nations Observer Mission in Liberia (1993); United Nations Mission in Haiti (1993); United Nations Assistance Mission for Rwanda (1993); United Nations Aouzou Strip Observer Group (1994); United Nations Mission of Observers in Tajikistan (1994); United Nations Angola Verification Mission III (1995); United Nations Confidence Restoration Operation in Croatia (1994); United Nations Preventive Deployment Force (1995); United Nations Mission in Bosnia and Herzegovina (1995); United Nations Transitional Administration for Eastern Slavonia, Baranja and Western Sirmium (1995); United Nations Mission of Observers in Prevlaka (1995).

[11]See, e.g. the UN Observer Mission in El Salvador which was mandated to use good offices to resolve a conflict between the Government and the liberation movement FMLN (UN 1993); see also the UN Mission in Mozambique, mandated to oversee implementation of a peace agreement between the Government and the resistance movement (UN 1992b).

could work more constructively with Member States to resolve conflicts, but also the growth of complex intra-state conflicts that required UN intervention to prevent spill-over into the surrounding regions. The delegation and expansion of good offices—implicit in the appointment of a Special Representative of the Secretary-General (SRSG) or Special Envoy—was a dominant story of the 1990s.

A second development in the 1990s was the dramatic growth of the so-called "groups of friends," established by Member States to support or work in parallel with UN peacemaking efforts. Between 1990 and 2009 the number of groups of friends ballooned from only four to more than 30.[12] While these groups were not mandated by the Security Council to provide good offices (in fact they have operated almost entirely outside Security Council mandates), their functions were largely to facilitate political agreements between conflicting parties, and to support the UN operations when a unified effort of particular Member States was necessary. Similar to the growth of UN operations, the rise of groups of friends resulted from post-Cold War global dynamics, but also from a recognition that the UN alone was often not capable of resolving the more complex conflicts of the day.[13] As such, the good offices work of the UN was not only delegated to more UN actors, but it was more entwined with these support groups and increasingly reliant on tailored constellations of Member States.

Following the downturn in violent conflict in the 1990s and early 2000s, there was a tripling of intra-state conflicts between 2004 and 2014, a parallel tripling of battle-related deaths, and a strong tendency for relapse into conflict by countries that had recently emerged from war (Einsiedel 2014). This trend was driven by significant changes in the nature of armed conflict, including a rise in the influence of non-state actors, the growing impact of transnational organised crime on state fragility and conflict, increased impact of global jihadi networks, and deepening linkages between regional conflicts and sub-national ones (Bosetti and Einsiedel 2015; Einsiedel 2014). The Arab Spring and US interventions in Afghanistan and Iraq were major watershed moments that fed into these conflict dynamics, particularly the tendency of regional players to become involved in conflicts within states. Other factors, such as

[12] Whitfield (2010b). For a comprehensive study of groups of friends, see also Whitfield (2007).

[13] Whitfield (2016), providing a history of the groups of friends following the Cold War.

food prices, climate change, demographic shifts and water scarcity have combined to create new drivers of conflict and a complex terrain for international mediators.

These changes in the nature of armed conflict have contributed to further shifts in how good offices are employed today. Firstly, the increasing regionalisation of intra-state conflict—by which I mean the role of regional states in affecting the trajectory of conflict within a given country—has led the UN to rely more heavily on regional partnerships and structures to resolve conflict. Examples of innovative partnerships include the AU/UN/Humanitarian Dialogue mediation support to Kofi Annan in Kenya in 2008; the joint mediation for Madagascar in 2009 bringing together the AU, SADC, the UN, and the Organisation de la Francophonie (Whitfield 2010c); and UN support to AU-led mediations in countries like the DRC where a more direct UN role may be counterproductive (UN 2016d). Another form of partnership with a lower likelihood of repetition is the so-called "hybrid" operation, such as the AU/UN operation in Darfur (UNAMID).

The UN's regional focus and partnerships have become more institutional as well, most significantly with the 2002 establishment of the UN Office for West Africa (expanded in 2016 to include the Sahel), the 2007 creation of the UN Regional Centre for Preventive Diplomacy for Central Asia, the 2010 establishment of a UN/AU office in Addis Ababa, and the 2012 UN Regional Office for Central Africa. With each of these offices granted a clear political mandate, good offices have been spread more broadly, and linked more closely with regional actors.

Perhaps the most important shift, however, has been the growth of large, multidimensional peacekeeping operations between the mid-1990s and today. Whereas traditional peacekeeping tended to be confined to monitoring and reporting on ceasefires and troop withdrawals across international boundaries, multi-dimensional operations are far more intrusive and complex. Sometimes, though not always, deployed to support the implementation of a peace agreement, large operations, such as those currently deployed in the Central African Republic, the DRC, South Sudan, Mali and Darfur, have sprawling mandates covering disarmament, demobilisation, and reintegration, security sector reform, justice sector reform, extension of state authority, support to institutional development, protection of civilians, human rights monitoring, policing, support to humanitarian operations, local conflict resolution, technical support to democratic processes, and *also* a political/good offices function. With mandates that are based in whole or in part on Chapter VII of the UN Charter, the largest of these missions typically have thousands of soldiers and police, dozens of field offices in remote locations, military aviation and ground assets, and annual budgets of over one billion dollars.[14] They are often deployed into situations of ongoing hostilities, where civilians are actively at risk of further violence, and where states are frequently the source of political intransigence and insecurity. At the same time, the missions often have extremely ambitious political objectives, such as to facilitate credible elections, help to resolve longstanding national-level disputes, support the establishment of accountable institutions, or implement complex regional peace agreements with little local buy-in.[15]

These shifts—proliferation of UN entities with a good offices function, increasing reliance on regional approaches, and the growth of multi-dimensional peacekeeping—combine with serious ramifications for the good offices of the UN. On the one hand, the UN has far more points of contact across the globe than it had forty years ago. With regional offices and large missions employing thousands of national staff in often conflict-prone areas, the UN is in principle able to keep its finger directly on the pulse of societies. And there is evidence that this has made the UN better at identifying the early tremors of conflict, if not necessarily acting immediately upon them.[16] Deepened partnerships and more sustained presence has also improved the UN's knowledge and relationships with key actors involved in preventing and managing armed conflict. As the next section will describe, this has resulted in some successes for UN good offices in high-risk situations.

But there are strong downsides to these shifts as well, particularly in the growth of the multidimensional peacekeeping mission. Heads of these missions are not only the chief political actor empowered to

[14]UNMISS' budget for 2016–2017 is roughly USD 1.1 billion (UN 2016e); UNAMID's is just over USD 1 billion (UN 2016f); and MONUSCO's is USD 1.2 billion (UN 2016g).

[15]See, e.g. Security Council Resolution 2277 (UN 2016a) and 2295 (UN 2016h).

[16]See International Crisis Group (2016); see also Zenko and Friedman (2011), arguing that there are a huge number of points of contact for gathering information, but criticizing the UN for failing to have a comprehensive method of bringing it together.

employ the good offices of the UN in country,[17] they are also managers of complex, expensive operations with troops, police, and civilians often spread out over huge territories. As a result, heads of large peacekeeping missions tend to be faced with two fairly bad options. Either they can immerse themselves in management, diving deep into the budgetary, human resources, asset deployment, and structural configuration of the mission. This may make for well-managed operations, but it often leaves very little bandwidth for engagement with domestic political actors. Alternatively, an SRSG can leave the mission management to a deputy and focus instead on the political activities required by the mandate, splitting the mission into essentially a special political office of the SRSG and a peacekeeping operation. The first option leaves the political mandate unattended; the second tends to bifurcate the mission into a political and an operational component. There are of course ways to tie these two elements of peacekeeping together, but there are few clear success stories in recent history where a large mission was able to achieve meaningful political traction. Instead, there is some evidence arising from the cases considered below that good offices may be best provided by smaller, more agile configurations, embedded in regional structures, rather than large peacekeeping operations.

Essential Elements for Success: Where Modern Good Offices Work, and Don't

If good offices are successful, violent conflict is averted before it escalates, or active violence is reduced rather than perpetuated. It is difficult to measure success in this counterfactual situation: how much worse would the violence have been in the absence of an intervention, or how good would the election have been without the UN's engagement? Nonetheless, by comparing a variety of recent cases, it is possible to identify key elements for successful political engagement, and some of the outcomes when these elements are not present. The essential elements are: (1) an in-depth understanding of the conflict based on sustained contact and relationships on the ground; (2) timing of the

[17] By definition, the Special Representatives of the Secretary-General are empowered to represent him, and thus provide his good offices.

intervention; (3) leverage over the key conflict actors; and (4) credibility of the mediator.[18]

Knowledge and Relationships

In-depth understanding of the situation, and relationships with the conflict actors are critical to any successful political engagement, and are often the result of a sustained presence on the ground. During the 2009–2010 crisis in Guinea following a military coup, the UN's Special Representative, Said Djinnit, conducted 45 missions to the region, meeting with all actors, including the military junta. His ground game and clear commitment to engaging with a broad array of stakeholders were viewed as crucial for the success of the mediation effort.[19] Similarly, the UN Office for West Africa (UNOWA) SRSG Ibn Chambas was present in country ahead of, and frequently during, the electoral crisis that gripped the Gambia in 2016,[20] and Special Envoy Jamal Benomar was lauded for having spent time in different locales in Yemen to better understand the players and dynamics during the 2011 crisis (Day and Fong 2017). Former Nigerian President Olusegun Obasanjo's success as a UN envoy in brokering a ceasefire in eastern DRC in 2008 was in part due to his deep experience in the region and broad set of relationships (Bright 2011).

Where there are limited relationships, diplomatic efforts are often stymied. The UN's experience in Darfur is one such example where, from 2007–2010 the Government's reluctance to engage on a meaningful

[18] The configuration of elements used here is drawn from Day and Pichler (2017). More broadly, the elements are included in a wide range of analysis of UN political engagement. See Babbitt (2012), focused on leverage and access as key elements; Chesterman (2017, p. 100), describing cases where leverage and legitimacy were key elements; Gowan et al. (2010), arguing that elements for success of diplomacy include anticipatory relationships, good understanding of elite actors, ability to anticipate political inflection points, and sufficient leverage; Lund (1996), identifying several factors for successful preventive diplomacy, including timing, support from major players, multifaceted action, and moderate leadership.

[19] United Nations (2011, para. 55); UN Department of Political Affairs internal report on Guinea intervention, on file with author.

[20] UNOWAS (2016); UN Department of Political Affairs internal report on Gambia intervention, on file with author.

political process with the rebel groups resulted in limited access for the AU/UN mediation with key state actors.[21] The fact that the joint AU/UN mediation was structurally separate from the peacekeeping operation and based almost entirely out of country with infrequent visits to Darfur also curtailed the day-to-day knowledge of the situation and the possible range of relationships. This is a typical shortcoming when the good offices function is located out of country: the Geneva-based Syria mediation, for example, has suffered since 2011 with a lack of granular knowledge, limited access to key players, and little credibility on the ground.[22]

The establishment of regional offices like UNOWA and the United Nations Regional Centre for Preventive Diplomacy for Central Asia (UNRCCA) has boosted the UN's ability to maintain strong relationships and deep knowledge of conflict-prone areas.[23] The use of well-respected envoys with an established track record in the region has also bolstered the UN's relationships in conflict settings.

Timing

It is particularly helpful for timing if the key parties to the conflict are ready for the UN to play a role. There are several examples where this has led to relatively successful outcomes, including the request by the Government and opposition for UN mediation support in Sierra Leone in 2009; the willingness on the part of the Maoists and the Nepalese Government for the UN to play a good offices role from 2003 (Einsiedel 2012); a request by the Malawian Government in 2011 for the UN to broker a deal with the opposition; and the willingness of both the DRC and Rwanda for the UN to broker a ceasefire with the CNDP— National Congress for the Defence of the People, a rebel group active in both countries—in 2008 due to the very poor relationship between the countries at the time.

The ability of the UN to respond quickly when there is an opportunity to engage diplomatically is essential to the success of its good offices (International Crisis Group 2016). Again, regional presence and

[21] Guéhenno (2015), Chapter 8 on UNAMID.

[22] Hinnenbusch and Zartman (2016), noting that the UN mediation for Syria suffered from a lack of access, consent on the ground, and credibility with key actors.

[23] See United Nations (2011), describing the successful interventions based out of the UN's regional offices.

partnerships have played an increasingly central role in recent years. For example, UN/ECOWAS (Economic Community of West African States) joint missions to Guinea in 2008 and to Burkina Faso in 2014 produced a clear and forceful reports on the likely deterioration of the situation in the period to follow and positioned the UN to be ready to act when the crisis struck.[24] Similarly, in responding to the 2010 crisis in Kyrgyzstan, the proximity of the UNRCCA facilitated early contacts as the situation developed, quick establishment of a new in-country office, and the rapid deployment of a senior reconciliation adviser (UN 2011, para. 23). Being present in the neighbourhood does not guarantee timely response by the UN, but it appears to help.

Leverage

Leverage is the most important of the factors, and perhaps the most elusive given that the UN "often appear[s] unable to do more than encourage contacts to behave responsibly" (International Crisis Group 2016, p. 18). Instead, the UN must rely more upon soft-power techniques, corralling international actors around common messages, finding pressure points via bilateral relations, and offering hesitant leaders discreet ladders to climb down from conflict (Wallensteen 2015; Ramsbotham et al. 2016, pp. 199–212).

However, often even the most well-coordinated messaging can fail to gain leverage by itself. In Gambia, SRSG Chambas was working to pressure incumbent President Jammeh to accept the results of the 2016 election, and during a single month Jammeh was made to receive similar messages from the King of Morocco, the presidents of Liberia, Mauritania, Chad and Nigeria, as well as from the Organization of Islamic Conference, the UN, and the AU.[25] But even this exceptionally well-coordinated approach did not appear to change Jammeh's calculations, and it was only when ECOWAS demonstrated its willingness to use force to back up its message that he agreed to step aside (Al Jazeera 2017). In terms of preventing major escalation, sometimes diplomacy backed by threat of force is necessary (Johnstone 2003).

[24] UN Department of Political Affairs internal report on Burkina Faso intervention, on file with author.

[25] UN DPA internal assessment of Gambia intervention, on file with author.

Short of use of force, other sticks can generate leverage when combined with diplomacy. In Burkina Faso, the threat of sanctions by the AU, along with suspension of AU membership and united messaging from the Security Council (Reuters 2015), together contributed to the leader's decision to step down and avoid further violence. In contrast, the AU's imposition of sanctions on the military junta in Guinea in 2009 appeared to have no impact; in fact, the incumbent head of state reportedly entrenched his position immediately following the sanctions.[26] There is no magic formula to gain leverage, but the combination of sustained international messaging, combined with something more coercive, has shown some success.

Often, a major bilateral actor or combination of actors can dramatically increase the leverage over a reluctant principal. In 2015, US Secretary of State John Kerry broke protocol and flew to see incumbent Nigerian President Goodluck Jonathan, urging him to respect the outcome of the elections (Shapiro 2015). There is anecdotal evidence that this may have played a role in Jonathan's decision to stand down. Richard Holbrooke's famous role in pushing Slobodan Milošević to accept the 1995 Dayton Accords is another such example, which also demonstrates the importance of threat of force behind diplomatic action (Holbrooke 1998). The growth of groups of friends described above in fact reflects the efficacy of getting the right constellation of Member States around a particular conflict setting, one of whom often possesses outsize leverage (Whitfield 2007).

A united Security Council is one of the most authoritative sources of leverage and, when it speaks with one voice, there is a far higher chance of success. But even a united Council cannot necessarily deliver. Strong, well-coordinated messaging on the need for both Presidents Kabila and Nkurunziza to step down in DRC and Burundi, respectively, have fallen on deaf ears, even in the face of widespread violence. And the Council has become increasingly notorious for its paralysis on key conflicts, most importantly Syria, but also arguably in its failure to place Myanmar, Ukraine, and Zimbabwe meaningfully on its agenda in recent years, thwarted by the use of a Permanent Member's veto. A united Security Council is often necessary, but seldom sufficient, to achieving leverage (Gowan 2017).

[26] UN DPA internal assessment of Gambia intervention (Day and Pichler 2018).

Finally, it is worth considering the potential leverage provided by the presence of large peacekeeping operations, which often deliver significant programmatic funds, deploy troops, and engage with a range of actors on the ground. While this kind of presence should ostensibly generate leverage for the UN, experience has if anything underscored the extremely limited political sway of even the biggest peacekeeping operation. The 2008 deployment of nearly 20,000 AU/UN troops into Darfur had no apparent impact on the Government's or rebels' positions with respect to the peace negotiations (which are unresolved nine years later). Nor did UNMISS' very large presence in South Sudan in 2013 appear to give it much influence over the protagonists of the civil war, and the 2016 relapse into open conflict there has shown the lack of leverage of the UN in brokering a political solution there. Likewise, MONUSCO's sprawling presence across the DRC and significant state-building support programs have not positioned the UN as a central player in the ongoing negotiations over the electoral process.[27] As the former Chief of the Department of Peacekeeping lamented, large missions like those in Darfur and the DRC frequently fail to use their presence as a fulcrum for gaining influence in country, due to "a lack of understanding of the political nature of peacekeeping, as if the conduct of military operations and the military posture could be divorced from the politics of the situation" (Guéhenno 2015).

Credibility

There is no formula for achieving credibility in a diplomatic process, and frequently it is highly personality-based. In some cases, the respect afforded to a seasoned official with a history of success in the region bestows credibility on a process. Here, the particular status of Djinnit in Guinea, Obasanjo in eastern DRC, and Ibn Chambas in Gambia and Nigeria have been cited as critical to the success of the diplomatic effort (Hara 2011). But even the most seasoned and respected officials are not always capable of delivering if the conditions are not right. Kofi Annan was highly successful in Kenya in 2008, but made very little progress as the Syria Envoy in 2012. Lakhdar Brahimi brokered major breakthroughs in Afghanistan, but he too was stymied by Syria. What is clear

[27] In fact, the SRSG of MONUSCO has been largely limited to a supportive role to the AU-led mediation on the elections crisis.

is that a lack of credibility will undermine the process, particularly if the mediator is seen as an unwanted intervention or too dependent upon biased actors. Here again, as described above, embedding mediation processes in regional structures like UNOWA and the UNRCCA may have had a salubrious effect on the UN's credibility to address recent conflicts.

Too Big, May Fail: Recommendations Toward Nimble, Effective Good Offices

The nature of violent conflict has radically changed since the inception of the UN in 1945, and the UN's role in preventing and resolving it has had to evolve as well. As the UN has become more deeply involved in intransigent civil wars, increasingly reliant on a broad range of international, regional, and local actors, and heavily invested in large peace operations, good offices have become only one of several tools available to peacemakers. In many ways, the waters of diplomacy have been muddied. But, as the HIPPO points out, the political work of the UN is *primus inter pares*, and political solutions must be at the heart of modern conflict prevention and management.

A crucial step in this regard is to build strategies based on the successful elements of past efforts, looking to deepen knowledge and key relationships, identify ripe moments when diplomatic intervention will have the most impact, and connect all the points of leverage into a coherent approach. The cases described above have demonstrated that the vaguely defined notion of good offices has allowed for innovative, entrepreneurial approaches and some tangible stories of success. The establishment of lean, relatively responsive regional offices has especially helped deliver diplomatic interventions in a flexible and bespoke fashion, and could be usefully replicated in regions including North Africa and potentially the Middle East.[28]

At the same time, it appears that the growth of multidimensional peacekeeping has not contributed substantially to politics-first approaches. In fact, the heavy administrative burdens and competing tasks of large missions may well have had a deleterious effect on SRSGs' capacity to focus on the political work of the mission. With much to lose and little demonstrable leverage, large missions appear to tend to become

[28]See Gowan et al. (2010), noting that the UN Secretariat had proposed the establishment of additional regional political offices for East Asia and Latin America, which had not been approved by Member States.

practical hostages of the host government, often sacrificing leverage and independence when the time comes to press for political outcomes. Perhaps ironically, it seems that missions mandated to build state institutions and capacity—such as in the DRC, South Sudan, and Mali—may have had the least success in gaining political traction in country. Further down the size scale, and considering missions such as those in Liberia, Sierra Leone, Mozambique, East Timor, and El Salvador, there may be instances where missions were able to employ their good offices more effectively. But there is little evidence that size matters when it comes to achieving political solutions in peace operations.

All of this leads to the conclusion that the UN's good offices appear best employed in a flexible, nimble fashion, unencumbered by overly ambitious peacekeeping mandates, and able to find leverage points outside of the UN, especially via regional players. In an era of paralysis within the Security Council and deepening divisions in many of the most fragile regions in the world, independent, entrepreneurial diplomats in the vein of Dag Hammarskjöld are sorely needed to carry out the demanding political work of the United Nations. In order to do so, protecting the good offices functions as "almost anything" (Whitfield 2010a) is perhaps more important than ever.

References

Adams, Robert, and Benedict Kingsbury (eds.). 1994. *United Nations, Divided World: The UN's Role in International Relations*, 2nd ed., revised. Oxford: Clarendon Press.

Al Jazeera. 2017. Gambia's Yahya Jammeh Confirms He Will Step Down. Al Jazeera, January 21.

Annan, Kofi. 2001. Dag Hammarskjöld and the 21st Century. Speech in Uppsala, September 6.

Babbitt, Eileen F. 2012. Preventive Diplomacy by Intergovernmental Organizations: Learning from Practice. *International Negotiation* 17 (3): 349–388.

Bosetti, Louise, and Sebastian Einsiedel. 2015. *Intra-State Based Armed Conflicts: Overview of Global and Regional Trends (1990–2013)*. Tokyo: United Nations University Centre for Policy Research.

Bright, Nancee Oku. 2011. Negotiating to Save Lives. *UN Chronicle*, vol. XLVIII, no. 2.

Chesterman, Simon. 2011. The Charter of the United Nations: A Commentary—Articles 97, 98, 99. In *The Charter of the United Nations: A*

Commentary, ed. Bruno Simma, Daniel-Erasmus Khan, Georg Nolte, and Andreas Paulus. Oxford: Oxford University Press.

Chesterman, Simon (ed.). 2017. *Secretary or General? The UN Secretary-General in World Politics.* Cambridge: Cambridge University Press.

Convention for the Pacific Settlement of International Disputes. 1899. *The Hague*, October 18.

Convention for the Pacific Settlement of International Disputes. 1907. *The Hague*, July 29.

Day, Adam, and Alexandra Pichler Fong. 2017. Diplomacy and Good Offices in the Prevention of Conflict: A Thematic Paper for the United Nations—World Bank Study on Conflict Prevention. Conflict Prevention Series, No. 3. United Nations University Centre for Policy Research, Tokyo.

Day, Adam, and Alexandra Pichler Fong. 2018. UN Preventive Diplomacy in the 2008–10 Crisis in Guinea. United Nations University, Centre for Policy Research, April 2018.

Einsiedel, Sebastian. 2012. *Nepal in Transition: From People's War to Fragile Peace.* Cambridge: Cambridge University Press.

Einsiedel, Sebastian. 2014. *Major Recent Trends in Violent Conflict.* Tokyo: United Nations University Centre for Policy Research.

Fischer, Thomas. 2002. *Switzerland's Good Offices: A Changing Concept.* Zürich: Center for International Studies.

Franck, Thomas M. 1995. The Secretary General's Role in Conflict Resolution: Past Present and Pure Conjecture. *European Journal of International Law* 6 (3): 360–387.

Franck, Thomas M. 1997. *Fairness in International Law and Institutions.* Oxford: Clarendon Press.

Gowan, Richard, Bruce D. Jones, Sara Batmanglich, and Andrew Hart. 2010. *Back to Basics: The UN and Crisis Diplomacy in an Age of Strategy Uncertainty*, 2010. New York: Center on International Cooperation.

Gowan, Richard. 2017. *Diplomacy in Action: Expanding the UN Security Council's Role in Crisis and Conflict Prevention.* New York: Center on International Cooperation.

Griffiths, Martin, and Teresa Whitfield. 2010. *Mediation Ten Years On: Challenges and Opportunities for Peacemaking.* Geneva: Centre for Humanitarian Dialogue.

Guéhenno, Jean-Marie. 2015. *The Fog of Peace: A Memoir of International Peacekeeping in the 21st Century.* Washington, DC: Brookings.

Hara, Fabienne. 2011. Preventive Diplomacy in Africa: Adapting to New Realities. *International Crisis Group*, op-ed, December 31.

Hinnenbusch, Raymond, and I. William Zartman. 2016. *UN Mediation in the Syrian Crisis: From Kofi Annan to Lakhdar Brahimi.* New York: International Peace Institute.

Holbrooke, Richard. 1998. *To End a War: The Conflict in Yugoslavia—America's Inside Story—Negotiating with Milosevic.* New York: Modern Library Paperbacks.

International Court of Justice. 1949. Reparation for Injuries Suffered in the Service of the United Nations. Advisory Opinion, April 11.

International Crisis Group. 2016. Seizing the Moment. Special Report No. 2. Brussels: International Crisis Group.

Jacobson, Harold K. 1979. *Networks of Independence: International Organisations and the Global Political System.* New York: Alfred A. Knopf Publishing.

Johnstone, Ian. 2003. The Role of the UN Secretary-General: The Power of Persuasion Based on Law. *Global Governance* 9 (4): 441–458.

Johnstone, Ian. 2010. Emerging Doctrine for Political Missions. New York: Center on International Cooperation.

Lund, Michael S. 1996. *Preventing Violent Conflicts: A Strategy for Preventive Diplomacy.* Washington, DC: United States Institute of Peace.

Michael, Michális S. 2009. *Resolving the Cyprus Conflict.* London: Palgrave Macmillan.

O'Donoghue, Aoife. 2014. Good Offices: Grasping the Place of Law in Conflict. *Legal Studies* 34 (3): 469–496.

Ramsbotham, Oliver, Tom Woodhouse, and High Miall. 2016. *Contemporary Conflict Resolution*, 4th ed. Cambridge: Polity.

Reuters. 2015. African Union Suspends Burkina Faso, Threatens Sanctions. *Reuters*, September 19.

Shapiro, Jeffrey Scott. 2015. Kerry Breaks Protocol, Flies to Nigeria to Discourage Election Violence. *The Washington Times*, January 25.

United Nations. 1945. *Report of the Preparatory Commission of the United Nations.* London: United Nations.

United Nations. 1946. *United Nations Security Council Resolution 2.* New York: United Nations.

United Nations. 1954. *United Nations General Assembly Resolution 906.* New York: United Nations.

United Nations. 1956a. *United Nations Security Council Resolution 118.* New York: United Nations.

United Nations. 1956b. *United Nations Security Council Resolution 119.* New York: United Nations.

United Nations. 1964. *United Nations Security Council Resolution 186.* New York: United Nations.

United Nations. 1980. *United Nations General Assembly Resolution 35/37.* New York: United Nations.

United Nations. 1982. The Manila Declaration on the Peaceful Settlement of Disputes Between States. *United Nations General Assembly Resolution 37/10.* New York: United Nations.

United Nations. 1988a. Declaration on the Prevention and Removal of Disputes and Situations Which May Threaten International Peace and Security and on the Role of the United Nations in This Field. *United Nations General Assembly Resolution 43/51*. New York: United Nations.

United Nations. 1988b. *The United Nations Handbook on the Peaceful Settlement of Disputes Between States*. New York: United Nations.

United Nations. 1992a. *An Agenda for Peace: Preventive Diplomacy, Peacemaking and Peace-Keeping*. New York: United Nations.

United Nations. 1992b. *United Nations Security Council Resolution 797*. New York: United Nations.

United Nations. 1993. *United Nations Security Council Resolution 832*. New York: United Nations.

United Nations. 2004. *Report of the Secretary-General on His Mission of Good Offices in Cyprus*. New York: United Nations Security Council.

United Nations. 2011. Preventive Diplomacy: Delivering Results. Report of the Secretary General. New York: United Nations.

United Nations. 2012. *UN Security Council Resolution 2039*. New York: United Nations.

United Nations. 2015. *Report of the High-Level Independent Panel on Peace Operations on Uniting Our Strengths for Peace: Politics, Partnership and People*. New York: United Nations.

United Nations. 2016a. *UN Security Council Resolution 2277*. New York: United Nations.

United Nations. 2016b. *UN Security Council Resolution 2299*. New York: United Nations.

United Nations. 2016c. *UN Security Council Resolution 2274*. New York: United Nations.

United Nations. 2016d. *Security Council Leadership Critical to Defusing Tensions in Democratic Republic of Congo, Deputy Secretary-General Stresses*. New York: United Nations.

United Nations. 2016e. *United Nations General Assembly Resolution 70/281*. New York: United Nations General Assembly.

United Nations. 2016f. *United Nations General Assembly Resolution 70/284*. New York: United Nations General Assembly.

United Nations. 2016g. *United Nations General Assembly Resolution 70/274*. New York: United Nations General Assembly.

United Nations. 2016h. *UN Security Council Resolution 2295*. New York: United Nations.

United Nations. 2017. Secretary-General Calls for Surge in 'Peace Diplomacy' at Munich Security Event, Noting Prevailing Impunity, Unpredictability, Unclear Power Relations. *Munich*, February 18.

United Nations Office for West Africa and the Sahel. 2016. Mohamed Ibn Chambas Calls for Inclusive, Credible and Peaceful Presidential Election in the Gambia. https://unowas.unmissions.org/mohamed-ibn-chambas-calls-inclusive-credible-and-peaceful-presidential-election-gambia. Accessed 28 Nov 2017.

Vienna Convention. 1985. *Vienna Convention on the Protection of the Ozone Layer*, United Nations adopted 22 March 1985. Vienna and New York: United Nations.

Wainhouse, David W. 1966. *International Peace Observation: A History and Forecast.* Baltimore: Johns Hopkins Press.

Waldheim, Kurt. 1980. *The Challenge of Peace.* London: Weidenfeld and Nicolson.

Wallensteen, Peter. 2015. *Understanding Conflict Resolution.* London: Sage.

Whitfield, Teresa. 2007. *Friends Indeed? The United Nations, Groups of Friends, and the Resolution of Conflict.* Washington, DC: US Institute of Peace.

Whitfield, Teresa. 2010a. *Political Missions, Mediation and Good Offices.* New York: Center on International Cooperation.

Whitfield, Teresa. 2010b. *Working with Groups of Friends.* Washington, DC: United States Institute for Peace.

Whitfield, Teresa. 2010c. *External Actors in Mediation: Dilemmas and Options for Mediators.* Geneva: Centre for Humanitarian Dialogue.

Whitfield, Teresa. 2016. Groups of Friends. In *The UN Security Council in the 21st Century*, ed. Sebastian von Einsiedel, David M. Malone, and Bruno Stagno Ugarte. Washington, DC: International Peace Institute.

World Trade Organization. 1994. Understanding on the Rules and Procedures Governing the Settlement of Disputes. Annex 2 in the *Marrakesh Agreement Establishing the World Trade Organization.* Marrakesh: WTO.

Zenko, Micah, and Rebecca R. Friedman. 2011. UN Early Warning for Preventing Conflict. *International Peacekeeping* 18 (1): 21–37.

Open Access This chapter is licensed under the terms of the Creative Commons Attribution 4.0 International License (http://creativecommons.org/licenses/by/4.0/), which permits use, sharing, adaptation, distribution and reproduction in any medium or format, as long as you give appropriate credit to the original author(s) and the source, provide a link to the Creative Commons license and indicate if changes were made.

The images or other third party material in this chapter are included in the chapter's Creative Commons license, unless indicated otherwise in a credit line to the material. If material is not included in the chapter's Creative Commons license and your intended use is not permitted by statutory regulation or exceeds the permitted use, you will need to obtain permission directly from the copyright holder.

CHAPTER 5

People-Centred Approaches to Peace: At Cross Roads Between Geopolitics, Norms, and Practice

Youssef Mahmoud

"We the Peoples" and the Act of Creation[1]

On the eve of the 2015 world leaders' summit that would unanimously adopt the 2030 Sustainable Development Agenda, "We the peoples," the emblematic first three words of the UN Charter, were on full display during an art exhibit at the United Nations. In 1953, the American painter, Norman Rockwell, had been so hopeful about the creation of the United Nations that he sketched a drawing entitled the United Nations after the newly formed organisation (Husain 2015). The sketch features in the foreground the representatives of the Governments of the United States, the United Kingdom, and the now-defunct Soviet Union. In the background, people of all ages and from different cultural and ethnic backgrounds looked over the shoulders of these representatives,

[1] See Schlesinger (2004).

Y. Mahmoud (✉)
International Peace Institute (IPI), Vienna, Austria

© The Author(s) 2019

C. de Coning and M. Peter (eds.), *United Nations Peace Operations in a Changing Global Order*,
https://doi.org/10.1007/978-3-319-99106-1_5

with anxious but hopeful eyes. Rockwell never finished this sketch. Instead, in 1961, he drew from it to complete his now famous painting "the Golden Rule" (Norman Rockwell Museum 2014), currently on permanent display at the UN headquarters, featuring the same figures of the people in the background but without the Government representatives in the front. A likely interpretation is that, after his original drawing eight years earlier, he had decided to de-emphasise governments (Reimers 2015): By giving "We the Peoples" centre stage, he wanted to convey the message that when people in their immense diversity and collective wisdom stand together in dignity and mutual respect, they can achieve the common goals enshrined in the Charter.

No one could have predicted that Rockwell's decision to remove government representative from the "Golden Rule" rendition of the "United Nations" would be a harbinger of the complex and, at times, tense state-society relations we are witnessing today in many parts of the world.

Many of the 50 founding states that had signed the Charter in June 1945 were undemocratic. Yet no one contested their right to speak for the people, who were admittedly exhausted from the ravages of World War II. Things are different today. While most governments are democratically elected, their remit to speak for "we the peoples" is regularly challenged (van Tongeren 2005). Aided by the democratisation of information, education, and the forces of globalisation, ordinary citizens and networks of interconnected people have become aware of the performance of their governments and thus do not shy away from vociferously making known their views about the quality of the services they expect from these governments. As attested by the wave of protest movements that swept over parts of Africa, the Middle East and several countries in Latin America, citizens are no longer content with the proposition that their right to change non-performing governments can only be exercised during election periods.

Global challenges such as development deficits, health pandemics, drug trafficking, food security, water, climate change, poverty reduction, criminal networks, and terrorism are no longer transnational problems for governments alone to worry about, echoing the conclusions of the Panel of Eminent Persons on United Nations-Civil Society Relations (UN 2004). This shift was in full display during the UN's 70th anniversary celebration where foreign policy discourse was not so much about augmenting the power of the state as about serving the people (Center for Strategic and International Studies 2015).

"We the Peoples" in Development and Peace and Security

People-centred approaches are not a novelty for the UN system. In the early nineties, the UN Development Programme (UNDP) struck a balance between state-centric and people-centred approaches, most notably in its Human Development Report (HDR). Now its flagship publication, the HDR, was first launched in 1990 with the Pakistani economist Mahbub ul Haq as a key instigator. The aspiration was to put people centre stage in debates on development, which goal was to provide people with opportunities and choices (United Nations Development Programme 2017). "People are the real wealth of a nation," Haq wrote in the opening lines of the first HDR (United Nations Development Programme 1990). "The basic objective of development is to create an enabling environment for people to enjoy long, healthy and creative lives." It is no surprise, therefore, that the UNDP's core mission is to empower people and build the resilience of nations.

The unanimous adoption in 2015 by the UN General Assembly of the 2030 Agenda for Sustainable Development and the Paris Agreement on Climate Change have been hailed as much as state achievements as a "peoples'" achievement. The first was touted as a global social contract between the peoples' world and their states, and the second a trilateral compact, a covenant between states, peoples, and the planet. Both constitute a remarkable proclamation of hope at a time when the world is torn by much strife and violent conflict. The intense engagement and mobilisation of grass root movements throughout the consultation process and the relentless pressure they exercised on world leaders account for the sense of collective ownership by all stakeholders of these two universal agendas (Leiva-Roesch et al. 2014). As the Panel of Eminent Persons on United Nations-Civil Society Relations concluded (UN 2004, p. 3), "constructively engaging with civil society is a necessity for the United Nations, not an option."

"We the Peoples" in Peace and Security

In the area of peace and security, integrating people- or community-centred approaches to manage conflict has been a slow process met with occasional pushback. Despite the pervasive awareness that contemporary conflicts are largely occurring within states and tend to be driven from below—often by non-state actors and citizens with unanswered grievances—the UN Security Council, designed to prevent and arbitrate interstate conflicts, has been struggling to adapt its state-centric approaches to these new realities. Its mandate design is still dominated by the assumption that fixing imperfect or weak states, securing their juridical legitimacy through elections, and extending their remit throughout a particular territory would yield peace dividends for citizens and communities. This dominant paradigm equates state-building with peacebuilding, impervious to the empirical evidence indicating otherwise (Call 2012). This point was not lost on the g7+ Group of countries, composed of mostly fragile and conflict affected states, when they agreed in 2011 together with their international development partners on the five peacebuilding and state building goals that should guide their collective action out of fragility (G7plus 2017). Thus it comes as no surprise that the first goal gave primacy to legitimate politics over state building. Their firm view was that no state authority is viable without inclusive, participatory governance and equitable delivery of basic services to the people.

HIPPO and the Challenges of People-Centred Approaches

It is against this background that the High Level Independent Panel on Peace Operations (HIPPO) set out to fulfil the mandate entrusted to it by the UN Secretary-Secretary in October 2014 (UN 2014). The High-Level Panel (henceforth the Panel) devoted considerable time in developing a shared and practical understanding of what was meant by people-centred approaches to peace operations before advocating these approaches as one of the essential shifts (UN 2015a, pp. viii and 16) that had to be embraced in the future in the design and delivery of UN peace operations. As a panel, we argued for a "renewed resolve on the part of United Nations peace operations personnel to engage with, serve and protect the people they have been mandated to assist." The Panel, not unlike the Advisory Group of Experts on the Review of the Peacebuilding Architecture and the High Level Advisory Group on the implementation of Security Council Resolution 1325, considered sustaining peace (UN 2015a, p. 34) as the ultimate objective of UN post conflict engagements in which inclusive politics and people in their plurality, particularly women and youth, played a central role.

Panel members were keenly aware that reaching out to people and engaging with local communities and ordinary citizens are common practices in many peace operations, notwithstanding the Council's half-hearted acceptance of the concept as outlined above. These field practices ranged from local perception surveys on mission performance, to communication and sensitisation outreach programs through UN radios.

However, the Panel felt that these practices tended to take the form of discrete activities, without sufficient strategic focus on their connections to self-sustainable peace. Whether stemming from Security Council mandates or conceived by field missions, community engagement activities appeared as mission-centric (e.g. winning hearts and minds of local populations) or as appendices to various state-centric goals that were judged to be far more critical to stability, such as sustaining a fragile peace agreement, holding elections, or restoring and extending state authority. The latter activity tended to be carried out in a way that emphasised control by the centre rather than empowerment of the peripheries and their forms of self-government, especially in areas that had escaped government control in the past and where invariably the state suffers from a trust deficit. The Panel was also aware that in peacekeeping missions, operating in hostile environments where much of the military assets are mobilised to prevent or counter asymmetric threats, the space for meaningful community outreach tends to be limited or compromised, at times even securitised.

In pointing out the above shortcomings and operational constraints, HIPPO members were equally aware that people-centred approaches, are not without dilemmas, challenges, or risks, particularly in complex conflict environments and notwithstanding normative advances, policy prescriptions, good practices, and guidance notes (UN 2015a, p. 66).

The central challenge for a state-centric instrument such as peacekeeping is to what extent it should have its own mechanisms for engaging and consulting directly with "we the peoples" without making government officials feel that their unique prerogative, as elected representatives to engage with their own people, has been usurped (van Tongeren 2005) and thus would insist on being involved. The flip-side of this dilemma is how to partner with the government in this endeavour without the latter capturing UN devised people-focused processes for narrow political gains, including using them to shore up any perceived lack of performance legitimacy.

Another challenge is that it is not easy to identify, outside elite circles, civil society representatives who genuinely speak on behalf of local people. Therefore, questions of who and when and how to engage become central. Reaching out to communities associated with insurgent movements or terrorist groups that UN peace operations are expected to keep at arms-length, or even neutralise, could put UN personnel at risk (de Coning et al. 2015).

An additional challenge is the lack of capacity for rigorous analysis of local realities. This would require among other things a shift from focusing only on the drivers of conflict and fragility to identifying the communities' endogenous capacities for peace and resilience. These usually include local norms, physical structures, traditional governance institutions, and networks through which information is collected and disseminated and mutual assistance is provided (UN 2015a, p. 35). It is these informal coping mechanisms that people turn to in times of national or local stresses, whether they are man-made or nature-induced (Interpeace 2016). And it is these very capacities that peace operations need to strengthen so as to help lay the foundation for less reversible and, hopefully, self-sustaining peace. In the absence of such analyses, missions tend to resort to ad-hoc programmatic interventions that are not well thought-out or that unwittingly may do more harm than good.

Another factor that has been found to contribute to unintended consequences is the tendency of the UN to value thematic expertise (DDR, SSR, electoral processes) over local knowledge. This legitimises the deployment of people to missions who do not speak any of the local languages, nor are fully versed or interested in the custom, norms, and behaviours of the host country. They tend to look at complex local problems through the lens of their expertise with supply-driven solution at the ready.

A further challenge that was brought to the attention of Panel members is that because of concerns for staff security and safety, particularly in hostile environments, there was and still is a tendency to gather information on local peace and conflict dynamics from expatriates living in fortified compounds (Autesserre 2015). Attempts to address this deficit by relying on information provided by national Community Liaison Officers or Assistants in the employment of the mission have sometimes backfired or endangered their lives. This is particularly the case when local communities that are hostile to the mission or the government start suspecting these local employees (particularly those attached to UN military compounds) of using their privileged access to their communities to spy on them. The increasingly explicit emphasis on enhanced human intelligence capabilities as a force multiplier or for security and effective mandate implementation has fuelled these suspicions.

HIPPO Specific Recommendations, UN SG's Follow-on Report, and Member States' Reactions

In order to overcome the above dilemmas and challenges, the Panel called for a number of shifts in mindset and operational practices and made several specific recommendations. The most salient of these are discussed below.

For the Panel, countries emerging from conflict "are not blank pages and their people are not 'projects'" (UN 2015a, p. 34). As outlined above, these people possess knowledge, expertise, and resilient mechanisms that help withstand the stresses of conflict. Therefore, the Panel called for a shift from merely consulting with these people in order to validate pre-conceived ideas and solutions, to actively engaging with them so as to hear their perspectives and monitor and respond to how they experience the impact of the peace operation and ensure that the mission does no harm (UN 2015a, p. 24). In this connection, the Panel stressed the need to allocate the appropriate resources to, on a regular basis, conduct "independent surveys of local perceptions of the mission and progress towards mission objectives" (UN 2015a, p. 39). They also called on missions "to develop strategies for community engagement at various stages of the mission cycle—from assessment, analysis, planning, implementation, review and evaluation—and make increased and judicious use of national staff in designing and implementing these strategies" (UN 2015a, p. 66).

With respect to analysis, the Panel recommends that missions should focus inter-alia on identifying the local structures for managing and mitigating conflict, resource flows, and revenue or illicit power networks (UN 2015a, p. 46). Missions should also engage in differentiated and gender sensitive conflict analysis to better understand the specific experience, rights, needs, perspectives, and roles of women and girls in conflict situations (UN 2015a, p. 67). This would in turn "inform strategies for their protection and participation," and enable missions to draw on the expertise of local women leaders, and women's organisations (UN 2015a, p. 67).

With respect to community dynamics in zones of conflict, the Panel recommended that peace operations "should maintain the closest possible interaction with the communities and support national initiatives regarding rural and local development. Missions should lend their assistance to the resolution of local conflicts, and support community efforts to move toward reconciliation" (UN 2015a, p. 39).

In his follow-up report "The Future of UN Peace Operations" (UN 2015b), Secretary-General Ban Ki-Moon endorsed the strategic shift for a people-centred approach to peace operations and highlighted the specific, practical initiatives the Secretariat was already engaged in to implement many of the recommendations outlined in the Panel's report under this rubric. These include public opinion surveys undertaken by many missions to regularly assess progress and evolving community priorities, to recruiting national staff and community liaison officers to help the missions foster public support for their mandates (UN 2015b, p. 27), to guidance notes on how to understand local perceptions.

In its 2016 substantive session report (UN 2016a), the Special Committee on Peacekeeping Operations (UN 2016a, p. 34) expressed its support for more people-centred approaches in peacekeeping, "including through local level analysis that draws on more strategic engagement with communities and an understanding of local perceptions and priorities" (UN 2016a, para. 131). It also noted that "effective mission-wide communication strategies can enable peacekeeping operations to build trust with local communities, manage expectations…and improve awareness of the work and contributions of UN personnel in complex and challenging environments" (UN 2016a, para. 133).

The Security Council has held several thematic debates on the contents and recommendations of the HIPPO report and the SG follow-on report, the most important of which took place on 20 November 2015 (UN 2015c). The ensuing Presidential Statement (UN 2015d), issued five days after intense negotiations among Council members, was rather bland and made no reference to people-centred approaches in peacekeeping. The Resolution (UN 2016b) the Council unanimously adopted on 27 April 2016 jointly with the GA on sustaining peace was, however, hailed a significant conceptual and policy shift on the part of the Council (Mahmoud 2016). It argues that sustaining peace be "broadly understood as a goal and a process to build a common vision of a society ensuring that the needs of all the segments of the population are taken into account." The joint resolution also emphasises that sustaining peace is "a shared task and responsibility that needs to be fulfilled by the government and all other national stakeholders." Throughout the resolution, civil society organisations, women's groups, youth organisations, and, where relevant, the private sectors were often mentioned as key strategic and operational partners in moving the sustaining peace agenda forward.

On 10–11 May 2016, the President of the General Assembly convened a High Level thematic debate on the synergies between the three peace and security global policy reviews mentioned in the first part of this paper and issued a Chair summary containing a series of conclusions and observations. In this summary, it is stated that "the two-day debate made it clear that civilians are the main stakeholders of peace operations with the most to gain from their successes and the most to lose from their failures. Communities should be front and centre in decision-making. Placing people at the centre means also that peace operations are accountable to the people they are meant to serve" (UN 2016c).

Notwithstanding the above conceptual convergence and policy consensus on the importance for people-centred approaches to peace and security and on its constituent elements such as inclusive ownership, the Council in its legislative work continues to shy away from using the exact "people-oriented" phrase, preferring instead to the generic terms "civil society, including women and youth." Where it appears under various guises, it tends to be confined to the preamble part of resolutions rather than in the operational one which has more binding power, with the exception of gender as a cross-cutting theme. A happy exception is the Security Council Resolution 2301 of 26 July 2016 renewing the peacekeeping operation in the Central African Republic (UN 2016d) in which local people's participation and consultations were welcomed. On the contrary, in the one extending the mandate of the peace mission in Mali (MINUSMA) (UN 2016e), people-centred approaches or variations of the phrase are nowhere to be found.

What Would a People-Centred Approach Look like on the Ground?

The purpose of the following paragraphs is to articulate, in light of what was outlined above, how best HIPPO recommendations and the emerging policy consensus on people-centred approaches can be best implemented on the ground. In doing so, the author draws on personal field experience, including a recent visit to the UN mission in Mali (MINUSMA), on current best practices by seasoned practitioners, guidance notes for community engagement and insights garnered from scholarly research conducted by de Coning et al. (2015) and Karlsrud (2015) among others. Outlined below are some strategic and programmatic considerations, as well leadership skills and attitudinal shifts which, if heeded, may help achieve this objective, bearing in mind they may need adaptation depending on a mission's political and operational environment.

A starting point for creating a propitious environment for people-centred approaches in peace operations is to secure the explicit acceptance and adherence of national authorities to the strategic importance of the policy of inclusive ownership that creates space for all national stakeholders to contribute to self-sustainable peace. This adherence could be a part of the development of a shared understanding of the specific mandate authorised by the Security Council for UN engagement in a particular country, both at the incipient and renewal stages. Where feasible, such a broad understanding of the principles of inclusivity and some of its practical modalities should be part of any agreement that may be drawn between the UN peace mission or the Security Council and the government regarding the practical modalities of implementing the mission's mandate. This contract would provide a measure of transparency in the mission's activities and avoid any misunderstanding with respect to the government's sense of ownership and legitimacy, however tenuous the latter may be. More importantly, it will foster trust and strengthen the initial consent given by host country for the deployment of the mission.

Secondly, and as the High-Level Panel recommended, one should develop a strategy for community engagement at various stages of the mission cycle, that is not only guided by the overall strategic objective of sustaining peace and the principle of doing no harm but also contains elements that address and mitigate some of the dilemmas, challenges, and risks outlined above. To be viable, such a strategy should contain the following:

1. A participatory context analysis that takes peace, and not conflict, as a principal referent that seeks to identify not only the factors that drive and sustain communal violence and the related dynamics, but also the resilience capacities touched upon earlier that communities resort to in times of stress, including local dispute management and reconciliation mechanisms and processes. The analysis, if properly

designed and conducted, could serve as a barometer for assessing the quality of state-society relations in a particular region or community and thus help guide the implementation of the state-centric provisions of the mission mandate in a context-sensitive manner. In addition, the analysis should include an assessment of risks that community engagement may unwittingly engender. Programmatic interventions, however well designed and intentioned, can be captured by governing elites, create new structures, challenge existing power relations and vested interest, and may even reinforce exclusionary practices. Such an assessment should also evaluate, as the Panel recommended, the impact on the mission mandate and staff security, particularly when local outreach involves engaging with communities targeted by aggressors or judged to be sympathisers of groups that are deemed spoilers or extremists. In other words, inclusivity, noble as it may be, is neither necessarily politically neutral nor always peace-friendly and may therefore cause harm to the mission or the people it is meant to serve.

2. Programmatic interventions devised on the basis of this analysis, including economic recovery and quick impact projects, should build on what people know and where they are, and must contain a self-sustainability clause at the design stage, to enhance ownership and prevent a dependency syndrome. Integrating these interventions within the overall UN Country Team-led reconstruction and development priorities may help achieve this self-sustainability objective, particularly if it is coordinated with other development actors. In this connection, people-centric approaches should be a UN system-wide endeavour. They should also be compatible with and reinforce other mandated mission priorities, such as the restoration and extension of state authority and other state-centric activities. They should serve as a means for enhancing the outreach capacity and legitimacy of the government vis-a-vis its people, and ideally contribute to better state-society relations, particularly in marginalised communities (de Coning et al. 2015). The MINUSMA stabilisation and recovery program has integrated some of the above programmatic considerations and safeguards in its design and implementation modalities, despite the high-risk security environment in which the mission has been deployed.
3. A communication strategy both within and outside the mission is critical. The strategy should be informed by listening sessions and

regular perception surveys of people who are at the receiving end of mission activities, as recommended by HIPPO and the UN Secretary General.

4. Another critical component of the strategy is a benchmarking component for monitoring and evaluating the effectiveness of community engagement activities and their impact on mission effectiveness.
5. Peace and conflict are gendered, both at the national and the grass roots levels. It is therefore imperative that a gender lens be systematically applied in the design and implementation of the above steps.

Thirdly, to implement a people-centred approach, one should establish, at mission Headquarters and in regional field offices, standing civil society advisory groups. These would include religious, academic leaders, women, and youth representatives, judged to be credible voices for their respective communities. Such groups, as de Coning and colleagues proposed, can provide inputs and/or feedback on the peace and conflict analysis outlined above, "contribute to the mission's self-evaluation of its programmes and initiatives … [and] enable [it] to stop and re-direct those actions that have harmful effects…" (de Coning et al. 2015, p. 6). "Involving the community," de Coning, Karlsrud, and Troost (Ibid.) add, "not only ensures that the mission's work is relevant to the society it serves, but can also help the peace operation to become a learning organization…". The analysis, as outlined above, if conducted properly, should help overcome the inclusivity and representativeness challenges inherent in the selection of the members of these advisory groups.

The above three prescriptions are not novel and certainly not exhaustive. But if they have a fighting chance of succeeding, they require leadership and attitudinal shifts.

Leadership Shifts

With respect to leadership, senior mission leaders should invest time and energy early on in their tenure to encourage the government and other national stakeholders to develop a medium to long-term vision of what sustaining peace and development would look like for the country, including some indications on the part to be played by local communities in crafting and achieving that vision. It is not uncommon for post conflict countries to devise such a vision. Liberia's and East Timor's 2020 vision are but two examples. Mission leaders should also be seen as engaging meaningfully and on a regular basis with these people-oriented processes both at the strategic and programmatic levels. People-centred activities must be treated as a UN system-wide priority. These activities should not be seen as ancillary, or ad-hoc technical exercises best left to less senior staff, usually under pressure to spend post-haste the funds allocated to these activities. Senior leaders should hold program manager accountable for the sustainability of the peace dividends they are purported to yield, in addition to the immediate goodwill and well-being effects they may generate. Some senior mission leaders tend to treat Security Council mandates as a ceiling and are therefore not inclined to engage in initiatives that are not contained in that mandate even when realities on the ground dictate otherwise. It is hoped that the emerging international consensus around the concepts of sustaining peace, inclusive ownership, and the primacy of politics will encourage these leaders to do what is right for the people they are deployed to serve, without prejudice to the primary responsibilities of the host government, however weak it may be.

Attitudinal Shifts

With respect to the attitudinal changes that need to take place, I will mention just two. First, there is a pressing need to forego the illusion that the UN builds national ownership by simply consulting people on the ground. The reality is that such consultations tend to be perfunctory, largely dictated by the pressing need to validate situational analyses and assessment that have been made in a hurry or seek the acquiescence for pre-conceived solutions. Not unlike genuine communication, consultation is a two-way street. And in order for that to happen, UN staff need to suspend the certainty that comes from thematic knowledge and expertise and let go of the comfort that past remedies provide. What the UN should do is to start investing in the business of listening—listening with the intent to understand, and not with the intent to solve, advise, or justify. Listening with intent might even help us understand what the UN is not good at and come to the inescapable realisation that building peace is what the local people do, not what outsiders do. A cursory look at any contemporary Security Council resolution should dispel the notion that the burden of building peace rests on outsiders' shoulders. Almost every single operative paragraph of these resolutions starts with the key word "support." This is plainly the case of the most recent resolution extending the UN peacekeeping mission in Mali (MINUSMA) (UNSC 2018). The critical message is that the primary responsibility for building peace rests with national actors.

Second, there is an equally urgent need to forego the prescriptive biases of liberal peace (Richmond and Mac Ginty 2014), including the notion that the solution to state imperfections or failures is state building and institutional building. The common assumption informing the state building enterprise where the focus is on technical expertise, and where the emphasis is on juridical legitimacy through elections rather than on performance legitimacy earned through the equitable provision of basic services to "we the peoples," without exclusion. Extending state authority without some degree of performance legitimacy is hardly the best recipe for sustaining peace which is a relational goal, and an integral part of rebuilding the social contract. It looks at the quality of the relationship between the state and the citizen. Context and gender sensitive as well as people-centred approaches to peace and development can help promote a different understanding of legitimacy and ownership and thus may prove more effective for achieving some measure of sustainable peace. In other words, we need to strike a balance between top-down, externally prescribed peace and popular, locally prescribed peace (Roberts 2010).

Conclusion and Recommendation to the Security Council

The world we live in is clearly no longer ordered by states alone, and the monopoly of violence is escaping the grasp of states. As mentioned above, many of the new and emerging threats to international peace and security such as terrorism, organised crime, and violent extremism tend to be driven from below by non-state actors, some with state aspirations. These threats, in addition to their tragic humanitarian consequences, are perceived to constitute a clear and present danger to states and to the state-based multilateral governance system. This partly explains why the UN Security Council tends to resort to state-centric approaches, often militarised, as default responses to counter these threats. These responses, invariably prescribed under Chapter 7, tend to populate the mandates of contemporary peacekeeping operations. Many of these mandates are guided by the illusory proposition that the best way to repair failing states is to build strong state institutions and extend their remit at all cost, without credible checks and balance mechanisms and a reform agenda to address the governance and leadership deficits at the origin of their failures. I am not suggesting that people-oriented peace approaches within a peacekeeping context constitute magic silver bullets. What I am advocating is that these approaches, if properly designed and carried out, can facilitate the capacity of fragile societies to self-organise (de Coning et al. 2015), help repair frayed social contracts and thus make fragile peace less reversible, while the country embarks on the long-term process of building capable, inclusive, and accountable state institutions.

For reasons outlined in this paper and given the resurgence of unhealthy geopolitics within the Council as well as the visceral mistrust of the Council by a majority of the rest of UN members, I do not expect the Council to have a change of heart and fully embrace a people-centred approach to peace operations. What I am encouraging the Council to do is to muster the residual political will and request, as a standard practice, under Chapter 6, nations that are hosts to a peace operation to develop with the support of the UN system on the ground and the Peacebuilding Commission, a *compact for sustaining peace* that would articulate the primary responsibilities of the host government, the contributions of civil society, and the supportive role to be played by international partners on the ground. All of which will be assorted with an exit strategy undergirded by performance benchmarks and timelines to ensure accountability and facilitate reporting to the Council upon mandate renewal. This will be a strategic framework, not unlike compacts facilitated by the Peacebuilding Commission for certain situations, and not unlike the type of compact proposed by the Panel (UN 2015a, pp. 38–39). It is through this contract, I hasten to add that all the three foundational pillars of UN engagement will flow in an integrated manner, as advocated by Security Council Resolution 2282 (UN 2016c) on sustaining peace, and that people-centred approaches will find a natural and uncontested home.

In the absence of such a framework for mutual accountability, peace operations, particularly in environments of asymmetric threats, will find themselves pressured to make up for the deficits of imperfect states, captured by the political elites, however well-elected they may be, and be far more concerned with power and the next elections than governance. Some of these governing elites might even use the pretext of fighting terrorism and organised violence to escape scrutiny and resist the implementation of the requisite reforms for effective governance and sustainable peace. And as a result, and as several ongoing situations attest, the Council will find itself caught between the hammer and the anvil, damned if it withdraws prematurely and doubly damned if it has no other choice but to extend the peace operation ad-infinitum, and observing rising costs and mounting risks to "We the peoples."

References

Autesserre, Séverine. 2015. Trouble in Peaceland. Argument, in *Foreign Policy*, October 6.

Call, Charles T. 2012. Building States to Build Peace? A Critical Analysis. *Journal of Peacebuilding & Development* 4 (2): 60–74.

Center for Strategic and International Studies. 2015. Smart Women, Smart Power: Integrating a "People-Centered" Approach in Foreign Policy. Video, 1:25:24, March 11. https://www.youtube.com/watch?v=myk7FDScMD0. Accessed 9 Nov 2017.

de Coning, Cedric, John Karlsrud, and Paul Troost. 2015. Towards More People-Centric Peace Operations: From 'Extension of State Authority' to 'Strengthening Inclusive State-Society Relations'. *Stability: International Journal of Security and Development* 4 (1): 1–13.

G7plus. 2017. New Deal Implementation. G7plus.org. http://www.g7plus.org/en/our-work/new-deal-implementation. Accessed 30 Nov 2017.

Husain, Zahra. 2015. Norman Rockwell's United Nations. UN Foundation Blog, June 30. http://unfoundationblog.org/norman-rockwells-united-nations/. Accessed 9 Nov 2017.

Interpeace. 2016. Strengthening Peace Through 'Resilience' in the 2030 Agenda For Sustainable Development. Policy Brief: Resilience and the SDGs. http://www.interpeace.org/wp-content/uploads/2016/06/2016-FAR-Brief-2-Resilience-and-the-SDGs.pdf. Accessed 9 Nov 2017.

Karlsrud, John. 2015. How Can the UN Move Towards More People-Centered Peace Operations? *Global Peace Operations Review*, September 23. http://peaceoperationsreview.org/thematic-essays/people-centered-reform-at-the-un/. Accessed 30 Nov 2017.

Leiva-Roesch, Jimena, Youssef Mahmoud, and Steve Nation. 2014. Building a Sustainable Future Requires Leadership from State and Citizen. International Peace Institute: Global Observatory. https://theglobalobservatory.org/2014/09/sustainable-future-leadership-state-citizen/. Accessed 9 Nov 2017.

Mahmoud, Youssef. 2016. *With New Resolutions, Sustaining Peace Sits at Heart of UN Architecture*. New York: International Peace Institute, Global Observatory.

Norman Rockwell Museum. 2014. Rockwell's 'Golden Rule'. Norman Rockwell Museum, Blog Post, February 5. http://www.nrm.org/2014/02/golden_rule/. Accessed 9 Nov 2011.

Reimers, Fernando. 2015. We the Peoples… and the United Nations 70th General Assembly. *The Huffington Post*, September 15.

Richmond, P. Oliver, and Roger Mac Ginty. 2014. Where Now for the Critique of the Liberal Peace? *Cooperation and Conflict* 50 (2): 171–189.

Roberts, David. 2010. From Liberal to Popular Peace? *openDemocracy*, October 29. https://www.opendemocracy.net/david-roberts/from-liberal-to-popular-peace. Accessed 9 Nov 2017.

Schlesinger, Stephen C. 2004. *Act of Creation: The Founding of the United Nations*. New York: Basic Books.

United Nations Development Programme. 1990. Human Development Report 1990. http://hdr.undp.org/en/reports/global/hdr1990. Accessed 9 Nov 2017.

United Nations Development Programme. 2017. About Human Development. New York: United Nations Development Programme. http://hdr.undp.org/en/humandev. Accessed 14 Nov 2017.

United Nations. 2004. *Report by Panel of Eminent Persons on United Nations-Civil Society Relations*. New York: United Nations.

United Nations. 2014. *Secretary-General Appoints High-Level Independent Panel on Peace Operations*. New York: United Nations.

United Nations. 2015a. *Report of the High-Level Independent Panel on Peace Operations on Uniting Our Strengths for Peace: Politics, Partnership and People*. New York: United Nations.

United Nations. 2015b. *The Future of UN Peace Operations: Implementation of the Recommendations of the High-Level Independent Panel on Peace Operations*. New York: United Nations.

United Nations. 2015c. 7564th Security Council Meeting. November 20. http://www.securitycouncilreport.org/atf/cf/%7B65BFCF9B-6D27-4E9C-8CD3-CF6E4FF96FF9%7D/s_pv_7564.pdf. Accessed 9 Nov 2017.

United Nations. 2015d. Statement by the President of the Security Council. November 25. http://www.un.org/en/ga/search/view_doc.asp?symbol=S/PRST/2015/22. Accessed 9 Nov 2017.

United Nations. 2016a. *Report of the Special Committee on Peacekeeping Operations*. March 15. New York: United Nations General Assembly.

United Nations. 2016b. Conclusions and Observations by the President of the Seventieth Session of the UN General Assembly. May 19. http://www.un.org/pga/70/wp-content/uploads/sites/10/2015/08/Thematic-Debate-on-UN-Peace-and-Security-Conclusions-Observations-20-May-2016-1.compressed.pdf. Accessed 9 Nov 2017.

United Nations. 2016c. *United Nations Security Council Resolution 2282*. New York: United Nations.

United Nations. 2016d. *United Nations Security Council Resolution 2301*. New York: United Nations.

United Nations. 2016e. *United Nations Security Council Resolution 2295*. New York: United Nations.

United Nations. 2018. *United Nations Security Council Resolution 2423*. New York: United Nations.

van Tongeren, Paul. 2005. People Building Peace: Key Messages and Essential Findings. In *People Building Peace II: Successful Stories of Civil Society (Project of the European Centre for Conflict Prevention)*, ed. Paul van Tongeren, Malin Brenk, Marte Hellema, and Juliette Verhoeven. Boulder: Lynne Rienner.

Open Access This chapter is licensed under the terms of the Creative Commons Attribution 4.0 International License (http://creativecommons.org/licenses/by/4.0/), which permits use, sharing, adaptation, distribution and reproduction in any medium or format, as long as you give appropriate credit to the original author(s) and the source, provide a link to the Creative Commons license and indicate if changes were made.

The images or other third party material in this chapter are included in the chapter's Creative Commons license, unless indicated otherwise in a credit line to the material. If material is not included in the chapter's Creative Commons license and your intended use is not permitted by statutory regulation or exceeds the permitted use, you will need to obtain permission directly from the copyright holder.

PART II

Mandates and Strategy

Check for updates

CHAPTER 6

What Are the Limits to the Use of Force in UN Peacekeeping?

Mats Berdal

Introduction

The use and utility of military force have been central, if sometimes underlying and unarticulated, themes in discussions about the purposes, practices, and, indeed, the very identity of United Nations peacekeeping since its inception. The precise historical and normative context within which those discussions have taken place has necessarily evolved over time. And yet, as the 2015 report of the High-Level Independent Panel on Peace Operations (HIPPO) makes clear, many of the key questions raised by the use of force in peacekeeping—be they of a practical or conceptual kind—are not fundamentally new (UN 2015). Chief among these is an overarching question that also frames and animates the present chapter, to wit, what are the limits to the use of force in UN peacekeeping? In approaching this question, the chapter and the arguments it advances have been divided into three closely connected parts.[1]

[1]Some of these arguments, especially in part three, draw upon and are more fully developed in Mats Berdal (2016).

M. Berdal (✉)
Department of War Studies, King's College London, London, UK

© The Author(s) 2019

C. de Coning and M. Peter (eds.), *United Nations Peace Operations in a Changing Global Order*,
https://doi.org/10.1007/978-3-319-99106-1_6

The first of these seeks to locate current preoccupations regarding the use of force within a wider historical context. To this end, it briefly traces both the thinking and practice around the use of force by UN blue helmets from the conceptual foundations laid in the era of "classical peacekeeping" to the focus on the protection of civilians (POC) and "robust peacekeeping" that have come to define the period since the Brahimi Panel Report of 2000 (UN 2000). It highlights how changes in geopolitical context and normative expectations have shaped and broadened the scope and aims of UN peacekeeping in important ways, with direct implications for the use of force. It also notes, however, that third-party involvement in civil war-like situations—as in South Sudan, the Central African Republic (CAR), Mali, Darfur, and the Democratic Republic of the Congo (DRC), where more than 80,000 peacekeepers are currently deployed—have brought to the fore cross-cutting challenges and policy dilemmas of a more fundamental kind when it comes to the application of military force by UN peacekeepers.

Developing the argument further, part two dwells on two sets of limitations to the effective use of force in UN operations. The first of these may be viewed as *structural barriers* to military effectiveness in UN operations, that is, limitations built in, as it were, to the very machinery and system for mounting, conducting, and sustaining UN peacekeeping operations. While some of the constraints thus imposed can be mitigated through reform of practices and procedures, to the extent that they are rooted in the intergovernmental and political character of the UN as an institution, they can never be fully overcome. This is an oft-neglected reality that will continue to place significant constraints on the effective use of force by blue helmets in the future. Indeed, as will be argued more fully, with UN missions now routinely deployed in conditions of actual or latent civil war, entrusted with POC responsibilities and given mandates that allow for the robust use of force, the debilitating impact of inbuilt capability constraints on force cohesion and military effectiveness has become ever more acute.

Added to these structural, seemingly quasi-organic impediments to effectiveness in UN peacekeeping is a second set of limitations. These are the political and practical challenges that inevitably present themselves to a peacekeeping force deployed as an impartial third party in conditions of on-going or unfinished civil war, that is, in conditions of persistent insecurity and violence fuelled by power struggles among political elites for control of territory, populations, and governmental authority.

Over time, and indeed wherever the UN has deployed, such conditions have also given rise to distinctive, complex, and frequently mutating political economies of conflict, the dynamics of which the UN, with its limited analytical capacities both at its headquarters in New York and in the field, has struggled to grasp, let alone factor into policy. Any assessment of the prospects for the effective use of force by UN peacekeepers, nearly all of which are now deployed in situations of internal conflict, must take these realities into account.

The third and final section of the chapter looks in greater detail at the record of "robust peacekeeping" and the kind of lessons that can reasonably be drawn from operations since the late 1990s. In brief, it argues that the use of force in Sierra Leone (2000), Haiti (2006–2007) and the DRC (2003) all suggest that, at the *tactical level*, a properly equipped and properly commanded force can be used with decisive, albeit short-term, effect in response to immediate crises or emergencies. The larger *strategic* lesson from the history of robust peacekeeping since 1999, however, is, fundamentally, a far more cautionary one; one that highlights the need for the activities of peacekeepers to be much more closely aligned than they have become over the past decade and half to the search for durable and inclusive political settlements to disputes. As such, it is a conclusion that echoes one of the central messages of the HIPPO, and which has also emerged as an early theme of Antonio Guterres' tenure as the ninth Secretary-General of UN.

From the Sinai to the Kivus

In a concise and intellectually compelling effort to distil from the UN's early forays into peacekeeping "certain basic principles and rules" that might "provide an adaptable framework for later operations," the then Secretary-General, Dag Hammarskjold, identified the "prohibition against any *initiative* in the use of force" as one of UN peacekeeping's defining characteristics (Hammarskjold 1958). Alongside the principles of consent and impartiality, this commitment to minimum use of force except in self-defence came to constitute one of the core principles of so-called classical peacekeeping, defining its character as a distinctive form of third-party intervention involving the deployment of lightly equipped troops drawn from different member states and placed under UN command. Although the UN's peacekeeping experience during the Cold War was richer and more varied than is often assumed, that experience did not lead to a fundamental questioning or re-examination of those principles. Indeed, even some of the most "painful peacekeeping" of the Cold War era—in the Congo in the early 1960s and South Lebanon between 1978 and 1982—were seen, in the final analysis, as a vindication of their importance (James 1983).

It was only with the changes in political climate spawned by the end of the Cold War that more radical ideas began to be floated about the future directions of UN operations and the sanctity of the principles on which these had traditionally been based. Between 1987 and 1992, the liberating impact of improvements in the international political landscape was demonstrated in a series of successful UN field operations from the Middle East and Asia to Central America and sub-Saharan Africa.[2] Although these operations were all, with one exception, comparatively modest in aim and small-scale in scope, they nonetheless contributed to a growing, if inchoate, sense that the long-established practices and functions of UN peacekeeping might now be developed in new and far more ambitious directions.[3] Thus, in *An Agenda for Peace*, released in June 1992 when the hopes and normative aspirations of international society were still closely aligned with the optimism of the early post-Cold War period, the newly appointed Secretary-General Boutros Boutros Ghali urged the Security Council to "consider the utilization of peace-enforcement units in clearly defined circumstances" (UN 1992b). More suggestive still, he defined peacekeeping as involving the deployment of a UN presence "*hitherto* with the consent of all the parties concerned," (ibid., para. 20, my emphasis) thus hinting that the self-denying ordinance governing the use of force was ripe for re-examination.

Such optimism as could be gleaned from *An Agenda for Peace* proved, however, to be short-lived. Between 1992 and 1995, the horrors of Angola, Somalia, Rwanda, and former Yugoslavia—all places where UN peacekeepers had been deployed yet conspicuously failed to halt mass

[2] These included the UN Iran-Iraq Military Observer Group (UNIIMOG), active from 1988 to 1991; the UN Good Offices Mission in Afghanistan and Pakistan (UNGOMAP) between 1988 and 1990; the UN Angola Verification Mission (UNAVEM I) from 1988 to 1991; the United Nations Observer Group (ONUCA) established in 1989 and successfully terminated in 1992; as well as the larger, more complex and, ultimately, successful, UN Transition Assistance Group in Namibia (UNTAG) between 1989 and March 1990.

[3] For a revealing sense of the climate of optimism at the time, see the various presentations made by member states at the Security Council summit, the first of its kind, held in late January 1992 (UN 1992a).

atrocities—ushered in a profound crisis of UN peacekeeping. Taking stock in early 1995, Boutros Ghali issued a *Supplement to An Agenda for Peace*; a document markedly different in tone from the optimism of three years earlier and, more significantly, gloomy in its conclusions regarding the prospects for the use of force in peacekeeping operations. In essence, Boutros-Ghali called for a return to "basic principles," arguing that "peacekeeping and the use of force (other than in self-defence) had to be seen as alternative techniques and not as adjacent points on a continuum, permitting easy transition from one to the other" (UN 1995, para. 36). Both more rigorous and cogent in its analysis of the real-world challenges of post-Cold War peacekeeping than its precursor document, the *Supplement* rightly emphasised the limits of UN-led operations in civil war-like situations, especially so when member states were only prepared, as they had repeatedly demonstrated over the previous three years, to will the ends and not the means. Even so, the Secretary-General's intervention in early 1995 did not settle the discussion about the use of force by UN peacekeepers. The nature and the scale of UN's peacekeeping failures between 1992 and 1995 meant that, at one level, there simply could be no "return to basics." This would become even clearer some six months after the release of the *Supplement*, when the UN "safe area" of Srebrenica in Eastern Bosnia was overrun by Bosnian Serb forces. The bloody and horrific aftermath of Srebrenica's capture, just one year on from the genocide in Rwanda, inevitably and quite understandably influenced the subsequent evolution of UN peacekeeping and the discussion about its purposes.[4] As the spate of new operations since 1999 has shown, the apparent determination to ensure that the horrors of Rwanda and former Yugoslavia would never again be repeated on the UN's watch has emphatically *not* resolved the deeper tension between ends and means highlighted by the *Supplement*, tensions which, if anything, have become more acute. What it plainly has done, however, is to influence the mandate and change the operational focus of UN peacekeepers, with important implications for the question of the use of force.

The single most important manifestation of this change is the growing centrality of the "Protection of Civilians" (POC) as a task formally

[4]Contributing powerfully to this, were two detailed and damning inquires into UN's role in Rwanda and Srebrenica, both of them published in 1999. See "The Fall of Srebrenica" (UN 1999a) and "Report of the Independent Inquiry in UN actions During the Rwanda Genocide" (UN 1999b).

entrusted to UN peacekeepers. The Security Council first expressed "its willingness to consider how peacekeeping mandates might better address the negative impact of armed conflict on civilians" in September 1999 (UN 1999c, para. 11). Since then, POC has become the subject of regular debates by the Council and, more significantly, beginning with the establishment of the UN operation in Sierra Leone in October 1999, missions have routinely and expressly been mandated under Chapter VII of the Charter "to afford protection to civilians under imminent threat of physical violence" (UN 1999d, para. 14). The growing focus on civilian protection is also a key factor behind the calls for more muscular, or robust, peacekeeping that have become such a notable feature of contemporary UN peacekeeping practice and discourse (UN 2009). Since 1999 the Council has given peacekeepers authority under Chapter VII of the Charter to "use all necessary means," or "take the necessary action," to accomplish their mission. In a number of individual operations, notably in Sierra Leone, Haiti, and the Congo, that authority has in turn provided the basis for taking the *initiative* in the use of force. The trend culminated in March 2013 when the Council decided that the UN's troubled Congo mission should be strengthened with the creation of a Force Intervention Brigade (FIB)—a "milestone" in the evolution of UN peacekeeping, according to the Secretary General at the time (UN 2014)—whose mandate would be "to carry out targeted offensive operations … in a robust, highly mobile and versatile manner" (UN 2013, para. 12b).

When the Secretary-General authorised his review of peace operations in 2014, five of the UN's largest missions—in Darfur, the DRC, the CAR, Mali, and South Sudan—were all operating under Chapter VII, and all were centrally focused on the protection of civilians. The distinctly uneven record of civilian protection in these operations, along with the absence of political progress towards lasting stability in each case, provided the immediate backdrop to the HIPPO and to the continuing discussions about the precise role of force, its limitations, and possibilities in UN peacekeeping.

Limitations to the Use of Force by UN Peacekeepers

Structural Barriers to Military Effectiveness

In a written submission to the HIPPO in March 2015, some twenty former UN Force Commanders offered a series of detailed recommendations whose implementation would, in their view, help ensure "success in future peace operations." Penned by Robert Mood, a respected officer with extensive UN experience, the letter stressed the need for "strengthened command and control, improved preparedness and mission design, use of modern technology, enhanced capabilities, improved mission information, and strengthened logistics and support" (Mood 2015). Designed to address long-standing capacity gaps and impediments to operational effectiveness, the proposals ranged widely. Unsurprisingly, given the breath of experiences shared by the signatories to the letter, the recommendations also made good operational sense.

To any long-time observer of UN field operations, however, very few of the deficiencies that the letter sought to address were fundamentally new. The haphazard and unreliable provision of key capacities and force enablers, notably in logistics, intelligence, engineering, aviation support, and reserves; the persistence of complex and cumbersome regulations governing finance, procurement, and human resources; the challenges of force generation and speed of deployment; and the "dysfunctional" nature of relations between the UN in New York and field headquarters, have all long plagued UN peacekeeping.[5] They have also proved remarkably resistant, if not entirely impervious, to substantive reform. The UN's system of human resources management—a distinctly unglamorous but nonetheless critically important area if one is genuinely concerned about improving the effectiveness of UN field operations—illustrates the nature of the problem.

The system was originally set up to cater for a largely static and headquarters-oriented organisation, employing career civil servants primarily engaged in providing administrative support for conferences and meetings among member states. In short, it was emphatically not designed for an organisation where, at present, more than 50 percent of secretariat staff is deployed on operations, many of which require a diverse and complex mix of technical expertise. And yet, the original model and the rules and regulations that go with it, have "never been fundamentally overhauled" (Chandran and von Einsiedel 2016, p. 3). In the words of Chandran and von Einsiedel, seasoned observers of the UN

[5]With regard to challenge of rapid deployment the HIPPO notes in passing that "since a UN standing capacity was first proposed, by the Secretary-General in 1948, no significant progress has been made" (UN 2015, para. 188). For an instructive illustration of the persistence of similar kinds of weaknesses and challenges in UN operations, see Goulding (1997).

scene, "it has proven impossible, again and again, to design a recruitment system that can both satisfy the process requirements for UN headquarters recruitment, while also supporting large, fast-moving field operations."[6] The failure to address these challenges, then, is not new, nor is there a shortage of ideas about how best to tackle them. The problem lies elsewhere: the bureaucratic and, above all, political obstacles to meaningful reform have simply proved too powerful. Indeed, according to the HIPPO, "in operating environments that demand more tailored and flexible UN peace operations it appears that human resources policies may be moving in the opposite direction" (UN 2015, para. 296).

None of this is to suggest that practical efforts to improve the machinery and the effective functioning of UN peacekeeping should be abandoned, nor is it to suggest that previous reform initiatives have all come to naught. Following the recommendations of the Brahimi Panel in 2000, for example, the Secretariat was given greater authority to spend money early in the planning stages of a mission, and important steps were taken to pre-position strategic stocks to ensure more rapid deployment of peacekeepers to the field (Durch et al. 2003). Both were genuinely valuable steps aimed at improving the day-to-day running and conduct of operations. Even so, there remains a natural limit—insufficiently recognised in much of literature on UN reform, including that generated by the Secretariat itself[7]—to which the weaknesses and deficiencies that have historically characterised UN field operations can ever be more than partially mitigated, let alone overcome. The reason for this lies, as noted above, with the *intergovernmental* and intensely *political* nature of the organisation, which will always limit the degree to which a UN Force can work as a truly integrated, cohesive, and effective military force. The implications for the conduct of operations are best illustrated by the perennial challenge of command and control in UN operations.

In their submission to the HIPPO, the former Force Commanders stressed the importance of "One mandate – one mission – one concept,"

[6] Ibid.

[7] See, for example, "Evaluation of the implementation and results of protection of civilian mandates in United Nations peacekeeping operations," UN Office of Internal Oversight (UNOIO 2014). While this report usefully collates and catalogues poor and inconsistent implementation of mandates by various missions, it proposes solutions that underplay, if not entirely disregard, the political character of peacekeeping and political sources of TCCs behaviour.

noting that the key to mandate implementation lay in "unity of command under the authority of the SRSG/Head of Mission" (Mood 2015). This insistence on a single chain of command and on maintaining the international character of any UN Force, is not new; indeed, it has been presented as a *sine qua non* of effective UN peacekeeping since its beginning in the 1950s. And yet, it has always come up against the reality of conflicting national priorities, risk-aversion among troop-contributing countries (TCCs), and uncertain loyalty from contingents, factors that have translated into the adoption, spoken or unspoken, of national caveats and a penchant for interfering in the UN chain of command. This has been the case especially when the perceived risks to peacekeepers have been high, and when questions regarding the use of force have been involved. Even so, as long as the peacekeeping environment has proved generally benign, and support from a united Security Council has been in place, UN missions have historically been able to function (with greater of lesser degree of effectiveness) notwithstanding continuing capacity gaps and weaknesses in command and control. Managing such inherent tensions has been a major role of Force Commanders and heads of mission. Indeed, their ability—through improvisation, ingenuity, and flexibility in mandate interpretation—to surmount and work around challenges thrown up by limited resources and a less than optimal system of administrative, managerial, and political support, is among the most important (and under-appreciated) qualities of mission leadership in UN operations.[8]

Developments over the past decade and a half, however, have placed altogether new strains on UN peacekeeping, posing challenges not only for mission leadership but to the very viability of missions themselves. A cursory survey of the five largest UN missions underway in early 2017—accounting for more than 80,000 out of a total of some 115,000 peacekeepers deployed on 16 missions worldwide—shows that operating environments are now, as a general rule, anything but stable and benign.[9] Instead, they typically include a combination or all of the

[8]For an example of how mission leadership helped shepherd an operation through to success *in spite* of the UN machinery designed to assist the mission, see Berdal (2015, pp. 416–429).

[9]These are the missions to South Sudan (UNMISS), Darfur (UNAMID), Mali (MINUSMA), CAR (MINUSCA) and the DRC (MONUSCO), see United Nations (2017). "Peacekeeping operations fact sheet." Accessed 9 November 2017. https://peacekeeping.un.org/en/peacekeeping-fact-sheet-oct-2017.

following characteristics: the absence of clear front lines; vast geographical distances amidst war-ravaged, even non-existent, infrastructure; the presence of large numbers of internally displaced; numerous armed groups, often poorly controlled and prone to preying on civilians; and persistent insecurity and on-going violence fuelled by both predatory political economies and power struggles among political elites. Now, the deployment of peacekeepers with a mandate to protect civilians and the authority to engage in robust peacekeeping in these conditions, have had two, partly conflicting, consequences.

First, these conditions have plainly heightened the operational importance of ensuring that UN missions actually do function as cohesive and integrated formations, properly resourced and with the most critical weaknesses—in the areas of tactical mobility, logistics support, and intelligence capacity—addressed. Of these weaknesses, arguably the most urgent requirement, given the non-permissive and volatile nature of contemporary peacekeeping environments, has proved to be the need for more systematic intelligence collection, assessment, and conflict analysis capacities by UN missions, the lack of which in zones of conflict has critically undermined attempts to grapple with underlying political economies of conflict and the way in which these often drive violence and encourage predation against civilian populations.[10] As noted above, however, plugging such capacity gaps has proved difficult to achieve even in the best of circumstances. The result when it comes to POC, as the Brahimi Panel Report perceptively foresaw back in 2000, has been to create a very "large mismatch between desired objective and resources available to meet it," as well as to guarantee "continuing disappointment with United Nations follow through in this area [of civilian protection]" (UN 2000, para. 63).

Second, these very conditions have also heightened differences among TCCs about how mandates should be interpreted and, specifically, over attitudes to the use of force. This, again, has further undermined efforts to achieve Force cohesion and unity of purpose, in many cases pushing the mission beyond the "outer limits for UN peacekeeping [as] defined by their composition, character and inherent capability limitations" (UN 2015, p. x). Significantly, TCCs that now provide the bulk of

[10]For this, see Kristof Titeca and Daniel Fahey's (2016) study of MONUSCO's failure to comprehend the character and dynamics driving the actions of the rebel group known as the Allied Democratic Forces (ADF) in the DRC between 2014 and 2016. For the consequences of relying on flawed intelligence, see also Fahey (2016, pp. 91–100).

peacekeepers, India, Bangladesh, and Pakistan, as well as many contributors from Latin America, remain deeply sceptical of the trend in favour of more robust use of force by UN peacekeepers (Modi 2015).

Limitations to the Third-Party Use of Force in Conditions of Civil War and Internal Conflict

The second set of limitations to the use of force connects still more directly to the context of internal conflict. A UN peacekeeping force that is deployed within the jurisdiction of a sovereign state where the host government is faced with internal challenges to its authority will, over time, find it increasingly difficult to remain above the domestic political fray, however much it may formally aspire to do so. Alan James, writing about the UN's involvement in Congo in the early 1960s, pinpointed the elemental reason for this: "On an internal scene a government is but one of the actors; in one degree or another the political balance is likely to be in constant movement; and the way in which a UN force responds may well have some impact on the balance, or – which in effect comes to the same thing – be seen as shifting the balance" (James 1994, p. 46). For UN peacekeepers to take the initiative in the use of force—especially, but not merely, when force is used in support of the host government—cannot but have an impact on that political balance, and will also affect the military and political calculations of other conflict actors. As such, it runs the risk of undermining the UN's chief asset as an interlocutor in internal conflicts and the search for political solutions: its perceived impartiality in relation to major disputants. In the words of Jean Marie Guéhenno, reflecting on the UN's post-Cold War experience in Congo:

> …if the UN becomes the auxiliary of a government whose legitimacy and representativeness is still questioned, it may lose not only its military but its political legitimacy, putting at risk what is potentially it most valuable contribution: the capacity to foster compromise among various groups as the indispensable base of lasting peace. (Guéhenno 2015, p. 147)

The UN's Congo experience highlights another inescapable risk associated with the enforced and prolonged proximity of UN missions to host governments in situations of on-going internal conflict. In all such cases, even if consent for the UN's presence remains formally in place, relations between missions and host governments have tended to deteriorate as host governments—often weak and beset by internal challenges, suspicious of outside meddling and protective of their sovereign rights—become ever more resentful of obstacles to their unfettered control over internal affairs. When, as is now overwhelmingly the case, the mandates given to UN missions are themselves politically intrusive and include potentially conflicting objectives, tensions have only been further heightened, with the result that both the credibility and leverage of UN missions have dwindled over time. Perhaps nowhere has this dynamic been more evident than in the DRC and South Sudan where the UN has been charged with protecting civilians as well as with monitoring government observance with human rights obligations and supporting security sector reform, and yet where, in both cases, government security forces have proved to be major sources of violence against civilians. Indeed, according to the UN's own reporting "the Congolese state was responsible for roughly 65% of the human rights violations [in 2016], and in many parts of the country the army is seen by local communities as the most dangerous armed group" (Day 2017, p. 2). Reviewing the period before the eruption of full-scale civil war in South Sudan in December 2013, an assessment of the UN Mission in South Sudan (UNMISS) concluded that "intractable problems, near-impossible dilemmas and difficult trade-offs will be a constant, especially given its decision to take on multiple, at times, conflicting roles" (Hemmer 2013, p. 8; da Costa and de Coning 2015). It is a finding equally applicable to other operations where the UN is deployed in intrastate settings in the absence of a viable political process.

Lessons in Robustness: The Use of Force from Haiti to the DRC

Mindful of these structural and political limitations to the use force by UN peacekeepers, what lessons for future operations should one draw from the experience of robust peacekeeping over the past decade and a half? The answer to that question needs to start with the recognition, or reaffirmation, of the importance of upholding the basic, albeit broad, distinction between what is essentially a peacekeeping operation and one that is premised on the logic of war-fighting and enforcement. It is equally important, however, to be clear about what exactly this means in practise, and what implications flow from it. The meaning of "essentially" in this context has little to do with whether or not a mission has been formally authorised under Chapter VII of the UN Charter; by now, almost all are as a matter of routine. The key to the distinction lies in whether or not achieving mission objectives—including the larger and key strategic objective of reaching a political settlement to end violence—is fundamentally dependent, in the final analysis, on building consent and support for the activities of peacekeepers among the parties. The history of peacekeeping since 1999 shows just how fragmentary and incomplete such consent can be, nowhere more so than when peacekeepers operate in conditions of civil war. Combining activities that rely on consent, cooperation, and access with offensive military operations, all within the same mission, have historically proved highly destabilising, politically as well as in humanitarian terms. For all its finely balanced and properly justified criticism of UN actions in Bosnia, that conclusion was also at the heart of the Srebrenica Report issued in 1999: "peacekeeping and war fighting are distinct activities and should not be mixed" (UN 1999a, 107). An inescapable corollary of this is that there will also be circumstances when the instrument of peacekeeping is not appropriate. The history of UN operations over the past decade and a half does not fundamentally alter these lessons.

Now, while the qualitative distinction between peacekeeping and enforcement must be reaffirmed, it does not follow from the above that the UN can or should *only* operate in environments where distinctions are clear-cut and simple, or that the use of force cannot, at the margins and in the right circumstances, be used with, potentially, decisive effect. There are instances since 1999 when properly equipped and properly commanded forces have scored tactical victories in response to immediate crises and emergencies: preventing the collapse of the UN mission Sierra Leone in 2000; dismantling the gang-structures Haiti in 2006–2007; securing Bunia in eastern DRC in 2003 and in defeating Laurent Gbabgo's violent challenge to the outcome of elections in Cote d'Ivoire in 2011. In evaluating these tactical successes, however, it is vital not to lose sight of the wider, and more critical, lessons offered by each case.

For one, all of these involved well-equipped, competently led and highly capable forces (drawn from the UK in the case of Sierra Leone, Brazil in the case of Haiti and France in the case of Bunia and Cote d'Ivoire), precisely what UN missions have tended to lack. Moreover, the military challenge faced in each case, though real enough, was mounted by marginal and, ultimately, militarily unimpressive actors. Still more important than these qualifications, however, is the fact that the long-term strategic outcome of these and similar actions depends critically on whether or not the use of force has been properly calibrated to support an overall strategy aimed at reducing violence, mitigating conflict, and fostering a political solution to the conflict at hand. Whether the actions of UN peacekeepers, including the use of military force, serve to advance these kinds of strategic objectives is, ultimately, the true measure of their effectiveness. And yet, with the partial exception of Sierra Leone, the all-important link between military action and political purpose has been weak to non-existent in UN operations since 1999.

In Sierra Leone, the UK military intervention in 2000 was able to check, at a critical moment, advances by the RUF and other armed groups in the country. Crucially, however, this short, sharp, and limited action was followed by concerted diplomatic moves aimed at shoring up the post-war political dispensation in the country; moves that included a sustained effort to galvanise others to contribute to a beefed up and reconfigured UN mission, as well as a serious and long-term commitment to reforming and professionalising the country's armed forces (Riley 2006, 2). As one detailed study of the use of force by British forces in Sierra Leone makes clear, even though the "use of force was critical in creating an opportunity for political progress, it was not in itself decisive or even that strategically significant"—long-term success was contingent on political follow-up at the UN and regionally, underpinned by a plausibly effective programme of security sector reform (Ucko 2016).

In Haiti, by contrast, "tactical success through the use of force led to only limited strategic payoffs in the larger state consolidation mission, with MINUSTAH struggling to integrate the use of force into a larger project for Haitian political and economic transformation."[11] A similar picture emerges from the various applications of robust force in the DRC, including *Operation Artemis* in 2003 and the Ituri campaign of 2005.[12] The record of MONUSCO's Force Intervention Brigade since 2013—the most ambitious attempt to conduct offensive operations

[11] Cockayne (2014, p. 738). Echoing these conclusions, see also Guéhenno (2015, pp. 261–262).

[12] Discussed more fully in Berdal (2016, pp. 11–17).

within a peacekeeping setting—has proved even more troubling, with mounting evidence in 2016 that the force through its actions has, if anything, contributed to a worsening of the security situation in eastern DRC.[13] In the words of one Senior Political Advisor working for in MONUSCO throughout 2016: "Not only has it failed to degrade the militias it was tasked to fight, but the FIB has potentially increased risks to civilians and diverted resources away from activities that might well serve them better."[14]

Taken together, what all of these cases do is to underline a basic lesson from the UN's experience of "robust peacekeeping": UN peacekeeping missions are structurally ill-equipped and politically ill-suited to use force effectively in support of strategic objectives, and when they have attempted to do so in a political vacuum without proper resources, the medium to long-term consequence of their actions have been, more often than not, to destabilise the operating environment and complicate the search for political solutions.[15] Even so, it is worth stressing again that none of this is to rule out the use of force by peacekeepers in all circumstances. The operations discussed here have all shown that in fluid and complex internal settings with multiple conflict actors, it will sometimes be possible and, indeed, necessary to differentiate between *major* disputants, loosely defined as political and militarily significant actors, and more marginal spoilers, distinguished by their predatory agendas and, crucially, their lack of local legitimacy. Decisive military action against the latter may have a stabilising effect in the short term. Any lasting effect or achievement resulting from the use of force, however, will always, in the final analysis, depend on whether or not military action is "framed as an enabling component of a political strategy" (Doss 2014, p. 730).

[13]Congo Research Group (2017). Since late 2016, there have been frequent clashes between the Congolese Army and the M-23, the Rwanda-backed rebel group which the FIB was initially credited with having successfully having defeated back in 2013.

[14]Day (2017, p. 2). This article provides an excellent assessment of the FIB's failure in the DRC.

[15]Although beyond the scope of the present chapter, it is worth noting that the war-fighting role given to the FIB in the DRC has also raised legal issues relating to the use of force that ought properly to be considered in any wider discussion of challenges and limitations to the use of force in UN peacekeeping. For an excellent discussion see Sheeran and Case (2014).

Concluding Thoughts: Re-establishing the Link Between Military Force and Political Purpose

When Jean-Marie Guéhenno, then head of the UN Department of Peacekeeping Operations (DPKO), visited the DRC in March 2006 to take stock of the challenges facing MONUC on the eve of the first elections in the country for 41 years, he used the occasion also to assess the impact of "the robust and unprecedented manner" in which UN military forces, operating alongside and in support of the Congolese army (FARDC), had sought out and engaged armed groups over the previous year. The results, he found, were decidedly mixed, with the "negative consequences" of UN military operations—including reprisals against civilians by armed groups targeted by the UN, new "waves" of internally displaced and uncontrolled looting, pillaging and abuses committed by the elements of MONUC's ally, the Congolese army—all suggesting the need to shift away from aggressive pursuit and "to start taking a longer-view." As he perceptively reported back to New York, "the reality is that foreign armed groups will need to be dealt with in the longer-term, in tandem with an economic and political strategy, and in a way that does not threaten civilian populations" (UN 2006). More than a decade on from Guéhenno's visit, with the DRC still faced with political stasis, violence and humanitarian crisis, his recommendations remain, sadly, just as appropriate as they were back in 2006 (Gowan 2016). They also point to wider lessons for UN peacekeeping that transcend the particular circumstances of the DRC.

In the end, perhaps the single most important implication to flow from the analysis above is that UN peacekeeping in and of itself—and most certainly robust peacekeeping of the kind attempted over the past decade and a half—can only ever play a very limited part in helping to address the deeper sources of violent conflict in fragile and conflict-ridden states. UN peacekeepers can undertake a range of ancillary tasks aimed at strengthening and helping in the search for lasting political settlement to conflicts. That range is now longer and more complex than it was in the era of "classical" peacekeeping and includes security sector reform, support for humanitarian relief operations, complex monitoring, and confidence-building tasks. When conditions require and resources permit—as operations in Sierra Leone, Haiti and even at times the DRC have shown—UN forces may also be in a position to respond locally to obstructionist violence or immediate emergencies and defeat "marginal actors" (Guéhenno 2015, p. 262). These are all important tasks and the scope for improving the quality of delivery in each is certainly there, especially in the vital area of security sector reform, which, too often, has been under-funded, overly technocratic in approach and ignorant of the political economies of conflict on the ground. But they are *ancillary* tasks in the sense that their lasting contribution to addressing conflict depends not only on how effectively they are delivered in a technical sense but, crucially, on whether they are aligned to and help advance the overriding objective of arriving at political agreements to end violence. A key and concluding implication to flow from this is that UN mission leaderships in the field, aided by the secretariat and backed by the Security Council, must—through improved political engagement, effective use of good offices, and enhanced analytical capacities—prioritise the search for political avenues and opportunities that promise ways out of conflict and protracted violence.

References

Berdal, Mats. 2015. The UN Operation in Mozambique, 1992–1994. In *The Oxford Handbook of UN Peacekeeping Operations*, ed. Joachim Koops, Norrie Macqueen, Thierry Tardy, and Paul Williams. Oxford: Oxford University Press.

Berdal, Mats. 2016. The State of UN Peacekeeping—Lessons from Congo. *Journal of Strategic Studies* 39 (2016): 1–30.

Chandran, Rahul, and Sebastian von Einsiedel. 2016. New Ideas for a New Secretary-General: Fixing the UN's Human Resources System, November 2. Tokyo: United Nations University Centre for Policy Research.

Cockayne, James. 2014. The Futility of Force? Strategic Lessons from Dealing with Unconventional Armed Groups from the UN's War on Haiti's Gangs. *Journal of Strategic Studies* 37 (5): 736–769.

Congo Research Group. 2017. As Violence Escalates Across the Congo, Who Is to Blame? Congo Research Group, March 2. http://congoresearchgroup.org/6209/. Accessed 9 Nov 2017.

da Costa, Diana Felix, and Cedric de Coning. 2015. UNMISS. In *The Oxford Handbook on UN Peacekeeping Operations*, ed. Joachim A. Koops, Thierry Tardy, Norrie MacQueen, and Paul D. Williams. Oxford: Oxford University Press.

Day, Adam. 2017. The Best Defence is No Offense: Why Cuts to the UN Troops in Congo Could Be a Good Thing. *Small Wars Journal*, April 8. http://smallwarsjournal/rpint/66367. Accessed 9 Nov 2017.

Doss, Alan. 2014. In the Footsteps of Dr. Bunche: The Congo, UN Peacekeeping and the Use of Force. *Journal of Strategic Studies* 37 (5): 703–735.

Durch, William, Victoria K. Holt, Caroline R. Earle, and Moira K. Shanahan. 2003. *The Brahimi Report and the Future of UN Peace Operations.* Washington, DC: The Henry Stimson Center.

Fahey, Daniel. 2016. Congo's 'Mr.X': The Man Who Fooled the UN. *World Policy Journal* 23 (2): 91–100.

Goulding, Marrack. 1997. Practical Measures to Enhance the UN Effectiveness in the Field of Peace and Security: A report submitted to the Secretary-General of the United Nations, June 30.

Gowan, Richard. 2016. The UN Is Caught in a Trap as Kabila Angles for Third Term in DRC. *World Politics Review*, May 2. https://www.worldpoliticsreview.com/articles/18650/the-u-n-is-caught-in-a-trap-as-kabila-angles-for-third-term-in-drc. Accessed 4 Dec 2017.

Guéhenno, Jean-Marie. 2015. *The Fog of Peace—A Memoir of International Peacekeeping in the 21st Century.* Washington, DC: Brookings Institution Press.

Hammarskjold, Dag. 1958. *Report of the Secretary-General: Summary Study of the Experience Derived from the Establishment and Operation of the Force.* New York: United Nations.

Hemmer, Jort. 2013. The UN Mission in South Sudan and Its Civilian Protection Strategy: An Early Assessment. CRU Policy Brief, No. 25, January, Clingendael Institute, The Hague.

James, Alan. 1983. Painful Peacekeeping: The United Nations in Lebanon, 1978–1982. *International Journal* 38 (4): 613–634.

James, Alan. 1994. The Congo Controversies. *International Peacekeeping* 1 (1): 44–58.

Modi, Narendra. 2015. PM Narendra Modi's Statement at the UN Peacekeeping Summit, September 29. http://www.thehindu.com/news/resources/statement-by-prime-minister-narendra-modi-at-the-un-summit-on-peace-operations/article7699430.ece. Accessed 9 Nov 2017.

Mood, Robert. 2015. *Force Commanders' Advice to the High-Level Independent Panel on UN Peace Operations.* Washington, DC: United Nations.

Riley, Jonathon. 2006. The UK in Sierra Leone: A Post-conflict Operation Success? Heritage Foundation Lecture 958, June 15.

Sheeran, Scott, and Stephanie Case. 2014. *The Intervention Brigade: Legal Issues for the UN in the DRC.* New York: International Peace Institute.

Titeca, Kristof, and Daniel Fahey. 2016. The Many Faces of a Rebel Group: The Allied Democratic Forces in the DRC. *International Affairs* 92 (5): 1201–1205.

Ucko, David H. 2016. Can Limited Interventions Work? Lessons from the British Success-Story in Sierra Leone. *Journal of Strategic Studies* 39 (3): 26–61.

United Nations. 1992a. Provisional Verbatim Record, Security Council Summit, January 31. New York: United Nations Security Council.

United Nations. 1992b. *An Agenda for Peace, Preventive Diplomacy, Peacemaking and Peace-Keeping: Report of the Secretary-General Pursuant to the Statement Adopted by the Summit Meeting of the Security Council on 31 January*. New York: United Nations.

United Nations. 1995. *Supplement to An Agenda for Peace: Position paper of the Secretary-General on the Occasion of the Fiftieth Anniversary of the United Nations*. New York: United Nations.

United Nations. 1999a. *Report of the Secretary-General Pursuant to General Assembly Resolution 53/35: The Fall of Srebrenica*. New York: United Nations.

United Nations. 1999b. *Report of the Independent Inquiry in UN Actions During the Rwanda Genocide*, December 16. New York: United Nations Security Council.

United Nations. 1999c. *United Nations Security Council Resolution 1265*. New York: United Nations.

United Nations. 1999d. *United Nations Security Council Resolution 1270*. New York: United Nations.

United Nations. 2000. *Report of the Panel on United Nations Peace Operations*. New York: United Nations.

United Nations. 2006. DRC: Report on Visit 6–15 March 2006. New York. United Nations DPKO.

United Nations. 2009. *DPKO-DFS Concept Note on Robust Peacekeeping*. New York: UN DPKO.

United Nations. 2013. *United Nations Security Council Resolution 2098*. New York: United Nations.

United Nations. 2014. *Secretary-General's Remarks at Security Council Debate*, June 11. New York: United Nations Security Council

United Nations. 2015. *Report of the High-Level Independent Panel on Peace Operations on Uniting Our Strengths for Peace: Politics, Partnership and People*. New York: United Nations.

United Nations. 2017. Peacekeeping Fact Sheet. www.un.org/en/peacekeeping/resources/statistics/factsheet.shtml. Accessed 9 Nov 2017.

United Nations Office of Internal Oversight. 2014. Evaluation of the Implementation and Results of Protection of Civilian Mandates in United Nations Peacekeeping Operations, March 7. New York: UNOIO.

Open Access This chapter is licensed under the terms of the Creative Commons Attribution 4.0 International License (http://creativecommons.org/licenses/by/4.0/), which permits use, sharing, adaptation, distribution and reproduction in any medium or format, as long as you give appropriate credit to the original author(s) and the source, provide a link to the Creative Commons license and indicate if changes were made.

The images or other third party material in this chapter are included in the chapter's Creative Commons license, unless indicated otherwise in a credit line to the material. If material is not included in the chapter's Creative Commons license and your intended use is not permitted by statutory regulation or exceeds the permitted use, you will need to obtain permission directly from the copyright holder.

CHAPTER 7

Protection of Civilians in the United Nations: A Peacekeeping Illusion?

Hilde Frafjord Johnson

Introduction

After the experiences of Rwanda and Srebrenica in the 1990s, and the United Nations' (UN) failure to act, the protection of civilians (POC) has taken an increasingly prominent role in international peace operations. The first mission to be mandated with an explicit POC-mandate was the UN Mission in Sierra Leone (UNAMSIL) in 1999. While the emphasis on POC may initially have been met with reluctance, both from traditional troop and police contributing countries (T/PCCs) and from within the system, the concept has increasingly taken a central role in UN peace operations after the Brahimi Report (UN 2000). More than 98% of military and police personnel currently deployed in peace operations have a mandate to protect civilians, as part of integrated mission-wide efforts.

Although the Security Council (UNSC) has recognised the progressive consideration of POC in armed conflict as a thematic issue since 1999 (UN 1999), for a number of years there was limited guidance on

H. F. Johnson (✉)
Norwegian Institute of International Affairs (NUPI), Oslo, Norway

© The Author(s) 2019

C. de Coning and M. Peter (eds.), *United Nations Peace Operations in a Changing Global Order*,
https://doi.org/10.1007/978-3-319-99106-1_7

how such mandates should be implemented. In an independent report on the protection of civilians in UN peacekeeping operations, it was made clear that missions largely lacked a clear definition of POC, and suffered from poor planning and implementation of protection mandates (Holt and Taylor 2009). That same year, the Security Council adopted a resolution that requested all UN missions with protection mandates to incorporate comprehensive protection strategies into overall mission implementation and contingency plans (UN 2009). This, together with other developments, led to an increased focus on guidance to the field, trying to improve the understanding and application of POC mandates. In 2010, an operational concept on POC was published by the UN Department of Peacekeeping Operations/Department of Field Support (DPKO/DFS), and the following year a Framework for Drafting Comprehensive Protection of Civilians Strategies in UN Peacekeeping Operations (UN 2010, 2011).[1]

Following this guidance framework and additional focus on POC by the Security Council, a POC Policy has been developed by DPKO/DFS (UN 2015a). The intention was to strengthen POC implementation in the field, making sure that there will be a common standard across the system, and that the capacities both on the civilian and military side are fit for purpose. In all these guidelines and policy documents, as well as in most Security Council Resolutions mandating missions with POC mandates, it is emphasised that the primary responsibility for the protection of civilians rests with the respective governments. The presence of a UN mission or other protection actors does not diminish the obligation of host governments to make every effort to protect their own civilians. However, the responsibility of the host government does not dilute the obligation of UN missions to act within their capabilities when the host governments are not willing or able to protect its citizens. There are many situations when governments do not take on their POC responsibility or lacks the capacity to do so. This poses significant challenges to UN missions.

This chapter provides an overview of the implementation of POC mandates in UN peace operations, drawing on my experience from the UN Mission in South Sudan (UNMISS) between 2011 and 2014 as Special Representative and Head of Mission. UNMISS had a broad

[1] See UN (2010, 2011), which sets out the full range of activities that fall within this mandated task.

POC-mandate, covering both military, police and civilian components. I will start with a focus on the capacity to protect through non-military means, and then move on to the capacity to provide physical protection. Third, I will address the responsibility of the host government. To conclude, I will offer a few recommendations for strengthening the protection of civilians in UN peace operations.

Protection of Civilians: Policy and Practice

Protection of civilians has for many years primarily been understood in military terms, and the ultimate test confronting peace operations has been to which extent they were able to physically protect civilians under imminent threat. It is important, however, to emphasise that the UN framework provides guidance on several aspects of POC, and include prevention through political action, as well as other civilian protection measures. This is also linked to capacity- and institution-building and is included in the following three tiers:

- *Tier I: Protection through dialogue and engagement*: Activities include dialogue with a perpetrator or potential perpetrator,[2] conflict resolution, and mediation between parties to the conflict, persuading the government and other relevant actors to intervene to protect civilians.
- *Tier II: Provision of physical protection*: Activities by police and military components involving the show or use of force to prevent, deter, pre-empt, and respond to situations in which civilians are under threat of physical violence.
- *Tier III: Establishment of a protective environment*: Activities to help create a protective environment for civilians, for example through the rule of law, human rights, and protection cluster activities, as well as Security Sector Reform (SSR) and Disarmament, Demobilization, and Reintegration (DDR). Many of these activities are undertaken alongside or in coordination with programmes by the United Nations Country Team or Humanitarian Country Team (UN 2015a).

[2] This may be a state actor, non-state actor, groups of actors or individuals, or all of the above.

While UN policy and guidance frameworks on the protection of civilians have been strengthened, no specific policy has been developed for UN Police, which is quite surprising given the focus on POC in almost all peace operations. Nevertheless, as the UN High-Level Independent Panel (HIPPO) observes in its Report (UN 2015b), significant progress has been made in promoting norms and frameworks for the protection of civilians.

Furthermore, the new 2015 POC Policy represents a more comprehensive approach and advises POC operations to be implemented along four operational phases: (i) prevention, (ii) pre-emption, (iii) response, and (iv) consolidation (UN 2015a, p. 9). This should be reflected in a comprehensive POC Action Plan, including all relevant components of missions.

Despite conceptual progress, results on the ground are at best mixed. The gap between what is asked for and what peace operations can deliver has widened, especially in the more difficult environments (UN 2015b, p. ix). In the following, I will analyse some of the reasons.

Protection Through Non-military Means

In South Sudan, UNMISS developed a POC strategy with interventions along all three tiers outlined above in consultation with the UNHQ and the Humanitarian Country Team, and every state office was obliged to do the same. The POC strategies at the state level helped the mission have a more systematic approach to threat assessments and a more coherent approach to the extensive protection work the mission engaged in.[3]

UNMISS tried to reduce the threat to civilians by engaging actively on multiple fronts to prevent inter-communal conflict; it supported mediation to end such conflicts, and, to prevent the communities from relapsing into violent conflict, it supported peace consolidation efforts where agreements were reached. The mission supported several institutions relevant to the POC Policy's 1st Tier, such as the Peace Commission of South Sudan and the National Reconciliation Committee, as well as peace advisors at different administrative levels.

[3] UNMISS Protection of Civilian Strategy, final draft approved by SRSG, 4 June 2012, since then replaced by the UNMISS Protection of Civilians Strategy, approved by SRSG, 15 September 2014.

However, it proved difficult to build the capacity of the host nation institutions to take responsibility for Tier 1 protection tasks.

Although some progress was made, the best results were not achieved in the formal institutions of Juba, but locally. It was most rewarding to work with leaders at state and county level, community leaders and also with religious leaders where conflicts were brewing, emerging, and in some cases escalating. The UN's collective efforts in trying to prevent or resolve inter-communal conflict bore fruit in several instances, for example in the Equatorian States and the Tri-State Area between Unity, Warrap and Lakes States. In one instance in the latter area a large-scale attack of thousands of armed youth was prevented. In another, significant efforts were invested in the peace process in Jonglei on multiple fronts. But despite signed peace agreements, the cycle of violence proved intractable and extraordinarily challenging to resolve. This frustration resulted in heavy-handed disarmament campaigns and military operations by the Sudan People's Liberation Army (SPLA) (UN 2012a, b). They were not successful, and only led to more tensions, unrest and eventually, conflict, in particular in the Pibor area. Only when an UNMISS-supported Church-led peace process succeeded was it possible to achieve some stability.[4] Later, however, also this peace process imploded, impacted by the ongoing civil war.

Creating a protective environment, an objective in Tier 3 of the POC Policy, was another major challenge in a country awash with weapons, and with significant security challenges including inter-communal violence and ill-disciplined and at times violent and abusive security services. Some training in international humanitarian law and POC was provided to the SPLA and police, but the scale in terms of numbers receiving courses was too limited to have any real impact. Similarly, such courses are less effective when the illiteracy levels of the participants are very high (UN 2015c).

While UNMISS was from the outset mandated to support the police and rule of law institutions, strengthening them and their protection role was necessarily a long-term effort. The current timelines and methodologies of military and police personnel in peace operations are not conducive for such capacity-building processes. The rotation of personnel is but one of the impediments in this regard. The supply-driven blue-print

[4] See Jonathan Agensky's chapter in this volume.

approaches usually applied in UN peace operations seldom deliver good and sustainable results in reforming and building the capacity of national police. Only through fundamental reforms in the way the UN Police operates can better outcomes be achieved. These points are reflected in the HIPPO report recommendations (UN 2015b, pp. 41–43) and in the UN Police review from end-May 2016.[5]

Despite these challenges, the mission found new ways of using existing UN Police mechanisms to provide capacity-building in some areas. Through unique, pre-negotiated arrangements with Uganda and Rwanda, training teams were deployed as UN Police to the Police College in Juba, providing training modules in key policing areas. We also used specialized teams from Kenya to help develop livestock police.

Throughout its first years, UNMISS worked on multiple fronts to create a more protective environment for people, amongst others by working to increase respect for human rights, and through partnerships with, for example, the Protection Cluster that brought together the humanitarian agencies working on protection as well as some NGOs. However, UN capacity-building efforts of government institutions delivered limited results. The human rights and humanitarian institutions of the country faced great challenges in making a real impact, despite the best efforts of the entire UN family in building their capacity. It would primarily be through Security Sector Reform and a transformation of both the SPLA and the Police Service that one could hope to see an improvement.

Tier 1 steps range from the local to the national, from dealing with inter-communal conflicts to national-level tensions. For instance, in UNMISS, the mission leadership took Tier 1-type preventive steps concerning the SPLM-leadership, starting already 18 months before the political crisis escalated in the country. The Sudan People's Liberation Movement (SPLM)-leaders and regional leaders also tried to prevent such an escalation. However, none of these attempts succeeded, and the country exploded into violent conflict on 15 December 2013 (UN 2014a).

[5]An independent review team was appointed on 28 December 2015 to follow up on many of these HIPPO recommendations. The Independent Core Review Team was tasked with assessing the UN's Police Division and its operations and delivered its report *External Review of the Functions, Structure and Capacity of the UN Police Division* on 31 May 2016. The report confirmed these systemic deficiencies in how UN Police operates, hence recommending capacity building and police reform. Hilde F. Johnson and Abdallah Wafy were co-chairs of the UN Police review.

Although the UN Security Council, UNMISS, and the international partners must shoulder some responsibility for failing to prevent the outbreak of violence in South Sudan, in the final instance, the lapse into conflict and then civil war was primarily caused by the high-risk behaviour of the South Sudanese leaders on all sides, across the core of the SPLM-leadership. It was the decisions of the two leaders, President Salva Kiir and former Vice President Riek Machar and their supporters, however, that led to the loss of thousands of lives, to the rape and torture of thousands more, to the disruption of the livelihoods of thousands, and later millions of civilians, who had to flee their homes in search of safety in UN compounds, or flee South Sudan all together to towards Ethiopia, Uganda, or Sudan.

The government and the warring parties in South Sudan completely failed to protect non-combatants, as required under International Humanitarian Law, and instead engaged in systematic targeting of civilians, as also documented by the UN Panel of Experts on South Sudan in their Final Report (UN 2016). As we shall see, when the fighting started in 2013 in Juba, the physical protection challenges were far beyond the capacity of UNMISS.

Opening the Gates: A Last Resort

As the fighting within the security forces spread into neighbourhoods, civilians of Nuer origin were in danger. For UNMISS to have intervened in the conflict by using force in a situation of active combat between two belligerent forces, would have required a new mandate from the Security Council. Even if we did get such a mandate, our resources were too limited given the scale of violence raging in Juba, to intervene militarily.[6] Almost all our UN forces had been deployed elsewhere in the country, not least to Jonglei, where, until then, civilians had been under greatest threat. Although our planning exercises had included worst-case scenarios for Juba in the event of a crisis, our forces located there were few and lightly armed—they were mainly soldiers guarding UN assets and staff, as well as engineering, aviation, logistics, and transport units and had

[6] Redeployment from Jonglei, of for example one battalion of 850 troops, would take 7–9 days. Adrian Foster from New York Headquarters remained at the Mission and made three recommendations: (i) political engagement, (ii) documentation of human rights violations, and (iii) protection of people seeking refuge.

limited capacity and equipment. We had only about 120 infantry soldiers who could engage in military operations outside the two UNMISS bases in Juba.[7]

It was my firm decision that leaving civilians to their fate where they were likely to be killed, was out of the question. In the early morning hours, thousands had flocked to us at the UN House in Tonyping, an area in Juba and outside the other UN compound in the Jebel area. They were screened for weapons, and let in. During the morning of 16 December, approximately eight thousand sought refuge at Tonyping, and at UN House in Jebel five-to-six thousand poured in. During the afternoon, the total number approached 14,000, and increased the following day.[8] Two days later, we realized that people would not return home soon, and we established a unique partnership with the humanitarian actors. Soon, they administered the Protection of Civilian-sites within our bases, providing lifesaving humanitarian aid.

Within four to five months, 85,000 civilians had sought protection in eight UNMISS compounds around the country (UN 2014a). Internally Displaced People (IDP) seeking refuge in UNMISS POC sites during times of violent surged, and reached 100,000 before my departure from the Mission in July 2014 (UN 2015c; UNMISS 2015). At the end of 2015, the number had doubled.

Protection within UNMISS-bases were never meant to be a long-term solution. Despite the establishment of additional POC-sites within and adjacent to these bases, the camps were unbearably over-crowded. Conditions were very bad, in particular during the rainy season, and people were suffering. Given the fighting and insecurity, they were too afraid to leave the bases. This put the Mission in a very difficult situation.

It has become clear that the civilians will not leave the POC-cites in the UN-bases unless they have a sense of peace and protection outside the bases. Cessation of hostilities has been promised repeatedly. Yet, these have been empty promises, as was a peace agreement signed in 2015, which later collapsed. Indeed, peace still seems to be far away.

[7]Some 250 Rwandan soldiers protected UN Headquarters and the two large bases and another company (150 soldiers) had guard and commando-post functions, transport, logistics and administrative tasks.

[8]The neighbourhoods of New Site, Manga, Mangaten, Mia Saba and Eden were all attacked by government forces (UNMISS 2014; Human Rights Watch 2014).

People will not return home until there is a new and credible peace agreement which appears to last. Civilians need to feel reassured that a lapse into violent conflict is unlikely. They will also need to see a protective environment, to be able to trust the peace. This implies that building a new police service will be critical for people to be willing to return to their communities.

In summary, and to relate to civilian protection strategies, active engagement under Tier 1 and 3 is critical and usually more effective than other protection work. Yet, the traditional focus of peacekeeping operations has been to rely on the deployment of uniformed personnel, often with mixed results. As was pointed out in the HIPPO-report, there are serious deficiencies in the assessment, analysis, and planning of missions to enable political primacy and to make sure that the right resources are deployed at the right time. This has serious consequences for the capacity of mission leadership to engage in the protection of civilians under Tier 1 and Tier 3. This also negatively impacts the implementation of POC-strategies. As the local capacity to protect civilians is very low at all levels, a lot of responsibility rests with UN peace operations. It is even more important, therefore, that missions have the capacity to act along all three Tiers.

Before reverting to these issues, I will analyse the possibilities to provide physical protection of civilians under threat through the use of force.

Physical Protection: A Peacekeeping Illusion?

Both prior to the crisis and during the civil war, the mismatch between the UNMISS' mandate and its resources were glaring, making it close to impossible for the mission to deliver on its mandate to provide physical protection to civilians under threat. However, as the HIPPO points out (UN 2015b, para. 93–94), UNMISS is not the only peace operation to face this problem. It is, therefore, imperative to address these challenges.

While a blanket protection of civilians mandate in military terms is not possible for any UN-mission—resources will never be adequate—there is still a strong expectation that military contingents act robustly and pro-actively when civilians are under threat. An evaluation conducted by the UN Office of Internal Oversight Services (UN OIOS 2014) has shown that these expectations are often not met, and that far too many missions are viewed as not acting to protect civilians quickly and robustly enough. While I have some methodological concerns with the evaluation, its findings still warrant attention and discussion: many UN missions are perceived to fail in the implementation of their physical protection-mandates. Whether this is the reason for the revised definition of the protection of civilians mandate in the new POC policy, is not known. The definition now contains the additional "and including the use of deadly force" (UN 2015a, para. 12–13). It reads as follows:

> In light of the above, the protection of civilians mandate for civilian, military and police components in United Nations peacekeeping is defined as follows: all necessary means, up to and including the use of deadly force, aimed at preventing or responding to threats of physical violence against civilians, within capabilities and areas of operations, and without prejudice to the responsibility of the host government. (UN 2015a, para. 13) (underscored by author)

The impact that this revised definition will have on the performance of the contingents, will largely depend on capabilities and the contingents' own willingness to take risk.

Physical protection is about resources, including the numbers of troops compared to the challenge and the military capabilities available, as well as ensuring that these are fit for purpose and with adequate mobility in difficult terrain. In classic military thinking, one would need two to three times the number of forces as the enemy to successfully counter the threat. One can compensate for the lack of numbers of troops with force multipliers such as attack helicopters and more advanced weaponry or high-performance mobile and technologically advanced military units. In most cases peace operations have neither; both troops and force multipliers are lacking.

It is not without reason, therefore, that larger peace operations deployed to small countries are more likely to succeed than those deployed to large countries, where the protection needs in many cases are in remote areas. As the HIPPO also pointed out, the resource constraints of many UN missions are dire, particularly in countries that are vast, with a difficult topography, poor infrastructure, and difficult climatic conditions, such as in the Democratic Republic of the Congo (DRC), Mali, and South Sudan (UN 2015b, paras. 93 and 210). All these missions are struggling to deliver.

UNMISS, for one, suffered major deficits on all of the abovementioned fronts. The challenges in South Sudan were grossly underestimated from the outset, despite the previous six-year UN-mission—UNMIS from 2005 to 2011. The number of troops in UNMISS were wholly inadequate for the task. The mission had one soldier per 100 km, almost three times fewer peacekeepers compared to other comparable UN missions.[9] Some would say that this is not a relevant comparison; it all depends on where one positions the troops and their mobility. In the case of South Sudan, however, the mobility constraints were even worse than in many comparable missions, constituting a major impediment to a timely response.

Sixty percent of the country's territory is inaccessible for six to eight months per year during the rainy season. The mission therefore needed a much more diverse set of mobility assets to have a chance to deliver on its mandate. Without means of river transport and without all-terrain vehicles that could move in the mud and the swamps, the mission was largely dependent on aviation. We were literally stuck in the mud. The lack of proper airstrips implied that the only realistic means of transport was helicopters.[10] This limited the numbers of troops that could be deployed and retained in remote locations significantly. The mission often suffered from a mobility crisis due to these aviation constraints. UNMISS saw columns of 5–8000 armed youth in military formation attack particular communities. The maximum number of troops the mission could deploy over time to face such a threat was 300–400. The resource deficits were particularly exposed in Jonglei, but the mission continued to have major challenges all over the country.

In April 2013, during a military capability review, UNMISS had problems convincing visiting colleagues of the urgent need for strengthening

[9]Johnson (2016, p. 326, footnote 75): UNMISS' ratio was 98:1 in late 2012. In 2011–2012, the figure was even lower. As the comparator for UN Stabilization Mission in the DRC (MONUSCO), the Eastern DRC was used as this is the primary area of operations for this mission, and the ratio of territory to soldier in 2012 was 17:1. For The UN-African Union Mission in Darfur (UNAMID), it was 29:1, and for UN Operation in Cote d'Ivoire UNOCI) it was 35:1. These comparators also do not account for the fact that UNMISS had less infantry and more engineering companies than most other missions. Even if all forces were moved to Jonglei state, UNMISS would have had a ratio of 1:19, which was worse than what MONUSCO already had as its presence in Eastern DRC.

[10]Constructing air-strips was high on the mission's agenda, but the engineering companies were delayed in their deployment to the mission, and had to concentrate on building military bases, which also were lacking. This implied that the construction of new airstrips were delayed.

the capabilities of the mission on several fronts, despite the threats to thousands of civilians. Only after the crisis hit in December 2013 was it possible to obtain the approval for a significant strengthening of the mission's capabilities, although the surge then took unacceptably long, an equally important obstacle in the UN deployment system.

The HIPPO makes strong recommendations that would, if implemented, enable missions to deliver better on their POC mandate. For example, the proposal to change the mandating process to a two-step process, in which any mandate would be revisited six months after the mission onset, would make it possible to tailor mandates to the needs on the ground. It is critical to make sure that the resources and capabilities match the mandates. If the necessary resources will not arrive, the mandates should change accordingly (UN 2015b, pp. 47–48).

Beyond lacking resources, another challenge is the performance of the contingents and their willingness to engage pro-actively in confronting threats to civilians with force. While some UNMISS contingents were more risk averse, with mission leadership at times having to directly instruct a more robust response, others delivered on the mandate pro-actively and effectively. When the crisis hit in December 2013, these differences became even more evident. The national caveats that had been applied by some contingents were later expanded and amplified, with new constraints, for example on mobility, positioning of assets and posture. Other contingents were on the other hand undeterred and engaged in protecting civilians through impressive and courageous efforts.

One example of the latter were the efforts of the UN forces in Bentiu, Unity State, where civilians were hiding in hospitals, churches, and mosques. More than 400 civilians were rescued from these locations by the Mongolian contingent whilst under fire. A safe corridor was also established to bring an additional 1000 or more people into safety. In Bentiu, this happened several times while the fighting was raging, in addition to the protection of 40,000 civilians within the UN-base. This shows that results on POC can be achieved, even by an overstretched and under-resourced mission and under dire circumstances. The degree to which troops are willing to engage robustly and proactively within their means when they are seeing civilians under threat, can thus make a huge difference.

The HIPPO panel also used strong language on the performance of peacekeepers, stating that national constraints imposed on contingents from their own capital or military headquarters were not acceptable and should be treated as disobedience of lawful command (UN 2015b, p. 28). It is incumbent upon the UN-leadership in New York to make sure that Troop and Police Contributing Countries do not get away with mediocre performance and the introduction of new caveats when the contingents are deployed to UN missions.

Resources and performance are key to the implementation of a POC-mandate. While expectations are often unrealistic, experience from both UNMISS and other peacekeeping operations shows that it is at times possible to deliver on POC-mandates even with such shortcomings.

Another aspect that has become of increasing concern, however, is the many cases where host governments are blocking access for UN peacekeepers to areas where civilians are at risk, preventing them from fulfilling their POC-mandate. Even worse are situations when security forces of host government themselves are the primary perpetrators of violence against civilians, or when they support non-state actors constituting similar threats. In South Sudan, for example, UNMISS has been barred access from a number of locations. Numerous UN-reports have also documented that the government's security forces have been a major perpetrator against civilians.

While the protection mandate is the same whoever the perpetrator is, UN guidelines are not clear on which actions a mission should take in situations when the host government is the primary perpetrator of violence against civilians. References are often made to the Status of Forces Agreement, which the UN signs with the host government to facilitate the presence and operations of the relevant UN Mission. If a peace operation were to confront the armed forces of the host government militarily, there is fear that the mission may find itself without a SOFA and be asked to leave the country. Most Troop Contributing Countries will have major problems with confronting host governments in such situations. In many cases they would be instructed by their respective governments to refrain from engaging with the security forces of the host government.

To many civilians subject to such threats, the UN peacekeepers' ability to protect them from threats to their lives will therefore remain an illusion. This dilemma is not being discussed openly in the UN system. The Security Council has also avoided this sensitive issue. With the increased complexity of conflicts in a number of countries, often involving host government forces, it is likely that more UN missions will be faced with this dilemma. In the case of UNMISS, for example, the lives peacekeepers could save through direct protection in situations where civilians are under threat by SPLA-forces (or non-state actors supported by them) would have to be weighed against the risks to the lives of more than 200,000 civilians under UNMISS' protection in the event that the Mission would be forced to leave.

This is also related to the interpretation of the Security Council mandate of peace operations. It is not made clear to missions what is expected of them in situations where host governments are the primary perpetrators of violence against civilians. It appears that direct engagement with government security forces would normally imply a peace enforcement mandate from the Security Council. Rather than leaving such difficult assessments to mission leadership, guidance should be developed which provides clarity to people in the field.

POC by the Host Government: Rhetoric or Reality?

As stated in the introduction, and despite what is stated above, the main responsibility for the protection of civilians rests unequivocally with the host government. When a civil war is raging, one must respect the Geneva Conventions; to clearly distinguish combatants from non-combatants (i.e. civilians). This is currently not the case in South Sudan, where violations of these conventions appear to be the rule and not the exception. In more stable settings, one should expect the uniformed forces of a host government to do their utmost to actively protect civilians. This, however, is not the case in most countries where the UN is deployed with a POC mandate. Here lies one of the greatest paradoxes in the UN's approach to POC in its peace operations.

Most peace operations deploy into countries emerging from conflict where the UN is faced with state and non-state armed actors. One can hardly talk about a professional army. Nevertheless, the principle is clear; any government has the primary responsibility to protect its own population. But very few government armies, whether professional conventional armies or those that have originated from liberation movements, militia, or guerrilla warfare, have experience in operations that involve the protection of civilians. Military operations are usually focusing on gaining control over territory and dominating it and protecting territory when this control is threatened. And in doing so, armed forces of all categories have often been the predators of the civilian population and not their protectors.

The more static modus operandi of traditional military operations is also different from protecting civilians. Hardly any traditional military unit has been trained in these types of mobile operations. Most armies see this typically as a job for police forces, formed police units, or gendarmerie. The tactics and operations of protecting civilians usually involve highly mobile units much more similar to the more robust armed police units, such as those conducting crowd control and riot control in highly professional police forces. Although there are differences, it is mostly this type of mobility—and that of counter insurgency units—that have certain similarities. Military contingents of peacekeepers are therefore not used to such operations, either. This has not been a topic of much discussion, however.

What is even more surprising is that there is no systematic investment enabling host governments to take civilian protection seriously. Hardly any efforts are being made to train forces of host governments to enable them to better conduct operations to protect civilians. Very limited investment is being made in developing the numbers of formed police units that more effectively could take on such tasks. Not even UN formed police units are being properly trained in a systematic manner for such operations according to agreed standards. Few have experience in POC related operations from their home countries.

That training of uniformed forces in the specifics of POC operations, whether military or police, is not given higher priority is surprising. But more importantly, it is a great paradox that host governments are not assisted with such training programmes to enable their police and military units to develop and build the type of capacities and institutions that are needed to better protect civilians. This is a serious concern. After all, host governments are supposed to have the primary responsibility for the protection of civilians. But without such support, the principle will remain an empty slogan.

Such POC training programmes can only succeed when they are developed as part of an overall SSR process, where fundamental issues such as professionalisation, command and control, competence and performance, and discipline and accountability are mainstreamed through the uniformed forces. It is also necessary to apply the UN's Human Rights Due Diligence Policy and other instruments (UN 2013). Civilians will not be protected by forces and institutions that are dysfunctional and of questionable quality and where behaviour will depend on the individual commander's whims. POC training, which would be a natural area for the UN to invest in, will therefore never work as a stand alone-measure, but will have to be imbedded in the strengthening of the institutions of the armed forces and the police.

To consolidate and sustain peace in a country, SSR may be the most critical intervention. As the HIPPO panel has highlighted, the security sector can be the greatest spoiler of peace (UN 2015b, p. 40). Yet, this is maybe one of the largest gaps in international peace efforts. While bilaterals engage in Defense Sector Reform (DSR), often in accordance with their own strategic interests, and with minimal transparency, hardly anyone, including the UN, supports overall SSR effectively, making sure there is a holistic approach, with coherence and coordination between the reform efforts in the different security sectors.

The HIPPO panel identified this as a major gap. While the more technical aspects of DSR is not an area where the UN is well positioned to engage, the UN can support aspects related to oversight and accountability. It is one of the biggest actors in police development and DDR. The HIPPO panel therefore stated that more efforts should be made to support SSR in a more effective and coordinated way. The *UN can and should play a convening and coordinating role in SSR*, if so requested by the government (UN 2015b, p. 40). This implies making sure coherent reform efforts take place in all security sectors.[11] This is also affirmed in a recent Security Council Resolution on this issue (UN 2014b).

A lot will have to be done to change the way UN peace operations work, if such efforts are to succeed. Fundamental reforms are needed (UN 2015b, p. 41, para. 156–157, recommendations 1, 2, 5, and 6). Moreover, in order to develop advisory functions in the SSR area there is a need to change the way that UN peace operations support institution-building. This is about capacity-building in one of the most difficult, yet most critical sectors.

The lack of reform in the SPLA in South Sudan was one of the main contributing factors to the escalation of violence in December 2013. While the origin of the crisis was political, it spun out of control largely due to the implosion in the security forces, and its rapid escalation was in no doubt caused by an institutionally weak and ethnically fragmented army. The responsibility for this rests squarely with the SPLM leadership, but it also illustrates how fundamental security sector reform is.

One of the core issues for any peace process in South Sudan going forward will be the total transformation of the country's security

[11] For such reform efforts in SSR to succeed, local ownership is critical. A convening and coordinating role for the UN should therefore not substitute such ownership and should be at the national authorities' request.

forces, integrating units and elements from all sides. The engagement of third party actors, across all security organs, whether army or police, will be imperative, such as the UN, the AU and regional actors. If such a transformation of the security sector is not implemented and coordinated effectively, it will have an immediate impact on the prospects for peace. The security sector is the lynchpin in these countries, not only for the protection of civilians, but also for peace itself.

Conclusion

UN peace operations must be significantly reformed in order to more effectively protect civilians. As reflected in HIPPO, this is related both to the selection of mission leadership, the way the mandate is formed, the capacities involved and not least, the emphasis on the primacy of politics. When the political dynamics are at the centre, capacity on the political and civilian side, preventive diplomacy and Tier 1-efforts must be given much higher priority. This is critical and usually a far more effective way to protect civilians than protective actions in the field through Tier 2-operations.

To be able to do the latter, however, we also need to see major reforms on the military and police side. For the military to act more robustly, a series of measures need to be undertaken, both with regard to appropriate resources and the strengthening of capacities, systemic deficiencies and the willingness of TCCs to act. On the police side, a series of necessary reforms are listed in the UN police review that was undertaken in 2016 (UN 2016). In order to deliver on protection mandates UN peace operations must have both the necessary means and the will to act. The Security Council should also contribute to further clarity on what a POC-mandate implies in situations when host governments are the primary perpetrators of violence against civilians.

Given the scale of the challenge, and the fact that there are limits to what UN peace operations can do to physically protect civilians, investment in security sector reform and providing training in POC operations to uniformed forces of host governments is critical. It can help make protection a reality for civilians in many countries. And it can help prevent these forces from becoming perpetrators.

The security sector is too important for achieving and sustaining peace to be left to random arrangements, depending on the situation in each country. At the very least, a significant effort must be made to make sure that there is coherence in reforming the different security actors by competent third parties. The current status of affairs cannot continue. If invested in, the UN is well positioned to engage in a convening and coordinating role in this area. The Security Council needs to take this concern seriously.

With the UN in such a role, one would kill two birds with one stone, both for the efforts to consolidate peace and in relation to strengthening the protection of civilians. After all, uniformed forces of host governments are supposed to be the primary protectors of the citizens. Without making this a priority, physical protection is likely to remain an illusion for the vast majority of civilians, even where the UN is present with its blue helmets. And even worse, if the UN continues its rather hesitant approach to support comprehensive security sector reform, it will be at risk of failing in its overall mandate in the achievement of peace and security.

References

Holt, Victoria, and Glyn Taylor *with* Max Kelly. 2009. *Protecting Civilians in the Context of UN Peacekeeping Operations: Successes, Setbacks and Remaining Challenges*. New York: Independent study jointly commissioned by the UN Department of Peacekeeping Operations and the Office for the Coordination of Humanitarian Affairs.

Human Rights Watch. 2014. *South Sudan's New War: Abuses by Government and Opposition Forces*. New York: Human Rights Watch.

Johnson, Hilde F. 2016. *South Sudan: The Untold Story, from Independence to Civil War*. London: I.B. Tauris.

United Nations. 1999. *Statement by the President of the Security Council*, February 12. New York: United Nations Security Council.

United Nations. 2000. *Report of the Panel on United Nations Peace Operations*. New York: United Nations.

United Nations. 2009. *United Nations Security Council Resolution 1894*. New York: United Nations Security Council.

United Nations. 2010. *Operational Concept on the Protection of Civilians*. New York: Department for Peacekeeping Operations and Department for Field Support.

United Nations. 2011. *Framework for Drafting Comprehensive Protection of Civilians Strategies in UN Peacekeeping Operations*. New York: DPKO and DFS.

United Nations. 2012a. *Report of the Secretary-General on South Sudan*, November 8. New York: United Nations Security Council.

United Nations. 2012b. *Report of the Secretary-General on the Sudan and South Sudan*, November 27. New York: United Nations Security Council.

United Nations. 2013. *Human Rights Due Diligence Policy*, A/67/775–S/2013/110, March 5. New York: United Nations General Assembly.

United Nations. 2014a. *Report of the Secretary-General on South Sudan*, March 6. New York: United Nations Security Council.

United Nations. 2014b. *United Nations Security Council Resolution 2151*. New York: United Nations Security Council.

United Nations. 2015a. *The Protection of Civilians in United Nations Peacekeeping*. New Nork: DPKO and DFS Policy.

United Nations. 2015b. *Report of the High-Level Independent Panel on Peace Operations on Uniting our Strengths for Peace: Politics, Partnership and People*. New York: United Nations.

United Nations. 2015c. *Report of the Secretary-General on South Sudan*, April 29. New York: United Nations Security Council.

United Nations. 2016. *Final Report of the Panel of Experts on South Sudan, Established Pursuant to SCR 2206 (2015)*. New York: United Nations.

United Nations OIOI. 2014. *Evaluation of the Implementation and Results of Protection of Civilians Mandates in United Nations Peacekeeping Operations*, Report of the Office of Internal Oversight Services, March 7. New York: United Nations.

UNMISS. 2014. *Conflict in South Sudan. A Human Rights Report*, May 8.

UNMISS. 2015. *Flash Human Rights Report on the Escalation of Fighting in Greater Upper Nile*, June 29.

UNMISS. Protection of Civilian Strategy, approved by SRSG, 4 June 2012.

UNMISS. Protection of Civilians Strategy, 2014/PoC/1, 15 September 2014.

Open Access This chapter is licensed under the terms of the Creative Commons Attribution 4.0 International License (http://creativecommons.org/licenses/by/4.0/), which permits use, sharing, adaptation, distribution and reproduction in any medium or format, as long as you give appropriate credit to the original author(s) and the source, provide a link to the Creative Commons license and indicate if changes were made.

The images or other third party material in this chapter are included in the chapter's Creative Commons license, unless indicated otherwise in a credit line to the material. If material is not included in the chapter's Creative Commons license and your intended use is not permitted by statutory regulation or exceeds the permitted use, you will need to obtain permission directly from the copyright holder.

Check for updates

CHAPTER 8

UN Peace Operations, Terrorism, and Violent Extremism

John Karlsrud

Introduction

In the last decade or so, terrorism and violent extremism have moved centre stage on the international policy agenda. Consequently, also the question of the United Nations peace operations' role vis-à-vis these threats has gained strength.

Historically, UN peace operations have been deployed in theatres where such threats have been present, but they have so far not confronted these threats directly. The UN stabilisation mission in Mali (MINUSMA), deployed in 2013, marked the beginning of a new era in this respect. MINUSMA has been the target of terrorist attacks from a number of different groups, and had at the time of writing suffered 95 fatalities and a number of injuries as a result (UN 2017a). But MINUSMA is also a notable case study because it has been mandated by the UN Security Council to take "direct action" to mitigate and respond to the asymmetric threats that the terrorist groups represent (UN 2016a, p. 8).

J. Karlsrud (✉)
Norwegian Institute of International Affairs (NUPI), Oslo, Norway

© The Author(s) 2019

C. de Coning and M. Peter (eds.), *United Nations Peace Operations in a Changing Global Order*,
https://doi.org/10.1007/978-3-319-99106-1_8

This chapter will first look at the evolving discussion on terrorism and violent extremism, seen from the perspective of UN peace operations. It will then use the case of MINUSMA to discern some arguments for and against giving UN peace operations a larger role in mitigating and responding to these threats. In conclusion, the chapter argues that although there may be good financial and political reasons to give UN peace operations a larger role in the global war on terrorism and violent extremism, this will be close to impossible to do in practice. Indeed, it will have unintended and negative consequences for the role the UN has in the humanitarian and political domains in countries emerging from conflict and the future role of UN peace operations in general.

A New Era of Terrorism and Violent Extremism?

The number of fatalities caused by terrorism has been rising steadily since 2000, from 3329 in 2000 to 32,685 in 2014 (IEP 2015, p. 2). A particularly dramatic increase was noted in 2014, with an 80% increase compared to 2013, largely because of the rise of the so-called Islamic State (IS) as well as Boko Haram (ibid.). 2015 was the second deadliest year on record with 29,376 deaths (IEP 2016, p. 2).

Some of the key groups behind terrorist attacks are Al Qaeda (e.g. Afghanistan, Iraq, and Syria), IS (e.g. Syria and Iraq), Boko Haram (Nigeria, Cameroon, Niger, and Chad), Al Shabaab (Somalia), AQIM (Mali), Al Mourabitoun (Mali), and Macina Liberation Front (Mali).[1] Not only have the number of victims increased exponentially over the last 16 years, but the acts that these groups have committed are aimed to shock the conscience of humanity, and many constitute war crimes and crimes against humanity (see e.g. UNHRC 2015). Transnational terrorist groups such as the IS are qualitatively different from previous terrorist groups because they are not seeking recognition from the international community. Instead they are seeking to establish a new caliphate, irrespective of existing borders, and willing to use extreme violence to achieve this objective. Another key characteristic of these groups is the

[1]These groups are changing frequently. The al Mourabitoun, for example, emerged from the Movement for Oneness and Jihad in West Africa and the Masked Men Brigade, and, in the beginning of 2017, Ansar Dine, Al Mourabitoun, and al Qaeda in the Maghreb (AQIM) announced their merger. For more, see e.g. Raineri and Strazzari (2015) and Haugegaard (2017).

use of modern tools of communication and technology to intimidate and communicate the atrocities they commit, and recruit and radicalise new followers on a global scale. The shockingly violent acts, including the use of rape, sexual slavery, and forced marriage as tactics of terror against civilians (UN 2015a), have created a new sense of urgency to deal with these rapidly growing threats.

The United Nations, Terrorism and Violent Extremism

Terrorism has for long been a controversial topic at the UN, and the member states have so far not been able to agree on a definition of terrorism. Nevertheless, violent extremism and terrorism have been rising on the international agenda since the 9/11-attacks in 2001. The UN Global Counter-Terrorism Strategy was adopted by the General Assembly in 2006 (UN 2006), and had four pillars:

> a. tackling conditions conducive to terrorism;
> b. preventing and combating terrorism;
> c. building countries' capacity to combat terrorism and to strengthen the role of the United Nations system in that regard; and
> d. ensuring respect for human rights for all and the rule of law while countering terrorism. (UN 2015b, p. 3)

In the following years, the strategy was revisited at regular intervals, but with limited coordination and integration with the rest of the tools in the UN peace and security toolbox. This gradually started to change in parallel with a discursive move from "terrorism" to countering and preventing violent extremism (PVE and CVE, here grouped together as 'PCVE'). Realising that the Global War on Terror (GWOT) initiated after the 9/11-attacks proved controversial, the US administration under former US President George W. Bush made a discursive move from GWOT to "Struggle against Violent Extremism" or SAVE (Fox 2005). This reconceptualisation, subsuming the counter-terrorist agenda under less ominous sounding concepts, proved less divisive and in the following years, in parallel with the rapid increase in incidents labelled terrorist attacks, preventing and countering violent extremism have become mainstream concepts and agendas.

This was evidenced when Ban Ki-moon, the former UN Secretary-General launched a *Plan of Action to Prevent Violent Extremism* in the beginning of 2016. He stated that

> [t]here is no single pathway to violent extremism. But we know that extremism flourishes when human rights are violated, political space is shrunk, aspirations for inclusion are ignored, and too many people – especially young people – lack prospects and meaning in their lives. (UN 2016b)

In the action plan, he lamented the fact that so far there has been "a strong emphasis on the implementation of measures under pillar II of the Global Strategy, while pillars I and IV have often been overlooked" (UN 2015b, p. 3). In the plan, the terms "extremism", "violent extremism," and "terrorism" were used interchangeably (Modirzadeh 2016).

In the above-mentioned pillar II, we find counter-terrorism operations. Currently, the UN is neither principally nor operationally set up to fight terrorist groups by force. Operationally, the High-Level Independent Panel on Peace Operations (HIPPO) report drew a red line with counter-terrorism operations, saying that "UN peacekeeping missions, due to their composition and character, are not suited to engage in military counter-terrorism operations. They lack the specific equipment, intelligence, logistics, capabilities and specialized military preparation required, among other aspects" (UN 2015c, p. 31). However, this quote could be interpreted as to say that if these shortcomings were amended, UN peace operations would be able to take on such operations. However, the main message of the report is the primacy of a political engagement—a UN peace operation should always seek to be part of a "robust political process" and "continuously seek to build consent to the UN role and presence through an impartial posture" (ibid., p. 33). The ability to facilitate a political dialogue, often in tandem with key members of the Security Council, is argued to be the comparative advantage of the UN. By becoming a party to the conflict, this advantage is in peril.

Terrorism and violent extremism are part of the same spectrum, but they are not the same thing. Both are willing to use violence to pursue political goals, but to different degrees. If the objective is to limit, counter, and prevent violent extremism it follows that a primary objective would be not to further alienate those that may have legitimate governance and development concerns, and who are yet not fully radicalised. Characterising all groups and individuals as terrorists, no matter where they are located on the spectrum, risks further radicalisation and strengthening the most extreme groups.

There is thus a need to appropriately nuance the understanding of and strategies for dealing with violent extremism. Violent extremism can stem from a variety of root causes—including injustice, marginalisation, under-development, governance structures undermined by corruption, lack of responsive governments and social cohesion, weak and limited state-society relations, and externally supported religious radicalisation. The UN Secretary-General has warned against a securitised approach to countering violent extremism, and has outlined a prevention agenda where the main goals must be to better understand the motivations for joining groups such as the IS; avoid using "terrorism" as a label to eliminate political opposition; and deal with root causes through strengthening governance, the respect for human rights, more accountable institutions, service delivery, and political participation (UN News Centre 2015). The multitude of root causes to violent extremism must be reflected in the register of tools and approaches of member states and global and regional institutions to deal with these challenges.

The UN is a state-centric organisation. In the states it is seeking to support, however, the governments often enjoy weak legitimacy among large parts of the population. Material and ideational resources are concentrated among the elites, and access to education and other basic services is often limited to urban centres, leaving room for radicalisation and recruitment to violent extremist groups to fester. Adding to this vulnerable starting point, weak governments are often pursuing militarised solutions to the challenges it is facing, perpetuating, fuelling, and becoming an ever more intrinsic part of the problem. Being a state-centric organisation, the UN is in risk of following the same pattern by supporting member states in the fight against violent extremism and terrorism.

Since 9/11, the UN has unfortunately also increasingly become the target of terrorist attacks. The attacks in Baghdad in 2003, Algiers in 2007, Kabul in 2009, Mazar-i-Sharif in 2011, Abuja in 2011, Mogadishu in 2013, a number of attacks in Mali from 2013 until today, in addition to a high number of smaller attacks have all made it clear that the UN is increasingly considered a participant in the global war on terror. With the increase in attacks, the UN has been adapting its risk posture, taking precautions on movement and deployment of staff in high-risk zones.

Member states and multilateral organisations have developed various doctrines and guidelines for countering and preventing violent extremism, ranging from military-oriented counter-insurgency and counter-terrorism guidance such as the US Counterterrorism doctrine and *NATO's military concept for defence against terrorism* (United States Department of the Army 2014; NATO 2011). The UN is currently in a state of flux when it comes to policy development on the issue of counter-terrorism and countering and preventing violent extremism, and there is increasing pressure from member states on the UN to take on a greater share of these challenges (Boutellis and Fink 2016; Karlsrud 2017, 2018). These member states request that UN peace operations should be more relevant to what are seen as challenges of the twenty-first century, and MINUSMA has become the laboratory for testing whether UN peace operations actually are able to take on these challenges.

MINUSMA: Between a Rock and a Hard Place

Although the UN has been the target for spectacular attacks previously, the frequency and consistency of attacks on the UN have increased with the more active role that the organisation has been given in for example Somalia and Mali. Until now, it has been special political missions and UN development presences that have been the main targets for these attacks, but with the deployment of MINUSMA to Mali a UN multidimensional peacekeeping mission has been given a direct role in stabilising a country that had been destabilised by inter alia violent extremist and terrorist groups (Karlsrud 2015). It is also the first time a multidimensional peacekeeping mission has been deployed in parallel with an ongoing counter-terrorism operation, the French *Opération Serval*, later transitioned into the current *Opération Barkhane* (Ministère de la Défense 2015).

In 2014, one year after deployment, the Force Commander of MINUSMA briefed the UN Security Council, saying that "MINUSMA is in a terrorist-fighting situation without an anti-terrorist mandate or adequate training, equipment, logistics or intelligence to deal with such a situation" (UN 2014, p. 4). MINUSMA was suffering from repeated attacks, and in 2014 alone, MINUSMA suffered 41 fatalities—"one of the highest one-year fatality rates for any peacekeeping operation in UN history" according to the Ban Ki-moon, the former UN Secretary-General (UN 2015d). However, at that juncture, MINUSMA had still not been tasked to take 'direct action' against asymmetric threats.

MINUSMA has e.g. had a task force on counter-terrorism and organised crime, with a mandate to "provide recommendations on the delivery of a common and comprehensive strategy to support the Government of Mali in counter-terrorism and in combating organized crime" (UN 2015e, p. 23). In the more robust end of the spectrum, the MINUSMA military troops have been preparing "targeting packs [...] on groups and individuals considered a threat to the mission," (Karlsrud 2017, p. 1224) and has been sharing information with the parallel French counter-terrorism mission *Opération Barkhane* (ibid.). Taken together, these practices suggest that MINUSMA may already have crossed the red line drawn by the HIPPO.

What, then, should be the way forward? When deployed to countries like Mali, the UN must be equipped to mitigate and prevent attacks against itself and the local population. In practice, this means militarily engaging violent extremists and terrorists. As I have already noted, this takes UN peace operations across the line drawn by the HIPPO-report. For MINUSMA, this is already the reality it is struggling to deal with. Future missions may be deployed to Libya, Somalia, Syria, and Yemen, and find similar mission environments and threats.

Use of Force: Burden-Sharing with Regional Organisations

Since similar ongoing operations are shouldered by the African Union (AU) and sub-regional organisations on the African continent, and that likely future operations of this kind will be in Libya, Yemen, and Syria, it may make more sense to undertake such operations in coalitions of the willing. This would give the lead regional organisation/group of states the space to decide on a range of issues that might be more constrained in a UN setting. Such missions should be sequenced to not further undermine traditional UN peace operations. Coalitions of the willing, and in some instances regional organisations, will remain the only options with the requisite political will, capabilities, doctrines, and staying power to conduct counter-terrorism operations, equipped with a UN mandate.

The AU and sub-regional organisations have proven that they are enhancing their competency and ability to conduct peace support operations, although the potential for improvement is still significant.

The AU has been either mandating or directly implementing counter-terrorist operations in a number of theatres—with for example its AU Regional Task Force for the elimination of the Lord's Resistance Army in Uganda, the AMISOM mission in Somalia, the African-led International Support Mission to Mali, the Multinational Joint Task Force established to fight Boko Haram, and the Group of Five Sahel Joint Force composed of troops from Burkina Faso, Chad, Mali, Mauritania and Niger.

AU peace enforcement missions also have the comparative advantage of participating states' strong political will and the ability to sustain significant losses over time, something UN peace operations simply cannot or will not be able to match. However, the funding, capability, and capacity issues remain unresolved. The initiative of the AU to increase the self-funding of AU peace operations to 25% over a five-year period (AU 2015), alongside strengthened accountability and human rights due diligence mechanisms and the development of a mission support concept, could unlock further support. However, also the AU is still suffering from weak capacity in many areas, with frequent reports on human rights violations committed by troops in Somalia as one example (see e.g. UN 2017b). Member states thus need to continue to build the capacity of the AU, sub-regional organisations, and African member states to counter and prevent violent extremism in a holistic manner, including a stronger emphasis on early peacebuilding and recovery programmes that can provide real opportunities and stop the recruitment into terrorist organisations.

Towards a Holistic Approach

The comparative advantage of the UN lies in its convening power and impartiality as well as in its ability to provide and coordinate comprehensive support across the peace and security, development, and human rights pillars. This gives the UN unique legitimacy from which it draws its strength. However, each of these elements are vulnerable to mission creep, overstretch, and inefficacy in implementation. The state-centric nature of the UN is both its advantage and its Achilles' heel.

Using force limits the ability of the UN to provide good offices, engage with armed groups, and be a legitimate actor in early peacebuilding, recovery, and development efforts. Taking active part in a conflict also significantly increases the risks of attacks against the soft targets of the UN—international and local staff, as well as contractors and other actors with real or perceived ties to the organisation.

Fortified UN compounds with Hesco barriers, barbed wire and limited freedom of movement are often apt responses to increased threats from violent extremists and terrorists. However, while increased security measures may be necessary, more limited engagement with local populations may lead to a weaker understanding of underlying political, economic, and social dynamics and increased vulnerability for attacks, perpetuating and increasing the gap between local populations and UN staff. The risk avoidance of troop contributing countries in hostile theatres will also contribute to weakening the legitimacy of UN peace operations, as seen in Mali.

A militarised strategy does not only risk fuelling further radicalisation, but also draws funding from potential prevention activities, leading to a negative spiral on local, national, regional, and global levels. A prevention agenda must engage national elites in a rethink of state-society relations that should include more and deeper dialogue with civil society and lead to more inclusive, participatory, and representative societies (de Coning et al. 2015). The UN thus needs to maintain an impartial stance vis-à-vis the government in power and counter efforts of instrumentalisation of the UN peace operation to fight political opposition labelled "terrorists".

To tackle the root causes of violent extremism and terrorism, UN peace operations and the UN system can partner with national governments, multilateral organisations, religious organisations, and NGOs to promote holistic approaches. There is a need to generate new platforms for political dialogue, inclusion, and community engagement. In view of the rapidly increasing interconnectedness and transnational character of the challenges the world faces, strategies must not only be national, but regional and global in scope. New partnerships are needed—particularly at the sub-regional and regional levels—that are holistic, comprehensive, integrated and based on a deep analysis of the societal challenges that the violent extremism stems from. Unfortunately, the responses are often frustrated by limited acknowledgment of underlying societal drivers and root causes, lack of cooperation, competition, and rivalry among member states on the sub-regional and regional level.

Due concern must also be given to the impact on women of violent extremism and militarised responses to these threats. "The rise of violent extremism, which is given much importance in the report, threatens women's lives and leads to a cycle of militarisation of societies" (Stamnes and Osland 2016, p. 17). Violent extremism, terrorism, and counter-terrorism put vulnerable groups between a rock and a hard place, narrows the space for engagement by women peacebuilders, and limits the funding for basic services and peacebuilding activities.

The religious dimension of radicalisation also deserves scrutiny. Gulf states have been exporting their particular kind of Islam to the rest of the world for many decades, fomenting and driving radicalisation. In Mali for example, Muslims are traditionally Maliki Sunnis and Sufis, but the more radical Wahhabi strand of Islam has rapidly taken hold with the financial support of key Gulf states such as Saudi Arabia. In this context, it is also curious to notice that Saudi Arabia is the main sponsor of the UN Counter-Terrorism Centre (UNCCT), part of the Counter-Terrorism Implementation Task Force (CTITF) (UN 2016c), endorsed by member states of the UN General Assembly through the Global Counter-Terrorism Strategy adopted in 2006 (UN 2006). The UNCCT and CTITF are both part of the UN Department of Political Affairs (DPA), also responsible for special political missions. The UNCCT received in 2014 a donation from Saudi-Arabia of $100 million to strengthen its "tools, technologies and methods to confront and eliminate the threat of terrorism" (UNCCT 2015). It is also partially funded by Germany, the UK, and the US. According to one UN official, the CTITF/UNCCT accounted for roughly half of the operational part of the DPA budget funding projects and activities in the field in 2015, and UNCCT has for example reached out to the UN mission in Mali, UN agencies, and others to develop projects, counting 31 projects at the beginning of 2016 (UN 2016c).

This apparent oxymoron points to an important point—the prevention and deradicalisation agenda is fairly well known, but implementation is either limited or ineffective. This shows the limited political will to deal with clear-cut and well-known challenges, such as the continued financing of the export of radical Islam by Gulf states. The thin and at times non-existent legitimacy of the regimes that are facing violent extremists is another clear challenge, severely limiting the will to engage in political dialogue.

The UN Security Council should maintain a central role for the UN in the mediation of conflict even where the UN is a party or considered to be a party to the conflict. Therefore it should nominate a separate Special Envoy to lead the negotiations to create the necessary space for engagement. The UN should not be barred from talking with any of the actors, even those beyond the pale, but keep communication channels open.

More capacity is needed to uncover and address linkages between organised crime, terrorist groups, and national elites (UN 2015a). For the UN, this is a particularly sensitive area, as a focus on corruption may lead to significant resistance and increase the hurdles the UN peace operation and the UN Country Team are facing. However, only continued emphasis on this is likely to make leaders accountable to their populations, and enable representative, inclusive, and legitimate regimes.

A UN peace operation should be working closely with the UN Country Team to devise peacebuilding and early recovery plans that use a combination of development data and intelligence to target particularly vulnerable populations such as youth and marginalised communities or ethnicities. Community violence reduction programmes have proved useful in for example Haiti, and are being tested in Mali "to address recruitment into the armed movements present in the country, including those allied to Al-Qaida" (UN 2015e, p. 22). UN peace operations should also consider limiting their military presence and focus on civilian activities in areas where they are seen as party to the conflict (Di Razza 2017).

Conclusions and Recommendations

The High-Level Independent Panel on Peace Operations report emphasised the primacy of political solutions. It stated, "there is a clear sense of a widening gap between what is being asked of [UN] peace operations today and what they are able to deliver" (UN 2015c, p. 9). Jean-Marie Guéhenno, the former head of UN peacekeeping, argues that robust peacekeeping has to be supported by a robust political strategy (2015). UN peace operations are operating in increasingly difficult theatres, facing the threats of violent extremism and transnational terrorist networks. This is partly due to the UN Security Council asking for deployment of missions long before the conditions are ripe, such as in Mali, and partly because of a structural development in technology and communication also propelling the nature of terrorist threats, with violent extremists and terrorists becoming far more interconnected and media-savvy.

These threats are likely to intensify, and in order to continue to operate in difficult and at times hostile environments, the UN will have to improve at all levels, even if it is not explicitly being asked to undertake counter-terrorism tasks. As it is likely that the UN will continue to be deployed in parallel with regional organisations that have a counter-terrorism mandate, the UN should be wary of the security, reputational, and legitimacy risks it will be facing in parallel deployments. It must mitigate increasing security risks by limiting engagement in military and substantive tasks where it is in parallel deployment with a counter-terrorism operation, intensify its efforts to establish a functioning and integrated intelligence concept for UN missions, strengthen its conflict prevention agenda, with particular emphasis on the engagement with those in risk of being radicalised. As borders are only lines in the sand, intermission cooperation must be intensified, with sharing of information, analysis, and capabilities on a regular basis.

While the UN can and should prepare for and be able to better respond to transnational terrorist threats, I have shown the limits of what UN peace operations are able to do operationally, principally, and politically. The growing capacity of regional and sub-regional organisations to deal with these threats should be supported by the UN and member states in the South and the North.

References

African Union. 2015. *Peace and Security Council 547th Meeting at the Level of Heads of State and Government*, September 26. Addis Ababa: African Union.

Boutellis, Arthur, and Naureen C. Fink. 2016. *Mind the Gap: UN Peace Operations and Terrorism and Violent Extremism Between Policy and Practice, Opportunities and Risks*. New York: International Peace Institute.

de Coning, Cedric, John Karlsrud, and Paul Troost. 2015. Towards More People-Centric Peace Operations: From 'Extension of State Authority' to 'Strengthening Inclusive State-Society Relations'. *Stability* 4 (1): 1–13.

Di Razza, Namie. 2017. *Reframing the Protection of Civilians Paradigm for UN Peace Operations*. New York: International Peace Institute.

Fox, Robert. 2005. Gwot Is history: Now for Save. *New Statesman*, August 8. Accessed 20 Dec 2017. http://www.newstatesman.com/node/195357.

Guéhenno, Jean-Marie. 2015. *The Fog of Peace*. Washington, DC: Brookings Institution Press.

Haugegaard, Rikke. 2017. Sharia as 'Desert Business': Understanding the Links Between Criminal Networks and Jihadism in Northern Mali. *Stability: International Journal of Security & Development* 6 (1): 1–15.

IEP. 2015. *Global Terrorism Index 2015*. Sydney: Institute of Economics and Peace.

IEP. 2016. *Global Terrorism Index 2016*. Sydney: Institute of Economics and Peace.

Karlsrud, John. 2015. The UN at War: Examining the Consequences of Peace Enforcement Mandates for the UN Peacekeeping Operations in the CAR, the DRC and Mali. *Third World Quarterly* 36 (1): 40–54.

Karlsrud, John. 2017. Towards UN Counter-Terrorism Operations. *Third World Quarterly* 38 (6): 1215–1231.

Karlsrud, John. 2018. *The UN at War: Peace Operations in a New Era*. Basingstoke: Palgrave Macmillan.

Modirzadeh, Naz K. 2016. If It's Broke, Don't Make It Worse: A Critique of the U.N. Secretary-General's Plan of Action to Prevent Violent Extremism, January 23. Accessed 28 Oct 2016. https://www.lawfareblog.com/if-its-broke-dont-make-it-worse-critique-un-secretary-generals-plan-action-prevent-violent-extremism.

Ministère de la Défense. 2015. Opération Barkhane, November 30. Accessed 8 Jan 2016. http://www.defense.gouv.fr/operations/sahel/dossier-de-presentation-de-l-operation-barkhane/operation-barkhane.

NATO. 2011. NATO's Military Concept for Defence Against Terrorism, January 2. Accessed 27 Jan 2016. http://www.nato.int/cps/en/natohq/topics_69482.htm.

Raineri, Luca, and Francesco Strazzari. 2015. State, Secession, and Jihad: The Micropolitical Economy of Conflict in Northern Mali. *African Security* 8 (4): 249–271.

Stamnes, Eli, and Kari Osland. 2016. *Synthesis Report: Reviewing UN Peace Operations, the UN Peacebuilding Architecture and the Implementation of UNSCR 1325*. Oslo: Norwegian Institute of International Affairs.

UN News Centre. 2015. Preventing Violent Extremism, Promoting Human Rights Go Hand-in-Hand, Ban Tells Washington Summit. UN News Centre, February 19. Accessed 11 Jan 2016. http://www.un.org/apps/news/story.asp?NewsID=50123#.VpOdrcmEr9d.

UNCCT. 2015. Kingdom of Saudi Arabia Donates USD 100 Million for the United Nations Counter-Terrorism Centre. *The Beam* 8: 1–3. Accessed 11 Jan 2016. http://www.un.org/es/terrorism/ctitf/pdfs/The%20Beam%20Vol%208.pdf.

UNHRC. 2015. *Report of the Office of the United Nations High Commissioner for Human Rights on the Human Rights Situation in Iraq in the Light of Abuses Committed by the So-Called Islamic State in Iraq and the Levant and Associated Groups*. New York: UN Human Rights Council.

United Nations. 2006. *The United Nations Global Counter-Terrorism Strategy*, September 30. New York: United Nations.

United Nations. 2014. *United Nations Peacekeeping Operations*, 7275th Meeting, October 9. New York: United Nations.

United Nations. 2015a. *Conflict-Related Sexual Violence: Report of the Secretary-General*, March 23. New York: United Nations.

United Nations. 2015b. *Plan of Action to Prevent Violent Extremism: Report of the Secretary-General*, December 24. New York: United Nations General Assembly.

United Nations. 2015c. *Uniting Our Strengths for Peace—Politics, Partnership and People*. New York: United Nations.

United Nations. 2015d. *Secretary-General Remarks at Wreath-Laying Ceremony for International Day of United Nations Peacekeepers*, May 29. New York: United Nations.

United Nations. 2015e. *Report of the Secretary-General on the Threat of Terrorists Benefiting from Transnational Organized Crime*, May 21. New York: United Nations.

United Nations. 2016a. *United Nations Security Council Resolution 2295*. New York: United Nations.

United Nations. 2016b. *UN Secretary-General's Remarks at General Assembly Presentation of the Plan of Action to Prevent Violent Extremism [As Delivered]*. New York: United Nations.

United Nations. 2016c. UN Counter-Terrorism Centre. United Nations. Accessed 11 Jan 2016. http://www.un.org/en/terrorism/ctitf/uncct/.

United Nations. 2017a. (4a) Fatalities by Mission, Year and Incident Type up to 30 November 2017. United Nations. Accessed 20 Dec 2017. https://peacekeeping.un.org/sites/default/files/statsbymissionyearincident-type_4a_2.pdf.

United Nations. 2017b. *Protection of Civilians: Building the Foundation for Peace, Security and Human Rights in Somalia*. Mogadishu and Geneva: UN Assistance Mission in Somalia and Office of the United Nations High Commissioner for Human Rights.

United States Department of the Army. 2014. *Joint Publication 3–26: Counterterrorism*. Washington, DC: U.S. Army. Accessed 28 Feb 2017. http://www.dtic.mil/doctrine/new_pubs/jp3_26.pdf.

Open Access This chapter is licensed under the terms of the Creative Commons Attribution 4.0 International License (http://creativecommons.org/licenses/by/4.0/), which permits use, sharing, adaptation, distribution and reproduction in any medium or format, as long as you give appropriate credit to the original author(s) and the source, provide a link to the Creative Commons license and indicate if changes were made.

The images or other third party material in this chapter are included in the chapter's Creative Commons license, unless indicated otherwise in a credit line to the material. If material is not included in the chapter's Creative Commons license and your intended use is not permitted by statutory regulation or exceeds the permitted use, you will need to obtain permission directly from the copyright holder.

Check for updates

CHAPTER 9

Peace Operations and Organised Crime: Still Foggy?

Arthur Boutellis and Stephanie Tiélès

Introduction

Two and a half years after the initial deployment of the United Nations Multidimensional Integrated Stabilization Mission in Mali (MINUSMA), the UN Secretary-General noted in his report to the Security Council that "while positive steps were taken towards the implementation of the peace agreement by the signatory parties, there was an increase in the number and geographical spread of activities by extremist and terrorist groups and organized crime networks" and that "MINUSMA convoys remained the primary target of extremist and terrorist groups and transnational drug traffickers on the main supply routes" (UN 2015a). The Council, when it first authorised MINUSMA in June 2013, had foreseen the "serious threats posed by transnational organized crime in the Sahel region, and its increasing links, in some cases, with terrorism" and

A. Boutellis (✉)
International Peace Institute (IPI), New York, NY, USA

S. Tiélès
Central Directorate of Judicial Police (International Relations Division), Nanterre France

© The Author(s) 2019

C. de Coning and M. Peter (eds.), *United Nations Peace Operations in a Changing Global Order*,
https://doi.org/10.1007/978-3-319-99106-1_9

underscored "the urgent need to address these issues." Yet, it did not give any specific tasks or guidance to the UN stabilisation mission in terms of organised crime and has instead encouraged "Member States of the Sahel region to improve coordination to combat recurrent threats in the Sahel, including terrorism, together with transnational organized crime and other illicit activities such as drug trafficking" (UN 2015b) or welcomed initiatives and "efforts of the Group of Five for the Sahel (G5) … to strengthen regional security cooperation …. and to establish a new counterterrorist centre" (UN 2016).

This reflects the increasing disconnect between the growing recognition by the UN system and Member States over the past decade that organised crime (OC) is a problem that cannot be ignored where the UN has peace operations on the ground. It also reflects the fact that the UN system and Member States are still uncertain about how to approach a phenomenon that lacks a precise definition[1] and, more importantly, refers to various criminal activities or threats understood differently based on contexts and perceptions. Although organised crime and trafficking are now considered a threat to security and stability in post-conflict countries in their own right, they also continue to be most often considered in their relation to terrorism and violent extremism (UN 2015c), which is not always helpful for developing realistic peace operations approaches to OC.

In recent years, the Sahel region witnessed the proliferation of international forces and regional ones[2] resulting in a securitisation of approaches when a number of experts called for more nuanced human security-based approaches to addressing the organised crime-terrorism threat: "States and regional organizations [need] to pause and reexamine their counterterrorism and counterinsurgency measures, which by militarizing the region are exacerbating the problems and fail to address the fundamental issues that affect the region" (Kfir 2016). There is also a

[1]The 2000 UN Convention against Transnational Organized Crime defines OC as *"a structured group of three or more persons, existing for a period of time and acting in concert with the aim of committing one of more serious crimes or offenses established in accordance with this Convention, in order to obtain, directly or indirectly, a financial or other material benefit."*

[2]International forces include the French counterterrorism force Barkhane and the UN mission MINUSMA and regional ones include the joint force of the Group of Five for the Sahel (G5 Sahel) which was just established and includes an explicit mandate to combat transational crime in addition to terrorism.

growing body of literature suggesting that OC may not always be the enemy of peace operations, and can indeed benefit from the minimal level of stability and both licit and illicit business opportunities provided by the presence of peacekeepers—themselves not immune—and/or sanctions regimes and embargoes.

Nowadays, almost three-quarter of UN peace operations—ranging from small political missions without armed components in Guinea Bissau, Afghanistan, Libya, Somalia, and most recently Colombia (including unarmed military observers) to large multidimensional peacekeeping operations like the ones in Haiti, Kosovo, the Democratic republic of Congo (DRC), the Central African Republic and Mali—operate in environments that are considered significantly affected by organised crime (OC). It was, however, only in 2010 that the UN Security Council invited the Secretary-General to consider the threats posed by organised crime in mission planning and reporting (UN 2010). Yet, of current UN peace operations, less than half have explicit mandates related to organised crime, fewer have mandates to tackle criminal groups spoilers directly, and those that do are still not well-prepared to face this threat in terms of policy, doctrine, strategic and operational guidance, and capacities (Kemp et al. 2013).

This chapter first looks back at how and why organised crime has increasingly become recognised as a threat to international peace and security and as a UN peace operations problem. It then reviews the dominant law enforcement and capacity-building approaches adopted so far for UN peace operations to deal with organised crime and their limits. It finally explores the way forward for how the UN could deal more realistically and effectively with transnational organised crime in the future. While taking a historical approach, the chapter focuses particularly on the Mali/Sahel example as the latest laboratory for (re-)defining the relationship between UN peace operations and organised crime.

The Growing Recognition of Organised Crime as a Strategic Threat

A number of studies and United Nations reports have over the past two decades demonstrated how armed groups—including terrorist groups—resort to illicit trafficking to finance their activities, and how organised crime can be an important driver of conflict and instability in some post-conflict and fragile states, particularly when it penetrates and/

or co-opts States institutions at the local and national levels. The 2004 *Report of the High-level Panel on Threats, Challenges and Change* recognised transnational organised crime as one of the six clusters of threats with which the world must be concerned now and in the decades ahead, because it facilitates many of the most serious threats to international peace and security. The Panel's recommendation at the time, however, solely focused on the need for better international regulatory frameworks and building State capacity in the area of the rule of law. The 2011 *World Development Report* also emphasised that the penetration by organised crime of the already vulnerable socio-political, judicial, and security structures in developing countries can be a serious obstacle to peacebuilding and economic development, and made the case for longer-term approaches to building effective state institutions.

The United Nations initially approached criminal activity and trafficking issues in relation to conflict situations already on the Security Council's agenda, particularly where UN peace operations were deployed in the Balkans, Central America, the DRC, Haiti, Somali, and West Africa. And while the link between drug trafficking and terrorism contributed to moving the issue up the Council's agenda in the 2000s, particularly in the context of Afghanistan, the Council later started considering whether drug trafficking and organised crime could constitute in themselves a threat to international peace and security. This was illustrated by a series of thematic debates, presidential statements and resolutions since 2009, and in December 2015, the Council added human trafficking to the list of criminal activities whose impact on conflict it has considered. The Council also "moved furthest, fastest, where the criminal activity in question threatened permanent members' interests, the country was already on the Council's agenda, and no state with influence in the Council had a particular reason to limit such experimentation" (Cockayne 2015).

These developments culminated with the 24 February 2010 Security Council Presidential Statement (PRST) noting the "serious threats" posed by drug trafficking and transnational organised crime and the financing of terrorism to international security, and noted that these "may threaten the security of countries on its agenda" and expressed its intention to "consider such threats, as appropriate." In the same statement, the Council also invited the Secretary-General "to consider these threats as a factor in conflict prevention strategies, conflict analysis, integrated missions' assessment and planning and to consider including in his reports, as appropriate, analysis on the role played by these threats in situations on its agenda" (UN 2010).

This was the basis for the establishment a year later of an internal UN System Task Force on Transnational Organized Crime and Drug Trafficking, co-led by the UN Office on Drugs and Crime (UNODC) and the UN's Department of Political Affairs (DPA) to develop an effective and comprehensive approach to the challenge of transnational organised crime (TOC) and drug trafficking and coordinate UN actions in these areas, primarily through assistance to states. While this task force has had a slow start and produced little guidance, it may have contributed to raising the profile of organised crime (traditionally a UNODC 'turf') more broadly within the organisation, as illustrated by the recent development of a UN "Transnational Organized Crime and Security Sector Reform" guidance note by the UN Inter-Agency Security Sector Reform Task Force. In 2013 the Secretary-General's Policy Committee requested the Task Force (in Decision 2013/3) to "share experiences across regions on what it means in practice to adopt 'comprehensive UN approaches' to drugs and crime, including lessons learned/good practices notes on thematic issues such as crime-sensitive … peacebuilding, and conflict prevention policies," and to "produce a guidance note on how to include issues related to drug trafficking and organized crime in conflict analysis and integrated assessment processes" but at the time of the writing of this chapter, the guidance note had still not been produced.

Persistent Hesitancy on How to Approach Organised Crime in UN Peace Operations

Organised crime is present in almost three quarter of the countries where the Security Council has authorised the deployment of UN peace operations—ranging from small political missions without uniformed components to large multidimensional peacekeeping operations. OC does, moreover, present a threat, sometimes direct (in terms of safety and security of UN personnel as in the case of Mali); but most of the time indirect, in that it hampers the implementation of the mandate and bolsters the spoiling capacity of certain groups in places like Guinea Bissau, Afghanistan, Libya, Somalia, Haiti, Kosovo, the DRC, etc. But despite the above-mentioned 2010 PRST, the Security Council has so far been hesitant to give specific mandates to its peace operations, with less than half of the resolutions mandating these operations to make reference to organised crime and fewer mandating UN operations to tackle criminal groups spoilers directly (Kemp et al. 2013).

While a number of reasons explain the Council's hesitation, it has led to a "chicken and egg" situation. The lack of a clear mandate (most references to organised crime are in the preamble of Council resolutions rather than in operative paragraphs) limits the ability of UN operations to focus and devote resources to analysing and possibly starting to address organised crime beyond limited capacity building efforts (in security sector, rule of law reform, and border management). And, in turn, it limits their ability to shed light on the issue and its far-reaching implications when reporting to the Council. That said, the lack of specific reference to organised crime in the mandate did not stop past leaderships from at certain times being proactive in the UN missions in Kosovo (UNMIK) and Timor-Leste (UNTAET)—notably under rare so-called "executive" mandates which have not been reiterated since—or Haiti (MINUSTAH, see below). Conversely, despite having a specific crime fighting mandate, the mission in Guinea Bissau (UNIOGBIS) has had little success in implementing it in part due to the lack of political will from the successive host governments and the limited leverage and capacities of the small UN political mission. The latest Security Council resolution 2343 (2017) on Guinea Bissau nonetheless reemphasised the issue of organised crime and the need to support the West Africa Coastal Initiative (WACI)—a regional programme co-led by UNODC, DPA/UN Office for West Africa and the Sahel (UNOWAS), the UN Department of Peacekeeping Operations (DPKO) and INTERPOL.

Generally, UN peace operations have been largely "flying blind" when it comes to transnational organised crime, particularly the UN Special Political Missions (SPMs) with the least resources and presence on the ground. A particular limitation has been that (host country) consent-based peace operations have not been mandated to "address the nexus between organized crime and national political or power dynamics, which increasingly constitute the driving force behind instability in various regions" (Cockayne and Kavanagh 2011). But while organised crime is obviously a challenge that goes far beyond the mandate and lifetime of a peace operation, the failure to look into the problem at an early stage arguably risks making it even more difficult to deal with later when it has further infiltrated the very government and state institutions that the UN seeks to strengthen. As Mats Berdal notes, many post conflict settings are characterised by the "ability of organized crime to take root and flourish in periods of transition from war to peace, to develop symbiotic relationships with local political elites and strengthen ties to transnational criminal networks" (Berdal 2009, p. 62). A recent review of the literature commissioned by the UK government's Stabilisation Unit indeed concluded to an emerging consensus among scholars that in conflict and post-conflict settings political and criminal actors are not necessarily adversarial, but may in fact collaborate and even merge (Scheye 2015, pp. 3–7). The traditional peace operations distinction between political and criminal actors would therefore be largely misleading.

Some of the more innovative UN approaches to organised crime may have come from the DPA regional offices, particularly the UN Office for West Africa (UNOWA)—recently renamed UN Office for West Africa and the Sahel (UNOWAS)—which has helped raise awareness on the threat represented by organised crime and drug trafficking in West Africa, including through its June 2011 reporting to the Security Council that the "corrupting effects [which] have further weakened already fragile State institutions and may finance armed or terrorist groups operating across West Africa and the Sahel." The West Africa Coastal Initiative (WACI) has also been praised for its regional approach combining a political level (with a High-Level Policy Committee chaired by the UNOWA head)—to encourage the political will of regional heads of states—and an operational level consisting of building Transnational Crime Units (TCUs) in Sierra Leone, Liberia, Côte d'Ivoire, Guinea-Bissau, and Guinea.

Initially launched in 2009 to support the implementation of the Economic Community of West African States' *Action Plan to Address the Growing Problem of Illicit Drug Trafficking, Organized Crime and Drug Abuse in West Africa*, the WACI was extended until 2017 with a possible enlargement to Benin and Togo. WACI contributed to enhancing both operational law enforcement capacities and inter-agency cooperation at the national level and international coordination by strengthening intelligence-based investigations. Since 2014, the first fully operational TCUs in Liberia, Sierra Leone and Guinea Bissau carried out joint operations and have been using INTERPOL tools and services. Notably, these TCUs continued operating during the 2014/2015 Ebola outbreak with UNODC's operational and logistical support. The strength of the model, which is its national ownership and empowerment, has, however, also become a challenge where host states are less supportive and even resistant of international involvement in some cases. Another major concern has been the vetting of TCUs personnel and the risk that they may not be immune from corruption by powerful criminal networks. The sustainability of such an onerous project is also at risk of a funding gap, which may be the result of donors refocusing their efforts on emerging threats on terrorism, violent extremism, and illegal migrations from the region.

Despite this growing recognition that criminal groups can act as a spoiler to peace processes and represent a strategic threat to the successful implementation of a mission's mandate and of the fact that peace operations could play a role in managing or disrupting organised crime, the question of whether peace operations are the right instrument to deal with organised crime at the operational level, and if so how they should deal with the problem, remains largely unanswered since the first major publication on peace operations and organised crime (Cockayne and Lupel 2011). The lack of UN success stories and so-called "best practices" in this specific area has also surely played a part. While some lessons could have been identified from earlier crime-fighting European missions such as EU Police Mission in Bosnia Herzegovina (2003) or the EU Rule of Law Mission in Kosovo, these contexts are very different from the ones UN missions now face on the African continent.

Amid this confusion and competing priorities, the UN has so far not invested in developing system-wide policy and strategic guidance that factors in organised crime. The most recent UN peacekeeping strategic documents, the 2008 Capstone Doctrine—which introduced the concept "robust peacekeeping" as a recognition that force may be used at the tactical level against spoilers in some cases—and the 2009 New Horizon—announcing that the UN is "working to identify essential early tasks as the first step to a coherent post-conflict stabilization strategy"—only make few passing references to organised crime, and have yet to result in a UN stabilisation doctrine which would factor in the destabilisation impact of such threats. Similarly, while the DPA 2016–2019 Strategic Plan mentioned TOC upfront alongside "violent extremism" as a major issue, no concrete policy responses are mentioned beyond the need for strengthening partnerships within the organisation to address such transnational and cross-cutting challenges.

The best illustration of such disconnect between the diagnosis and the prescription is the United Nations Multidimensional Integrated Stabilization Mission in Mali (MINUSMA). The issue of peace operations and organised crime has arguably never before been as relevant as in the Mali/Sahel context, with the 2012 Mali crisis illustrating the potentially destabilising impact of criminal networks in the region, not only because illegal trafficking became the dominant economy of Northern Mali overtime and contributed to financing activities of armed groups, but also because the increasing profits from drug trafficking and kidnapping-for-ransom activities led to the corroding of State institutions eventually leading to the collapse of the Malian State (Lacher 2012). Yet, despite broad recognition among member states and UN Secretariat that organised crime is a problem in Mali, the mandate given to MINUSMA was not different from that of other UN missions. Three years into the mission, Resolution 2295 of June 2016 (UN 2016), although it authorised a more "proactive and robust posture" in an attempt to prevent asymmetric attacks, did not give any specific instructions to MINUSMA as to what to do about trafficking in weapons, drugs and humans, which at least in some cases are linked to terrorist networks. With most of the mission's military assets dedicated to self-protection, and no obvious solution to trafficking in areas beyond the government's control, organised crime easily falls down the agenda.

The Limitations of Consent-Based Peace Operations

Beyond the lack of mandate and strategic guidance, one must acknowledge the many risks and inherent limitations for peace operations to address the issue of organised crime effectively. First of all, this is because organised crime takes very different shapes and forms from one place to another and evolve over time to adapt to changing realities. UN peace operations, on the other hand, are deployed for a finite period of time which limits its ability to adapt and adopt effective longer-term strategies (that in many cases would imply the transformation of economic and power structures) against organised crime. This is rendered even more complex by the fact that the leadership of UN operations are faced with many competing tasks and priorities—for instance supporting the political process and the restoration of state authority—with urgent issues often prioritized over the important OC issues.

Haiti is a good example. Here, the UN Stabilization mission (MINUSTAH) carried out robust intelligence-led operations against gangs in 2006 and 2007 in support of the government, which have largely been successful in taming the challenge to stability posed by political violence and armed gangs. The UN mission later refocused its efforts away from enforcement towards the development of the capacities of the Haitian National Police but without addressing the underlying causes of organised crime and trafficking. As a result, while the UN may have been a strong deterrent for violence since, it has not been a deterrent for illicit activities and the UN risks now withdrawing MINUSTAH and leaving a country where organised crime has become further embedded in state institutions, including security forces that may be profiting from crime rather than fighting it.[3]

The fact that most UN peace operations (with the notable exception of regional offices) are geographically limited to one country is also a serious limitation to analysing organised crime and trafficking that profit from operating across borders and regions. A further concern has been the limited resources, tools, and expertise available to date to peacekeepers in terms of criminal intelligence and political economy analysis but also the lack of a legal framework for developing such "supranational" capacities. In many cases, the host government may not consent to the UN mission investigating criminal networks, which in many cases would lead to uncovering links—support, penetration, or co-optation—to both armed groups and the government itself, which would naturally strain relations with the host State. This may partly explain why until now the Security Council has preferred mandating independent Panels/Groups of Experts monitoring sanctions regime to look into issue of illegal arms and minerals trafficking. The recent resolution 2374 creating a sanctions regime in Mali targeting actors derailing the peace process actually lists organized crime and traffics as possible sources of financing for spoilers.[4]

Another recurrent challenge raised by both troop and police contributing countries (TCCs/PCCs) is the safety and security of the personnel in UN peace operations. Indeed, in most cases organised crime does not represent a direct threat to peacekeepers until peacekeepers either get involved, or attempt to expose, contain, or disrupt its illegal activities. While in some cases UN missions may have the ability to deal

[3] See Haiti case study in Kemp et al. (2013, p. 32).

[4] "supporting or financing individuals and entities … including through the proceeds from organized crime, including the production and trafficking of narcotic drugs and their precursors originating in or transiting through Mali, the trafficking in persons and the smuggling of migrants, the smuggling and trafficking of arms as well as the trafficking in cultural property" (UN 2017).

militarily with some spoilers (the local gangs in Haiti or armed groups in the eastern DRC), in other cases, "going on the offensive" against powerful organised crime and trafficking networks with links to armed groups would likely result in direct retaliations against the UN mission and personnel on the ground. Similarly, UN police starting to investigate organised crime—even in support of their national counterparts—could present potentially serious security concerns for UN personnel. Some may even themselves become involved or complicit of powerful OC and trafficking networks when UN operations still have no security clearance and/or counter-intelligence systems in place.

A Constrained Police Capacity-Building Approach

In the midst of this quasi absence of UN strategic guidance for peace operations on organised crime and in light of the challenges above, the UN Police Division has taken the lead in promoting a law enforcement capacity-building approach. Its February 2014 *DPKO/DFS Policy on United Nations Police in Peacekeeping Operations and Special Political Missions* states that "addressing organized crime and strengthening the rule of law have taken on greater importance in most peacekeeping operations and special political missions and is an important entry point for engaging with national authorities to take action." Activities suggested include to "support the planning and implementation of host State and regional operational and analytical capacity-building activities" in partnership with UNODC, the United Nations Development Programme (UNDP), INTERPOL and other relevant actors, as well as "anti-corruption initiatives; assessments and engagement with the public [...] and strengthen the capacity of the criminal justice system" (UN Police 2014). The 2016 External Review of the UN Police Division confirmed this tendency by suggesting the better factoring of OC at headquarters in order to better support missions in the field in an exhaustive manner.

The Security Council endorsed this approach in November 2014 when "highlighting the important role that United Nations Police Components can play in building the capacity of host-State policing and other law enforcement institutions, as mandated, to address organized crime, particularly through support in the areas of border, immigration and maritime security and crime prevention, response and investigation." It however also encouraged information sharing between Special Representatives of the Secretary-General, DPKO including the Police

Division, DPA, Counter-Terrorism Committee Executive Directorate, UNODC, Counter-Terrorism Implementation Task Force and UNDP "within existing mandates and resources, when considering means to address, in a comprehensive and integrated manner, transnational organized crime, terrorism and violent extremism which can be conducive to terrorism" (UN 2014a), thereby emphasising the need for a UN system-wide approach.

The following month, the Council issued a resolution calling on "relevant entities of the UN and other relevant international and regional organizations to support the development and strengthening of the capacities of national and regional institutions to address terrorism benefitting from transnational organized crime, in particular law enforcement and counter-terrorism agencies" and reiterated that peace operations "may, if mandated by the Council, assist in capacity-building for host governments, as requested, to implement commitments under existing global and regional instruments and to address the illicit trafficking of weapons" (UN 2014b, paras. 16 and 18). While that same resolution reaffirmed the lead role of the UN in coordinating international efforts in combating "international peace and security caused by terrorists profiting from involvement in transnational organized crime," this continues to be a challenge in practice with many international actors—bilateral, regional, and international—often driving competing agendas through capacity building projects in support of national authorities.

One of the challenges will indeed be for UN peace operations to reconcile a fairly narrow law enforcement capacity-building police approach with the need for a UN system-wide approach to preventing and addressing organised crime—and its links to terrorism and violent extremism—that remains to be defined. In Mali for instance, the UN Police component played a leading role and developed unprecedented initiatives. It created a twenty-five people Serious and Organized Crime unit dedicated to supporting Malian authorities with counterterrorism and TOC training and equipping, including the newly developed Malian Judicial Division specialised in the fight against terrorism and transnational crime. The UN Police has been considering and appealing to PCCs for some years already for the deployment of readily formed specialised team. With the increasing consideration given recently to Serious and Organized Crime, the UN aims at fostering the recruitment of specialised teams of law enforcement practitioners in peace operations. The specific nature of such police work requires specific expertise and specialisation. The lack of international standards on how to tackle organised crime groups might, however, challenge the pressing need of supporting host state security forces when threatened by complex criminal organisations. In Mali, by dedicating specialised crime advisers covering a wide range of police technics against illegal activities, the United Nations Police increased its ability to provide an in-depth expertise in the complex fields of forensics, criminal intelligence and large scale investigation. The UN Police also established a MINUSMA Task Force on Counter-Terrorism and Organized Crime in Mali in mid-2014—which includes representatives from UNODC and a number of MINUSMA Sections, as well as UNDP. The Action Plan it designed, however, disregarded the linkage between security and development by focusing only on supporting the Malian law enforcement agencies, judiciary, and corrections sectors, and does not in itself constitute a UN system-wide strategy to organised crime in Mali.

A study by the international non-government organisation Transparency International (TI) submitted that "International involvement in defense operations that doesn't take corruption into account can exacerbate the problem, and security assistance can make a country less secure if it isn't accountable [...] In Mali, security assistance was focused on tactical training and equipping troops, but didn't address structural and institutional weaknesses like corruption" (TI 2015). Indeed, in addition to the need for the UN to adopt a more integrated approach to justice and security sector reform, any strategy to prevent and combat transnational organised crime should consider the fight against state corruption as a foremost concern to be first addressed at the macro level, before any action is taken at the operational level to strengthen the capacity of local law enforcement agencies. Short of this, the UN risks strengthening security and political institutions that are part of the problem rather than the solution because they are already corrupted by criminal groups. Meanwhile, the UN could do more at the micro/local level to mitigate factors bolstering OC and trafficking and to build local communities' resilience particularly where and when the state is absent.

Academic research advises refocusing security sector reform on the needs of individuals and communities in order to avoid building the capacity of government structures which can inadvertently supports officials connected to crime (Jesperson 2016). Furthermore, such an approach would reinforce the confidence of the local population in their national institutions and deter them from relying on alternatives provided by criminal or armed groups. In cases where the host country authorities may be part of the problem or lack political will, some research has also suggested to better acknowledge the penetration of organised crime by encouraging development actors to make smarter use of a range of tools to determine when to engage and where to prioritise efforts. A detailed assessment of interests and stakeholders would enable development actors to determine political obstacles to engagement (Kavanagh et al. 2013). Nevertheless, the high turnover in mission leadership and lack of longer term strategies (partly due to mandates that are renewed every year) also affects the ability of the mission to make a difference.

The fairly narrow police capacity building and law enforcement approach to organised crime adopted so far, however, seems to be more of a default position resulting from both the complexity of the issue at stake and the lack of clarity and strategic guidance from Member States and the UN Secretariat on what the role and approach of peace operations could and should be beyond policing. The deployment of a UN stabilisation mission in Mali with unprecedented analytical and uniformed capacities has brought the issue of organised crime back on the radar of UN peace operations and made MINUSMA a new laboratory. Already in an October 2013 report, the UN Secretary-General mentioned "the fight against corruption and organized crime" as an equally important governance challenge to the effective functioning of the Malian state, alongside security sector reforms, national dialogue, and reconciliation and justice (UN 2013, para. 82). So if the UN were serious about organised crime, what could/would it do?

The Way Forward: A More Strategic and Holistic Approach to Organised Crime in Peace Operations?

First and foremost, the UN needs to develop better information collection and analysis capacities when it comes to organised crime. In Mali, the NATO-standard All Sources Information Fusion Unit (ASIFU) brought unprecedented analytical capabilities to the UN mission but information collection itself was not well integrated into the mission's existing information and intelligence infrastructure.[5] Similarly, the military

[5] In the course of 2017, ASIFU was merged with the Military Intelligence Unit (U2) in an attempt to better integrate the mission's various information collection and analysis capacities.

intelligence subscribes to a different methodology and purpose that can be incompatible with the kind of criminal intelligence and political economy analysis required for analysing criminal networks and their impact and better understand the political, criminal, and terrorist nature of diverse armed groups. A more effective approach may be to develop mission-wide OC analytical capacities so that various staff within the mission (political affairs/mediation, civil affairs, Joint Mission Analysis Center (JMAC), police, justice, Disarmament, Demobilization, and Reintegration (DDR), etc.) are able to detect, collect and analyse relevant information on an ongoing basis, in liaison with regional UN offices—such as UNOWAS and UNODC in the case of MINUSMA—and the Panel of Experts when they exist, to factor in cross-border regional issues. Such information should then be centralised—Ideally within the JMAC, which combines civilian, police and military personnel—to produce forward-looking strategic analysis identifying opportunities and suggesting both strategic and operational responses to prevent, avert, or mitigate threats to mandate implementation for mission leadership. In April 2017, DPKO released a Peacekeeping Intelligence policy meant to address some of these systemic challenges and is envisaging creating Criminal Intelligence Unit (CIU) comprised of specialised intelligence police officers within missions, but member states remain divided on even the use of the term intelligence.

A number of assessment tools already exists—such as the one used by UNODC-DPA for regional TOC Threat Assessment (UNODC 2010) and *Spotting the Spoilers: A Guide to Analyzing Organized Crime in Fragile States* (Shaw and Kemp 2012)—that can be used to train and sensitise relevant mission staff. Early literature on peace operations and OC suggested that peacekeeping missions should adopt a "spoiler management" approach to avoid excluding certain actors or reverting to a law enforcement approach by labelling them as criminal. Instead, one ought to focus on the mission's attention on "managing" spoiling behaviour and activities rather than the impossible task of fighting OC in general (Cockayne and Lupel 2011). The problem of course is that, often, OC may not produce violence in the short term—and may even contribute to stability. But in the medium to longer run, however, organised crime can effectively undermine the very objective of stability and the building of functioning state institutions.

In the first comprehensive review of UN peace operations since the 2000 "Brahimi report," the 2015 High Level Independent Panel on

Peace Operations (HIPPO) may have overlooked the issue of the impact of criminal agendas on the work of peace operations, but nonetheless made three recommendations that can be helpful in adopting crime-sensitive approaches in the future: First, it recommends to strengthen the underlying analysis towards designing better and more effective political strategies, mandate sequencing to allow for better informed strategic planning, and more "people-centric" operations. The UN Secretary-General subsequently established a small centralised analysis and planning capacity in his office, which could play an important role on mainstreaming organised crime into analysis and planning before preparing strategic considerations and options for possible UN responses (UN 2015d). For example, the presence of violent criminal actors may suggest the need for a uniformed component with more qualified police over military. Second, the HIPPO recommends a sequencing approach that could, for instance, allow a better "tailoring" of a mission as the UN develops a better understanding of the impact of organised crime but also of the political will and capacities of the host government—which in some cases may be part of the problem—with whom the UN could establish "Compacts."[6] Third, it recommends a "people-centric" approaches to peace operations, in that it could help adopt measures to address and prevent OC that risk alienating communities—including by depriving them of economic opportunities and hurting their livelihood—and instead help peace operations strengthen resiliency (UN 2015e).

Amid lots of attention on the OC issue in Mali and the Sahel, the HIPPO report also recognised that transnational organised crime "is a mission-wide concern and a strategic risk to sustaining peace" but its only recommendations was that the UN acquire police expertise in this area "when requested and in partnership with others to support national police capacity" (UN 2015e, para. 160).

Beyond technical fixes, research points to a more fundamental shift in addressing organised crime in fragile state by moving away from the traditional dominance of security and law enforcement approaches—so far

[6]The idea of "Compacts" was put forward by the 2015 HIPPO Report suggesting that UN "mission leadership should be empowered and supported to assess- through broad consultations with national actors, the UN Country Team and other international actors as required—the context and the most appropriate package of measures to help sustain peace, to be reviewed together with mandate renewal. This package should form the basis of a compact between the UN and the host government" (UN 2015e, para. 146).

used by the UN—to a greater role for development actors and partnerships. Instead of solely reforming the security sector, capacity building programmes should involve more civil society to monitor the practices of the security sector, and focus more on citizen security rather than state security (Jesperson 2016). The development response to drug trafficking in West Africa studied by the US Agency for International Development (Dininio 2015), has tabled suggestions in that sense for how development actors can better assess when and where to provide support in countries where trafficking is prevalent. USAID suggests that development programmes should include adequate flexibility to be able to adapt to emerging threats by closing activities, shifting locations, or introducing complementary programming activities especially in areas where government counterparts are identified as complicit. This flexibility would require the UN missions to undertake a continuous and meaningful analysis of the impact of organised crime and less bureaucratic rules to have a nimble ability to support accordingly.

Some existing peace operations activities could, however, benefit from adapting some of the "traditional" UN peace operations tools. For instance, James Cockayne (2013) has suggested the strengthening of mediation to deal with criminal agendas and armed groups involved in illicit activities, which if ignored could spoil peace processes. In Mali for instance, the parallel "business deals" between politico-military leaders and businessmen at the head of armed groups seen in late 2015, taking place outside the formal international mediation process, carry the risk of the reestablishment of a militarised political-economic system that was the source of much of the violence in the first place in northern Mali (International Crisis Group 2015). But conversely, if such deals come in support of a national peace process—as seems to have been the case in November 2017—they could also contribute to stability. DDR and Community Violence Reduction (CVR) programmes could also be used in innovative ways to provide at least short-term alternatives to illicit economies. Indeed, while UN peace operations cannot transform the political economy of a country, incentive-based, more people-centric, and non-repressive approaches are essential complements to the law enforcement capacity building approaches described above.

Recent research by the United Nations University (UNU) suggests peace operations should adopt a more holistic "Crime-Proofing Peace-Making" approach. It gives practical but ambitious pointers on what the UN could do to protect electoral processes from penetration by criminal financiers, how it could tailor the use of sanctions to address crime-politics connections and avoid unintended consequences, make use of strategic communications to disrupt and degrade criminal legitimacy, and use gender smart approaches (Bosetti et al. 2016). Naturally, the issue of OC goes beyond the mandate, capacities, and time span of peace operations, and require better Member State cooperation as well as longer-term and system-wide approaches both within the UN (including the UN development system) and beyond (INTERPOL, International Financial Institutions, etc.).

Some have, however, also highlighted the limitations of current State-based bilateral and multilateral law enforcement approaches and of the tools to fight transnational and multidimensional networks. Notably, the *Global Initiative Against Transnational Organized Crime* initiated in 2011, which brings together senior law enforcement officials, representatives of multilateral organisations, development practitioners, and policy-makers in a "network to counter networks," has been calling for a more strategic and proactive global approach to counter transnational crime and trafficking (The Global Initiative 2011). UN operations, in the relatively short time they are deployed, could benefit from closer collaboration with such networks of experts. Whenever faced with a new issue, the tendency of the UN has too often been to expand the bureaucracy by creating new specialised units and posts when sometimes it may be best to partner with others or bring temporary thematic (political economy, criminal intelligence etc.) and region/country-specific (with necessary language skills) expertise on board for shorter periods of time.

Conclusion

In conclusion, despite the recognition by the UN system and Member States that organised crime is a threat to peace and stability, particularly when in conjunction with terrorism and violent extremism, there is still much uncertainty about how to address it, and even more uncertainty about what UN peace operations could and should do about it. The field of peace operations and organised crime remains relatively new, with literature on the issue dating less than a decade. Moreover, the UN started officially considering the threats posed by organised crime in mission planning and reporting on it only in 2010. And the issue has become front and centre, with almost three quarters of UN peace operations now operating in environments significantly affected by organised crime, particularly in the West Africa and Sahel contexts.

Much of the debate until now, however, has remained at the conceptual level around the fact that OC could represent a strategic threat to the successful implementation of a mission's mandate, and little has been experimented at the operational level on how a peace operation could practically deal with the problem. Yet, the story of UN peace operations is one of trial and error at the field level leading to lessons that eventually make it into policy through a bottom-up approach rather than the reverse. In that sense, recent experiments with the regional WACI project, a specialised Serious and Organized Crime police unit in MINUSMA, and the increasing acceptation of the need for UN missions to collect and analyse 'intelligence' (including criminal intelligence) are useful developments that will generate further lessons. Much can also be achieved through adapting some of the existing UN tools (such as mediation and DDR but also assessments, elections, strategic communication etc.) and generate greater coherence between missions, UN Country Teams, Regional Offices, UNDP, and UNODC, to ensure that the mission's efforts are part of a longer-term strategy.

Such developments at the operational level however need to be accompanied by a broader strategic thinking on when and where to engage, based on a thorough analysis of opportunities and risks that should factor in the political economy of the country, corruption of state institutions, and the political will of the host government (or lack thereof) so that the mission's efforts do not become part of the problem rather than of the solution. UN peace operations also need to become more people-centric and focus more on prevention—rather that the elusive goal of countering OC—by mitigating factors bolstering trafficking and facilitating the strengthening of communities' resiliency through partnerships with UN development actors and international and local non-governmental organisations. This chapter does not suggest that every mission deployed in an environment significantly affected by organised crime should make it one of the mission's top priority, and it certainly does not suggest that UN peace operations can tackle the issue on their own. However, whether and what to do about it, and whom to partner with in this endeavour, should be a deliberate decision based on an informed analysis.

References

Berdal, Mats. 2009. *Building Peace After War*. London: Routledge.

Bosetti, Louise, James Cockayne, and John de Boer. 2016. Crime-Proofing Conflict Prevention, Management, and Peacebuilding: A Review of Emerging Good Practice. Occasional Paper 6, United Nations University Centre for Policy Research, Tokyo.

Cockayne, James, and Adam Lupel. 2011. *Peace Operations and Organized Crime: Enemies or Allies?* London: Routledge.

Cockayne, James, and Camino Kavanagh. 2011. Flying Blind? Political Mission Responses to Transnational Threats. *Review of Political Missions 2010*. New York: Center for International Cooperation.

Cockayne, James. 2013. *Strengthening Mediation to Deal with Criminal Agendas*. Geneva: Center for Humanitarian Dialogue.

Cockayne, James. 2015. Confronting Organized Crime and Piracy. In *The UN Security Council in the 21st Century*, ed. Sebastian von Einsiedel, David M. Malone, and Brunos S. Ugarte. New York: Lynne Rienner.

Dininio, Phyllis. 2015. *Organized Crime, Violent Conflict and Fragile Situations Assessing Relationships Through a Review of USAID Programs*. Arlington: Management Systems International.

International Crisis Group. 2015. *Mali: Peace from Below?* Africa no. 115, December 14, International Crisis Group, Dakar and Brussels.

Jesperson, Sasha. 2016. *Rethinking the Security-Development Nexus: Organised Crime in Post-conflict States*. Routledge Studies in Conflict, Security and Development.

Kavanagh, Camino, Kwesi Aning, Vanda Felbab-Brown, James Cockayne, Enrique Desmond Arias, Charles Goredema, Sampson B. Kwarkye, John Pokoo, and Summer Walker. 2013. *Getting Smart and Scaling Up: Responding to the Impact of Organized Crime on Governance in Developing Countries*. New York: Center on International Cooperation.

Kemp, Walter, Mark Shaw, and Arthur Boutellis. 2013. *The Elephant in the Room: How Can Peace Operations Deal with Organized Crime?* New York: International Peace Institute.

Kfir, Isaac. 2016. *Organised Criminal-Terrorist Groups in the Sahel: Why a Counterterrorism/Counterinsurgency-Only Approach Ignores the Roots of the Problem*. Institute for National Security and Counter-terrorism.

Lacher, Wolfram. 2012. *Organized Crime and Conflict in the Sahel-Sahara Region*. Washington, DC: Carnegie Endowment for International Peace.

Scheye, Eric. 2015. *Organised Crime in Stabilisation Contexts*. London: UK Stabilisation Unit.

Shaw, Mark, and Walter Kemp. 2012. *Spotting the Spoilers: A Guide to Analyzing Organized Crime in Fragile States*. New York: International Peace Institute.

The Global Initiative. 2011. *The Global Initiative Against Transnational Organized Crime.*

Transparency International. 2015. Tackle Instability and Terrorism by Fighting Corruption, February 4. https://www.transparency.org/news/feature/tackle_instability_and_terrorism_by_fighting_corruption. Accessed 13 Nov 2017.

UN. 2010. *Statement by the President of the Security Council.* S/PRST/2010/4. New York: United Nations.

UN. 2013. *Report of the Secretary-General on the Situation in Mali.* S/2013/582. New York: United Nations.

UN. 2014a. *Security Council Resolution 2185.* New York: United Nations.

UN. 2014b. *Security Council Resolution 2195.* New York: United Nations.

UN. 2015a. *Report of the Secretary-General on the Situation in Mali.* S/2015/1030. New York: United Nations.

UN. 2015b. *Security Council Resolution 2227.* New York: United Nations.

UN. 2015c. *Report of the Secretary-General on the Threat of Terrorists Benefiting from Transnational Organized Crime.* S/2015/366. New York: United Nations.

UN. 2015d. *Report of the Secretary-General on the Future of United Nations Peace Operations: Implementation of the Recommendations of the High-Level Independent Panel on Peace Operations.* New York: United Nations.

UN. 2015e. *Report of the High-level Independent Panel on Peace Operations on Uniting our Strengths for Peace: Politics, Partnership and People.* New York: United Nations.

UN. 2016. *Security Council Resolution 2295.* New York: United Nations.

UN. 2017. *Security Council Resolution 2374.* New York: United Nations.

UN Police. 2014. *DPKO/DFS Policy on United Nations Police in Peacekeeping Operations and Special Political Missions.* New York: United Nations.

UNODC. 2010. *The Globalization of Crime - A Transnational Organized Crime Threat Assessment.* Vienna: United Nations Office on Drugs and Crime.

Open Access This chapter is licensed under the terms of the Creative Commons Attribution 4.0 International License (http://creativecommons.org/licenses/by/4.0/), which permits use, sharing, adaptation, distribution and reproduction in any medium or format, as long as you give appropriate credit to the original author(s) and the source, provide a link to the Creative Commons license and indicate if changes were made.

The images or other third party material in this chapter are included in the chapter's Creative Commons license, unless indicated otherwise in a credit line to the material. If material is not included in the chapter's Creative Commons license and your intended use is not permitted by statutory regulation or exceeds the permitted use, you will need to obtain permission directly from the copyright holder.

CHAPTER 10

UN Policing: The Security–Trust Challenge

Kari M. Osland

Introduction[1]

Despite few success stories (Osland 2014), international police reform is considered increasingly important in contemporary conflict resolution (UN 2014, 2015a, b, 2016a, b).[2] While the breakdown of law and order may trigger the deployment of a UN peace operation, it is often the (re-)establishment of the rule of law institutions, including policing, that indicates a mission is completed and allows for an exit.[3]

The more robust mandates in UN operations, such as in Mali, the Democratic Republic of Congo, the Central African Republic, and South Sudan, require the international police contribution to not only perform its "traditional" tasks, such as mentoring and training, but also

[1]This chapter was prepared as part of the Community-Based Policing and Post-Conflict Police Reform Project (ICT4COP), which has received funding from the European Union's Horizon 2020 research and innovation programme under grant agreement No. 653909.

[2]Also reflected in investments by the EU and the UN (Peake and Marenin 2008, p. 61; Devon 2016, p. 1).

[3]Exemplified in Timor-Leste, Sierra Leone, and Liberia (UN 2016b, pp. 4 and 9–10).

K. M. Osland (✉)
Norwegian Institute of International Affairs (NUPI), Oslo, Norway

© The Author(s) 2019

C. de Coning and M. Peter (eds.), *United Nations Peace Operations in a Changing Global Order*,
https://doi.org/10.1007/978-3-319-99106-1_10

to take on new tasks, such as protecting civilians, promoting reform, and providing operational support, in addition to an increased focus on developing host-state capacity in countering transnational organised crime, sexual and gender-based violence, and violent extremism (UN 2016b, p. 4). The fact that most UN missions operate amid on-going war and conflict, appears to have hardened the UN Police's (UNPOL) "shell." Today, Formed Police Units (FPU) constitute 66% of UNPOL. They do not respond to military threats as such, but well-trained FPUs are supposed to operate in high-risk environments and have become the main unit responsible for protection of civilians (UN Police 2017a; UN 2016c, p. 3; Sebastian 2015).[4]

However, the 2016 report on the "External Review of the Functions, Structure and Capacity of the UN Police Division" (henceforth the External UN Police Division Review) calls for a paradigm shift in UNPOL's operating model in order to have a better chance of achieving results (UN 2016a). This is partly based on an understanding that, while there has been a steady escalation of tasks to be performed by the police (UN 2000a, 2015a), this has not been matched by a change in the operating model of UNPOL, resulting in a large expectation-implementation gap (2016b, pp. 2 and 12).[5] For instance, while some of the tasks are short-term, such as the protection tasks, others focus more on the restoration of trust, requiring a transformed behaviour if not attitude, and thus asks for a long-term perspective. There seems to be a delicate balance between enforcing security on the one hand and establishing trust on the other. Is the UN set up to achieve both?

In this chapter, I start by looking closer at the role of the police in society with a particular focus on trust, before exploring the role of UNPOL, its history, and toolbox. I will then investigate principal reform initiatives in and doctrinal development on UN Policing during the last decades, before I analyse closer what I call the 'security–trust challenge'. I will end by reflecting on whether the UN is indeed able to both provide security and build trust.

[4]UNPOL homepage on FPU, see https://police.un.org/en/formed-police-units-fpus. See also UN (2016c, p. 3; Sebastian 2015).

[5]For more on the contextual-conceptual divide, see Chana (2002), Sedra (2010), and Osland (2014, p. 4).

The Role of the Police in Society

Most definitions on policing recognise the police as having a responsibility to prevent and detect crime, to keep public order, and to protect the people. The police can be used as a *tool* of power; it can also be perceived as a *projector* of power "with the ability to constrain freedom as well as protect it under its capacity as both a political and a social institution" (Devon 2016). As a projector of power, the police empower individuals and groups through its practices—intended and unintended. Police reform is, therefore, a very political endeavour, challenging the most sensitive sector of the state, namely its instrument of power (Osland 2014, p. 28).

The police are supposed to serve the people—as a police *service*—and at the same time, they are meant to protect the interests of the state—as a police *force* (i.e. service vs coercion). Mawby (2008) argues that police systems at the control-dominated end of the spectrum tend to be centralised nationally and have a military-like approach, hardly providing public services that address communities. In contrast, at the other end of the spectrum are community-oriented police (COP) systems, whose main function is to provide a service that addresses the wider needs of the community.[6] In this latter system, although maintaining order is important, crime is seen as symptomatic of wider social problems and the police service enjoys a high level of legitimacy. In the control-dominated system, the legitimacy of the police force fails to be recognised by the general population. In all types of systems, the police are part of the interface between state and society and constitute an important component of the social contract between the state and its people. In numerous authoritarian states, and in particular in countries experiencing war and conflict, there is no recognised contract between the state and the society, and the police are used by the ruling elite to protect its own interests, habitually violating international human rights. Whether the police are perceived as a projector of power or as a tool of power, and whether there is a recognised contract between state and society, is to a large extent a matter of trust between the people and their governors.

According to most research on trust between the police and the citizens, people's trust in the police is related to the legitimacy of police

[6]The concept of community-oriented policing is somewhat vaguely defined. For more, see Rosenbaum (1994), Brogden and Nijhar (2005), Reisig (2010). See also the EU2020-funded project, Community Based Policing and Post-Conflict Police Reform (ICT4COP).

actions and ultimately, to the effectiveness of the police (Lea and Young 1984; Lyons 2002; Sunshine and Tyler 2003); if the citizens view the police as legitimate—or trustworthy—cooperation with the police in ways that assist effectiveness is more likely (Goldsmith 2005, p. 444). However, trust in the police is ultimately linked to trust in government—these should be considered interdependent. In cases with strong indicators of social disorganisation and socio-economic inequality, public trust in the police tends to be lacking (Goldsmith 2005, p. 444). This is the case in most post-conflict societies, where the police have served the rulers and not the people, and where its practices in dealing with the people has not served the purpose of establishing trust, but rather fear (del Frate 1998; Mishler and Rose 1998).[7]

The UN defines "policing" as

> …a function of governance responsible for the prevention, detection and investigation of crime; the protection of persons and property; and the maintenance of public order and safety. Policing must be entrusted to civil servants who are members of police and other law enforcement agencies of national, regional or local governments, within a legal framework that is based on the rule of law. Police and law enforcement officials have the obligation to respect and protect human rights. (UN 2016b, pp. 5–6)

Further, in the same document, the UN Secretary-General states that the aim of UN police is to "…enhance international peace and security by supporting Member States in conflict, post-conflict and other crisis situations to realise effective, efficient, representative, responsive and accountable police services that serve and protect the population" (ibid.).

Per both quotes, the police's two key responsibilities seem to be trust and civilian *service*. One would maybe then assume that (re-)establishing *trust* in civilian police would be a key task for UNPOL. Nonetheless, the context in which the international police officers are to perform their duties is very often one characterised by fear and distrust between the people and its police—with longstanding histories of abuse and neglect by the police—and where parts of the country may still suffer from war. Since the international police forces most often are perceived as the

[7] I use the concept 'post-conflict' in this chapter, reflecting not only those countries where war has stopped, but also those where there has been a relapse of conflict in parts of the country and the UN has a policing presence.

prolonged arm of the state, given that their main role is to assist the national police, there is reason to believe that these forces are perceived with negative connotations by the people.

UNPOL: A Hardening Shell?

The first international civilian police *officer* was deployed from 1960 to 1964 to the UN Operation in the Congo (ONUC) (UN 2003a, p. 84).[8] In 1964, the first police *component* was deployed to the UN Peacekeeping Force in Cyprus (UNFICYP). Over the next 25 years, civilian police were used in UN peacekeeping operations to monitor and report on local police activities. This started to change following the deployment of police to Namibia in 1989, as part of the UN Transition Assistance Group (UNTAG). In 1995, the Centre for Human Rights in cooperation with the Department of Peacekeeping Operations (DPKO) Training Unit introduced the 'SMART' concept—an acronym describing the core of civilian police tasks in peace operations: supporting human rights and humanitarian assistance; monitoring the performance of the local law enforcement agencies, prisons, courts, and implementing agreements; advising the local police on humane effective law enforcement, according to the international standards laid down in the conventions, covenants, and treaties on human rights; reporting on situations and incidents; and training the local law enforcement in the best practice for policing and human rights (Hartz 2000, p. 31).

While civilian police officers continued to monitor, mentor and advise local police, they also started to assist in the development and restructuring of law-enforcement structures. In the cases of Kosovo and Timor-Leste, and more recently, to a limited degree, in the Central African Republic, they also acted as the authority for law enforcement.[9] In addition, in some missions there have been blurred lines between political actors, violent extremist groups, and transnational criminal networks, and the UN has been involved in strengthening host-state capacities to combat violent extremism, and transnational organised crime, as well as,

[8]From its first deployment in 1960 and for 45 years following, the UN police forces were termed CivPol (Civilian Police). In 2005, the name was changed to UN Police (UNPOL).

[9]EULEX, the EU's mission in Kosovo, also has executive policing authority under UNSC Resolution 1244 (UN 1999).

sexual and gender-based violence, for instance in Cote-d'Ivoire, Haiti, Mali and the Democratic Republic of Congo (UN 2016b, p. 5). Further, and as mentioned above, the UN plays an increasingly important role in protecting civilians (Sebastian 2015). Hence, there has been a steady increase, in the numbers of police officers, the complexity of police tasks, and in the number of operations where the police form an integrated part, reflecting the general growth in peace operation but also the relative importance of policing within these missions.

Furthermore, the United Nations Development Programme (UNDP) has an important advisory role in the planning and implementation of police reform around the world and has a more long-term focus compared to DPKO. Since 2012, UNDP is designated together with DPKO as the joint Global Focal Point on Police, Justice and Corrections Areas in the Rule of Law in Post-Conflict and Other Crisis Situations (GFP). Other key partners are the United Nations High Commissioner for Refugees, the United Nations Office on Drugs and Crime, the UN Office of the High Commissioner for Human Rights and the UN Women.

It is not only the mandates that have changed, but also the policing toolbox of the UN has transformed during the last decades. Today, UN police teams range in size from just a few officers to more than 3500. At the time of writing, there are 11,034 officers, of whom 10% are women, coming from 87 UN Member States and deployed in 16 out of 23 UN operations (UN 2017a, b). The main policing instruments of the UN are: Formed Police Units (FPUs), currently 66%, and individual police officers, currently 34%, including specialised police teams, contracted seconded police, and civilian experts. In addition, comes the Standing Police Capacity.

Individual Police Officers are normally police officers but can also be other law enforcement personnel of various ranks and experience assigned to serve with the UN on secondment by governments of Member States.[10] Individual Police Officers mentor and train national police officers; they provide specialisation in different types of investigations and in several countries, they help law enforcement agents to address transnational crime. In some cases, they develop community-oriented policing in refugee or internally displaced persons camps.

[10] As of November 2017, the five largest police contributing countries are (in decreasing order): Senegal, Rwanda, Egypt, Bangladesh and Jordan (UN Police 2017b).

Most police officers serving in UN peacekeeping operations are deployed as part of a Formed Police Unit.[11] These consist of approximately 140 police officers who are trained to operate in high-risk environments. The core responsibilities of FPUs are public order management, protection of UN personnel and facilities, and support to police operations requiring a concerted response (ibid.). The FPUs are normally more heavily equipped in contrast to individual UN police officers, who are unarmed (Hansen 2011, p. 2). The UN deployed its first *modern* FPU in 1999, to the UN Mission in Kosovo (UNMIK).[12] The numbers of FPUs has increased from 9 units in 2000 to 71 in 2016.[13]

The Standing Police Capacity is the rapid deployment unit of the UN, based in Brindisi, Italy. It has an approved operational capacity of 40 staff members and its core task is to provide technical assistance and start-up capacity to field missions, as well as in non-mission settings through the Global Focal Point arrangement (UN 2016b, p. 7). The Standing Police Capacity consists of people with specialised knowledge and leadership experience, and is to assist in the fulfilment of the strategic mission of the UN Police.

Increasingly, UN Member States have established specialised police teams that are deployed in peacekeeping operations. For instance, since 2010 Norway has a specialised police team on investigating sexual and gender-based violence (SGBV) assisting the UN mission in Haiti (Caparini and Osland 2016a, b). Furthermore, some UN Member States have other instruments available, such as the Spanish Guardia Civil, the French Gendarmerie, the Italian Carabinieri, the Portuguese National Republican Guard, and the Dutch Royal Marechaussee, all of which form part of the European Gendarmerie Force, established in 2006.[14] Several UN Member States also have a growing private industry offering policing and security services across the globe, including towards UN

[11] As of November 2017, FPUs are deployed in 7 missions. The FPU contributors include Bangladesh, Benin, Burkina Faso, Burundi, Cameroon, China, Djibouti, Egypt, Ghana, India, Indonesia, Jordan, Mauritania, Nepal, Nigeria, Pakistan, Republic of Congo, Rwanda, Senegal and Togo. See UN (2017a).

[12] The first FPU (from Ghana) was deployed as part of the UN Operation in the Congo (ONUC) from 1960 to 1964 and a similar unit was established in Bosnia and Herzegovina in 1998, called Multinational Specialised Unit (Hansen 2011, p. 1).

[13] UNPOL https://police.un.org/en/formed-police-units-fpus (accessed 21 April 2017).

[14] For more, see Treaty of Velsen (2007), Arcudi and Smith (2013).

peacekeeping operations. For instance, in the UK the private security industry offering such services overseas, is now valued at £1 billion (Ellison and Sinclair 2013, p. 3).

It seems like the shell of UNPOL has hardened. This is an expected development given the more insecure situations the UN faces. One would assume this is to promote the security of both the UNPOL itself and the people it is there to assist, but what impact can this have on the (re)-establishment of trust? Before going into that discussion, let us now turn to the different reform initiatives and doctrinal developments particularly relevant for UN Police.

Reform Initiatives and Doctrinal Development

The most important reform initiatives the last decades in the field of policing have come with the Brahimi Report (UN 2000a), the Secretary-General's two reports on UN Police (UN 2011, 2016b), the report of the High-Level Independent Panel on Peace Operations (HIPPO) (UN 2015a), the subsequent Secretary-General report (2015b), and the External UN Police Division Review (UN 2016a). In addition, as for doctrinal development, the UN Security Council (UNSC) Resolutions 2185 (UN 2014) and 2382 (2017c) as well as the Strategic Guidance Framework for International Police Peacekeeping (SGF) should be mentioned. These will be briefly explored in chronological order.

The 2000 Brahimi Report called for a doctrinal shift in the use of police and other rule of law elements to support a greater focus on reform and restructuring activities. Following the Brahimi Report, the General Assembly created the UN Standing Police Capacity, whose purpose was to initiate police components in new missions and assist such in existing missions.[15]

Given the growth in scale and scope for UN Police peacekeeping, the need for more strategic thinking was stressed by the UN Secretary-General in his first report on UN Police in 2011 (UN 2011). On 20 November 2014, the UNSC unanimously voted for Resolution 2185, the first ever dedicated to policing in peace operations (UN 2014). The discussion showed an overwhelming engagement where every member of the Security Council took the floor (Feller 2014). In this resolution,

[15] Operational in October 2007 with the UN Mission in Chad (MINURCAT).

the Security Council stressed the importance of international policing in peace operations and requested that the Secretary-General further promote professionalism, effectiveness, and system-wide coherence in the policing-related work of the UN, including through the development and implementation of standards and guidance through the SGF.

The work on the SGF, started in 2009 by the UN Police Division, has consisted of the elaboration of a set of policies, associated guidelines, and manuals that are to provide a cohesive and coherent framework for UN Police. With the SGF, effective as of February 2014, "…for the first time in the history of United Nations police peacekeeping, the mission of the United Nations police and what core functions and organizational structure should comprise police peacekeeping have been defined" (UN Police 2014).[16] In addition to an overarching policy, the SGF consists of four guidelines on police administration, police capacity building and development, police command, and police operations. Mainstreaming the UN's approach towards international policing should, needless to say, not be confused with applying the same blueprint for all missions.

While the HIPPO report in 2015 promoted the police components as one of the areas to improve sustainable peacebuilding, it also noted that "United Nations police officers are not usually trained to deliver police reform, and the United Nations model of short-term police deployments is supply-driven and unsuited for capacity development. A significant change in approach is needed" (UN 2015a, para. 162). It recommends that police strategies should be based on capacity assessment in the country, reflected in mission planning, staffing and recruitment, including specialised teams and long-term civilian experts. It also focuses on completing the SGF, consistent monitoring and evaluation of police development efforts, and an increased availability and effectiveness of FPU's (ibid., para. 54–56 and para. 161–168). On the FPU's, there are disturbing stories being told from several missions that many of these units cannot be used for policing purposes because they are too militarised in their approach, often coming from countries where regulations for the treatment of the general public are close to non-existent.[17]

[16]Earlier documents with a comparable function were the UN Civilian Police Principles and Guidelines (2000b), the UN Police Handbook (2005), and the UN Criminal Justice Standards for UN Police (2009).

[17]Interview May 2016 in New York with two Police Commissioners in ongoing UN missions in Africa.

An external review of the UN Police Division was recommended by both the HIPPO report and the subsequent Secretary-General implementation report, on how to improve UN police contributions. In January 2016, a seven-member independent team was assigned to conduct this review and in May, the External UN Police Division Review was delivered.[18] One of the challenges identified in the report, is that the current model relies on having a high number of Individual Police Officers deployed on a short-term rotation to fulfil a capacity- and institution-building mandate that they are not trained to perform and that is complex and long-term in nature (UN 2016a, para. 34a).

The need to strengthen the gender focus and the number of female police officers in UN peace operations is another challenge mentioned in the HIPPO report (UN 2015a, para. 165), in the 2015 Global Study on the implementation of UNSC Resolution 1325 (UN Women 2015), and in the 2015 review of the Peacebuilding Architecture (UN 2015c). Police officers are more efficient when the different needs, concerns and experiences of women and men are taken into account when assisting in rebuilding the police in post-conflict societies; it increases the overall trust in the police, and presents opportunities to promote gender equality by, for example, establishing more inclusive national police services (Osland 2017a, b). As of November 2017, there are 1081 or 10% female police officers deployed, hence, there is still a long way to go (UN 2017a).

In 2016, the UN Secretary-General's second report on policing was launched.[19] There, a vision for a "…people-centred, modern, agile, mobile and flexible, rights-based and norm-driven" UN police was presented, and 14 recommendations were put forward to realise that vision (UN 2016b, pp. 2–3). These recommendations were further emphasised with the UNSC Resolution 2382, adopted in November 2017. The resolution stressed the role of UN policing in peace operations throughout the conflict cycle. It further recognises that improved performance of UN policing can contribute to the success of exit strategies and to the protection of

[18]The Under-Secretary General of Peacekeeping Operations, Hervé Ladsous, appointed the team, consisting of Hilde Frafjord Johnson, Norway (co-chair); Abdallah Wafy, Niger (co-chair); Ahmad Alsayaydeh, Jordan; Benazir Ahmed, Bangladesh; Janine Rauch, South Africa; Serge Rumin, France; and Mark Kroeker, United States.

[19]This report was a response to the External Review (2016a) as well as to Security Council Resolution 2185 (UN 2014).

civilians, including in preventing and addressing sexual and gender-based violence. Also, it supports implementation of the SGF, the need to give clear, credible, achievable, appropriately resourced mandates for policing-related activities, and emphasise the need to ensure a UN system-wide approach to the rule of law, including through the Global Focal Point. It also urges police-contributing countries to ensure comprehensive training for deployed police and to substantially increase the numbers of women officers and their representation in leadership positions.

Through all of these reports and resolutions, much knowledge about challenges and best practices has been put on the table. However, there is still a large gap between this and what is being implemented.

Why Is It so Hard?

One of the main reasons why it is so difficult to succeed is simple: UN policing is an enormously challenging endeavour. It was never easy, but the increase in tasks to be carried out, combined with a system that is not set up to manage the new reality of tasks, mandates, and problems, only adds to the challenge.

If looking at what is being done in UN missions on policing, one might get the impression that the main purpose is to strengthen the existing police, whatever type of police that may be. This is because a large part of the activity consists of rebuilding, equipping, and training the police forces. UNSC resolutions occasionally state that peacekeepers will assist in reforming the national police in line with the principles of democratic policing but more often, they mandate peacekeepers to train police forces. In the original mandate for the UN Mission in Liberia (UNMIL) it is stated that the mission shall do both "…assist the transitional government of Liberia in monitoring and restructuring the police force of Liberia, consistent with democratic policing, to develop a civilian police training programme, and to otherwise assist in the training of civilian police…" (UN 2003b, para. 3n). However, the implementation of these mandates seems to focus on the more "technical" parts, stressing the training, rebuilding, and equipping of the national police forces, and less on the more long-term issues that will contribute to (re-)establishing trust (Osland 2014). There are several reasons why this is the case (ibid.).

First, it is not uncommon that the most basic of police equipment is lacking, that there are none or devastated police stations or training centres, and that the war has lasted so long that it is imperative to start afresh, establishing a new force with updated training etc. Second, the mandates are normally not long-term, and the training, rebuilding, and equipping of the police can be expected to show relatively quick and tangible results. On the other hand, the reforms to make the police more accountable, in accordance with democratic standards, and increasing the trust of the people, demand a long-term perspective. The progress and results of this latter work is almost by definition very difficult to measure. Third, while there may be much disagreement between the national government and international actors on the goal and strategies for the way ahead, it is frequently the case that national and international actors would concur on the need for new equipment and buildings—they are not perceived as very sensitive. Fourth, the changes can be performed relatively independent of other reform initiatives.

While all of these activities may contribute to a necessary re-building and investment, if this is the *only* thing that is done, it mainly contributes to *one part* of what seems to be the main goal for the international intervention; it contributes to increasing the security part but it does very little as for the trust-building part, except for the fundamental fact that if people do not experience basic security, trust will not prevail. This leads us to what I will call the security–trust challenge.

Simplified, I would argue that there are two main challenges for international police forces who are to assist in peace operations: on the one hand, increase the sense of security of the people and, on the other hand, assist in increasing the trust between the police and the people. Both challenges would normally require a long-term perspective, but while (re-)establishing trust could require a generational perspective, in cases where it is non-existent (re-)establishing a sense of security is somewhat more short term—albeit that these two goals are clearly related. Democratic countries, who have a police *service* understanding of policing, would tend to be both high on the trust and the security end of the scale. More authoritarian countries would be high on security but low on trust, while post-conflict countries and countries where conflict is still ongoing, would be low on both security and trust. This can be exemplified in the following Model 10.1:

The UN and other international actors such as the EU and the AU, take a Weberian state-centric understanding as its point of departure. This does not necessarily imply that the *only* way forward is to pursue a top-down approach to police reform. Research has proven that this is not very successful (Osland 2014). For the international community to succeed in

Model 10.1 The security–trust challenge

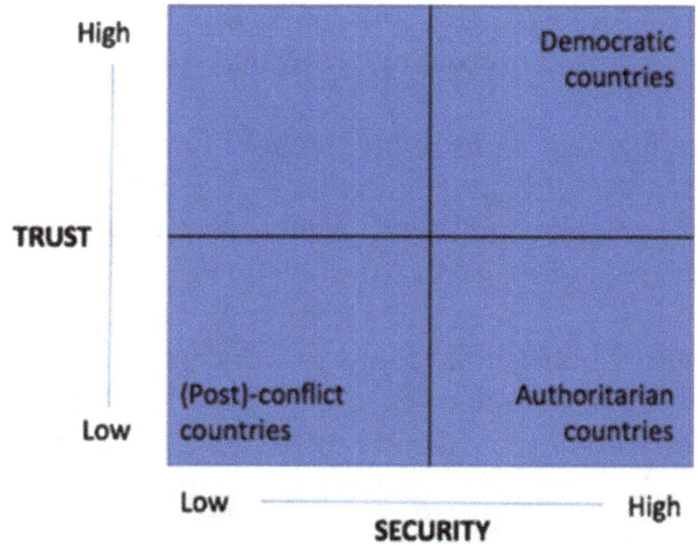

assisting in *also* building trust between the local police and its people, a bottom-up approach would be an important contribution and community-oriented policing holds promise in this regard. This is intertwined with one of the most difficult areas for international interveners, to establish national ownership. National ownership in this setting represents a paradox: we only talk about national ownership when there are external actors as part of the equation—as such, national ownership is a utopia. In an ideal world, national ownership is locally initiated and externally supported—external actors are supposed to assist and complement national actors, to provide options and not answers. In reality, most plans and strategies are created by outside actors, and then afterwards one tries to make local governmental actors agree to those plans and implement them. In order to answer the External UN Police Divisions Review in their call for a paradigm shift, I would argue that to start focussing on community-oriented policing would be a change in the right direction—towards a more bottom-up approach, towards more local ownership—and in the end, towards more trust between the people and their police; *and* increased sense of security for the people. Some recent internal reviews have started endorsing this approach (UN 2014, para. 49; UN Police 2016, para. 22). According to the SGF Guidelines on Police Operations of 2016, there are four cornerstones of community-oriented policing (UN Police 2016, para. 30):

- consulting with communities,
- responding to communities,

- mobilizing communities, and
- solving recurring problems.

While this is promising, it should not be forgotten that the launching of reports and strategies are only the mid-point of a reform path; if it is to be implemented, you need strong and consistent champions to follow it through (Thakur 2016). The needed reforms and their accompanying initiatives will not fly unless some dedicated Member States make a real effort in promoting them, over time.[20]

If the purpose for the UN work on policing does not include (re-) establishing such trust, then that needs to be made clear from the beginning. The HIPPO report echoes the need for realism as for what can be achieved within its lifespan (UN 2015a, para. 161). Also, the External UN Police Division Review is clear in its criticism in this regard: "a paradox exists between the supply of a large number of regularly rotating personnel, usually police generalists, who are deployed to United Nations missions, and the long-term qualitative and structural challenges they are expected to address" (2016a, p. 8).

Concluding Remarks

Compared to 20 years ago, there has been considerable progress in some areas, for instance, a larger focus on local ownership as imperative for sustainable reforms (Donais 2015); an understanding that more technical reforms are also highly political through the empowering of some and disempowering of others (Osland 2014); as well as an increased understanding that police reform, like reform of the larger security sector, implies a changed way of thinking about reforms rather than a given set of actions (Osland 2015, pp. 31–33). Nevertheless, the ongoing changing landscape of conflicts merits a continuous process of change in our understanding of how to handle these new challenges. During the last two decades, both the mandates and the tools of the UNPOL have changed: with nine Formed Police Unites (FPUs) in 2000, to 71 authorised FPU's in 2016. This development has happened in a context of a constant lack of resources; more robust mandates focusing more on protection of civilians and combatting violent extremists' groups, on which

[20] Norway has been one of the driving forces behind the SGF-process, as one such example.

the police officers often have received little specific training; UNPOL officers from 87 countries, all with their own principles and structures, not to forget the context that is often characterised by distrust between the general public and the police in the host-state. It goes without saying that assisting in the restoration of state authority in such a context, represents a very serious challenge; in particular seen from the perspective of those citizens who are not represented by the political elite at a given time, but also seen from the perspective of the UN, that not assisting in restoring state authority is not perceived as an option since the alternative is that non-state and often criminal actors will take advantage of any security and governance vacuum. What may represent an even greater challenge is the restoration or establishment of trust between the host-state police and its people. In order to achieve this, a different timeframe is needed and probably also a different approach—less top-down and more bottom-up. An increased focus on community-oriented policing is a step in the right direction. The extent to which external actors, such as the UN, can indeed contribute towards increased trust between people and its police, is a different matter.

So, is UNPOL fit for purpose? At first glance, it is tempting to make a connection between the equipment used by the police—and argue that its hardened shell represented by its increasing number of FPUs—will be counterproductive to establishing trust. Yet, this is a simplified argument; it is about how the police behave, not how they are equipped. If the operational situation requires a more robust set-up, it will not contribute to establishing trust if the police is neither equipped nor organised to handle the challenges, quite the contrary. For the police to be perceived as legitimate, it needs to simultaneously be perceived as efficient. Trust is first and foremost connected to attitudes and behaviour and how the police treat the people it is set to serve. However, if UNPOL is supposed to be a community-oriented service, as stated in the SGF, something that could in fact contribute towards increased national ownership and hence, add to the security–trust challenge, then UNPOL is *not* fit for purpose. While the strategies are there, saying that community-oriented policing should be an overarching approach for international assistance in post-conflict countries, the *implementation* of a community-oriented policing strategy is lacking.

We live in an era where there is a lot of scepticism about the UN and its ability to perform in the peace and security arena. While the UN often gets blamed for the failures, the ultimate responsibility lies with Member

States. The UN Secretariat can support Member States, but they cannot replace them or make up for the lack of political will among them.

References

Arcudi, Giovanni, and Michael Smith. 2013. The European Gendarmerie Force: A Solution in Search of Problems? *European Security* 12 (1): 1–20.

Brogden, Mike, and Preeti Nijhar. 2005. *Community Policing: International Models and Approaches*. Cullompton: Willan Publishing.

Caparini, Marina L., and Kari M. Osland. 2016a. MINUSTAH's Specialized Police Team to Combat Sexual Violence in Haiti. NUPI Working Paper, no. 867. Oslo: Norwegian Institute of International Affairs (NUPI).

Caparini, Marina L., and Kari M. Osland. 2016b. SGBV Capacity-Building in Peace Operations: Specialized Police Teams. NUPI Policy Brief, no. 35. Oslo: NUPI.

Chana, Jane. 2002. Security Sector Reform: Issues, Challenges and Prospects. Adelphi Paper, no. 344. London: International Institute for Strategic Studies.

del Frate, Anna Alvazzi. 1998. *International Victimization Survey*. Rome: UN Interregional Crime and Justice Research Institute.

Devon, Shai A. 2016. Police Reform and Power in Post Conflict Societies: A Conceptual Map for Analysis. *European Journal of Policing Studies* 4 (3): 269–298.

Donais, Timothy. 2015. Ownership: From Policy to Practice. In *Handbook of International Security and Development*, ed. Paul Jackson, 227–247. Cheltenham: Edward Elgar.

Ellison, Graham, and Georgina Sinclair. 2013. *Entrepreneurial Policing? International Policing Challenges*. Southampton: The Open University.

Feller, Stefan. 2014. An Insider's View of UN Policing. *Huffington Post*, May 12.

Goldsmith, Andrew. 2005. Police Reform and the Problem of Trust. *Theoretical Criminology* 9 (4): 443–470.

Hansen, Annika S. 2011. Policing the Peace: The Rise of United Nations Formed Police Units. Policy Briefing. Berlin: Zentrum für Internationale Friedenseinsätze.

Hartz, Halvor A. 2000. CivPol: The UN Instrument for Police Reform. In *Peacebuilding and Police Reform*, ed. Tor Tanke Holm and Espen Barth Eide, 27–42. London: Frank Cass.

ICT4COP. https://www.nmbu.no/en/faculty/landsam/department/noragric/research/clusters/chsd/projects-and-activities/ict4cop and https://communitypolicing.eu/.

Lea, J., and J. Young. 1984. *What Is to Be Done About Law and Order?* London: Penguin.

Lyons, William. 2002. Partnerships, Information and Public Safety: Community Policing in a Time of Terror. *Policing: An International Journal of Police Strategies and Management* 25 (3): 530–542.

Mawby, Rob I. 2008. Models of Policing. In *Handbook of Policing*, 2nd ed., ed. Tim Newburn, 17–46. Cullompton, Devon: Willan Publishing.

Mishler, William, and Richard Rose. 1998. *Trust in Untrustworthy Institutions: Culture and Institutional Performance in Post-communist Societies*. Glasgow: Centre for the Study of Public Policy.

Osland, Kari M. 2014. *Much Ado About Nothing? The Impact of International Assistance To Police Reform in Afghanistan, Bosnia and Herzegovina, Kosovo, Serbia and South Sudan: A Comparative Case Study and Developing a Model for Evaluating Democratic Policing*, 1–419. Oslo: Faculty of Social Sciences, University of Oslo/Akademika Publishing.

Osland, Kari M. 2015. Security Sector Reform. In *United Nations Peace Operations: Aligning Principles and Practice*. NUPI Report, no. 2, ed. Mateja Peter. Oslo: NUPI.

Osland, Kari M. 2017a. *Norsk politi i Internasjonal tjeneste 1989–2016*. NUPI Rapport, no. 2. Oslo: NUPI.

Osland, Kari M. 2017b. Norwegian Police in International Operations 1989–2016. NUPI Policy Brief, no. 3. Oslo: NUPI.

Peake, Gordon, and Otwin Marenin. 2008. Their Reports Are Not Read and Their Recommendations Are Resisted: The Challenge for the Global Police Policy Community. *An International Journal* 9 (1): 59–69.

Reisig, Michael D. 2010. Community and Problem-Oriented Policing. *Crime and Justice* 39 (1): 1–53.

Rosenbaum, Dennis P. (ed.). 1994. *The Challenge of Community Policing: Testing the Promises*. London: Sage.

Sebastian, Sofia. 2015. The Role of Police in UN Peace Operations: Filling the Gap in the Protection of Civilians from Physical Violence. Stimson Center Policy Brief, no. 3. Washington, DC: Stimson Center.

Sedra, Mark (ed.). 2010. *The Future of Security Sector Reform*. Waterloo: Center for International Governance Innovation.

Sunshine, Jason, and Tom R. Tyler. 2003. The Role of Procedural Justice and Legitimacy in Shaping Public Support for Policing. *Law and Society Review* 17: 513–547.

Thakur, Ramesh. 2016. High-Level Panels. In *The Oxford Handbook of International Organizations*, ed. Jacob Cogan, Ian Hurd, and Ian Johnstone, 859–880. Oxford: Oxford University Press.

Treaty of Velsen. 2007. *Treaty on Establishing the European Gendarmerie Force*, October 18. Velsen, the Netherlands.

UN Police. 2014. *DPKO/DFS Policy on United Nations Police in Peacekeeping Operations and Special Political Missions*. New York: Department of Peacekeeping Operations/Department of Field Support.

UN Police. 2016. *DPKO/DFS Guidelines on Police Operations in United Nations Peacekeeping Operations and Special Political Missions*. New York: Department of Peacekeeping Operations/Department of Field Support.

UN Police. 2017a. Formed Police Units (FPUs). United Nations Police. https://police.un.org/en/formed-police-units-fpus. Accessed 3 Jan 2018.

UN Police. 2017b. Police Contributing Countries. United Nations Police. https://police.un.org/en/police-contributing-countries. Accessed 3 Jan 2018.

UN Women. 2015. *Preventing Conflict, Transforming Justice, Securing the Peace: A Global Study on the Implementation of United Nations Security Council Resolution 1325*. New York: UN Women.

United Nations. 1999. *United Nations Security Council Resolution 1244*. New York: United Nations.

United Nations. 2000a. *Report of the Panel on United Nations Peace Operations*. New York: United Nations.

United Nations. 2000b. *UN Civilian Police Principles and Guidelines*. New York: Department of Peacekeeping Operations/Department of Field Support.

United Nations. 2003a. *Handbook on Multidimensional Peacekeeping Operations*. New York: UN Department for Peacekeeping Operations.

United Nations. 2003b. *United Nations Security Council Resolution 1509*. New York: United Nations.

United Nations. 2005. *UN Police Handbook: Building Institutional Police Capacity in Post-conflict Environments*. New York: UN Department for Peacekeeping Operations.

United Nations. 2009. *UN Criminal Justice Standards for UN Police*. New York and Vienna: Department of Peacekeeping Operations/UN Office on Drugs and Crime.

United Nations. 2011. *Report of the Secretary-General on United Nations Police*, December 15. New York: UN General Assembly.

United Nations. 2014. *United Nations Security Council Resolution 2185*. New York: United Nations.

United Nations. 2015a. *Report of the High-Level Independent Panel on Peace Operations on Uniting Our Strengths for Peace: Politics, Partnership and People*. New York: United Nations.

United Nations. 2015b. *The Future of UN Peace Operations: Implementation of the Recommendations of the High-Level Independent Panel on Peace Operations*. New York: United Nations.

United Nations. 2015c. *The Challenge of Sustaining Peace: Report of the Advisory Group of Experts for the 2015 Review of the United Nations Peacebuilding Architecture*. New York: United Nations.

United Nations. 2016a. *External Review of the Functions, Structure and Capacity of the UN Police Division*, May 31. New York: United Nations.

United Nations. 2016b. *Report of the Secretary-General on United Nations Police*. New York: UN General Assembly.

United Nations. 2016c. *Revised Policy on Formed Police Units in United Nations Peacekeeping Operations*. New York: Department of Peacekeeping Operations/Department of Field Support.

United Nations. 2017a. Mission and post, 30 November. United Nations Peacekeeping. https://peacekeeping.un.org/sites/default/files/mission_and_post.pdf. Accessed 3 Jan 2018.

United Nations. 2017b. Peacekeeping Fact Sheet Oct 2017. United Nations Peacekeeping. https://peacekeeping.un.org/sites/default/files/pk_fact-sheet_10_17_e_3.pdf. Accessed 3 Jan 2018.

United Nations. 2017c. *United Nations Security Council Resolution 2382.* New York: United Nations.

Open Access This chapter is licensed under the terms of the Creative Commons Attribution 4.0 International License (http://creativecommons.org/licenses/by/4.0/), which permits use, sharing, adaptation, distribution and reproduction in any medium or format, as long as you give appropriate credit to the original author(s) and the source, provide a link to the Creative Commons license and indicate if changes were made.

The images or other third party material in this chapter are included in the chapter's Creative Commons license, unless indicated otherwise in a credit line to the material. If material is not included in the chapter's Creative Commons license and your intended use is not permitted by statutory regulation or exceeds the permitted use, you will need to obtain permission directly from the copyright holder.

PART III

New and Old Partnerships

CHAPTER 11

Africa and UN Peace Operations: Implications for the Future Role of Regional Organisations

Cedric de Coning

Introduction

Over the past decade and a half, Africa has developed a significant peace operations capacity. This is reflected in the number of peacekeepers African countries contribute to African-led and United Nations (UN) peace operations. African countries contributed only 10,000 troops to UN peacekeeping operations in 2000, when the African Union (AU) was established (Lotze 2013). Today, African countries contribute about 50% of the UN's approximately 100,000 peacekeepers.[1] This means that Africa has now replaced South East Asia as the largest regional contributor to UN peace operations. Since the AU was launched, it has deployed

[1] Peacekeeping statistics are constantly changing, both in the short term due to routine rotations, and longer term due to the kind of changes addressed in this paper. The UN provides monthly updates at (UN 2018).

C. de Coning (✉)
Norwegian Institute of International Affairs (NUPI), Oslo, Norway
e-mail: cdc@nupi.no

© The Author(s) 2019

C. de Coning and M. Peter (eds.), *United Nations Peace Operations in a Changing Global Order*,
https://doi.org/10.1007/978-3-319-99106-1_11

eight peace operations of its own, including to Burundi (AMIB), the Central African Republic (MISCA), the Comoros (AMISEC and MAES), Mali (AFISMA), Somalia (AMISOM) and Sudan (AMIS I and II). In addition, it has provided support to ad hoc regional security coalitions against the Lord's Resistance Army (LRA), Boko Haram and instability in the Sahel region. In total, African countries contributed approximately 85,000 military, police and civilian personnel to UN and African-led peace operations in 2018. The main reason why Africa's peace operations capacity has significantly increased over the past decade and a half is because the AU and the sub-regional organisations in Africa, with significant support from international partners, have invested in establishing and developing the African Standby Force. This project has generated political support in Africa and internationally for a significantly scaled-up African role in peace operations on the African continent. It has been successful in focussing the support of international partners, including the UN, on building African peace operations capacities. The success of this project to date has boosted the confidence of the AU and the sub-regional organisations, and today they are playing a much more prominent role in conflict management in Africa than ever before.

One of the implications of this more assertive African posture is that the UN has less freedom to manoeuvre than it enjoyed in the past. A decade and half ago the UN was the most important actor when it came to the deployment of peace operations in Africa. Today, it is unthinkable that the UN would consider deploying a new peace operation in Africa without close consultation with the AU and relevant African countries and sub-regional organisations. In fact, the UN would probably only consider deploying a peace operation in Africa if the AU or the relevant sub-region is unable to take the lead itself, and even then the UN mission is likely to have a significant African character. Africa is thus no longer only the recipient or host of UN peace operations, the AU and the sub-regional organisations in Africa have now become an integral part of the global peace and security architecture. This has changed the role of UN peace operations in Africa. As approximately 75% of UN peacekeepers are deployed in Africa, and approximately the same amount of the UN peacekeeping budget is spent on peace operations in Africa, this means that these changes are likely to profoundly affect UN peace operations in the years ahead.

This chapter will explore the future direction that AU and African-led peace operations may take, and consider its impact on the strategic relationship between the UN and the AU. We will assess the capacities the AU has developed to date, and are likely to continue to develop, as well as several decisions the AU has taken recently regarding re-organising the Union and improving the way its peace operations are financed. Based on these considerations we will assess the implications of these developments for the relationship between the UN and regional organisations.

African-Led Peace Operations

The peace operations led by the AU, the Regional Economic Communities (RECs), Regional Mechanisms (RMs) or African-led ad hoc coalitions, are all deployed under the legal framework of the AU Constitutive Act and the UN Charter. The AU's Peace and Security Protocol have established a comprehensive African Peace and Security Architecture (APSA), which include elements such as the Continental Early Warning System, the Panel of the Wise, the Peace Fund, and the African Standby Force (ASF). Three RECs, namely the Economic Community of West African States (ECOWAS), the Economic Community of Central African States (ECCAS) and the Southern African Development Community (SADC), and two RMs, namely the East African Standby Force (EASF) and the North African Regional Capacity (NARC), make up the five regional standby arrangements of the ASF.

The practice that has emerged over the past decade and a half is that there are three main types of African-led peace operations, namely those deployed by the AU, those deployed by RECs/RM and those undertaken by an ad hoc coalition (de Coning 2017). The AU-led operations include the operations in Burundi (AMIB, 2003), Darfur (AMIS, 2004), Comoros (MAES, 2007), Somalia (AMISOM, 2007–), Mali (AFISMA, 2012), and the Central African Republic (CAR) (MISCA, 2013). The AU has also deployed a mission to West Africa to stop the spread of Ebola in 2014 (ASEOWA).

Examples of REC/RM-led operations include ECOWAS' ECOMOG missions in Liberia and Sierra Leone in the 1990s, the ECCAS missions in CAR, such as FOMUC (2002–2008) and MICOPAX (2008–2013), and the more recent ECOWAS missions to Guinea-Bissau and the Gambia (2017) and the SADC mission to Lesotho (2017).

Examples of African-led ad hoc security coalitions operations include the Regional Cooperative Initiative against the Lord's Resistance Army

(RCI-LRA), the Multinational Joint Task Force (MNJTF) that is combatting Boko Haram in the Lake Chad Basin, and the G5 Sahel Force that combats violent extremism and organised crime in the Sahel. These coalitions differ significantly from the traditional notion of a peace operation. The MNJTF is essentially a counter-insurgency and counter-terrorism operation where countries from the region, including Cameroon, Chad, Niger, and Nigeria undertake their own national operations—mostly within their own borders, and occasionally in hot pursuit across their borders—but in a coordinated manner with a shared political-strategic mandate and a joint multinational headquarters that coordinate the overall effort. The G-5 Sahel Force follows the same logic and is a regional initiative consisting of Chad, Burkina Faso, Mauritania, Mali, and Niger. Together they counter transnational organised crime and violent extremism in the Sahel region. The AU's role is to provide strategic-political direction and authority, via mandates from the Peace and Security Council (PSC), to coordinate international backing, including financial contributions, and to provide technical support for the multinational headquarters.

The observations and recommendations of the UN's Independent High-level Panel on Peace Operations (HIPPO) regarding the primacy of politics is also highly relevant for African-led peace operations. These African-led peace operations are meant to be part of a larger political intervention where the role of the military operation is to contain violence and generate stability, so that political solutions can be pursued. In reality, however, the security effort is often not matched sufficiently with political and development efforts. It often takes a few years for those responsible for deploying such operations to realise that the military or security dimension is insufficient to bring about and end to hostilities, and that a much more comprehensive approach is needed to sustain the peace. In Somalia, for instance, where AMISOM is engaged in stabilisation, counter-insurgency, and counter-terrorism operations, it took the AU and the Troop Contributing Countries (TCCs) approximately a decade to understand that whilst AMISOM may be able to temporarily stabilise a situation by winning selected battles and by controlling some towns, it cannot ultimately defeat Al Shabaab militarily. They can only be defeated in the long-term if the Government of Somalia can provide better security, governance, and social-economic opportunities than what Al Shabaab can offer. As a result of these lessons, there are initiatives underway in the Sahel and Lake Chad Basin to embed the G5 force and the

MNJTF into larger regional stabilisation strategies that are politically-led and that include development, socio-economic, governance and rule of law dimensions. It also means that these African-led operations would need to be part of larger international networked stabilisation and development strategies, because they would not be able to achieve their missions on their own. The UN plays a leading role in coordinating these regional strategies and networks.

Most AU- and REC-led peace operations to date have included political and civilian components that have the task of providing the mission leadership with advice and support on the roles these missions should play in the political and civilian realms, as well as in participating in the larger regional and international networks that are needed to achieve their missions' mandate. The ASF has had a dedicated effort to develop the civilian dimension of African peace operations since 2006 (de Coning and Kasumba 2010). However, these efforts have lagged behind the investment in the military capabilities of the ASF, and will need to be significantly scaled-up if they are going to have an impact on the way AU- and REC-led peace operations are planned and managed (de Coning et al. 2017). The UN has been slow to grasp the importance of the civilian dimension of African peace operations. Initially the UN has discouraged the AU from developing a civilian component for, for instance AMISOM. It saw AMISOM as a military operation and it wanted the UN political mission to provide the civilian expertise. Eventually the UN accepted that the AU needed to have its own political and civilian expertise in order for it to meaningfully engage in a larger comprehensive strategic framework (de Coning et al. 2017).

Two other operations deserve to be mentioned, because the first reflects how African-led capabilities have also augmented UN peace operations and the second reflects on the level of maturity the African peace and security architecture. The first is the Force Intervention Brigade (FIB) that was deployed to enhance the UN Stabilization Mission to the Democratic Republic of the Congo (MONUSCO) in 2013. The FIB was given the mandate to neutralise the M23 and other rebel groups, and is a rare example of a UN peace operation that has been tasked to do peace enforcement (Karlsrud 2015). The International Conference on the Great Lakes Region (ICGLR), SADC, and the AU concluded that MONUSCO was not effective enough in countering the M23 and other rebel groups in Eastern DRC, and proposed to establish an AU or SADC force. Once the UN Security Council was convinced that such a force had clear political support from all the stakeholders in the region, the UN suggested that such a force should be incorporated into the existing UN mission. This was agreeable to the countries in the region because it resolved the complications that would arise from having two different forces operating in the same area of operations, and it also solved the challenge of financing and supporting the FIB if it was an AU or SADC operation.

The FIB is widely regarded as having been effective in supporting the Congolese armed forces in containing the M23 rebel group (Peter 2015). This success was due to a number of factors. All the FIB's TCCs—Malawi, South Africa, and Tanzania—as well as the host nation DRC, are members of SADC. They have participated in joint training exercises under the auspices of the SADC Standby Arrangement of the ASF, which meant that they had a common understanding of the doctrine and command and control. The FIB was deployed with a clear political will to use force. With the full support of the DRC, TCCs, SADC, ICGLR and the AU, the UN Security Council deployed the FIB with a clear mandate to use offensive force, if necessary, to contain the rebel groups. Finally, the FIB was deployed with its own enablers and force multipliers including artillery, attack helicopters, and specially trained troops. It is the combination of these factors that enabled the FIB to undertake the kind of offensive enforcement actions that it did initially take against the M23. When some of these factors waned, for instance when the DRC, TCCS, ICGLR, SADC, the AU and the UN failed to reach a similar common understanding on how best to deal with some of the other rebel groups, the FIB became less effective.

As a result of the early successes of the FIB in the DRC, the AU and UN also considered deploying an African FIB-type mission to Northern Mali, and a Regional Protection Force in Juba, South Sudan, which would be tasked with protecting civilians to support the UN Mission in South Sudan. The protection force was authorised in August 2016, but deployment began first in August 2017 because the government of South Sudan objected to its composition and deployment modalities (Williams 2016). The plan for a FIB-type mission for Northern Mali morphed into what is now the G-5 Sahel Force. These developments may indicate the start of two news trends, namely on the one hand where regionally led and composed forces are used to augment UN peacekeeping operations, and on the other hand, where UN peacekeeping or dedicated support missions are used to support regional forces, such as in the case of AMISOM and the G5-Sahel force.

The second operation is the January 2017 intervention of ECOWAS in The Gambia. In this case a constitutional crisis developed when the then President Yahya Jammeh, first recognised and then later disputed the victory of Adama Barrow in the 2016 presidential election. ECOWAS, the AU, and the international community recognised the outcome of the 2016 presidential election. A constitutional crisis loomed as President Jammeh refused to step down and hand over power on 19 January 2017 (Al Jazeera 2017). To avert a crisis, several heads of state from the ECOWAS region travelled to The Gambia to convince Jammeh to hand over power. When he continued to refuse, ECOWAS prepared for a military intervention. On 19 January, Adama Barrow was inaugurated as President in the Gambian Embassy in Senegal. His first act at President was to request ECOWAS to help ensure that the constitutional order is preserved in The Gambia. On the same day the UN Security Council approved Resolution 2337, which expressed support for ECOWAS' efforts to find a political solution to the crisis in The Gambia. Shortly before the ECOWAS Mission in The Gambia (ECOMIG) started to enter The Gambia from neighbouring Senegal, the Gambian army chief pledged allegiance to President Barrow and declared that the Gambian army will not resist the ECOWAS intervention. Before ECOMIG reached the capital Banjul, it halted its advance to give more time to find a negotiated solution. After further diplomatic interventions by the Presidents of Mauritania and Guinea, Jammeh finally agreed to step down, and he left the country on 21 January (Cocks and Jahateh 2017).

As President Barrow requested help from fellow ECOWAS countries, ECOMIG was not a non-consensual intervention, and thus did not require UN Security Council authorisation. The Gambian experience reflects how far ECOWAS and the AU has come in the development and application of the APSA. Firstly, ECOWAS and the AU followed the election in The Gambia closely, including through election observation missions, and thus had their own information that led them to credibly recognise the outcome of the elections. Secondly, both ECOWAS and the AU took several decisions that signalled very clearly to Jammeh and the international community their intent to recognise the election and thus Barrow as the elected President. ECOWAS signalled early that it would pursue a peaceful transfer of power, but use force if necessary. The AU also clearly signalled that it would no longer regard Jammeh as President after 19 January. The AU has a long-standing policy to reject unconstitutional changes of government, and the consistent application of this norm further helped to create a political context in which it was clear to all, and finally also to Jammeh, that he had no option other than to hand over power to newly elected President Barrow. Thirdly, the mustering of ECOMIG signalled to Jammeh, the Gambian army, and all others involved that ECOWAS was serious in its intent to use force if necessary. Fourthly, ECOWAS was careful to ensure that it acted according to international law and the constitution of The Gambia, further ensuring that the mission was seen by all as legitimate and credible. Lastly, ECOMIG managed to intervene with a credible mustering of force and firm resolve, carefully synchronised with clear political support and direction, and this enabled it to achieve its mission without the need to use force. The Gambia case demonstrated how ECOWAS and the AU used its political, diplomatic, and military tools in a sophisticated and coordinated way to prevent and manage a significant crisis. The alternative could have been a costly civil war that could have destabilised an already fragile region.

The AU and the sub-regional organisations have thus developed a significant peace operations capacity over the last decade and a half. This capacity has been used to deploy AU, sub-regional and ad hoc coalition operations, and it has contributed significantly to UN peace operations. At the same time, as the Gambia case show, African institutions have developed the ability to coordinate sophisticated international, regional and sub-regional networks, as well as to align its political, diplomatic and peace operations efforts, to prevent and manage crisis and conflicts. African is thus no longer only a recipient or host of UN peace operations, but it has now become a strategic partner and enabler for the UN.

AU Reforms

There are three aspects that will have a significant impact on the future direction of African-led peace operations. Firstly, the AU should adapt its current Peace Support Operations (PSO) doctrine, as well as the ASF concept, to better reflect the kind of operations the AU and RECs have undertaken over the past decade, and is likely to undertake in future. The AU PSO doctrine and ASF concept was developed between 2003 and 2008, when the AU had little experience of its own. As a result, its PSO doctrine and ASF concept largely reflect the doctrinal and policy assumptions of NATO, EU, and the UN at the time. Since then, a unique African model of peace operations has emerged (de Coning et al. 2016), and NATO, EU, and UN approaches to peace operations have also undergone considerable adaptations (de Coning et al. 2017). The AU should thus review and update its doctrine, concepts and policy frameworks to reflect the changes in the global system and its own experiences and lessons.

Secondly, another important aspect that needs to be addressed is the ambiguous relationship between the AU and the RECs. Various AU reports and decisions have highlighted the need to clarify the relationship between the AU and the RECs (African Union 2017; Assogbavi 2017). Should the relationship be based on the principle of subsidiarity, where the RECs have the primary responsibility for peace and security in their regions? There are two issues that complicate this question. Firstly, how should the AU and RECs deal with crises that lie on the border of two regions? Secondly, how should the response account for the fact that not all regions are equally developed?

The AU operation in Mali has highlighted the challenges when a REC, in this case ECOWAS, has to manage a crisis on its border, when key neighbours and stakeholders, for instance Algeria and Chad, are not part of the REC. In such instances the role of the AU can be a key factor in ensuring regional coherence and synergy. The operation in Mali also highlighted that in the absence of a functioning REC in North Africa, the AU had to go beyond the regional building block model and find innovative ways to engage all the stakeholders. The planning for the 2016 MAPROBU mission in Burundi also showed that although the Eastern African Standby Arrangement should have been the appropriate regional mechanism to carry out the mission, various political factors resulted in the AU having to look beyond the regional building block model for TCCs. These cases show that the AU cannot always depend on the subsidiarity-based REC regional building-block model of the ASF. In fact, despite the progress made with the ASF, most African-led operations to date have been ad hoc coalitions of the willing (de Coning et al. 2016, p. 120). The AU-REC/RM experiences in Burundi, CAR, Mali and Somalia have thus shown that each situation is unique and that no one model of subsidiarity can accommodate each situation. Instead, in each case, a particular division of work emerged based on the actual relations and comparative advantages of the different actors on the ground. Instead of trying to find one predictable model, the AU and RECs/RMs should invest in institutionalising predictable coordination and cooperation mechanisms and processes, including regular information exchanges, joint assessment missions, joint analysis, joint planning, joint deployments, co-location, and joint evaluations.

Thirdly, the AU has decided to embark on a significant structural reform process during its January 2017 Summit, based on a set of proposals submitted by a team led by President Paul Kagame of Rwanda (Assogbavi 2017). The reform proposals require that the AU refocus itself around fewer priorities, of which peace and security is recognised to be at the core of the AU's mandate and role. Another important dimension is the financing of the African Union and specifically the funding of peace operations.

The AU has become reliant on partners for approximately 98% of its programme budget and 99% of its peace and security expenditure (African Union 2016a). This is problematic, because the AU's dependency on external resources denies it the freedom to independently take decisions on the strategic, operational, and even tactical aspects of the PSO it is responsible for. Any action that has cost implications requires prior negotiation with partners to mobilise the resources necessary for it to be implemented. As a result, the AU has only been able to undertake those operations where there was a convergence of interests with its partners.

The financial problems of the AU reached a critical stage in 2015, and that year the AU Member States, at both the January and July AU Summits, committed themselves to self-finance 100% of the AU's regular budget, 75% of its programme budget, and 25% of its peace and security budget, in particular the cost of its peace operations, by the year 2020 (African Union 2016a). This commitment was followed-up at the AU Summit in Kigali in June 2016, where a historic decision was reached to implement a 0.2% levy on eligible imports into all AU member states (African Union 2016b, para. 5b). In addition to the decision to introduce an import levy, the July 2016 Summit also approved recommendations for the revitalisation of the Peace Fund.

If successful, this new funding arrangement will significantly strengthen the ability of the AU to take ownership of its own operations. It will also result in a more balanced relationship between the AU and the UN, because the AU will be able to co-fund—with at least 25% of its operations—those peace operations the UN Security Council authorises it to undertake. The funding generated by the import levy may enable the AU to shift its relations with partners away from one defined by financial necessity, to one informed by strategic choice.

There are thus reforms underway at the level of the AU and the RECs that has the potential to further strengthen the capacity of the AU and RECS/RMs to undertake peace operations. The AU-UN relationship is thus likely to be characterised by a further strengthening of African capabilities and a willingness of African institutions to take up an even greater share of responsibility for African peace and security.

Implications for the Strategic Partnership with the United Nations

The AU–UN relationship used to be more like a donor-recipient relationship where the UN's role was to build the capacity of the AU. The AU took a conscious decision to change that a decade and a half ago, and have since succeeded in transforming the AU–UN relationship into a functioning strategic partnership.

The peace operations that the AU undertakes under UN authorisation needs to be understood as regional responses to global problems. Most African conflicts are global in the sense that they are heavily influenced by external factors like the global war on terror; fall-out and spill-over from the interventions in Iraq, Afghanistan, Libya, and Syria; the exploitation of natural resources by multinational companies; capital flight facilitated and solicited by the international financial system; and transnational organised crime, driven by markets in the West and Asia for narcotics, human trafficking, timber, and illegally caught fish (Africa Progress Report 2013). African peace operations thus represent a significant contribution to the global common good.

For this reason, the AU has been arguing consistently for many years that, together with other regional organisations, it is effectively part of a collective global peace and security architecture. Therefore, when the AU is asked to help the UN maintain international peace and security in Africa, the UN should use its assessed contribution system to support the peace operations that the AU is undertaking on behalf of the UN (African Union 2016a). From an AU perspective, the UN assessed contribution budget for peace operations is the most effective and efficient global burden-sharing arrangement for peace operations, as all members of the international system contribute to the budget against a pre-agreed scale of assessment. However, to date, the prevailing view in the UN Security Council is that the UN should assist the AU to mobilise resources by encouraging partners and by facilitating the establishment of Trust Fund arrangements, but that its obligation does not extend to directly financing AU operations. However, in Sudan, Mali, CAR and Somalia the UN Security Council has authorised, on a case-by-case basis, the UN to assist AU peace operations with various form of direct and indirect support, utilising the UN's assessed contribution budget. The issue that is currently being considered is whether the UN Security Council should make an in-principle commitment to finance AU peace operations.

In this debate a number of pre-conditions have been identified, namely that the AU take steps to ensure that its peace operations adhere to international human rights, international humanitarian law, and related conduct and discipline standards, that the AU provide access to UN auditors, and that the AU finances at least 25% of the cost of its peace operations itself. The AU has taken steps towards meeting these pre-conditions, and the UN Secretariat and a number of UN Member States have expressed satisfaction with the progress made. It is likely that the AU, the UN Secretary-General and several UN Member States will keep this issue on the agenda of the UN Security Council, but it is unlikely that the Council will commit itself in-principle, to directly financing AU peace operations authorised by the UN Security Council in the short- to medium term.

At the UN a number of reforms are also underway, and there is thus a need for the AU and UN to remain closely coordinated, at all levels, to ensure that both can adapt their relations to their respective reform processes, as well as in response to the existing and emerging operational challenges they face.

Meanwhile, at the operational level, a symbiotic division of work has developed between the AU and the UN, and this has been further strengthened in a strategic partnership agreement between the AU and UN that was signed in 2017. The UN is good at implementing peace agreements and consolidating peace processes, but it is not well suited for enforcement actions. The AU has demonstrated that it is willing and able to undertake stabilisation and counter-terrorism operations, but it lacks the broad sets of capacities necessary to implement comprehensive peace agreements. The UN and AU thus have mutually reinforcing capabilities that serve as the basis for a strategic partnership in which the UN and AU complement and augment each other. The AU and sub-regional organisations have acted as first responders in Burundi, CAR and Mali. When these situations have been sufficiently stabilised, the UN has taken over with a peacekeeping operation to consolidate the peace. In Burundi, CAR, and Mali, the African military and police personnel that served in the AU operations were re-hatted and became UN peacekeepers. In other cases, like Somalia, where the UN Security Council has authorised enforcement, the AU has deployed and managed the operations, but with financial and logistical support from the UN and other partners.

At the strategic level, the UN and the AU need to foster a common narrative that is mutually re-enforcing and respectful of each other's roles and comparative advantages. The members of the UN Security Council and the AU's PSC have started to meet regularly. However, these kinds of meetings need to be further deepened so as to ensure even greater coherence between the approaches of the UN Security Council and the AU PSC on the many conflicts that are on their mutual agenda.

At the operational level, the UN and AU have been meeting regularly at the desk-to-desk level, but these meetings now need to start delivering specific outcomes, such as developing guidelines for joint assessments, shared analysis, joint planning, AU–UN inter-mission coordination and cooperation, mission support, best practices, join evaluations, and joint Standard Operating Procedures for transitions between AU and UN operations.

Almost all AU peace operations will be accompanied by UN special political missions, similar to the way UNSOM and AMISOM have operated side-by-side in Somalia. At the same time, most UN peacekeeping operations in Africa will be accompanied by AU special political missions, such as has been the case with MINUSMA and African Union Mission for Mali and Sahel (MISAHEL) in Mali and MINUSCA and AU Mission for the CAR and Central Africa (MISCA) in CAR. A set of pre-agreed joint guidelines will make it easier for both organisations to involve each other from the earliest stages in assessments, planning, coordination mechanisms, mission support, benchmarks, and evaluation. This is especially important in those cases where AU peace operations transition into UN peacekeeping operations, or vice versa.

One of the AU's serious challenges is the capacity to support its own operations. The AU lacks a mission support concept and the staff/personnel, systems, and resources necessary to implement such a concept. The AU, with the support of the UN, has embarked on a process to develop a mission support policy. It will take several years for the AU to develop and refine its missions support capacity, and in the meantime it will rely on the UN and partners to support its operations.

This is especially challenging when the AU needs support for stability, counter-insurgency, and counter-terrorism operations—all peace enforcement operations in UN context—whilst its main partner in this regard, the UN, is geared to provide support to peacekeeping operations. Both institutions will need to develop fixes to cover this gap, until the AU has developed its own capacity in this area.

The AU and the UN has developed a functioning strategic partnership. This partnership plays out at the political, policy and operational levels, and reflect the reality that neither the AU nor the UN will deploy peace operations in Africa without close consultations and some form of cooperation with each other.

Conclusion

In this chapter, we explored the major factors that are likely to influence the future direction that African-led PSO may take, and considered what the impact may be of these developments for the strategic partnership between the UN and the AU. We argued that Africa's peace operations capacity has significantly increased over the past decade and a half because the AU, with significant support from the UN and its other partners, have invested in establishing and developing the ASF. As a result of this investment, Africa is now the largest regional contributor to UN peace operations.

When the ASF was designed, the AU had little peace operations experience of its own. Over the last decade the AU has undertaken eight operations of its own and has supported several others. In addition to contributing troops and police officers to UN peacekeeping missions, African countries are also likely to continue to provide African-led stabilisation brigades to augment UN peacekeeping missions in contexts like Mali and South Sudan, drawing on the success of the FIB model used in the DRC.

One of the implications of the significant capabilities that the AU and African sub-regional organisations have developed, is that the UN can no longer deploy peace operations of its own in Africa, without at least close consultations with the AU and sub-regional bodies. This is, however, not seen as a negative development. The increased capacity and willingness of the AU and other African regional bodies and coalitions to play an even greater role in African peace and security is seen as a positive development that opens the door for more specialisation, based on comparative advantage, as well as greater burden sharing. As discussed in several other chapters in this book, many of the challenges facing UN peace operations relate to the fact that the UN peacekeeping model is not well suited to enforcement or counter-terrorism type operations. Nor is the UN peacekeeping model well suited to deal with transnational challenges such as organised crime or regional manifestations of, for instance, violent extremism. The AU and other African bodies, such as the MNJTF in the Lake Chad Basin or the G5 force in the Sahel seem to be better suited to address these kinds of challenges. These African capabilities thus help to relieve the pressure on the UN on some fronts, which enable it to re-focus its efforts in other areas.

In the context of the larger shifts underway in the global order, the emerging role of African-led peace operations in Africa—where it has taken on a significant portion of the peace and security burden that the UN would otherwise have had to carry on its own—raises the question whether a new global peace and security architecture is emerging? In the past, Chapter VIII of the UN Charter, that deals with regional arrangements, was understood as providing for exceptional cases where the UN may need to turn to a regional organisation for help. As a result of the role the AU plays in Africa—and the European Union (EU) plays in Europe—the question arises whether the UN and regional organisations should establish a more formal global peace and security architecture that is based on burden-sharing and the principle of subsidiarity. This means that threats to international peace and security should be dealt with at the most immediate (or local) level that is consistent with their resolution.

At the moment, the relationships between the UN and regional organisations are undefined. Although the primary responsibility of the UN Security Council is not questioned, this does not amount to a hierarchal system where regional organisations such as the AU or the EU are subsidiary parts of a global peace and security architecture. Such an architecture would have a pre-agreed division of roles and responsibilities, where regional organisations are responsible for maintaining peace and security in their own regions, and where the UN is responsible for those aspects of international peace and security that the regional organisations are not able to address, or that is trans-regional. Rather, at present, the UN and regional organisations co-exist in a loosely defined manner that requires voluntary coordination and causes both tension and competition. A global peace and security architecture approach would imply that the UN and regional organisations, like the AU, agree to a more clearly defined division of roles under a burden-sharing arrangement. Such predictability would enhance cooperation, coordination, and efficiency and significantly alter the way we understand the role of the UN and regional organisations like the AU in the global peace and security architecture.

References

Africa Progress Report. 2013. *Equity in Extractives: Stewarding Africa's Natural Resources for All*. Geneva: Africa Progress Panel.

African Union. 2016a. *Securing Predictable and Sustainable Financing for Peace and Security in Africa*. Addis Ababa: African Union.

African Union. 2016b. *Decision on the Outcome of the Retreat of the Assembly of the African Union, July*. Addis Ababa: African Union.

African Union. 2017. *The Imperative to Strengthen Our Union: Report on the Proposed Recommendations for the Institutional Reform of the African Union*. Addis Ababa: African Union.

Al Jazeera. 2017. New Gambia President Adama Barrow Takes Oath in Senegal, Doha. Al Jazeera, January 19.

Assogbavi, D. 2017. Key Decisions of the AU Summit. https://assodesire.com/2017/01/31/key-decisions-of-the-au-summit/. Accessed 5 Feb 2018.

Cocks, Tim, and Lamin Jahateh. 2017. Gambia's Former Leader Jammeh Flies into Exile in Equatorial Guinea. *Reuters*, January 21.

de Coning, Cedric. 2017. Peace Enforcement in Africa: Doctrinal Distinctions Between the African Union and United Nations. *Contemporary Security Policy* 38 (1): 145–160.

de Coning, Cedric, and Yvonne Kasumba. 2010. *The Civilian Dimesion of the African Standby Force*. Durban: ACCORD and the African Union.

de Coning, Cedric, Linnea Gelot, and John Karlsrud. 2016. *The Future of African Peace Operations: From Janjaweed to Boko Haram*. London: Zed Books.

de Coning, Cedric, Chiyuki Aoi, and John Karlsrud. 2017a. *UN Peacekeeping Doctrine in a New Era*. London: Routledge.

de Coning, Cedric, Irene Limo, James Machakaire, and Jide M. Okeke. 2017b. The Role of the Civilian Component in African Union Peace Operations. In *The African Standby Force—Quo Vadis?* ed. Francois Vrey and Thomas Mandrup. Stellenbosch: Sun Media.

Karlsrud, John. 2015. The UN at War: Examining the Consequences of Peace-Enforcement Mandates for the UN Peacekeeping Operations in the CAR, the DRC and Mali. *Third World Quarterly* 36: 40–54.

Lotze, Walter. 2013. *Strengthening African Peace Support Operations: Nine Lessons for the Future of the African Standby Force*. Berlin: German Peace Operations Center (ZIF).

Peter, Mateja. 2015. Between Doctrine and Practice: The UN Peacekeeping Dilemma. *Global Governance* 21: 351–370.

United Nations. 2018. Peacekeeping Fact Sheet. www.un.org/en/peacekeeping/resources/statistics/factsheet.shtml. Accessed 12 Mar 2018.

Williams, Paul. 2016. *Key Questions for South Sudan's New Protection Force*. New York: IPI Global Observatory.

Open Access This chapter is licensed under the terms of the Creative Commons Attribution 4.0 International License (http://creativecommons.org/licenses/by/4.0/), which permits use, sharing, adaptation, distribution and reproduction in any medium or format, as long as you give appropriate credit to the original author(s) and the source, provide a link to the Creative Commons license and indicate if changes were made.

The images or other third party material in this chapter are included in the chapter's Creative Commons license, unless indicated otherwise in a credit line to the material. If material is not included in the chapter's Creative Commons license and your intended use is not permitted by statutory regulation or exceeds the permitted use, you will need to obtain permission directly from the copyright holder.

Check for updates

CHAPTER 12

The European Union and UN Peace Operations: What Global–Regional Peace and Security Partnership?

Thierry Tardy

Introduction

The European Union entered the world of crisis management in 2003 when it launched its first police mission—in Bosnia and Herzegovina—and, a few months later, its first military operations—in Macedonia and then in the Democratic Republic of the Congo (DRC). This came after a five-year period of conceptualisation of what was then called the European Security and Defence Policy (ESDP), which aimed to give the EU an autonomous capacity in the broad area of crisis management. ESDP was partly an answer to the EU's inability to respond meaningfully to the Yugoslav conflicts and to implement the ambitious goal of an EU Common Foreign Policy (defined in the 1992 Maastricht Treaty).

Over the last fifteen years, more than 30 EU operations have reflected and shaped a certain "EU approach" to respond to crises that is in various manners distinct from other international organisations' approaches. But the

T. Tardy (✉)
NATO Defence College, Rome, Italy

© The Author(s) 2019

C. de Coning and M. Peter (eds.), *United Nations Peace Operations in a Changing Global Order*,
https://doi.org/10.1007/978-3-319-99106-1_12

EU's approach also features typical crisis management activities and is therefore in many ways similar to the United Nations' crisis management style.

In fact, analysing the EU crisis management policy cannot be done while ignoring parallel developments at the UN level or simply ignoring the UN as a reference point for evaluating/assessing the EU's incremental engagement in crisis management. Indeed the very first EU operations in Bosnia and the DRC were sequential with (Bosnia) or in support of (DRC) UN operations, and, since then, most EU missions have in some ways cooperated with UN operations, most recently in Mali and in the Central African Republic (CAR). Furthermore, field cooperation was from the start accompanied by a parallel process of institutionalisation of the UN-EU relationship that has not been observed to the same extent between the UN and any other regional organisation.

This being said, the EU and the UN sometimes diverge on policy, and may find themselves as competing crisis management actors. Differences in capacities (financial and military), structure (membership and mandate) and political culture can also create asymmetries and hamper full reciprocity between the two actors. In the field over the last twenty years, UN operations have also suffered from a quasi-absence of European states as troop contributors. EU member states significantly finance UN peacekeeping, and have operated a comeback to UN operations in Mali, yet they have largely preferred other institutional frameworks for their own crisis management activities.

One of the four "essential shifts" identified by the 2015 High-Level Panel on Peace Operations is the need for a "stronger, more inclusive peace and security partnership" (UN 2015a, p. viii). Likewise, the Secretary-General's report in response to the High-Level Panel makes "global-regional partnerships" one of three pillars of the UN action plan on strengthening peace operations (UN 2015b, paras. 28–32). In response, the 2016 EU Global Strategy for Foreign and Security Policy defines four categories of "vital interests" for the EU, the fourth one being a "rules-based global order with multilateralism as its key principle and the United Nations at its core" (European Union 2016, p. 15).

This chapter aims at locating the EU's crisis management role in the broader framework of the UN's general mandate of "maintaining international peace and security." What is the EU's approach to managing crises? To what extent does the EU converge with and support the UN peacekeeping agenda? How are EU member states' own institutional choices being shaped and what do these choices tell us about the

UN-EU relationship or, in other words, about the global-regional peace and security partnership?

This chapter starts by providing an overview of EU crisis management operations, including their objectives and specific character. It then looks at how EU operations relate to the UN in legal, political, and operational terms, and presents similarities and differences between EU and UN operations. Third, the chapter sheds light on why the two institutions started cooperating and how this cooperation has shaped their relationship. Finally, the chapter looks at the issue of EU member states' contribution to UN peacekeeping; it takes stock of the European participation in the UN mission in Mali as of 2014, and it assesses how EU member states' institutional preferences may evolve in the coming years.

The EU Crisis Management Approach

The development of the EU crisis management policy came as a response to a need, expressed in the midst of the Kosovo conflict in the late 1990s and in the broader framework of the post-Cold War systemic evolutions, to provide the EU with the means to contribute to international security governance (Howorth 2007; Grevi et al. 2009; Biscop and Whitman 2012). In 1992, the Maastricht Treaty—that formally created the European Union and replaced the European Economic Community—had already laid the ground for a Common Foreign and Security Policy (CFSP). Yet the EU foreign policy stumbled over the Balkan conflicts in Croatia and then Bosnia and Herzegovina, while the US' (and NATO's) role in unblocking the situations both in Bosnia (in 1995) and Kosovo (in 1999) confirmed the limitations of the EU political and security ambitions. For European leaders—most prominently the French and the British—the EU was to be given a "capacity for autonomous action, backed up by credible military forces, the means to decide to use them and a readiness to do so, in order to respond to international crises" (Joint Declaration on European Defence 1998, art. 2). This commitment led to the design of a ESDP. In essence, ESDP has developed as a policy to manage crises occurring outside the EU, and excluding any collective defence mandate which should remain the prerogative of NATO for European states that are members of the Alliance (European Union 2007, art. 42.7). In practice, ESDP pushed the deployments of military and civilian assets in the management of crises in the Balkans, in Sub-Saharan Africa, and to a lesser extent in the Middle East and Asia. ESDP was then renamed Common Security and Defence Policy (CSDP) by the Lisbon Treaty (European Union 2007).

In 2017, CSDP operations are the most visible activity of the EU in the international security domain, and have been the most tangible examples of the coming to age of CSDP as well as EU security "actorness" (Tardy 2015, p. 51). In EU parlance, CSDP military activities are called "operations" while civilian activities are called "missions." By design, EU crisis management operations are either of a military or of a civilian nature. Although the Treaty on European Union (TEU) does not preclude the establishment of operations that could combine military and civilian elements, the EU planning and conduct structures, together with the relevant financial regulations, have so far prevented the creation of integrated military-civilian operations.

According to the Lisbon Treaty (European Union 2007, art. 42.1), CSDP shall provide the Union with an "operational capacity drawing on civilian and military assets" that can be used on "missions outside the Union for peace-keeping, conflict prevention and strengthening international security in accordance with the principles of the United Nations Charter." CSDP operations are further defined in Article 43.1 in the TEU (European Union 2007), which proposes a list of tasks to be carried out that includes "joint disarmament operations, humanitarian and rescue tasks, military advice and assistance tasks, conflict prevention and peace-keeping tasks, tasks of combat forces in crisis management, including peace-making and post-conflict stabilisation." The article adds that all these tasks "may contribute to the fight against terrorism, including by supporting third countries in combating terrorism in their territories."

Since 2003, the EU has launched and run 35 operations and missions, 23 of which were civilian and 12 military (Howorth 2014, Chapter 5; European Parliament 2012; Bund et al. 2017). In total, there are 16 on-going CSDP operations as of November 2017, ten civilian and six military. Civilian missions include the Kosovo rule of law mission (EULEX Kosovo), the monitoring mission in Georgia (EUMM Georgia), and capacity-building missions in Niger (EUCAP Sahel Niger), Mali (EUCAP Sahel Mali), Ukraine (EUAM Ukraine) and the Horn of Africa (EUCAP Nestor). Two of the military operations are maritime operations (Operation Atalanta off the coast of Somalia and Operation EUNAVFOR Med-Sophia in the south Mediterranean), and three are training missions (EU Training Missions in Somalia, Mali, and the Central African Republic) (Table 12.1).

Table 12.1 On-going CSDP operations and missions as of November 2017

Civilian missions	*Date of launching*
EUBAM Rafah	Nov. 2005
EUPOL COPPS/Palestinian Territories	Nov. 2005
EUMM Georgia	Oct. 2008
EULEX Kosovo	Dec. 2008
EUBAM Libya	May 2013
EUCAP Nestor—Horn of Africa	July 2012
EUCAP Sahel Niger	July 2012
EUCAP Sahel Mali	Jan. 2015
EUAM Ukraine	Dec. 2014
EUAM Iraq	Nov. 2017
Military Operations	*Date of launching*
Althea—Bosnia and Herzegovina	Dec. 2004
EUNAVFOR Atalanta—Gulf of Aden	Dec. 2008
EUTM Somalia	April 2010
EUTM Mali	Feb. 2013
EUTM RCA	July 2016
EUNAVFOR Med—Sophia	June 2015

In the civilian domain, EU crisis management focuses on the rule of law, good governance, and security sector reform; it proceeds through capacity-building and advisory tasks, often in cooperation with other crisis management actors.[1] Civilian missions fall within the three broad categories of strengthening missions, monitoring missions, and executive missions, although this latter category counts only one operation. Strengthening missions are mainly about capacity-building in the field of rule of law. They aim at assisting the recipient state in the reform and strengthening of its judicial and law enforcement institutions. This is done through monitoring, mentoring, and advising, as well as training and in some cases the provision of equipment. All civilian missions established since the entry into force of the Lisbon Treaty in 2009 are categorised as strengthening missions. Monitoring missions provide third-party observation of an activity or a process, be it the performance of a given sector (police, justice, border, etc.) or the implementation of an agreement (cease-fire line, peace agreement, etc.). The third category

[1] For a presentation of past and on-going EU civilian missions, see the European External Action Service (2017) at https://eeas.europa.eu/headquarters/headquarters-homepage/area/security-and-defence_en.

of civilian missions is that of executive missions, i.e. operations that can exert certain functions on behalf of the recipient state. The only example is EULEX Kosovo that has executive responsibilities in the areas of war crimes, organised crime and high-level corruption, as well as property and privatisation cases.

In the military domain, CSDP operations fit into the definition of crisis management in the sense that they fall short of war-fighting or openly coercive operations.[2] Maybe with the exception of the newly-created mission in the South Mediterranean Sea (EUNAVFOR Med-Sophia), EU operations are third-party interventions that are not supposed to take sides, or identify and militarily defeat an enemy. Some operations, like Atalanta, contain a coercive dimension to defeat pirates operating in the Gulf of Aden. Yet these operations do not have peace enforcement mandates, which makes them conceptually distinct from operations such as the NATO-led operation in Libya in 2011 or the French-led operation in Mali since 2013. The operation against migrants smugglers (Operation Sophia) is potentially different in the sense that it is the first EU operation that could theoretically lead to peace enforcement-type activities. The operation's mandate provides for the possibility of resorting to force against "spoilers" in a way that had never been contemplated in previous CSDP military operations. More precisely, the authorisation to "take all necessary measures" against a vessel and related assets, including through "disposing of them or rendering them inoperable" (Council of the European Union 2015a, art. 2.2.c)—and this after a phase of intelligence gathering—implies that the operation can proactively chase the smugglers and possibly resort to force against them in cases other than self-defence. Yet its implementation is conditioned upon either the consent of the Libyan state or the blessing of the UN Security Council, none of which had been obtained as of November 2017. In any case, given EU member states' general risk aversion, even the full implementation of EUNAVFOR Med's mandate would not make the mission a peace enforcement operation similar to the ones deployed in the last decade by states or by NATO.

Thirty-five CSDP operations attest to the existence of a certain EU conception of security policy that is distinct from any other institution's

[2] For a presentation of past and on-going EU military operations, see the European External Action Service website (2017) at http://www.eeas.europa.eu/csdp/missions-and-operations/index_en.htm.

conception. This refers to a specific EU security culture—defined in terms of shared ideas and beliefs in the security domain that would lead the organisation to act in a specific manner and of which CSDP operations and missions are an expression. This security culture reflects a certain way to handle crises, through a mix of civilian and military responses, a focus on rather short-term and consensual activities, almost always in support of existing state authorities, and in accordance with international legal instruments and a set of values and principles.

CSDP is about projecting security outside of the EU area in order to contribute to the stabilisation of states or regions that may potentially be the source of further destabilisation or more directly threaten EU societies. Such a security culture has been developed by design as much as by default; it results both from the difficulty to embrace a broader spectrum and from the desire to act at a particular level and through EU-specific tools or methods.

In this broad context, CSDP has over the last years evolved to more clearly respond to direct threats to European security, be it with operation Sophia and its migration-focused mandate or missions in the Sahel that also partly embrace an EU anti-terrorism or migration agenda.

EU vs. UN Operations: How Similar? How Different?

The EU has—more or less intentionally—developed its crisis management policy in reference to other international organisations, most notably NATO and the United Nations. The EU political-military structure (with the Political and Security Committee, the Military Committee, and the Military Staff) was copied from NATO's, while the NATO operations in Bosnia (IFOR then SFOR) in the implementation of the Dayton Peace Agreement and the NATO operation in Kosovo (KFOR) following the spring 1999 air campaign provided templates of what the EU should be able to do in the security domain.

Similarly, the UN was early on a source of inspiration and a point of reference for the EU's ESDP. At the legal level, all EU documents explicitly refer to the necessity for the EU to act in accordance with the UN Charter. Moreover, CSDP operations are established on the basis of a combination of a decision of the Council of ministers of the EU and either an invitation by the host state or a UN Security Council (UNSC) resolution under Chapter VII of the UN Charter (that allows for some sort of coercion). In practice, all civilian missions (with the exception of EULEX Kosovo) have been established on the basis of an invitation of the recipient state.

Military operations, for their part, fall into two categories. The first category includes those created with UNSC Resolutions referring to Chapter VII of the UN Charter. These include Althea in Bosnia, Atalanta in the Gulf of Aden, EUFOR RCA, as well as in the past the two operations in the DRC (2003 and 2006) or the one in Chad (2008–2009). The second category includes those created on the basis of an invitation, such as EUTMs in Mali, Somalia, and CAR.

Quite a few of the military operations not created on the basis of a UNSC resolution, as well as some civilian missions, are nonetheless referred to in UNSC resolutions. Such reference provides a degree of legitimacy to the EU endeavours. It also helps in future coordination with other international and local actors as various EU entities can draw on the UNSC text to justify their presence. In all cases, the host government has consented to the EU deployment.

In the field, EU and UN operations exhibit some similarities across levels. First, both EU and UN peace operations are consent-based and support rather than substitute local authorities. Although the EU's approach towards the use of force can be more robust than the UN's, both institutions are risk-averse and resent peace enforcement. Indeed, the three key principles of UN peacekeeping—impartiality, limited resort to force, and consent—by and large apply to EU-led operations. Interestingly, the EU and the UN are closer on the issue of the use of force than either organisation is to NATO or even the AU, which are both more comfortable with the idea of "enforcing peace" through military operations.

The scope of activities is equally large in both institutions that embrace the whole conflict spectrum, encompassing prevention, peacekeeping, peacebuilding, and stabilisation. Within this framework, the type of activities carried out are conceptually close. Both institutions seek to bring stability to a given place by using similar tools, i.e. a mix of military and civilian instruments that aim at providing security, strengthening the rule of law and governance institutions, reforming the security sector, facilitating economic recovery, supporting mediation and reconciliation, promoting human rights, etc. In doing so, the EU and the UN follow the "liberal peace" agenda by which the overall objective of their presence is the establishment of sustainable peace that should result from the combination of a democratic system and a market economy.

Finally, the UN and the EU are confronted with the same type of difficulties, ranging from a weak political support from their own member states to the difficulty to embed their operations in a broader political/strategic framework, the faltering consent of the host state and local actors, or the difficulty to operate and produce an impact in highly volatile environments (where there is no peace to keep) (Koops et al. 2015; UN 2014). The parallel UN and EU debates on the necessity to be "more strategic," the effectiveness and impact of the operations, the imperative of "delivering as one" or acting through a "comprehensive/integrated approach," and the insistence on local ownership and the critique of "imposing the liberal peace" all attest to similarities in the UN and EU's respective agendas and associated challenges.

In this context though, UN and EU operations also differ in certain ways. First, the UN global and universal mandate creates an expectation to respond to crises, an expectation that exists in no other regional organisation. The UN does not always intervene, but it certainly intervenes less selectively than the EU.

More practically, UN peace operations are significantly larger than EU operations. As an example, the latest two UN operations in Mali and CAR have over 10,000 uniformed personnel, which is more than the total strength of the 16 EU operations. The largest EU operation to date, operation Althea in Bosnia and Herzegovina, counted 7000 troops at its deployment in 2004, which would represent a modest size for any UN peacekeeping operation. Also, most EU civilian missions count less than 200 personnel, which makes them comparable to UN political missions rather than to peacekeeping operations.

Third, UN operations tend to be longer than EU operations, although recent trends indicate that EU operations' duration is increasing. While a few EU operations have indeed lasted a decade or more, most operations last less than five years. In contrast, UN operations often exceed a decade, for both good (the long-term needs of the host countries) and bad (structural difficulties to terminate them) reasons. This difference also accounts for variations in the two institutions' crisis management policies: a more crisis response-oriented for the EU vs. a longer-term structural approach for the UN.

Fourth, the combination of size and length creates a difference in the level of ambition and expected impact. Although CSDP operations can be quite ambitious, because of their format and duration, they can hardly be expected to generate the kind of strategic impact that UN operations may produce or aspire to have (Tardy 2015, pp. 32–33). The type of political, economic, and social engineering that characterises quite a few of the multidimensional UN operations is seldom at play within EU operations.

Fifth, the degree of political control is tighter over EU missions than over UN operations. Member states play a much more central role in the EU decision-making and planning processes than within the UN. This relates to the decision-making structure itself: while the UN Security Council is composed of a very limited number of states, and few with veto power, the EU Political and Security Committee comprises 28 members states with make decisions unanimously. In terms of planning, but also of command and control, the level of interference by or scrutiny of the political level is also more evident on the EU side. This implies a more politicised—and also more selective—EU approach, while UN operations can have a life on their own without much interference from the member states.

Sixth, as mentioned earlier, UN operations are more integrated than EU missions. For various reasons, it is not possible for EU operations to be of a civil-military nature; hence the typology of military operations vs. civilian missions. Following the release in 2016 of the EU Global Strategy for Foreign and Security Policy, the concept of an "integrated approach to conflicts and crises" has been framed within the EU to replace that of a "comprehensive approach." The EU "integrated approach" aims to further ensure the coherence and coordination of EU activities through a "multi-phased," "multi-dimensional," "multi-level," and "multi-lateral approach" (European Union 2016, p. 18). However, the civil-military caesura is there to stay within the EU and the type of integration of the military and civilian components within UN operations will remain unmatched in the EU.

Finally, the nature of troop contributors shapes the type of capabilities that are made available to the two organisations. Theoretically, UN operations could benefit from the military capabilities of European states if these states were contributing to UN operations. However, the quasi-absence of Europe—and as a matter of fact of most countries with high-tech military equipment—from UN operations deprives these operations from the equipment that EU or NATO operations benefit from.

The EU and the UN: Natural Partners?

In many ways, the relationship between the United Nations and the European Union has during the last decade developed into the most closed-knit institutionalised partnership between two independent organisations.

From a UN perspective, the EU aspiration to become a fully-fledged crisis management actor was initially perceived with cautious optimism and mixed feelings. On the one hand, it was hoped that this new capacity could be harnessed for supporting the UN with desperately needed resources and expertise; on the other hand, it was feared that the development of CSDP could further estrange Europeans from engaging directly in UN peacekeeping (Koops 2011, pp. 246–250). Both hopes and concerns turned out to be true.

In addition to civilian missions taking over or operating alongside the UN in Bosnia and Kosovo, the EU has launched four military operations directly in support of UN peacekeeping missions: Artemis and EUFOR RD Congo in support of MONUC in both 2003 and 2006, EUFOR Tchad/RCA in support of MINURCAT in 2008–2009, and EUFOR RCA as a bridging operation to the UN Mission in the Central African Republic in 2014.[3] In all four instances, the EU demonstrated that it could provide key resources and support to UN-led peacekeeping at critical junctures. Particularly operation Artemis, which was deployed less than two weeks after the UN Security Council's authorisation, highlighted the EU's (and most notably France's) willingness to support UN peacekeeping in a robust manner, although for a very short period of time and on strict EU terms (Gegout 2005). In 2006, EUFOR RD Congo once again reinforced MONUC's presence and posture during the DRC's first democratic elections. While posing a far more difficult logistical and political challenge, EUFOR Tchad/RCA marked a further step in EU-UN inter-organisational peacekeeping cooperation through the co-deployment during the first year and substantial re-hatting of EU troops to MINURCAT in 2009. More recently, EUFOR RCA acted as

[3] Artemis was a French-led EU mission, deployed from June to September 2003 to provide robust support to MONUC in Ituri. See United Nations Peacekeeping Best Practice Unit (2004). On EUFOR Tchad/RCA, see Mattelaer (2008).

a bridging operation before the MINUSCA took over. In addition, EU civilian missions (such as EUPOL and EUSEC RD Congo) supported MONUC through small-scale security sector reform and police reform, while the EU's largest civilian mission—EULEX Kosovo—has been working closely with UNMIK. In Mali, the two EU operations also play a role of burden-sharing with the UN operation (MINUSMA).

Second, interaction in the field has led to the formalisation and institutionalisation between the two Secretariats. Two UN-EU Joint Declarations signed in 2003 and 2007 respectively have laid the basis for this institutionalisation (Council of the European Union 2003, 2007). While the 2003 Declaration was a direct follow-up to the cooperation experience in the context of the EU Operation Artemis, the 2007 Joint statement reiterated the EU's commitment to UN peacekeeping and linked the partnership to joint capacity-building efforts vis-à-vis the African Union. Both documents advanced joint communication and coordination channels, such as desk-to-desk dialogue and regular video conferences on thematic issues and emerging security threats. The 2003 Declaration also called for a 'UN-EU Steering Committee' to convene twice a year in order to bring together key officials from both organisations with a view to strengthen inter-organisational relations. In 2011, the UN Department of Peacekeeping Operations (DPKO) and the Department of Political Affairs (DPA) opened a joint UN Liaison Office for Peace and Security (UNLOPS), establishing a permanent presence in Brussels and an additional layer of the UN's institutionalised cooperation with the European Union and to a lesser extent with NATO.

In the same vein, the EU issued in 2012 an "Action Plan on CSDP support to UN peacekeeping" (Council of the European Union 2012) that helped revitalise the partnership at a moment of rather low CSDP activity. The Action Plan defined a series of actions to move the relationship forward, with the hope on the UN side that the partnership would also take the form of national European contributions to UN peacekeeping operations. In 2014–2015, the deployment of EUFOR RCA as well as EUCAP Sahel Mali, in both cases in parallel with UN operations, allowed for renewed cooperation between the two institutions. In parallel, in 2015 a new framework on the "UN-EU Strategic Partnership on Peacekeeping and Crisis Management" covering the period 2015–2018 was being elaborated. The new plan identifies six priority areas: rapid response; support to the African Peace and Security Architecture; Facilitating EU member states' contributions to UN peacekeeping; Cooperation in Rule of Law and Security Sector Reform (SSR); Cooperation in Support and Logistics; Enhanced information and analysis exchange (Council of the European Union 2015b).

On the UN side, both the UN Secretary-General report "Partnering for peace: moving towards partnership peacekeeping" (UN 2015c), the High-Level Independent Panel on Peace Operations (UN 2015a), and the Secretary-General's report in response to the High-Level Panel (UN 2015b) emphasise the necessity to strengthen the "global-regional partnerships," in which the European Union, together with the African Union, play an important role.

Yet expectations are not always met and the initial concern about CSDP developing at the expense of UN operations has partly been vindicated. The UN Secretariat regularly calls for European national contributions to UN operations, in particular through "strategic enablers" such as helicopters, intelligence assets, or medical units. The possibility for the UN to rely in a semi-automatic manner on the deployment of the EU Battle Groups as a "first response capacity" that could serve as a "bridging force" until "the UN can mobilise and deploy a follow-on UN peace operation" is also regularly put forward (UN 2015b, para. 192). So far, however, this has been to no avail.

Indeed, before a come-back in Mali as of 2014–2015 (see below), the development of CSDP was also to an extent accompanied by a certain disengagement of European states from UN operations. In parallel, the evolution of crisis management and the respective roles of the UN and the EU in this field raised the issue of complementarity of these different frameworks, and even of competition between them.

Competition has been observed in areas where both organisations have a comparative advantage or where they both need to demonstrate their relevance. Parallel operations in the DRC, Chad, Kosovo, and Mali have shown how the organisations are eager to preserve their autonomy, access to information, or relation with the local actors, sometimes to the detriment of inter-organisational cooperation. UN-EU relations are also hindered by political divergences in their strategic assessments of particular crises as well as their conception of their own role or of peace operations. They are also mirrors of member states' priorities or institutional preferences. Finally, technical differences can be obstacles to smooth cooperation between institutions that have difficulties to interact for administrative or human resources reasons.[4]

Overall, while the UN-EU partnership has delivered tangible results, the two institutions are also fora and instruments of international politics, which carries incentives for cooperation as much as for defection.

Time for Europe to Return to UN Peacekeeping?

Stricto sensu, EU-UN cooperation does not include the issue of EU member states' contributions to UN operations. States participate in UN operations in their national capacity, and the idea that the EU as an institution could contribute to a UN-led operation has so far not happened.

However, the EU-UN relationship is in many ways dependent on EU member states' policies, their institutional preferences, and their perception of complementarity between UN and EU crisis management. As a matter of fact, while the 2012 EU-UN Action Plan, as well as the latest 2015 document, mention "national contributions" to UN peacekeeping operations as a key element of the partnership, this seems not to reflect reality. Indeed, European countries have largely moved away from UN peacekeeping as a result of the lessons drawn from their commitment to such operations in the early 1990s, mainly in Bosnia, Rwanda, and Somalia.

In 2017, EU states collectively financed between 35 and 40% of the UN peacekeeping budget, and played a central role in UN operations' mandate design, most notably through the two European permanent members of the Security Council (Tardy and Zaum 2016). But before the situation changed in 2014, when some European countries started to participate in the UN operation in Mali, European troop contributions had over the last twenty years remained minimal, oscillating between four and eight percent of the total.

As of December 2013, prior to the comeback of some European states to UN peacekeeping in Mali, the 28 EU member states were contributing 4819 military personnel and police—i.e. 4.9%—out of the 98,200 uniformed personnel deployed in the 16 UN peacekeeping operations. The bulk of the European contribution was deployed in the operation in Lebanon (UNIFIL). As of May 2017, that figure had raised to 6577 out of 96,617 uniformed personnel, that is 6.8%, as a result

[4] See for example Richard Gowan (2009).

of the contribution of Germany, the Netherlands, and Sweden to the MINUSMA in Mali (UN 2017).

European states have remained by and large committed to peace operations, but have favoured frameworks—such as the EU, NATO, or coalitions of states—that better suit their political and military requirements in terms of strategic cultures, command and control structures, or interoperability among troop contributors. For most of them, the UN has lost the trust placed in it right after the end of the Cold War, and is perceived as ill-equipped for complex crisis management. The command and control structure has received the most criticism and distrust. From a military point of view, the diversity of military cultures combined with the weak authority of Force commanders over the contingents deployed could only weaken the credibility of the UN chain of command and therefore the trust placed in it by units on the ground.

Since the mid-1990s, efforts have been made to try to reform the UN, with the hope that by making it more efficient, one could entice countries that formerly distanced themselves from the institution to reconsider their position and possibly return to UN operations. Lately, the argument has often been that "a lot has changed" within the UN and that the flaws of the early 1990s were now fixed, therefore allowing reticent countries to consider coming back to UN peacekeeping. The debate was particularly prominent in 2013–2014 in the context of the termination of the International Security Assistance Force (ISAF) in Afghanistan around the idea that some of the Western or European states present in ISAF might switch to UN operations once they pulled out their troops from Afghanistan (Johnson 2014, pp. 85–96; Smith 2014; Byers 2012). And indeed, a few of them approached the UN DPKO to explore further this option.

It is in this context that the Netherlands, and then Sweden and Germany, announced their participation in the UN operation in Mali (MINUSMA), mainly through Intelligence, Surveillance and Reconnaissance units. In parallel, a few European countries—among them the Netherlands, Sweden, Norway, Denmark, Germany, Finland, and Estonia—have contributed personnel to an intelligence fusion cell integrated into the MINUSMA (Karlsrud and Smith 2015). As of May 2017, the Dutch, German and Swedish contributions to the MINUSMA were 273, 618, and 199 respectively (UN 2017).

This shows to an extent a return of European states to UN peacekeeping, or at least openness towards the UN as a political and operational crisis management actor.[5] Indeed the UN displays comparative advantages that may trigger renewed interest given the complexity of contemporary threats. Most prominently, the UN provides a unique framework for cooperation between Western and non-Western states at a time when the former may want to reach out to the latter in their security policies (Gowan 2015). UN operations may also be seen as operational responses to states' fragility and this fragility's possible consequences in terms of political destabilisation or youth's radicalisation. In the case of Mali, contributing to the UN operation can be a way to participate in the broad international stabilisation efforts of the Sahel without being involved in the direct military confrontation with the armed groups operating in Northern Mali.

Whether this comeback is a prelude to a more significant return to UN peacekeeping remains to be seen; at least three obstacles exist.

First, mistrust *vis-à-vis* the UN still tends to prevail within European ministries of defence where the thinking is still influenced by the 1990 engagements in Bosnia, Rwanda, and Somalia. The idea that the UN has, through several processes of reform, become a more effective crisis management actor is up for debate. Ministries of foreign affairs might be more agnostic on the virtues of the UN in peacekeeping, but military officials by and large still see the organisation as unfit to the task of complex crisis management. The UN institutional culture and the command and control structure are recurrently invoked as obstacles to a renewed European commitment. As a matter of fact, the Report of the High-level Independent Panel on Peace Operations acknowledges that the UN still suffers from "weak command and control" and has not sufficiently invested in this field (UN 2015a, paras. 35, 115).

Second, a comparative analysis of the various existing institutional channels does not portray the UN in the most favourable manner, as institutions such as NATO or the EU would in most cases be seen as more appropriate. The Mali situation—with a significant contribution from two European countries—provides an exception to this rule. The analysis in the Netherlands, Sweden, and Germany was that the UN, because of the nature of its operation in Mali, was the most appropriate recipient for the type of assets that they were willing to deploy. Such a

[5] See on this the Special Issue of *International Peacekeeping* by the editors Joachim Koops and Giulia Tercovich (2016), with chapters on Germany (Joachim Koops), the Netherlands (Niels van Willigen), and Sweden (Claes Nilsson and Kristina Zetterlund).

scenario can be replicated elsewhere with other European States. Yet the incentives to opt for the UN rather than the EU, NATO, or multilateral operations are not obvious and in reality, European states are likely to prefer the more restricted clubs, both as a path dependency choice and for political reasons.

The EU itself may not always come up as the best option, and recent EU operations have shown that the EU could also suffer from a certain level of disaffection. How this may incentivise European states to look at the UN in a more positive way is very uncertain. In this context, the type of lessons that the Europeans will draw from their experience in the MINUSMA will in part determine both their own long-term commitments and a possible come back for other European states. The literature that is appearing on these issues, often based on the Mali situation, seems to indicate that the European states that have contributed to the MINUSMA are more vindicated in their mistrust *vis-à-vis* the UN than reassured that the UN is one option amongst several. What the MINUSMA has also revealed is the emergence of a two-tier operation in which the Europeans and the non-European contingents hardly communicate with one another, and where the African and Asian contingents benefit very little from the intelligence gathered by the Europeans (Albrecht et al. 2017). This is in itself an interesting conclusion as it tends to undermine the assumption by which Europeans are needed in UN operations because of the enablers that they bring.

Finally, a possible European "comeback to UN operations" is also to be analysed for what it would imply for the EU CSDP. Given the general restrictions on force projection resources, any scenario that would mean a significant European contribution to UN operations would most likely play to the detriment of the political and operational prominence of CSDP, as much as CSDP can develop at the expense of the UN. European states commit assets to UN or EU operations, but probably not to both at the same time. The last fifteen years have indeed shown that assets provided to the EU (troops, enablers, etc.) were de facto not provided to the UN. Typically, the principle of bridging operations means that EU member states decide not to participate in UN operations but rather to support them through EU operations. Paradoxically, it is possibly precisely because European states are not in the UN mission that the bridging operation becomes necessary.

Conclusion

As highlighted by the various studies or reports on UN peace operations released in 2015, the crisis management landscape has evolved into a multi-actors endeavour that calls for an inclusive "global-regional partnership"[6] (UN 2015a, p. viii; 2015b, paras. 28–32).

The United Nations has a key role to play in materialising such partnerships and building coherence out of the various institutions' priorities and activities. Similarly, the European Union is one of the main pillars of this effort, and the latest EU Global Strategy clearly reasserts the European commitment to promote a "rules-based global order" with the "United Nations at its core" (European Union 2016, p. 10). Indeed, the EU has become an autonomous crisis management actor that in most cases operates alongside the UN and potentially can support UN operations in different ways.

Yet the degree of compatibility between the UN and the EU is to be evaluated in light of the two institutions' respective agendas and constraints. The EU has embraced a conception of crisis management that is close to the UN's and is a priori willing to support the "global-regional peace and security partnership"; also, EU operations need the UN for legitimacy and in their transition strategies, in particular when the UN takes over from the EU and practically enables the EU to withdraw.

But the EU is also a highly politicised and state-dominated organisation that aspires to ensure its own visibility and independence. Besides, despite recent developments in Mali with significant European contributions to the UN operation, EU member states continue to view the UN with a certain level of suspicion and are overall reluctant to participate directly in UN operations. In this context, this chapter poses the following two questions for further research and strategic policy deliberation: (1) how long can the absence of European states from UN peacekeeping be prolonged without truly undermining the UN-EU peace and security partnership, and beyond it the North-South dialogue? and (2) do UN peace operations respond to evolving security threats in a way that makes European states want to re-investing in them?

[6] See ibid., p. viii, and 'The future of UN peace operations: implementation of the recommendations of the High-level Independent Panel on Peace Operations', Report of the Secretary-General, A/70/357, 2 September 2015, paras. 28–32.

References

Albrecht, Peter, Signe Marie Cold-Ravnkilde, and Rikke Haugegaard. 2017. *African Peacekeepers in Mali*. Copenhagen: Danish Institute for International Studies.

Biscop, Sven, and Richard Whitman (eds.). 2012. *The Routledge Handbook of European Security*. London: Routledge.

Bund, Jakob, Daniel Fiott, Thierry Tardy, and Zoe Stanley-Lockman. 2017. *EUISS Yearbook of European Security 2017*. Paris: European Institute for Security Studies. https://www.iss.europa.eu/content/euiss-yearbook-european-security-2017. Accessed 16 Nov 2017.

Byers, Michael. 2012. After Afghanistan: Canada's Return to UN Peacekeeping. *Canadian Military Journal* 13 (1): 33–39.

Council of the European Union. 2003. Joint UN-EU Declaration on Cooperation in Crisis Management, September 24. New York: European Union.

Council of the European Union. 2007. Joint Statement on UN-EU Cooperation in Crisis Management, June 7. Brussels: European Union.

Council of the European Union. 2012. Plan of Action to Enhance EU CSDP Support to UN Peacekeeping, June 14. Brussels: European Union.

Council of the European Union. 2015a. *Council Decision (CFSP) 2015/778 of 18 May 2015 on a European Union Military Operation in the Southern Central Mediterranean (EUNAVFOR MED)*. Brussel: European Union.

Council of the European Union. 2015b. Strengthening the UN–EU Strategic Partnership on Peacekeeping and Crisis Management: Priorities 2015–2018. European External Action Service, March 27. Brussels: European Union.

European External Action Service. 2017. Security and Defence. European Union. https://eeas.europa.eu/headquarters/headquarters-homepage/area/security-and-defence_en. Accessed 16 Nov 2017.

European Parliament. 2012: CSDP Missions and Operations. Lessons Learned Processes. European Parliament Think Tank. http://www.europarl.europa.eu/thinktank/en/document.html?reference=EXPO-SEDE_ET(2012)457062. Accessed 16 Nov 2017.

European Union. 2007. *Consolidated Version of the Treaty on European Union, 13 December*. Lisbon: European Union.

European Union. 2016. Shared Vision, Common Action: A Global Strategy for the EU's Foreign and Security Policy, June. Brussels. https://europa.eu/globalstrategy/sites/globalstrategy/files/eugs_review_web.pdf. Accessed 16 Nov 2017.

Gegout, Catherine. 2005. Causes and Consequences of the EU's Military Intervention in the Democratic Republic of Congo. *European Foreign Affairs Review* 10: 427–443.

Gowan, Richard. 2009. ESDP and the United Nations. In *European Security and Defence Policy. The First Ten Years (1999–2009)*. Paris: EUISS.

Gowan, Richard. 2015. UN Peace Operations and European Security: New Strategic Dynamics. European Council on Foreign Relations, Commentary, February 25.

Grevi, Giovanni, Damien Helly, and Daniel Keohane (eds.). 2009. *European Security and Defence Policy. The First Ten Years (1999–2009)*. Paris: EUISS.

Howorth, Jolyon. 2007. *Security and Defence Policy in the European Union*. Basingstoke: Palgrave Macmillan.

Howorth, Jolyon. 2014. *Security and Defence Policy in the European Union*, 2nd ed. London: Palgrave-Macmillan.

Johnson, Adrian. 2014. After Afghanistan: A British Military Return to Peacekeeping? In *New Trends in Peacekeeping: In Search for a New Direction*, 85–96, International Symposium on Security Affairs, November 5. Tokyo: National Institute for Defense Studies.

Joint Declaration on European Defence. 1998. Joint Declaration issued at the British-French Summit, December 4. Saint-Malo.

Karlsrud, John, and Adam Smith. 2015. European Military Participation in MINUSMA. Experiences and Lessons-Learned. New York: International Peace Institute.

Koops, Joachim A. 2011. *The European Union as an Integrative Power: Assessing the EU's 'Effective Multilateralism' Towards the United Nations and NATO*. Brussels: VUB Press.

Koops, Joachim, and Giulia Tercovich. 2016. A European Return to UN Peacekeeping? Special Issue. *International Peacekeeping* 23 (5): 597–609.

Koops, Joachim, Norrie McQueen, Thierry Tardy, and Paul D. Williams. 2015. Introduction: Peacekeeping in the Twenty-First Century. In *The Oxford Handbook of UN Peacekeeping Operations*. Oxford: Oxford University Press.

Mattelaer, Alexander. 2008. The Strategic Planning of EU Military Operations—The Case of EUFOR Tchad/RCA. IES Working Paper No. 5, Institute for European Studies, Brussels.

Smith, Adam. 2014. European Military Capabilities and UN Peace Operations: Strengthening the Partnership. *Policy Briefing*. Berlin: ZIF.

Tardy, Thierry, and Dominic Zaum. 2016. France and the United Kingdom at the UN Security Council. In *The UN Security Council in the 21st Century*, ed. Sebastian von Einsiedel, David M. Malone, and Bruno S. Ugarte. Lynne Rienner: Boulder.

Tardy, Thierry. 2015. CSDP in Action. What Contribution to International Security? *Chaillot Papers* No. 134, May, EUISS, Paris.

United Nations. 2015a. *Report of the High-Level Independent Panel on Peace Operations on Uniting Our Strengths for Peace: Politics, Partnership and People*. New York: United Nations.

United Nations. 2015b. *The Future of UN Peace Operations: Implementation of the Recommendations of the High-Level Independent Panel on Peace Operations.* New York: United Nations.

United Nations. 2015c. Partnering for Peace: Moving Towards Partnership Peacekeeping. Report of the Secretary-General to the Security Council. New York: United Nations.

United Nations. 2014. New Challenges and Priorities for UN Peacekeeping. Speech by United Nations Under-Secretary-General Hervé Ladsous, June 17. The Brookings Institution.

United Nations. 2017. Troop and Police Contributors. United Nations Peacekeeping. https://peacekeeping.un.org/en/troop-and-police-contributors. Accessed 5, 11 Dec 2017.

United Nations Peacekeeping Best Practice Unit. 2004. Operation Artemis: The Lessons of the Interim Emergency Multinational Force, October. New York: United Nations.

Open Access This chapter is licensed under the terms of the Creative Commons Attribution 4.0 International License (http://creativecommons.org/licenses/by/4.0/), which permits use, sharing, adaptation, distribution and reproduction in any medium or format, as long as you give appropriate credit to the original author(s) and the source, provide a link to the Creative Commons license and indicate if changes were made.

The images or other third party material in this chapter are included in the chapter's Creative Commons license, unless indicated otherwise in a credit line to the material. If material is not included in the chapter's Creative Commons license and your intended use is not permitted by statutory regulation or exceeds the permitted use, you will need to obtain permission directly from the copyright holder.

CHAPTER 13

China Rising and Its Changing Policy on UN Peacekeeping

Yin He

The[1,2] past four decades we have witnessed China's increasingly active participation in United Nations Peacekeeping Operations (PKOs). The existing literature on this issue has an obvious feature: many writers have focused on policy analysis or review (Stahle 2008; Gill and Huang 2009; International Crisis Group 2009; Lanteigne 2014). According to those analysts, China's active participation in PKOs is largely driven by a long list of pragmatic needs or interests ranging from belief in multilateralism and image building to more traditional concerns such as isolating separatist forces in Taiwan and securing its overseas investments (Gill and Huang 2009). Hence, it has been very difficult for different writers to agree on the core reason behind China's changing attitude towards UN peacekeeping. Some writers have applied theoretical analysis to their

[1] The views expressed in this chapter are the author's personal opinions. They do not represent the views of the China Peacekeeping Police Training Center or the Chinese Ministry of Public Security.

[2] This research was supported by the China National Social Sciences Fund project "China's Strategy on Participation in UN Peacekeeping Operations" (16ZDA094).

Y. He (✉)
China Peacekeeping Police Training Center, Langfang, China

© The Author(s) 2019

C. de Coning and M. Peter (eds.), *United Nations Peace Operations in a Changing Global Order*,
https://doi.org/10.1007/978-3-319-99106-1_13

research in China's peacekeeping behaviour (Sicurelli 2010), but they have failed to find the most important variable driving China's changing peacekeeping behaviour. In the 1970s, China opposed PKOs; today, it is a major supporter of UN peacekeeping. Is there any fundamental variable shaping this significant change? If there is, what is it, and how has it affected China's attitude towards the UN peacekeeping regime? This chapter explores the cause and effect of China's changing policy on UN peacekeeping, and argues that changes in China's national identity have led to changes in the country's foreign policy, including that on UN peacekeeping.

The first section of this chapter presents an analytical framework, and proposes the hypothesis that China's national identity is the most important factor shaping its behaviour within the UN peacekeeping regime. The second section discusses how China's international identities have affected its policy on UN peacekeeping during the period from 1971 to 2000. The third section analyses China's national identity and policy on UN peacekeeping in the twenty-first century. The last section concludes by raising questions for further research.

Analytical Framework

Many researchers believe that China's current policy of increasingly active participation in UN peacekeeping is largely driven by a long list of pragmatic needs or interests (Lynch 2014; Lanteigne 2014; Fung 2016). According to them, China's policy on peacekeeping is the result of a reactive response to those pragmatic needs or interests.

One cannot deny that national interests, especially the immediate ones, can affect a state's policy on international affairs. However, one will also find it hard to believe that a realism-oriented policy analysis can show the full picture of China as an active peacekeeper, especially given China's rise over the past four decades. In fact, many arguments based on policy analysis are easy to falsify. For example, some point to South Sudan and argue that China's participation in UN peacekeeping is driven by its increasing need for natural resources, such as oil (Lynch 2014). However, the deployment of substantial numbers of peacekeeping troops to places like Darfur, Lebanon, and Haiti—which lack significant stocks of natural resources—surely limits the strength of this argument. For another example, some analysts argue that Beijing's One China policy is the most important factor affecting the country's peacekeeping behaviour (International Crisis Group 2009). This might have been true in the 1980s and 1990s. However, as shown in its continuous support for the UN peacekeeping efforts in Haiti, a poverty-stricken Caribbean state which has long adopted a pro-Taiwan policy, geopolitical factors are not the most significant variable affecting present-day China's peacekeeping behaviour.

Any state's interests in international affairs are subject to change over time. This has been the case with China's interests in UN peacekeeping. In the 1970s, China stayed away from UN peacekeeping due to its normative stance on state sovereignty and non-intervention. From the 1980s to the 1990s, China's gradual adjustment of its attitude towards UN peacekeeping was mainly due to its need for a favourable international environment that could benefit its own economic development-oriented reform and opening up strategy. In the new century, China's increasingly active participation in UN peacekeeping serves three major interests: being a responsive power, strengthening the UN, and sharing common concerns for peace and security (He 2007).

To explore the fundamental reason behind China's changing policy on UN peacekeeping, one needs to look beyond China's pragmatic interests and answer the following question: Why has China shown different interests in UN peacekeeping affairs over the past four decades? Constructivism provides an insightful perspective for answering the question. According to this theoretical perspective, identity defines interests (Wendt 1999; Finnemore 1996). Applying this idea to the case of China's engagement in UN peacekeeping, the changing policies in this area derive from key shifts in China's national identity. Moreover, as constructivism also holds that interests define behaviour, there are causal relations between identity and behaviour. This chapter analyses the link between China's evolving national identity and its changing policy on UN peacekeeping in terms of causal relations.

However, in this chapter, the concept of "identity" is based on, but not limited to, the way in which it appears within the constructivist literature. Rather than the idea of a shared culture that is largely unaffected by material factors, here identity is conceptualised as being affected by both ideational and material factors (Kratochwill 1989; Ruggie 1998). Although the chapter does not take a purely theoretical stance, it adopts an eclectic analytical framework which draws theoretical support from mainstream international relations meta-theoretical approaches, including realism, institutionalism, and constructivism. To be more specific,

China's national identity is mainly constructed by three factors: the country's increasing comprehensive national strength, its increasingly active participation in the international institutions, and its increasing socialisation within the international community (Johnston 2008).

China's Changing National Identity and Policies on UN Peacekeeping Before the Twenty-First Century

Significant political, military, and social changes tend to generate shifts in a state's national identity (Qin 2005). During the period from 1971 to the end of the twentieth century, China's national identity has undergone two distinctive phases: from a semi-revolutionist state largely staying out of the international community dominated by the Western powers in 1970s, to an integrated member of the international community in 1980s and 1990s. Each of these phases had led China to develop different policies on UN peacekeeping. These two identities were later on replaced by a third and current one; that of a rising power, which also brought with it stronger Chinese engagement with UN peacekeeping operations.

A Semi-revolutionist State in 1970s

In the 1970s, China was to some degree a revolutionary state, or a semi-revolutionary state, in that it kept a sceptical eye on the existing international community dominated by the Western powers. Despite having returned to the UN in 1971 and gradually improved relations with the Western powers, especially after Richard Nixon's historic visit in 1972, China's international outlook had not changed significantly. It continued to regard itself as a victim of the imperialist behaviour of the two superpowers—the United States (along with other Western capitalist powers) and the Soviet Union—as it did in the 1960s, and identified itself with the Third World (Choedon 2005). During this period, revolution and struggle were still the banners of China's diplomacy. China wished to fulfil its international moral responsibility towards other Third World countries by strictly adhering to the Westphalian norms of state sovereignty and non-intervention. As a state which to a great extent remained outside the international community dominated by the West, China did not have much interest in accepting the rules and norms of the international system. As a result, it condemned and opposed the creation of new PKOs and the continuation of the existing missions, refused to share the burden of the peacekeeping budget or contribute personnel to ongoing operations, and abstained from UNSC voting (He 2007). The People's Liberation Army (PLA) was preoccupied with its traditional task of safeguarding China's territorial integrity and had no interest in international operations like peacekeeping. As a result, throughout in the 1970s China remained opposed to UN peacekeeping.

An Integrated Member in 1980s and 1990s

In the 1980s and 1990s, as China sought to become an integrated member of the international community, it began to selectively embrace the UN peacekeeping regime. Beijing's adoption of economic reform and opening up policy, starting at the end of the 1970s, shifted its focus from domestic as well as international revolution to development, especially economic development. After re-establishing diplomatic relations with the major Western states, especially the United States, China found its international security environment greatly improved (Kim 1987), which enabled it to allocate limited resources towards development-oriented reform and to its opening-up strategy. This in turn improved China's international status and self-confidence as a participant in international affairs. During the 12th National Congress of the Communist Party of China (CPC) held in 1982, an "independent foreign policy of peace" (*duli zizhu de heping waijiao zhengce*) was formulated, marking China's new willingness to play down its ideological disagreement with the West and its determination to seek peaceful coexistence (He 2007). China's adoption of the independent foreign policy of peace reflected its pragmatic strategy of integrating into the international community. Despite changes in both the international and domestic environment, Beijing largely stuck to this strategy throughout 1980s and 1990s. To this end, China needed to make good use of its limited domestic and international resources. As a veto-wielding permanent member in the UNSC, China found that its policy on UN peacekeeping, if well designed, could generate precious diplomatic capital, especially to break the isolation imposed by the Western states after 1989. As a result, Beijing gradually became engaged in UN peacekeeping.

This shift entailed several measures. First, China adjusted its attitude towards UN peacekeeping by providing financial support for PKOs and by participating in UNSC voting. In 1981, China voted in the UNSC for the first time, in favour of Resolution 495, which extended the ongoing UN Peacekeeping Force in Cyprus (UNFICYP). In 1982, China began to pay its dues for peacekeeping. Then, it began to show interest in participating in UN peacekeeping. In November 1988, China joined the UN Special Peacekeeping Committee. Five months later, in an unprecedented move, China's ambassador to the UN, Yu Mengjia, called on the international community to give powerful support to UN peacekeeping. Finally, in 1990, China became a peacekeeper by deploying five military observers to the UN Truce Supervision Organization (UNTSO) in the Middle East.

China's policy on UN peacekeeping in 1980s and 1990s largely reflected a balance between its traditional normative position and pragmatic concerns for its national interests, in particular those regarding its strategy of becoming an integrated member of the international community. During this period, especially in the 1990s, China had shown a certain degree of flexibility in its policy on UN Peacekeeping, in particular on the principle of use of force. Thirty-six PKOs were established between 1988 and 1998. China voted in favour of all operations that carried out traditional peacekeeping tasks as well as the continuation of all ongoing traditional PKOs that were established during the Cold War era. At the same time, it had not vetoed any PKOs mandated under Chapter VII of the UN Charter. Most notably, after Iraq invaded Kuwait, in November 1990 China chose abstention rather than a veto during the voting on UNSC Resolution 678, which authorised Member States to use all necessary means to restore international peace and security in Kuwait.

Being eager to get integrated into the international community, China would often react to deeds of other countries that challenged its membership. In 1997, China vetoed a UNSC draft resolution to deploy military observers to verify the implementation of ceasefire agreements in Guatemala, which had been active in pushing for Taiwan's membership in the UN. In 1999, Macedonia shifted its recognition from Beijing to Taipei 17 days before the UNSC intended to deliberate upon the extension of the UN Preventive Deployment Force (UNPREDEP). Beijing was enraged and vetoed the UNSC draft resolution.

China's National Identity and Policy on UN Peacekeeping in the Twenty-First Century

The third and current Chinese identity is one of a rising power, which is coupled with a stronger engagement in UN peacekeeping operations. China, indeed, is a rising power in the twenty-first century (Ikenberry 2008). It needs a foreign policy fitting into its strategy for peaceful rise. This section examines China's new national identity and policy on UN peacekeeping in the new century. Key questions to be answered include: how has the new national identity come into been?, and how has it affected China's policy on UN peacekeeping?

A Rising Power in the Twenty-First Century

China's strategy of being an integrated member of the international community in 1980s and 1990s proved a success. Continuous adoption of the development-oriented policy and increasing socialisation into the international community have contributed to rapid growth of national strength. Entering the twenty-first century, China's further integration into the global economy, marked by its participation in the World Trade Organization, among other things, secured the prospect of continuous high-speed economic growth. In the first decade of the twenty-first century, China's national strength had reached a new height. As is shown in Chart 13.1, according to statistics provided by the United Nations Statistics Division (2016), China's Gross Domestic Product (GDP) surpassed those of Germany, France, and the United Kingdom in around 2005. In 2010 it overtook Japan to become the second largest economy.

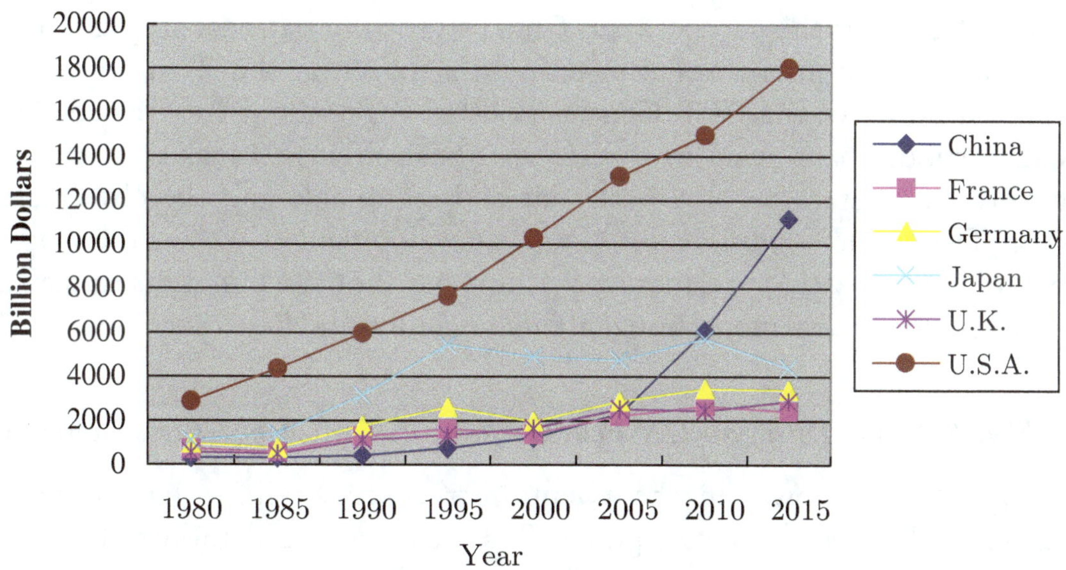

Chart 13.1 China and Major Western Powers' GDP (*Source* Author's own calculation based on data from United Nations Statistics Division 2016)

Enhanced national strength encourages China to rethink its identity in the international arena. In 1999, after China successfully tided over the Asian Financial Crisis, then Chinese Premier Zhu Rongji declared that China wanted to be a "responsible power" (*fuzeren daguo*). In late 2003, Zheng Bijian, then executive vice-president of the Party School of the CPC Central Committee, introduced the term of "peaceful rise" (*heping jueqi*) at the Boao Forum for Asia (Xinhua 2004). The term was accepted by the Chinese leadership (Medeiros 2004). However, as a rising power concerned about its international image, China cannot ignore the doubts and misgivings from outside such as the "China Threat" debate (Munro 1992; Yee and Storey 2002; Callahan 2005). The Chinese leadership might have recognised that the assertiveness reflected in "peaceful rise" could fuel perceptions that China was a threat to the established order dominated by the West. As a result, the concept "peaceful rise" gradually faded away in the Chinese political discourse and was replaced by the term "peaceful development" (*heping fazhan*). In May 2004, China's President Hu Jintao used "peaceful development" in a speech at the Boao Forum for Asia. In December 2005, The State Council Information Office (2005) of People's Republic of China issued a white paper titled *China's Peaceful Development Road.*

After Xi Jinping became the General Secretary of the CPC in November 2012, Beijing has become more confident in expressing its dissatisfaction at the gap between China's growing national strength and its status in the international system. In a speech at the 27th collective study meeting of the CCP Central Politburo, President Xi stressed that China should participate in the international efforts to make the global governance system become more fair and reasonable and thereby create more favourable conditions for China's development as well as the world peace (Xinhua 2015). To that end, China has shown willingness to play a more active role in international affairs, including UN peacekeeping.

China's Active Policy on UN Peacekeeping in the Twenty-First Century

Being a rising power in the twenty-first century, China has adopted an active UN peacekeeping policy. The activeness is demonstrated not only in its strong support for UN peacekeeping operations and relevant affairs, but also in its evolving doctrine on UN peacekeeping.

As of 31 August 2017, China had 2654 peacekeepers, including 2417 troops, 81 UN Military Experts on Mission (UNMEM) and staff

Table 13.1 China's contribution of peacekeeping personnel to ongoing UN PKOs, as of 31 March 2017

Operations	*Host country*	*Individual police*	*Formed police unit*	*UNMEM & Staff officer*	*Contingent troop*	*Total*
MINURSO	West Sahara			11		11
MINUSMA	Mali			8	395	403
MONUSCO	The DRC			16	218	234
UNAMA	Afghanistan	1				1
UNAMID	Darfur, Sudan			10	365	375
UNIFIL	Lebanon			8	410	418
UNFICYP	Cyprus	7				7
UNMIL	Liberia	1	140	1		142
UNMISS	South Sudan	7		23	1029	1059
UNTSO	Middle East			4		4
Total		**16**	**140**	**81**	**2417**	**2654**

Source Author's own calculation based on data from United Nations (2017a)

officers, and 156 police officers, in 9 of the 15 ongoing United Nations PKOs and one special political mission (see Table 13.1).[3] It ranked 11th among the 124 troop and police-contributing countries and number one among the five UN Security Council permanent members (P5) in terms of the contribution of personnel (United Nations 2017b). So far China has contributed a total of more than 35,000 military and police peacekeepers to the UN-commanded PKOs and special political missions. As is shown in Chart 13.2, back in 2000, China had the lowest number of UN peacekeepers among the permanent members. However, the last 15 years, China's contribution of UN peacekeepers has increased rapidly while contributions of all the other four P5 have either remained at a low level or significantly decreased.

China's assessment rate in contribution to UN peacekeeping in the 2016–2018 fiscal years is 10.28% (United Nations 2015). As is shown in Chart 13.3, back in 2001, its assessment rate was merely about two percent. However, since then, China's assessment rate has rapidly increased

[3] It should be noted that uniformed personnel, including military observers, and police officers on political missions commanded by the UN Department of Political Affairs are UN peacekeepers too.

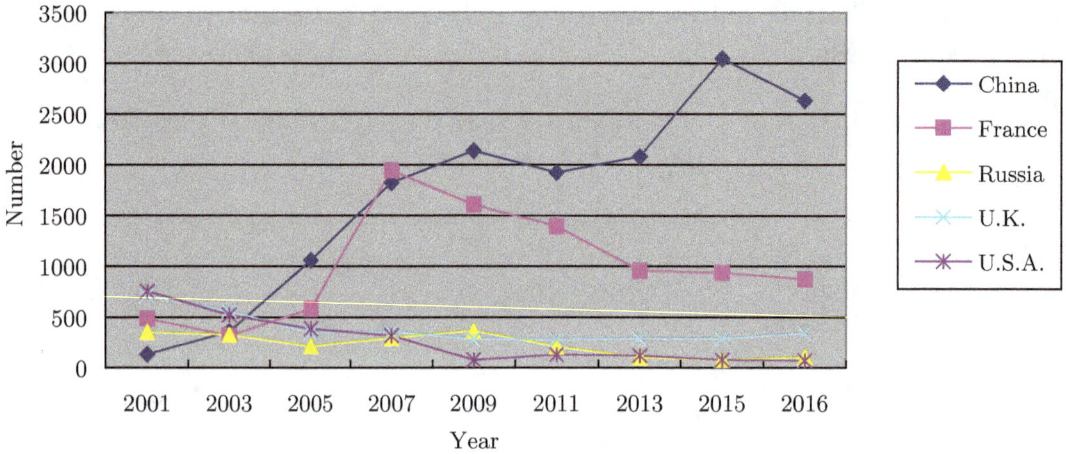

Chart 13.2 UNSC permanent members' contribution of UN Peacekeepers (2001–2016) (*Source* Author's own calculation based on data from United Nations 2017c)

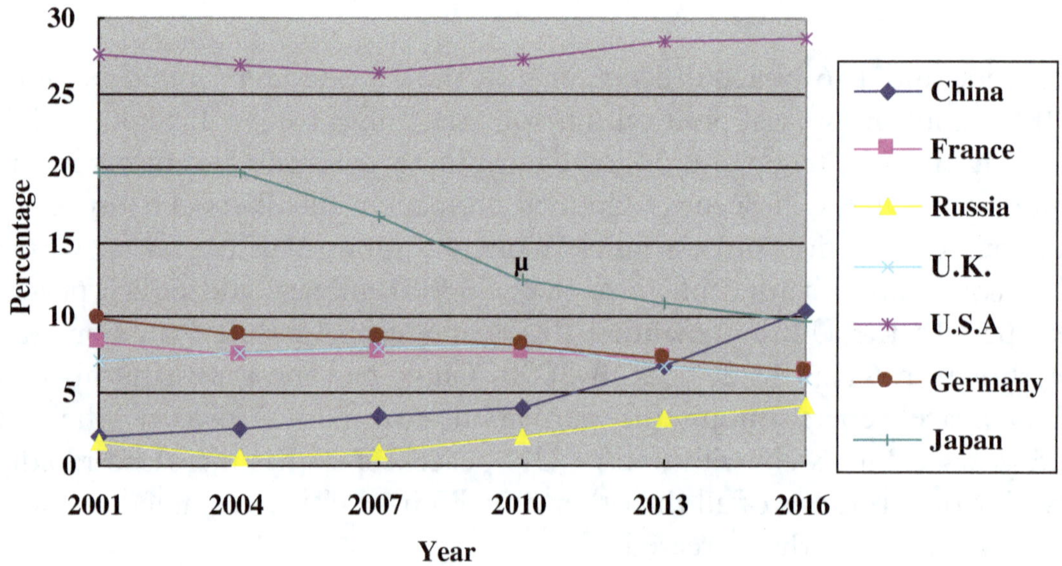

Chart 13.3 Major Power's assessment rate in contribution to UN Peacekeeping (2001–2016) (*Source* Author's own calculation based on data from United Nations 2015)

while most other major power's assessment rates have declined. China is now the second largest UN peacekeeping budget contributor among all the 193 UN Member States, and the largest among the developing countries (United Nations 2015).

China also attaches great importance to peacekeeping personnel training. It has invested heavily in setting up peacekeeping training facilities and uses them, among other things, as institutions for relevant international cooperation. China established China Peacekeeping Police Training Center in 2000 and the Ministry of Defense Peacekeeping Center in 2009. Both training centres have advanced facilities, which showcases China's increased material capabilities as well as strong political will of participating in UN peacekeeping.

Since 1990s China has been to learn the field of peacekeeping. It often sends delegates to participate in training courses, academic workshops and seminars held in other UN Member States, including those held in Western states such as the United Kingdom, France, Australia, the United States as well as in Nordic countries. It has also received peacekeeping training assistance from United Kingdom, France, and other states. However, in recent years, as China gradually gained more and more experience in peacekeeping, it is no longer merely a "participant" or "learner" of various peacekeeping-related international activities, but also an increasingly active organiser. Both the Chinese police and military peacekeeping training institutions often host international training courses and academic exchange activities.

China's strong support for UN peacekeeping is also reflected in its active engagement in hotspot issues that affect international peace and security. Working together with their international colleagues including those from the United States and Europe, the Chinese special representatives and minister of foreign affairs have made significant contributions to the peace process in South Sudan, Darfur in Sudan, the eastern part of the Democratic Republic of the Congo (DRC), Mali, Afghanistan, and the Middle East.[4] Besides, China has given strong support for the UNSC Resolution 1816 (UN 2008), which calls for international efforts to fight pirate activities in the Gulf of Aden. It has deployed the PLA Navy ships to conduct escort missions in the region's international waters since 2008. On 4 January 2014, one Chinese frigate Yancheng joined

[4] Interview with an official from the Chinese Ministry of Foreign Affairs, Beijing, 18 June 2014.

the international escort mission for the disposal of Syrian chemical weapons in response to appeals from the UNSC and the Organization for the Prohibition of Chemical Weapons (Xinhua 2014a).

The PLA, China's armed forces, has included peacekeeping as one of its major missions. In March 2013, the MND issued a white paper called The Diversified Employment of China's Armed Forces, which for the first time systematically explained the PLA's missions in the twenty-first century (State Council Information Office 2013). The white paper states that the PLA has diversified its missions to include defending national sovereignty, security, and territorial integrity, supporting national economic and social development, and safeguarding world peace and regional stability. It explains that the PLA should assume its due international responsibilities, and play an active role in maintaining world peace, security, and stability (State Council Information Office 2013).

Most significantly, on 28 September 2015, in his statement at the General Debate of the 70th Session of the UN General Assembly and remarks at the UN Peacekeeping Summit, Chinese president Xi Jinping (2015a, b) announced six important commitments to support the improvement and strengthening of UN peacekeeping:

First, China will join the new UN peacekeeping Capability Readiness System and set up a permanent peacekeeping police squad and build a peacekeeping standby force of 8000 troops. Second, China will give favorable consideration to UN requests for more Chinese engineering soldiers and transportation and medical staff to take part in UN PKOs. Third, in the coming five years, China will train 2000 peacekeepers from other countries, and carry out 10 demining assistance programs which will include training and equipment provision. Fourth, in the coming five years, China will provide free military aid of US$100 million to the African Union to support the building of the African Standby Force and the African Capacity for Immediate Response to Crisis. Fifth, China will send the first peacekeeping helicopter squad to UN PKOs in Africa. Sixth, China will establish a 10-year, US$1 billion China-UN peace and development fund to support the UN's work, advance multilateral cooperation and contribute more to world peace and development. Part of the fund will be used to support UN PKOs.

These six Chinese measures show that China has decided to expand its contribution to UN peacekeeping and relevant international efforts of maintaining peace and security. Considering its rising power identity as well as being a key UN Member State, China's huge support package is of special significance. Although during the 2015 UN Summit and afterwards, many other Member States have also made similar promises to support the UN peacekeeping, so far none of them have given support as significant as that of China.

As most of the ongoing PKOs are operating in volatile places, increasing contribution of peacekeepers can mean increasing possibilities of fatalities and injuries. On 1 June 2016, terrorists attacked the barracks of the Chinese peacekeeping security unit located in Gao, Mali with a vehicle bomb, leading to the death of one Chinese peacekeeper and four injuries. A few weeks later, on 10 July, another two Chinese peacekeepers were killed and five more injured in a mortar exchange between the government forces and the rebel army in Juba, South Sudan. Although both accidents have aroused heated discussion among the Chinese public on security of peacekeepers, Beijing has not shown any signs of withdrawing troops from Mali or South Sudan or intention to reduce its contribution of peacekeeping personnel. In October 2016, China announced that the equipment of a 140-person PLA air unit with four multifunctional helicopters was been transported to the African Union/United Nations Hybrid Operation in Darfur (UNAMID). In September 2016, a 150-person Chinese police unit passed the UN selection process to serve as the first standby Formed Police Unit in the organisation's history. By November 2017, PLA has organized a standby peacekeeping force of 19 units with 8000 troops. Apparently, a rising China is determined to be an active UN peacekeeper despite increasing fatalities and injuries of Chinese peacekeepers.

China's Peacekeeping Doctrine in the Twenty-First Century

China's new identity of a rising power in the twenty-first century also shapes its peacekeeping doctrine. An analysis of China's interpretation and practice of basic UN peacekeeping doctrine, such as the three fundamental peacekeeping principles and the concept of responsibility to protect (R2P), helps understand this country's UN peacekeeping policy.

Three Fundamental Peacekeeping Principles

UN peacekeeping has three core principles—consent, impartiality, and non-use of force—which China believes are fundamental to winning the confidence and support of Member States for peacekeeping operations and ensuring their smooth conduct (Chinese Ministry of Foreign Affairs 2014). Although today's China still insists that peacekeeping should adhere to these principles, it's approach to and practice of them have undergone some changes.

While insisting that the consent of a host country is a prerequisite to establishing a PKO, Beijing also agrees that sometimes consent cannot be obtained without efforts of the international community. In recent years, China has become increasingly willing to participate in those efforts. For example, it is believed to have joined the international community in persuading Sudan, South Sudan, the DRC, and Syria to accept UN peacekeeping or cooperate with the UN in recent years.[5]

Regarding impartiality, although China maintains this principle should be abided by in peace efforts by the international community, it does not practice the principle in a rigid way. For example, Beijing insists that the internal affairs of any state should not be interfered with by outside forces. However, it is willing to play an active role in many conflict-affected countries' peace processes through different means, including engaging with opposition parties under special circumstances.

In early June 2011, China confirmed that its ambassador to Qatar, Zhang Zhiliang, had met with the chairman of Libya's National Transitional Council, Mustafa Abdel Jalil (Xinhua 2011). One retired Chinese diplomat noted that China's engagement with the Libyan opposition leader before the fall of Gaddafi's government showed flexibility in its principle of non-intervention.[6] The special representative of the Chinese government on African affairs has had talks with South Sudan's conflicting parties since 2012.[7] On 5 February 2013, the Chinese ambassador to Egypt, Song Aiguo, met with Syrian National Coalition for Opposition and Revolutionary Forces chairman Ahmed Moaz Al-khatib in Cairo (Xinhua 2013). Chinese Foreign Ministry spokesperson Hua Chunying noted during a press conference: "What is the core is that we should push both sides in Syria to blaze a 'middle

[5] Interview with a Chinese diplomat, Beijing, 18 June 2014.

[6] Interview with a Chinese retired diplomat, Langfang, China, 25 May 2016.

[7] Interview with a Chinese retired diplomat, Beijing, 12 June 2014.

way' by keeping in mind Syria's national conditions and the interests of all parties" (Xinhua 2014b). When asked to confirm the report about an Afghan Taliban delegation's visit to Beijing in late November 2014, another Chinese foreign spokesperson, Hong Lei, said:

> As a friendly neighbor of Afghanistan, China attaches great importance to developing relations with Afghanistan, hopes to see Afghanistan achieve lasting peace, stability and development at an early date, supports the 'Afghan-owned' process towards peace and reconciliation and wishes to play a constructive role to that end. (Chinese Ministry of Foreign Affairs 2015)

China maintains that peaceful settlement of international disputes and non-use of force in international relations is an important principle of the UN Charter and a basic norm of international law (Chinese Ministry of Foreign Affairs 2005). Nevertheless, Beijing does not rule out the necessity of using force under exceptional circumstances. When use of force is necessary, Beijing insists that use of force should meet two basic requirements: "one is the authorization of the UNSC, the other for the purpose of self-defense or defense of the mandate" (Chinese Ministry of Foreign Affairs 2005).

China's changing attitude towards the principle of use of force is well reflected in its contribution of security troops to PKOs in recent years. The international community has long expected China to contribute "combat troops" to PKOs (International Crisis Group 2009; Gill and Huang 2009). Since the early 1990s, China had for a long period of time refrained from contributing security troops to PKOs. However, this stance has gradually changed in the twenty-first century. In 2004, China deployed a 125-person peacekeeping Formed Police Unit to the United Nations Stabilization Mission in Haiti (MINUSTAH). In December 2013, China for the first time deployed a security company to a PKO, the United Nations Multidimensional Integrated Stabilization Mission in Mali (MINUSMA). More significantly, in 2015 China deployed a 700-person infantry battalion to the UN Mission in South Sudan (UNMISS) (Xinhua 2014c). In the new millennium, although China still has concerns regarding the use of force, it no longer minds being directly engaged in use of force in UN-commanded PKOs when there is UNSC authorisation and the situation on the ground deems it necessary to use force.

R2P

Entering the twenty-first century, the post-Westphalian interventionist concept of responsibility to protect (R2P) has begun to challenge Westphalian norms of sovereignty and non-intervention. Although Beijing has in principle endorsed R2P by supporting the 2005 World Summit Outcome, it has never embraced the interventionism embodied in the concept. According to the 2005 World Summit Outcome, R2P has three pillars:

> *Pillar One*: Each individual state has a responsibility to protect its population from mass atrocities.
>
> *Pillar Two*: The international community has a responsibility to assist the state to protect its population.
>
> *Pillar Three*: If the state fails to protect its citizens from mass atrocities and peaceful measures have failed, the international community has the responsibility to intervene through coercive measures. But military intervention is the last resort (UN 2005).

China insists that most of the weight of R2P should fall on Pillar One. It is concerned that R2P may serve as a sharp tool for the West, which prefers Pillars Two and Three, to skip the consent of host countries and penetrate the wall of traditional sovereignty (He 2014a). On 24 July 2009, the Chinese ambassador to the UN, Liu Zhenmin, made a statement at the plenary session of the General Assembly on the question of R2P, insisting that

> The government of a given state bears the primary responsibility for protecting its citizens. The international community can provide assistance, but the protection of the citizens ultimately depends on the government of the state concerned…there must not be any wavering over the principles of respecting state sovereignty and non-interference of internal affairs.…it is necessary to prevent 'R2P' from becoming another version of 'humanitarian intervention. (Permanent Mission of the People's Republic of China to the UN 2009)

According to one retired Chinese diplomat, the government largely regards R2P as a concept or a good wish, which solely has significance as political morality.[8] Nevertheless, China has not adopted a rigid policy

[8] Interview with a Chinese retired diplomat, Langfang, China, 13 December 2012.

on R2P that would rule out international intervention under special circumstances. It does recognise that the concept of R2P can apply to the four international crimes of "genocide, war crime, ethnic cleansing, and crimes against humanity" (Permanent Mission of the People's Republic of China to the UN 2009).

One major concern of the supporters of R2P is with the concept of protection of civilians (PoC). As is shown in China's support for the UN guiding principles on the use of force, which makes it clear that force can be used only as a last resort in implementing UNSC authorisation, China basically agrees to the concept PoC. Chinese peacekeepers in places like Mali and South Sudan are carrying on PoC tasks according to their mission mandates.

In recent years, the Chinese academic community is becoming increasingly interested in discussing R2P. In 2012, Ruan Zongze, a senior researcher at the China Institute of International Studies (CIIS), a top Chinese think tank affiliated to the Chinese Ministry of Foreign Affairs (MFA), coined the concept of responsible protection (RP) vis-á-vis R2P (Ruan 2012a). RP has six elements:

1. Any intervention should protect innocent civilians in the country concerned as well as regional peace and stability, rather than specific political factions or armed forces;
2. The UN Security Council is the only body with the legitimacy to implement "humanitarian intervention";
3. The necessary precondition for the implementation of force must be that all diplomatic and political means of settlement have been exhausted;
4. The goal of protection should be to prevent or alleviate a humanitarian disaster, rather than the overthrow of a government;
5. National reconstruction after intervention and protection should be given sustained support;
6. The UN should establish a monitoring mechanism, and an effective evaluation and accountability system (Ruan 2012b).

Although the concept of RP has not been officially endorsed by the Chinese Government, it has attracted great international attention. As the six elements of RP are basically in line with China's official discourse regarding R2P, some international academics regard RP as expressing the Chinese protection approach in relation to R2P (Evans 2014; Thakur 2013).

RP was coined and discussed under the background that a rising China seeks to be an international norm contributor. Since 2014, the Chinese leadership has begun to introduce a concept called "Chinese Approach" (*zhongguo fangan*), which advocates that China has both the capabilities and willingness to help improve global governance by providing solutions with Chinese characteristics.

Some Chinese academics have also done research in China's normative contribution to UN peacebuilding. For example, since the beginning of the new century, many Western academics have criticised "liberal peace," the paradigm of international peacebuilding efforts. Liberal peace as a peacebuilding norm has two pillars, one is Western liberal democracy-oriented institution building, and the other liberal market economy. Critics point out that liberal peace-dominated peacebuilding has created "virtual peace" in many post-conflict states (Paris 2004; Richmond 2006; Taylor 2007; Richmond and Franks 2009; Mac Ginty and Richmond 2009; Mac Ginty 2010; Salih 2010; Campbell et al. 2011). He Yin coined "developmental peace", claiming that both China's peaceful rise as well as its international aid practice demonstrates a peace norm significantly different from liberal peace. Developmental peace advocates political and social stability supported by strong institutions and an economic development-oriented national development strategy. Liberal peace and developmental peace are two peace norms differing widely in their ways and contents. One seems to be a contrast to the other, competing for attention and resources in peacebuilding as well as legitimacy in international norm system. However, a comparison study of the peacebuilding practice in Haiti and Liberia shows that when the two peace norms are promoted at the same time, they can not only co-exist peacefully, but also improve the effect of peacebuilding efforts (He 2014b).

Both RP and developmental peace are coined by Chinese academics, which symbolises a turn of China's attitude towards international norms, from passive acceptance or rigid rejection in the past to today's increasingly active participation in debate. Being a rising power in the twenty-first century, China "increasingly sees itself as a norm-shaper and norm-maker with the international system" (Garwood-Gowers 2016; He 2014b).

Conclusion

Since China's return to the UN, great changes have taken place to the country's national identity, from a semi-revolutionary state in the 1970s and an integrated member of the international community in the 1980s and 1990s, to a rising power in the twenty-first century. The country's policy on UN peacekeeping has changed accordingly, from opposition in the 1970s to gradually expanded reactive participation in the 1980s and 1990s, to increasingly active participation in the twenty-first century. China's new identity of a rising power in the twenty-first century also shapes its doctrine on peacekeeping. It can show certain degree of flexibility or be creative in practicing the three fundamental principles of peacekeeping and the concept of R2P in order to play a constructive role in UN peacekeeping affairs, especially when the authority of the United Nations Security Council (UNSC) can be secured or when Beijing considers the specific circumstances to be exceptional.

As a rising power as well as one of the P5, China's support for UN peacekeeping benefits not only the country's peaceful rise strategy, but also the UN peacekeeping efforts and global security governance. However, although the UN and international community have reasons for applauding China's active policy on UN peacekeeping, some challenges should not be ignored. The first and foremost of these challenges is about China's role in the UN peacekeeping regime in the new millennium. Today's China is the second largest UN peacekeeping budget contributor among all UN Member States and the most active UN peacekeeper among the P5. However, research shows that China's discursive power in the UN peacekeeping affairs is in great deficit when compared to that of other major powers (He 2016). As a veto-wielding Member State in the UNSC, China has big influence in the high politics of UN peacekeeping affairs. However, when it comes to the bureaucratic or operational level, China is lagging behind many other major powers, including some non-P5 Member States. For example, China only ranks number 14 among all the 193 Member States in terms of number of civilian employees in the UN Secretariat (He 2016). Moreover, there are only 11 Chinese nationals occupying D1 or above level posts in the UN Secretariat, whereas the numbers of the United States, United Kingdom, and France are 50, 24 and 17 respectively (He 2016). China is also under-represented in all kinds of policy consultation activities initiated by the UN (Prodi 2014). For example, since 2000, the UN has nominated six important expert panels to review and advise on UN peacekeeping affairs. China has only been invited to participate in two of them (He 2016). Back in 2000, there was no Chinese representative in the Panel on the United Nations

Peace Operations (United Nations 2000). In 2015, China was almost once again excluded from the High Independent Panel for United Nations Peace Operations (HIPPO).[9]

Being a rising power as well as an active supporter for UN peacekeeping, China will never be satisfied at being regarded as merely a peacekeeping personnel and budget contributor. Through actively supporting UN peacekeeping, China wishes to share with the rest of the world its material success, but also intellectual achievement accumulated in its peaceful rising, including as they relate governance. China is ready to contribute with a "Chinese Approach" to global governance, including UN peacekeeping. To further this establish China's role in the international peacekeeping regime, two questions ought to be asked, researched, and finally tackled: How to improve China's representation in the UN peacekeeping regime so that more Chinese experts can participate in advising, designing, and running PKOs? And, how to welcome China's enthusiasm for UN peacekeeping and find it a comfortable position in the UN peacekeeping regime, which is undergoing critical reform and transformation?

References

Callahan, William A. 2005. How to Understand China: The Dangers and Opportunities of Being a Rising Power. *Review of International Studies* 31: 701–714.

Campbell, Susanna, David Chandler, and Meera Sabaratnam. 2011. *A Liberal Peace? The Problems and Practices of Peacebuilding*. London: Zed Books.

Chinese Ministry of Foreign Affairs. 2005. Position Paper of the People's Republic of China on the United Nations Reform, June 7. Beijing.

Chinese Ministry of Foreign Affairs. 2014. Foreign Ministry Spokesperson Hong Lei's Remarks on the UN Security Council's Vote on the Draft Resolution to Refer the Situation in Syria to the International Criminal Court, May 23. Beijing.

Chinese Ministry of Foreign Affairs. 2015. Foreign Ministry Spokesperson Hong Lei's Regular Press Conference, January 14. Beijing.

Choedon, Yeshi. 2005. China's Stand on UN Peacekeeping Operations: Changing Priorities of Foreign Policy. *China Report* 41 (1): 39–57.

[9] Interview with a Chinese diplomat at the Chinese Ministry of Foreign Affairs, Beijing, 2016.

Evans, Gareth. 2014. The Consequence of Syria: Does the Responsibility to Protect Have a Future? In *E-International Relations*, Edited Collection—R2P, Syria and Humanitarianism in Crisis. www.e-ir.info/2014/01/27/the-consequence-of-non-intervention-in-syria-does-the-responsibility-to-protect-have-future. Accessed 26 Apr 2017.

Finnemore, Martha. 1996. *National Interests in International Society*. New York: Cornell University Press.

Fung, Courtney J. 2016. What Explains China's Deployment to UN Peacekeeping Operations. *International Relations of the Asia-Pacific* 16: 409–441.

Garwood-Gowers, Andrew. 2016. China's "Responsible Protection" Concept: Reinterpreting the Responsibility to Protect (R2P) and Military Intervention for Humanitarian Purposes. *Asian Journal of International Law* 6 (1): 89–118.

Gill, Bates, and Chin-hao Huang. 2009. China's Expanding Role in Peacekeeping: Prospects and Policy Implications. SIPRI Policy Paper 25, Stockholm International Peace Research Institute, Stockholm.

He, Yin. 2007. China's Changing Policy on UN Peacekeeping Operations. Asia Paper, Institute for Security and Development Policy, Stockholm.

He, Yin. 2014a. China-EU Cooperation on UN Peacekeeping: Opportunities and Challenges. In *Europe and China in 21st Century Global Politics: Partnership, Competition, or Co-evolution?* ed. Frauke Austermann, Xiaoguang Wang, and Anastas Vangeli, 43–61. London: Cambridge Scholars.

He, Yin. 2014b. Norms Competition and Complementation: Peacebuilding as Case Study. *World Economics and Politics* 4: 105–121.

He, Yin. 2016. UN Peacekeeping Affairs and China's Discursive Power. *World Economics and Politics* 11: 41–62.

Ikenberry, John. 2008. The Rise of China and the Future of the West: Can the Liberal System Survive. *Foreign Affairs* 87 (1): 23–37.

International Crisis Group. 2009. China's Growing Role in UN Peacekeeping. Asia Report No. 166. International Crisis Group, Beijing, New York and Brussels.

Johnston, Alastair I. 2008. *Social State: China in International Institutions, 1980–2000*. Princeton: Princeton University Press.

Kim, Ilpyong. 1987. *The Strategic Triangle: China, the United States & the Soviet Union*. Saint Paul: Paragon House.

Kratochwill, Friedrich. 1989. *Rules, Norms, and Decision: On the Conditions of Practical and Legal Reasoning in International Relations and Domestic Affairs*. London: Cambridge University Press.

Lanteigne, Marc. 2014. China's Peacekeeping Policies in Mali: New Security Thinking or Balancing Europe? MFC Working Paper No. 11, MFG Research Group, Berlin.

Lynch, Colum. 2014. UN Peacekeepers to Protect China's Oil Interests in South Sudan. *Foreign Policy*, June 16.

Mac Ginty, Roger, and Oliver P. Richmond. 2009. *The Liberal Peace and Post-War Reconstruction: Myth or Reality?* London: Routledge.

Mac Ginty, Roger. 2010. Hybrid Peace: The Interaction Between Top-Down and Bottom-Up Peace. *Security Dialogue* 14 (4): 391–412.

Medeiros, Evan S. 2014. China Debates Its "Peaceful Rise" Strategy. *Yale Global*, June 22. https://yaleglobal.yale.edu/content/china-debates-its-peaceful-rise-strategy. Accessed 20 Apr 2017.

Munro, Ross H. 1992. Awakening Dragon: The Real Danger in Asia Is from China. *Policy Review* 62: 10–16.

Paris, Roland. 2004. *At War's End: Building Peace After Civil Conflict.* Cambridge: Cambridge University Press.

Permanent Mission of the People's Republic of China to the UN. 2009. Statement by Ambassador Liu Zhenmin at the Plenary Session of the General Assembly on the Question of Responsibility to Protect, July 24. New York.

Prodi, Romano. 2014. Forword. In *China's and Italy's Participation in Peacekeeping Operations*, ed. Andrea de Guttry, Emanuele Sommario, and Li-Jiang Zhu, xiv–xvii. Lanham: Lexington Books.

Qin, Yaqing. 2005. National Identity, Strategic Culture and Security Interests: On Three Hypotheses of the Relations Between China and International Society. *World Economics and Politics* 1: 10–15.

Richmond, Oliver P. 2006. *The Transformation of Peace.* Basingstoke: Palgrave Macmillan.

Richmond, Oliver P., and Jason Franks. 2009. *Liberal Peace Transitions: Between Statebuilding and Peacebuilding.* Edinburgh: Edinburgh University Press.

Ruan, Zongze. 2012a. Responsible Protection. *China Daily*, March 13.

Ruan, Zongze. 2012b. *Responsible Protection: Building a Safer World.* Beijing: China Institute of International Studies.

Ruggie, John Gerard. 1998. *Constructing World Polity: Essays on International Institutionalisation.* London: Routledge.

Salih, Mohamed. 2010. A Critique of the Political Economy of the Liberal Peace: Elements of an African Experience. In *New Perspectives on Liberal Peacebuilding*, ed. Edward Newman, Roland Paris, and Oliver P. Richmond, 133–158. Tokyo and New York: United Nations University Press.

Sicurelli, Daniela. 2010. Competing Models of Peacekeeping: The Role of the EU and China in Africa. Paper prepared for the Fifth Pan-European Conference on EU Politics. Porto, June 23–26. http://citeseerx.ist.psu.edu/viedoc/download?doi=10.1.462.9906&rep=rep1&type=pdf. Accessed 26 Apr 2017.

Stahle, Stefan. 2008. China's Shifting Attitude Towards United Nations Peacekeeping Operations. *The China Quarterly* 195: 631–655.

State Council Information Office. 2005. China's Peaceful Development Road. http://en.people.cn/200512/22/eng20051222_230059.html. Accessed 20 Apr 2017.

State Council Information Office. 2013. The Diversified Employment of China's Armed Forces. www.china.org.cn/government/whitepaper/node_7181425.htm. Accessed 20 Apr 2017.

Taylor, Ian. 2007. What Fit for the Liberal Peace in Africa? *Global Society* 21 (4): 553–566.

Thakur, Ramesh. 2013. A Chinese Version of 'Responsible Protection.' *Japan Times*, November 1.

United Nations. 2000. *Report of the Panel on United Nations Peace Operations*. New York: United Nations.

United Nations. 2005. *2005 World Summit Outcome*. New York: United Nations General Assembly.

United Nations. 2008. *United Nations Security Council Resolution 1816*. New York: United Nations.

United Nations. 2015. *Implementation of General Assembly Resolutions 55/235 and 55/236: Report of the Secretary-General: Addendum 1*. New York: United Nations.

United Nations. 2017a. UN Mission's Summary Detailed By Country, August 31. http://www.un.org/en/peacekeeping/contributors/2017/aug17_3.pdf. Accessed 22 Oct 2017.

United Nations. 2017b. Ranking of Military and Police Contributions to UN Operations, August 31. http://www.un.org/en/peacekeeping/contributors/2017/aug17_2.pdf. Accessed 22 Oct 2017.

United Nations. 2017c. Troop and Police Contributors Archive (1990–2016). http://www.un.org/en/peacekeeping/resources/statistics/contributors_archive.shtml. Accessed 20 Apr 2017.

United Nations Statistics Division. 2016. GDP and Its Breakdown at Current Prices in US Dollars (all countries for all years). http://unstats.un.org/unsd/snaama/dnlList.asp. Accessed 20 Apr 2017.

Wendt, Alexander. 1999. *Social Theory of International Politics*. Cambridge: Cambridge University Press.

Xi, Jinping. 2015a. China Is Here for Peace. Remarks by H.E. Xi Jinping of the People's Republic of China at the United Nations Peacekeeping Summit, September 28. New York.

Xi, Jinping. 2015b. Working Together to Forge a New Partnership of Win-Win Cooperation and Create a Community of Shared Future for Mankind. Statement at the General Debate of the 70th Session of the UN General Assembly, September 28. New York.

Xinhua. 2004. Peaceful Rise: Strategic Choice for China. *Xinhua News Agency*, April 25.

Xinhua. 2011. China Ready to Receive Libya Opposition NTC Envoys: Diplomat. *Xinhua News Agency*, June 9.

Xinhua. 2013. Chinese Ambassador Meets Syrian Opposition Leader in Cairo. *Xinhua News Agency*, February 6.

Xinhua. 2014a. Chinese Frigate Starts Escort Mission for Chemical Weapons: FM. *Xinhua News Agency*, January 8.

Xinhua. 2014b. China Backs UN Syria Mediation. *Xinhua News Agency*, June 23.

Xinhua. 2014c. China to Send 700 Peacekeepers to South Sudan for UN Mission: Defense Ministry. *Xinhua News Agency*, September 25.

Xinhua. 2015. Xi Jinping: Stresses Urgency of Reforming Global Governance. *Xinhua News Agency*, October 13.

Yee, Herbert, and Ian Storey. 2002. *The China Threat: Perceptions, Myths and Reality*. London: Routledge.

Open Access This chapter is licensed under the terms of the Creative Commons Attribution 4.0 International License (http://creativecommons.org/licenses/by/4.0/), which permits use, sharing, adaptation, distribution and reproduction in any medium or format, as long as you give appropriate credit to the original author(s) and the source, provide a link to the Creative Commons license and indicate if changes were made.

The images or other third party material in this chapter are included in the chapter's Creative Commons license, unless indicated otherwise in a credit line to the material. If material is not included in the chapter's Creative Commons license and your intended use is not permitted by statutory regulation or exceeds the permitted use, you will need to obtain permission directly from the copyright holder.

CHAPTER 14

Religion, Governance, and the 'Peace–Humanitarian–Development Nexus' in South Sudan

Jonathan C. Agensky

Introduction

The July 2011 independence of the new Republic of South Sudan marks the successful outcome of a long-time struggle, encompassing a wide spectrum of local and international activities. Included among them is a variety of UN-supported peace and relief operations like the Intergovernmental Authority on Development (IGAD)-led peace process, the UN-led Operation Lifeline Sudan (OLS), the UN Advance Mission, the UN Mission in Sudan (UNMIS), and, following independence, the UN Mission in South Sudan (UNMISS). Nevertheless, deep-rooted Southern animosities quickly upended the internal peace on which secession relied, troubling both international and local efforts toward sustainable peace and security. Early post-independence eruptions of violence exposed the precariousness of the new state. By 2014, the potential of a South Sudanese civil war came to fruition with the

J. C. Agensky (✉)
Ohio University, Athens, OH, USA
e-mail: agensky@ohio.edu

© The Author(s) 2019

C. de Coning and M. Peter (eds.), *United Nations Peace Operations in a Changing Global Order*,
https://doi.org/10.1007/978-3-319-99106-1_14

defection of senior figures from the South Sudanese parliament and its subsequent dissolution. Factional and interethnic violence have withstood various peace accords from 2015 to 2017, leading to widespread human rights abuses, devastating humanitarian crises, famine, and pervasive threats to human security. Amid widespread bi- and multilateral support, questioning how South Sudan become a newly independent state plagued by violence and contestation speaks to the intended and unintended consequences of peacebuilding in Africa, the impact of peace-seeking activities that parallel and overlap UN peace processes, and the wide range of non-state actors critical to securing peace outcomes.

This chapter highlights practices in the wider peacebuilding field that seek similar outcomes as UN peace operations or otherwise affect the background conditions necessary for their success. It treats South Sudan as an illustrative case study that uniquely reflects processes that shape and regulate sites of conflict, chronic emergency, and limited statehood across postcolonial sub-Saharan states. I argue that, despite the 'view from above', South Sudan's independence ultimately depended on two interconnected peacebuilding frameworks: a well-recognised top-down and centralised approach based on peacekeeping and diplomacy, and a lesser-known diffuse and multi-dimensional approach rooted in a nexus of religion, humanitarianism, and networked wartime governance. Focusing on the latter, I illustrate how the incorporation of religious institutions into postcolonial global and regional aid-based governance networks enables church-based actors to pursue political, social, and structural interventions critical to UN peace operations. In doing so, I emphasise the impact of religion, aid, and governance on peacebuilding in Africa, with a view toward contributing to discussions about holistic, integrated, and people-centered approaches to sustainable peace.

Recent literature on religion and peacebuilding increasingly emphasises the positive impact of religious actors, ideas, and institutions on international peace. Numerous religiously-identified activities in areas of wartime governance, aid, refugee and displaced persons assistance, track-two diplomacy, and civil mobilisation parallel UN operations across sub-Saharan Africa. Well known examples include Sudan, Uganda, Nigeria, Mozambique, the Democratic Republic of Congo (DRC), and Liberia. Throughout the second Sudanese civil war (1983–2005) and into South Sudan's independence (2005–2011), local and international

Christian groups utilised their roles within regional and international aid networks to conduct multi-track peace diplomacy, conflict management, and local governance. They helped minimise internal fragmentation, establish the viability of a southern state, and secure the conditions necessary to advance the South toward secession. Considering recent critiques of state-centric approaches and emphases on 'people-power,' these activities demonstrate the importance of parallel peace processes undertaken by non-state actors, and, notably, religious actors, in securing peace outcomes.

Religious actors and institutions are often uniquely situated to provide social services to populations in crisis and publicly legitimate governing parties. I argue this reflects modes of postcolonial governance, envisioned here as constituting a 'religion–governance interface': a context in which religious groupings are relied upon to perform sovereign functions, encompassing local and transnational actors and institutions responsible for the delivery of public goods and the provision of civilian livelihood. At the same time, these activities encompass their own sets of problems. In the case of South Sudan, issues included problematic tradeoffs and spillover effects as the church became increasingly undercut by overly instrumentalised relationships with the principal South Sudanese rebel group, the subsequent Government of South Sudan, and the international community. Attention to how the 'religion–governance interface' enables activities in times of war and crisis, therefore, uncovers sites in which external coordination across long-term peacebuilding efforts should be strengthened in ways that better reflect the political and institutional realities of postcolonial sub-Saharan states and, more specifically, the institutional arrangements of religion in the region.

This chapter has three sections. First, I discuss practices of international peace against the backdrop of human security, multidimensional peacebuilding, and calls for 'people-centered' approaches. Second, I outline the central roles played by the Church and Christian NGOs in postcolonial governance and statehood. Third, I illustrate the importance of a 'religion–governance interface' for the successes and failures of peacebuilding in South Sudan. More than simply a matter of South Sudanese politics, this history lays bare the heterogeneity of peacebuilding in Africa and the religious institutions and practices that overflow mainstream discourses and centralised operations.

Beyond State-Centric Approaches to International Peace

Considerable scholarship addresses changes in twenty-first century global security and the role of the UN in protecting international peace, securing welfare, and promoting human development. A principal theme concerns state failure in the global South and the struggle for control by opposing non-state groups. Across sub-Saharan Africa (and elsewhere), political violence occurs in societies that have limited state power, lack political stability and effective political institutions, and are unable to establish authority over large portions of territory (for example Somalia, Angola, DRC, Mali, Nigeria, and Sudan). Conflicts are driven by a complex interaction of private interests, group identities (i.e. ethno-national and ethno-religious sectarianism), and large-scale social cleavages (i.e. social, political, economic, and cultural). They tend to be protracted, blurring the boundaries between civilians and combatants, resulting in mass civilian death and displacement.

Although international actors historically intervened into war-affected societies in postcolonial Africa (for example Congo, Nigeria, and Sudan), only in the post-Cold War period were themes of medium- and long-term peacebuilding placed on the international policy agenda, reflecting an institutional shift toward multilateral solutions for international peace. Over this period, a 'protection of civilians' agenda emerged making civilian security in post-conflict environments "critical to the legitimacy and credibility of UN peacekeeping missions, the peace agreements they are deployed to help implement, and the institution of the United Nations itself" (UN 2009, p. 1). This is now part of an overarching human security framework subject to a diverse policy and implementation environment composed of states, multilateral organisations, and humanitarian and other non-state actors, with UN peace operations at the center. In contrast to state-centric security, human security requires effective civilian protection, inclusive political institutions, and a functional civil society, fostering complex relations between security providers.

As global security regimes focus on the wellbeing of populations and the conditions underlying 'weak' and 'failed' states, they disproportionately concentrate on postcolonial settings, especially in Africa. Beginning with the 1999 UN mission in Sierra Leone (UNAMSIL), UN peacekeeping missions across the continent have intensified their interactions with host states, humanitarians, and other non-state actors (for example MONUC in DRC; UNOCI in Côte d'Ivoire; and UNMIS and UNAMID in Sudan). Peacekeepers are now authorised to pursue actions beyond monitoring the implementation of peace agreements, becoming increasingly networked with various other actors to achieve specific political outcomes (for example operations in the Central African Republic and DRC). UN peacekeeping intersects political missions and peacebuilding operations, deploying offensive force and state-building mandates that push "the scope of activities beyond what the UN peacekeepers are accustomed to" (Peter 2015, p. 350). It has become part of a broader attempt to identify and support structures capable of strengthening peace and prevent relapse into conflict by balancing the interests of states and societies.

UN peace operations are now "multidimensional, addressing the full spectrum of peacebuilding activities, from providing secure environments to monitoring human rights and rebuilding the capacity of the state" (UN 2009, p. 2). Traditionally distinct practices intermingle, necessitating effective platforms to synergise across sectors and manage transitions from conflict to post-conflict settings. However, UN peace operations exhibit a 'coherence and coordination deficit'. Despite recognition that various "dimensions of peacebuilding systems are interlinked," practical integration has proven difficult (de Coning 2007, pp. 1–2). Accordingly, a range of policy recommendations seeks to strengthen both internal and external coherence among UN clusters and non-UN interventions and establish common strategic plans and shared priorities. This is most recently reflected by the High-level Independent Panel on Peace Operations (HIPPO), which advocates "innovative approaches that integrate conflict prevention, governance, development and human rights" (UN 2015, p. 21).

However, sustainable peace also requires local engagement and expertise as well as deepened commitment to safeguarding the lives of those in conflict-affected countries. There is a need to eschew 'white SUV culture' in favor of "a more human face that prioritizes closer interaction with local people to better understand their concerns, needs and aspirations" (UN 2015, p. 15). To that end, HIPPO promotes a 'people-centered' approach, aiming to link UN field-based personnel and local communities for improved mandate implementation and a stronger culture of protection. HIPPO suggests 'UN peace operations' be conceptualised as a "single spectrum of peace and security missions and other initiatives" and that the UN itself "become a more field-oriented and people-centered organization in its peace operations" (ibid.).

The 2016 UN 'Peace Promise' echoes these ideas by emphasising the need to "work together across silos and at the peace-humanitarian-development nexus in addressing the drivers of violent conflict, delivering humanitarian assistance and developing institutions, resilience and capacities simultaneously in a complementary and synergetic way" (UN 2016).

Calls for stronger field-oriented and 'people-centered' capabilities focus on utilising a wider range of international, regional, and local actors across a wider range of activities. These policy developments also echo recent scholarship on strategic and sustainable peacebuilding that emphasises the importance of integrating ideas, institutions, and 'people-power', for which religious actors are considered a principal resource (Philpott and Powers 2010). Although policy orthodoxy conventionally treats religion as a problem rather than solution for international crises, the participation of religious actors, organisations, and institutions is increasingly recognised as a significant part of international aid and peace, crosscutting what UN Peacebuilding calls the 'Peace-Humanitarian-Development Nexus.' Peacebuilding now encompasses aid and development efforts not automatically associated with peacebuilding by actors with considerable social capital to transform conflict dynamics. This is especially the case for religious actors in Southern states who are often deeply invested in these activities and embedded within overlapping networks. The question here is the extent to which these actors have been and could be effectively incorporated into strategic peacebuilding designs.

Church, Governance, and the Postcolonial State

Religion is central to contemporary discussions about democratisation, aid, and security across the African continent (Ranger 2008, pp. 4–5; Commission for Africa 2005, p. 27). As mechanisms of peace and international order increasingly rely on religious organisations to manage episodes of crisis, these discussions harmonise with broader 'post-secular' framings that highlight the social and political roles of religion and new accommodations between the secular state and religious actors in the post-Cold War period (de Vries and Sullivan 2006; Habermas 2008). With respect to contemporary peacebuilding, for example, Powers (2010, p. 328) argues that religious leaders at the local, national, and international level uniquely exemplify the potential of 'people power,' embodying a degree of moral credibility that "allows them to be effective advocates for peaceful social change, to mediate between conflicting parties, and to provide new visions for the future in societies torn by conflict." More generally, religious actors and institutions are widely acknowledged to be densely networked at local, regional, and global levels and to possess valuable material, social, cultural, and ethical resources. For those concerned with strategic approaches to sustainable peace, they represent an underutilised resource.

For sub-Saharan states, the public power of religion stems from a long trajectory of postcolonial governance in areas of security, aid, and development. Differences notwithstanding, religiously identified interventions are common features of postcolonial struggles and overlap the regional presence of international NGOs following decolonisation. Liberal internationalism has long depended on religious groupings to perform sovereign functions in colonial and postcolonial settings, encompassing local and transnational actors and institutions responsible for public goods and civilian livelihood. Postcolonial states defy 'Weberian' ideals of statehood modeled on European polities that cement public authority entirely within the secular state. They comprise multiple order-producing systems coterminous with state power (Mampilly 2011, p. 239). Across contexts (for example Afghanistan, Somalia, Libya, Sierra Leone, and Sudan), control over violence and provision of law, order, security, and health is subject to "dispersed, fragmented and overlapping structures that substitute for the weakness of the central and legally constituted state" (Podder 2014, p. 215). This pattern is exemplified by the sub-Saharan Church, which, as a broadly construed social, religious, and political institution, is embedded in overlapping regional and international networks, both religious and governmental. The global peacebuilding field needs to be reconceptualised in ways that reflect these political and institutional realities and, more specifically, the institutional arrangements of religion in the region.

Following decolonisation, the Church entrenched itself as a principal source of social service, advocating on behalf of economic and political inclusion and providing services to needy populations. This constituted a pattern across the continent, seen in Sudan, Kenya, Malawi, Zimbabwe, Congo, Mozambique, and elsewhere. Examples include the Relief and Rehabilitation Commission established by the Sudan Council of Churches; rural education administered by the National Christian Council of Kenya; and agricultural development by the Zimbabwe Council of Churches—to name a few (Gifford 2009, p. 50). The Church accrued widespread credibility and moral authority, contrasting the rampant patrimonialism, corruption, and 'politics of the belly' that characterised many postcolonial African states (Bayart 1993, p. 21).

Decolonisation, uneven development, and violent conflict also led to an intensified international NGO presence. By the 1980s, numerous African governments were unable to fulfill basic governance. International NGOs took their place, many of which were Christian identified and evolved from church-based relief and development structures. Western donors, adopting neoliberal approaches to foreign aid and weary of limited state capacity, channeled aid through NGOs and local churches. In South Sudan, for example, bi- and multilateral development aid organisations like the United States Agency for International Development (USAID), the British Department for International Development (DfID), and the World Food Programme funded a variety of international partners to provide services from water, sanitation, and hygiene to healthcare and education. In Mozambique, religious and secular NGOs were at times more powerful than the state. Church-affiliated NGOs like World Vision International and Christian Care entered Zimbabwe as relief organisations in the early 1970s, coming to play central roles in the development of the postcolonial state.

The interpenetration of religion, governance, and aid created an environment conducive to religiously identified public activity. It vested Christian-identified organisations with local credibility, authority, and social capital, strategically positioning the Church within overlapping networks of security, aid, and governance. For international stakeholders, the NGO sector was crucial for the democratisation of African countries and the creation of a pluralistic civil society, for which Christian NGOs were especially well-positioned. This overlapped and informed the Church's role in providing social service and local governance; its increasing orientation toward relief and development; and its growing entanglements in global aid regimes. Religious and secular NGOs thus became implicated in sustaining state power and economic development while also creating conditions enabling governments to streamline and limit their own role in civil services. Paradoxically, this both supported and undercut state legitimacy while also jeopardising the independence and autonomy of the Church and expending its own social and political capital.

Reconceptualising *political order* within postcolonial spaces is therefore critical for understanding how religious institutional configurations impact peace outcomes. The interface between religion and governance encompasses three dimensions relevant to peacebuilding Africa. First, there is a governance–brokerage dimension in which religious organisations subcontract social services, infrastructure, social capital, and legitimacy. Second, there is a political–strategic dimension in which they formulate their own organisational and strategic mandates and conduct various forms of political entrepreneurship and mobilisation. Third, there is an instrumental–organisational dimension in which the selective and limited engagement of these organisations by state, rebel, and international actors leads to potential trade-offs and spillover effects that can negatively impact both long-term peace outcomes and organisational integrity.

Political Fragmentation, Violence, and the New Republic of South Sudan

Prior to South Sudan's independence, conflict between Sudan's Khartoum-based government (the 'North') and southern insurgent groups (the 'South') produced two civil wars. These wars were part of a broader conflict system that displaced millions of people, intensifying the effects of environmental crisis and famine. The second Sudanese civil war between the North and South began in 1983. It was fought mainly between the North and what had become the primary southern rebel group, the South Sudan People's Liberation Movement/Army (SPLM/A). It was also fought among various southern factions, often through northern support. The war formally ended in 2005 with the 9 January signing of the Comprehensive Peace Agreement (CPA). The principal signatories were the Sudanese state and the SPLM/A. The CPA formalised a series of protocols established through a peace process led by IGAD (comprised of Djibouti, Eritrea, Ethiopia, Kenya, Somalia, and Uganda), 'Troika' states (USA, UK, and Norway), and the African Union. At its core was the possibility of southern secession through referendum following a six-year interim period of southern autonomy and national power sharing. It also afforded the bulk of southern political representation to the SPLM/A, which transitioned into the interim southern government and, after independence, has dominated the Government of South Sudan.

South Sudan's independence depended on two interconnected peacebuilding frameworks. The first, exemplified by the CPA, reflects a top-down centralised approach based on peacekeeping and diplomacy. It facilitated the negotiated settlement between Khartoum and the South and established the formal parameters for an internationally recognised secession. This framework became the principal referent for pre-independence peace operations, like UNMIS, which focused mainly on CPA protocols and the ceasefire between North and South. The second framework, exemplified by reconciliation among rebel factions and local support for the SPLA, reflects a more diffuse and multi-dimensional approach rooted in a nexus of religion, global humanitarianism, and networked wartime governance. It unified the southern insurgency; undercut the Khartoum-sponsored proxy war in the South; and constituted the SPLA as the legitimate political voice of South Sudan. Importantly, this framework secured the conditions necessary for both the negotiated settlement as well as secession itself. However, it also allowed the SPLA to channel funds derived through oil revenue and bilateral arrangements into security and military expenditures; unintentionally enabled the formation of local patron–client networks; and contributed to widespread corruption.

Violence between principal parties escalated following the referendum, propelled by the incomplete implementation of core CPA milestones. However, violence also escalated within the South. The CPA did not include all relevant parties (i.e. civil society and political and military factions) other than Khartoum's National Congress Party and the SPLM. At least 36 militias under the umbrella of the South Sudan Defense Forces) were excluded from the peace process. Nor did the CPA address the broader conflict system active throughout both the North and the South, leaving unresolved many core issues with respect to power sharing, equity, human rights, and security. Armed southern factions protested the SPLM- and Dinka-dominated government. Disgruntled politicians and political entrepreneurs traded on their abilities to mobilise, if by force, large militias to extract political concessions from the Government of South Sudan. Government efforts to resolve these issues through political concessions and ministerial posts, disarmament campaigns, immunity programs, and assassinations were unsuccessful. Violence was, and continues to be, fuelled by an admixture of political interests and entrepreneurship on the one hand, and tribal and ethnic rivalries, on the other—exacerbated by chronic underdevelopment, abject marginalisation, and war. The push to end the conflict and secede suppressed these issues. They forcefully resurfaced in the absence of a unified enemy and competition for post-independence dispensation.

Conflict, Aid, and Development

Outbreaks of large-scale violence and fragmentation expose multi-layered and multi-scalar tensions that have historically impeded peace and security in South Sudan. Throughout the second civil war and post-conflict period, these tensions crystalised into an increasingly autonomous local conflict system driven by rent-seeking, political entrepreneurship, and tribal and ethnic rivalries. Much of the death and displacement ascribed to Sudan's second civil war stemmed from factional fighting and mobilisation within the south, exploited by Khartoum through a sustained proxy war. The SPLA relied on international patronage to secure itself as the de facto governing entity of South Sudan, a status formalised through the CPA. It was far from the unproblematic political and military expression of the people's will, against which it often found itself. In order to achieve recognition and position itself as a quasi-sovereign actor in the international system, the SPLA required various means to manage factional struggles, suppress rival claimants, and establish political authority.

Although southern groups faced and resisted marginalisation, isolation, and exclusion by the northern elite, they also faced challenges from each other. The South always lacked a coherent ethnic or political basis from which its own polity could easily be formed, despite its representation in colonial materials, international treaties, local and regional peace-accords, and missionary cartography. South Sudan continues to encompass diverse ethno-national and ethno-social identities. Sudan's civil wars demonstrate this, fuelled by differing intersubjective cartographies, primordialist appeals, instrumental agendas, and emancipatory politics (Jok and Hutchinson 1999; Hilhorst and van Leeuwen 2005; Maitre 2009; Branch and Mampilly 2005, p. 4). Despite varying degrees of political autonomy and multiple civil wars, South Sudan remains an internally contested space, organised around interethnic lines that, in turn, create precarious boundaries traversed by raiders, pillagers, and militias that recruit men and boys at gunpoint. Considerable efforts on the part of local and international groups attempted to address these matters, but ended up only deferring them in favor of promoting independence.

Church, Aid, and Wartime Governance in South Sudan

Many international, regional, and local actors and agendas shaped the peacebuilding field in South Sudan. In the final phases of the IGAD-led peace negotiations, the UN authorised the Advance Mission in

Sudan (UNAMIS) to support peace talks and prepare for a subsequent UN peace operation. After the signing of the CPA, the United Nations Mission in Sudan (UNMIS) was mandated as an observer and verification force to assist principal parties with implementation of the agreement in cooperation with the AU and international partners. Following independence, UNMIS was replaced by the UN Mission in South Sudan (UNMISS), focused on supporting South Sudan's new government as well as protecting civilians and promoting development, peacebuilding, and recovery.

During the conflict, UN relief and development activities also incorporated peacebuilding objectives. In addition to repatriation of internally displaced persons, area development, and civil society support, for example, the UN Development Programme (UNDP) disseminated information on peacebuilding and engaged in community-level conflict transformation. UNICEF provided support for social services, infrastructure, local NGOs, and civic education while implementing peacebuilding programs and promoting humanitarian principles and human rights compliance. In partnership with the World Food Programme, UNICEF also established OLS, an umbrella organisation for a consortium of UN agencies and NGOs that created an organised framework for international aid and relief. OLS included most of the aid agencies working in Sudan, many of whom developed peacebuilding programs offering "peace education and training in conflict analysis, facilitating dialogue between warring parties, or promoting reconciliation and preventing conflict through reconstruction or economic development" (Bradbury et al. 2006, p. 23).

UN activities both supported and intersected grassroots peacebuilding initiatives, addressing 'second-tier' conflicts indirectly related to war between Khartoum and the SPLM/A. At the center of these initiatives were local and international Christian groups like the New Sudan Council of Churches (NSCC), the Presbyterian Church of Sudan, and various international Christian NGOs. Through its humanitarian mandate, this constellation of actors supported the IGAD peace process by conducting public messaging and awareness campaigns and community-level peacebuilding, pioneering a 'people-to-people' approach to peace. From 2000 to 2002, the NSCC took part in 'strategic linkages conferences' in South Sudan, Kenya, and Uganda that paralleled IGAD meetings. Based on their success, several large secular organisations adopted the people-to-people approach, including Pact Sudan, USAID's Sudan Peace Fund, UNDP, and UNICEF.

According to a Rift Valley Institute report, church-driven peacebuilding took place within a 'governance gap,' "on the periphery of the state, where local forms of governance exist, but central government and the opposition movements have little or no formal administrative capacity and limited control" (Bradbury et al. 2006, p. 22). However, this would be better conceptualised within a framework of postcolonial statehood, which has traditionally relied on a religion-governance interface. Accordingly, various church-based organisations utilised their positions within global and local governance networks to conduct aid, advocacy, and peacebuilding. They worked closely with the SPLM/A and the Government of South Sudan, international relief organisations, and various international churches and para-church groups. Globally, their labours reinforced the SPLM/A's standing as the central political voice of the South, effacing internal fragmentation and establishing the viability of a potentially independent southern state. Locally, they facilitated and fulfilled governance, delivered aid, and conducted peacebuilding initiatives that held the South together. From this perspective, the SPLA demonstrates patterns common to postcolonial insurgencies (and states) with respect to subcontracting legitimacy, drawing on religious structures, and mobilising both grassroots and transnational support.

I argue the peacebuilding field in South Sudan cannot be fully understood without attention to these activities, their embeddedness in a global and regional nexus of religion, aid, and governance, and the role of religious organisations in establishing order and authority throughout the conflict. In the remainder of this chapter, I provide three empirical snapshots that flesh this out, focusing on the crystallisation of the religion–governance in South Sudan following the first Sudanese civil war, the role of the church in wartime governance, and post-CPA struggles.

First, during Sudan's first civil war (1955–1972), the World Council of Churches (WCC), All Africa Conference of Churches, and the interdenominational American humanitarian agency Church World Service provided relief aid and financial support for southern Sudanese refugees in Uganda, Ethiopia, the Central African Republic, and Zaire/Congo. Having previously conducted aid and advocacy targeting Biafra's secession, they negotiated with Khartoum to create humanitarian space for aid delivery in the South. A decade into the conflict, they expanded their activities to more actively encompass peacebuilding and political advocacy. With support from the Khartoum-based Sudan Council of Churches, officials toured neighboring refugee camps seeking endorsement of a draft peace proposal that would ultimately form the basis of the final settlement. With much success, churches and relief agencies lobbied for support across Europe, including the WCC, Lutheran World Federation, and Norwegian Church Aid.

These activities cemented a nascent religiously identified humanitarian–peacebuilding nexus, for which the 1973 Addis Ababa peace agreement was a milestone (Collins 2008, p. 108; Howell 1978, pp. 430–435; Werner et al. 2000, pp. 391–394). They demonstrated the ability of the international Church to intervene into the postcolonial politics of sub-Saharan African states; to do so in conjunction with the delivery of aid and within an overarching humanitarian framework; and to successfully secure political outcomes. In conjunction with the agreement's provisions, they also facilitated an influx of new international groups into southern Sudan, both religious and secular, creating the conditions through which the Sudanese Church became implicated in the provision and implementation of international aid and governance.

Second, church-based actors became central to wartime governance, aid, and local peacebuilding in the post-Cold War phase of Sudan's second civil war. A hub for international aid and peacebuilding, the NSCC was established by the major Christian denominations to build governance capacity, provide social services, and manage international funds secured through the UN-sponsored OLS humanitarian initiative. The NSCC was part of the WCC ecumenical framework, deriving funding from European, North American, and regional ecumenical bodies. It was also operationally and financially supported by a group of church-based aid organisations, exemplifying the institutional effects of regional humanitarian governance and its overlap with the wider peacebuilding field. The NSCC became increasingly central to governance and institutional reform in the South. It was tasked with resolving internal southern violence and facilitating peace and reconciliation by the SPLA's newly created political wing, the SPLM, which strategically revised its relationship with the Church in the attempt to establish effective civil administration in areas liberated from the North.

This new relationship was exemplified by the 1997 joint SPLM and NSCC conference at the Kajiko parish center of the Episcopal Church of Sudan. The Kajiko conference utilised the NSCC's social capital to mitigate tensions between ethnic groupings and help resolve a devastating SPLA split that had been exploited by Khartoum and became responsible for the bulk of death and destruction during the war.

It also strengthened links between the SPLM/A and the Church, endorsing a set of common objectives on local peace and liberation (the 'Yei Declaration'). Kajiko reaffirmed the Church's commitment to the insurgency and mandated the NSCC with facilitating southern reconciliation. It laid the foundation for the Church-led 'Person-to-Person' peace process, which culminated in the 1999 Wunlit agreement that reunited the SPLA—paving the way for the IGAD-led peace negotiations between North and South.

Third, in the post-CPA period, as UNMIS and its international partners focused on CPA protocols, local and international Christian groups provided civic education and grassroots peacebuilding, helping advance the South through a timely and organised referendum and independence. Christian humanitarian NGOs like World Vision International, Tearfund UK, Norwegian Church Aid, and Catholic Relief Services incorporated longer-term developmental frameworks that centered on matters of governance—including supporting local governments through decentralisation. In terms of local peacebuilding, their efforts included the establishment of conflict early warning and response systems and a civil society track empowered to monitor and respond to internal southern violence. However, these organisations faced 'cold' relations with South Sudan government, as the SPLM asserted its political autonomy. They also faced unresolved southern grievances and the absence of an effective South Sudanese national identity. Throughout the war, social reassurances in the face of repressive tactics by Khartoum, the SPLA, and other rebel militias were not found in the certitudes of ethnic or national identification typically associated with civil or secessionist war. Instead, they were partly provided by a religion–governance interface, for which internal fragmentation was an enduring problem.

After its long history of providing aid, governance, and social services to the southern population, these issues symbolised the Church's broader struggle to find its public and private footing amid the impending normalisation and formalisation of southern governance. Indicating the importance of humanitarianism and governance to its institutional identity, the local Church reaffirmed its commitments to four key areas of activity: (1) repatriation and resettlement of internally displaced persons, through its social wing of the Emergency Relief, Rehabilitation and Development Agency; (2) peacebuilding and reconciliation, by establishing forums across the South at various levels; (3) advocacy and lobbying, by targeting various national, regional, and international partners with which it was already engaged; and (4) civic and voter education, by conducting campaigns at the grassroots and other levels, as well as engaging international observers and monitors (Sudan Council of Churches 2010). Despite their immediate successes, however, they failed to achieve much beyond secession.

After a prolonged history of productive entanglements, Church, aid, and the future of South Sudan had become inextricable. They created a nexus infused with complex global social dynamics, mixed mandates, and relations of dependency. The organisational capacity and competence of the principal ecumenical body weakened and it experienced issues with management and leadership. In many ways, internal Church dynamics mirrored social and institutional development across the South. Socially, the Church had become fragmented. Institutionally, it had become prone to corruption. Consequently, it faced a crisis of legitimacy. Humanitarian-centered ministry played a large role in the Church's vision of the future but the Church faced a double struggle. First, it was concerned not to be beholden to the guidelines and objectives of the common donor platform of bi- and multilateral agencies that were releasing new funds oriented to longer term, development goals in the South. Second, it struggled with being, and being perceived to be, impartial and independent of the government. Both struggles affected the public legitimacy and trust of the Church, exemplifying longer-term societal and institutional effects of the religion governance interface.

Conclusion

This chapter located South Sudan's precarious peace within an aid-based postcolonial order crystallised across sub-Saharan states. By calling attention to South Sudan's humanitarian past, it emphasised the historical importance of religious agency within this order for regulating and *producing* international spaces. Empirically, this paper questioned how South Sudan became a newly independent state plagued by violence and contestation, facing a prolonged and intractable civil war. Conceptually, it questioned how we think about the wider peacebuilding field with respect to intersections of religion, aid, and governance. Emphasising how these activities encompassed problematic tradeoffs and spillover effects, it pinpointed sites in which external coordination across long-term peacebuilding efforts should be both strengthened and more effectively utilised. Attention to how these relationships take shape is critical for discovering ways to *strategically* incorporate the full-spectrum of relevant actors into peacebuilding frameworks.

Military and humanitarian action alone are insufficient for achieving international peace in the absence of effective governing and political institutions. The HIPPO advocates better coordination between missions and humanitarian actors as well as deeper engagement of communities and non-governmental organisations. Calls for stronger field-oriented and 'people-centered' capabilities address this by focusing on how to utilise a wider range of actors across a wider range of activities. I have suggested that thinking about these questions from the perspective of a postcolonial 'religion–governance interface' calls attention to the unique ways religious agency impacts the 'Peace-Humanitarian-Development Nexus' in Africa. This lays bare the limits of state-centric—and *secular*—approaches to peacebuilding. Attending to the political and institutional realities of statehood in postcolonial spaces is critical for stabilising South Sudan and better utilising 'people-power' in support of UNMISS and related operations. It is also relevant for empowering other contemporary operations across the continent and beyond, with respect to multidimensional integrated missions mandated to protect civilians, extend state authority, and stabilize governments (e.g. MINUSCA in the Central African Republic, MINUSMA in Mali, and MONUSCO in DRC).

References

Bayart, Jean-François. 1993. *The State in Africa: The Politics of the Belly*. London and New York: Longman.

Bradbury, Mark, John Ryle, Michael Medley, and Kwesi Sansculotte-Greenidge. 2006. *Local Peace Processes in Sudan: A Baseline Study*. Nairobi: Rift Valley Institute.

Branch, Adam, and Zachariah Cherian Mampilly. 2005. Winning the War, but Losing the Peace? The Dilemma of SPLM/A Civil Administration and the Tasks Ahead. *The Journal of Modern African Studies* 43 (1): 1–20.

Collins, Robert O. 2008. *A History of Modern Sudan*. Cambridge: Cambridge University Press.

Commission for Africa. 2005. *Our Common Interest: Report of the Commission for Africa*. Commission for Africa.

de Coning, Cedric. 2007. Coherence and Coordination in United Nations Peacebuilding and Integrated Missions—A Norwegian Perspective. In *NUPI Report Security in Practice*, no. 5. Oslo: NUPI.

de Vries, Hent, and Lawrence Eugene Sullivan. 2006. *Political Theologies: Public Religions in a Post-secular World*. New York: Fordham University Press.

Gifford, Paul. 2009. *Christianity, Politics, and Public Life in Kenya*. Oxford: Oxford University Press.

Habermas, Jürgen. 2008. Notes on Post-secular Society. *New Perspectives Quarterly* 25 (4): 17–29.

Hilhorst, Dorothea, and Mathijs van Leeuwen. 2005. Grounding Local Peace Organisations: A Case Study of Southern Sudan. *The Journal of Modern African Studies* 43 (4): 537–563.

Howell, John. 1978. Horn of Africa: Lessons from the Sudan Conflict. *International Affairs (Royal Institute of International Affairs 1944–)* 54 (3): 421–436.

Jok, Jok Madut, and Hutchinson Sharon Elaine. 1999. Sudan's Prolonged Second Civil War and the Militarization of Nuer and Dinka Ethnic Identities. *African Studies Review* 42 (2): 125–145.

Maitre, Benjamin R. 2009. What Sustains 'Internal Wars'? The Dynamics of Violent Conflict and State Weakness in Sudan. *Third World Quarterly* 30 (1): 53–68.

Mampilly, Zachariah Cherian. 2011. *Rebel Rulers Insurgent Governance and Civilian Life During War*. Ithaca: Cornell University Press.

Peter, Mateja. 2015. Between Doctrine and Practice: The UN Peacekeeping Dilemma. *Global Governance: A Review of Multilateralism and International Organizations* 21 (3): 351–370.

Philpott, Daniel, and Gerard Powers. 2010. *Strategies of Peace: Transforming Conflict in a Violent World*. New York: Oxford University Press.

Podder, Sukanya. 2014. Mainstreaming the Non-state in Bottom-Up State-Building: Linkages Between Rebel Governance and Post-conflict Legitimacy. *Conflict, Security & Development* 14 (2): 213–243.

Powers, Gerard. 2010. Religion and Peacebuilding. In *Strategies of Peace: Transforming Conflict in a Violent World*, ed. D. Philpott and G. Powers, 317–352. New York: Oxford University Press.

Ranger, Terence O. 2008. *Evangelical Christianity and Democracy in Africa*. Oxford: Oxford University Press.

Sudan Council of Churches. 2010. *A Time to Keep Balance: A Vision for Peaceful Sudan: Sudanese Church Position on the Current Situation of the Internally Displaced People's in Regard to Upcoming Referenda and Popular Consultations in 2011 and Beyond*. Juba: The Sudan Council of Churches.

United Nations. 2009. *Protecting Civilians in the Context of UN Peacekeeping Operations: Successes, Setbacks and Remaining Challenges*. New York: United Nations.

United Nations. 2015. *Report of the High-Level Independent Panel on Peace Operations on Uniting our Strengths for Peace: Politics, Partnership and People*. New York: United Nations.

United Nations. 2016. Peace Promise: Commitments to More Effective Synergies Among Peace, Humanitarian and Development Actions in Complex Humanitarian Situations. http://www.un.org/en/peacebuilding/pbso/pdf/THE%20PEACE%20PROMISE.v.3.pdf. Accessed 17 Dec 2017.

Werner, Roland, William Anderson, and Andrew C. Wheeler. 2000. *Day of Devastation, Day of Contentment: The History of the Sudanese Church Across 2000 Years*, vol. 10. Nairobi: Paulines Publications Africa.

Open Access This chapter is licensed under the terms of the Creative Commons Attribution 4.0 International License (http://creativecommons.org/licenses/by/4.0/), which permits use, sharing, adaptation, distribution and reproduction in any medium or format, as long as you give appropriate credit to the original author(s) and the source, provide a link to the Creative Commons license and indicate if changes were made.

The images or other third party material in this chapter are included in the chapter's Creative Commons license, unless indicated otherwise in a credit line to the material. If material is not included in the chapter's Creative Commons license and your intended use is not permitted by statutory regulation or exceeds the permitted use, you will need to obtain permission directly from the copyright holder.

CHAPTER 15

UN Peace Operations and Changes in the Global Order: Evolution, Adaptation, and Resilience

Cedric de Coning

Introduction

At the end of the twentieth century, most peacekeepers were engaged in implementing comprehensive peace agreements. Today, only a decade and half into the twenty-first century, most UN peace operations have undergone a significant phase-shift and are now focused on stabilisation and protection of civilian roles. Why have peace operations changed its core role from conflict resolution to conflict management, and what further changes may be likely in the coming years? With this volume we wanted to understand how peace operations have been adapting, especially since the turn of the century, in response to macro-level systemic changes, and we wanted to explore if we can detect any trajectories that help us anticipate how peace operations are likely to continue to evolve over the coming decades.

C. de Coning (✉)
Norwegian Institute of International Affairs (NUPI), Oslo, Norway
e-mail: cdc@nupi.no

© The Author(s) 2019

C. de Coning and M. Peter (eds.), *United Nations Peace Operations in a Changing Global Order*,
https://doi.org/10.1007/978-3-319-99106-1_15

We have brought together a multidisciplinary and geographically diverse group of scholars and practitioners—some established authorities, others rising stars—to analyse the challenges and opportunities that UN peace operations are facing as a result of the uncertainty and turbulence of a global order in transition. Our ambition was to use this diversity of contributors to generate a variety of perspectives on the influences that shape peace operations. Together we have covered a range of topics that we thought are most critical to the evolution of peace operations in the twenty-first century.

Many of the contributing authors were engaged in some or other way with the UN High-level Independent Panel on Peace Operations (HIPPO) appointed by then UN Secretary-General Ban Ki Moon in 2014, to assess the state of peace operations. Ban Ki Moon tasked the Panel with making recommendations that would ensure that UN peacekeeping became fit for purpose again. The Panel produced its report in 2015, during a period when there was a sense in the diplomatic and research communities that the UN, and in particular its peace operations, was struggling to live up to its expectations (Peter 2015). The prevailing view was that the scope and complexity of the challenges that have emerged have outgrown the capabilities of the UN (van der Lijn and Smit 2015).

The HIPPO Panel published its report in 2015 with far reaching recommendations for strengthening and revitalising the UN's approach to peace and security, and especially UN peace operations (UN 2015; Boutellis and Connolly 2016). At the same time as the HIPPO Panel undertook its review of UN peace operations, a ten-year review of the UN peacebuilding architecture took place (de Coning and Stamnes 2016), as well as a review of the implementation of UN Security Council Resolution 1325 on Women, Peace and Security.[1] When these three reviews are read together, they provide a comprehensive overview and analysis of the key challenges facing UN peacekeeping, peacebuilding and the women, peace and security agenda a decade and half into the twenty-first century. Among others, they clearly show how inter-connected these agendas and approaches are, despite the fact that each is driven by its own political, bureaucratic, and scholarly interest groups.

In January 2017, a new Secretary-General, António Guterres, assumed office. The new UN Secretary-General immediately introduced a number

[1] For a summary of the major issues that these three reviews addressed, see Eli Stamnes and Kari Osland (2016).

of changes to the way the UN is managed and coordinated. He opted for a cabinet-style executive committee to oversee the day-to-day management of the UN. He has appointed a special advisor on prevention and re-organised the executive office of the Secretary-General so that it can better serve as a central coordinating hub for the UN system. He has also instructed the geographical desks of the departments that deal with prevention, mediation, and peacekeeping, as well as the department that supports such operations and missions, to co-locate. The Secretary-General followed-up on these initial changes a few months later with three significant reform packages, one each on management, development, and peace and security. Many of these changes have been inspired by the recommendations of the peace operations, peacebuilding, and 1325 reviews, and is meant to make the UN more resilient in its ability to respond to some of the key challenges that have been highlighted and analysed in this volume.

Taken together, these reforms represent a significant system-wide effort to adapt the UN to both changes in the global order as well as the new emerging challenges facing the UN, and to enhance the effectiveness and efficiency of the United Nations. It is unlikely that António Guterres would have been able to introduce such sweeping changes to the way the UN system is managed and coordinated, if the ground work was not already done through the peace operations, peacebuilding and 1325 reviews, and the subsequent political direction from UN member states, which is reflected in, for instance, the sustaining peace resolutions that was approved by the Security Council and General Assembly in 2016 (UN 2016a, b). It is not certain, however, that these reforms will all be implemented. Several aspects of the reforms are experiencing push-back from certain member states or interest groups within the UN system. The degree to which the UN system will thus be able to adapt to both the challenges it faces in the short- to medium-term, and the changes underway over the medium- to long-term, is thus still very much an open question.

The various chapters in this volume explain why the UN system in general, and peace operations in particular, is under significant strain at this point in its evolution. We identify and analyse the scope and complexity of a number of the most significant drivers that place the UN system under stress. The preceding chapters explain how a combination of several interlinked factors—including the destabilising effects of violent extremism and the emergence of transnational organised crime as a conflict driver in areas such as the Sahel—meant that the UN, and its peace operations, had to manage increasingly complex conflict environments. If we add to these additional factors such as the impact of climate change, the increase in large-scale humanitarian emergencies, and the unprecedented high numbers of refugees and internally displaced persons they have generated, then the challenges the UN system as a whole has to deal with increase even further in scope and complexity.

These challenges have been compounded by internal UN stressors, such as the UN's failure to prevent the sexual abuse and exploitation committed by some of its peacekeepers; its inability to prevent South Sudan from relapsing into violent conflict despite the presence of a UN peacekeeping operation; its powerlessness to help consolidate the peace processes in Darfur and the Democratic Republic of Congo despite a decade long sustained effort by two of the largest operations in the history of the UN, and especially its mixed track record when it comes to protecting civilians in these conflicts.

There are also a number of deep structural tensions that undermine the credibility and effectiveness of UN peacekeeping. The most significant of these is the North–South divide between those who contribute the bulk of the peacekeepers, those that contribute most of the funding, and the patterns this creates when it comes to the kind of capabilities the UN has at its disposal, and those it cannot ever seem to get enough of, such as air assets and other force multipliers. Among others, these patterns—both those that influence the stock and flow of peacekeepers and those that restrict the resources necessary to enable them to achieve their mandates, and safeguard them while doing so—determine which countries bear the brunt of the burden when it comes to peacekeepers losing their lives in the interest of protecting the lives of others, and in maintaining international peace and security on behalf of all of us.

All these developments, and the new reforms introduced by Secretary-General António Guterres, are taking place in the context of significant changes—what Adriana Abdenur refers to in her chapter in this volume as 'tectonic shifts'—that are underway at the global systems level. These changes are transforming the balance of power in the global order. In the last hundred years, we have seen the global order transform from a multipolar system into a bipolar order after the Second World War. At the end of the Cold War the global system changed again from a bipolar to a unipolar system, dominated by the United States and its allies. For the system of international governance, this meant that one ideology—neo-liberalism—became the global norm, and global institutions like the UN became agents for the dissemination, implementation, and enforcers of this ideology.

Currently we are witnessing yet another phase-shift. The unipolar era is waning in the face of a significant increase in the economic and political influence of countries like China and India in the global system. It is still uncertain what may replace it, but the next stage in the transition seems to be another multipolar era, in which several states—the United States, China, Germany, India, and Russia, to name a few—each have access to networks and forms of power sufficient to prevent any of the others from dominating the global order (de Coning et al. 2015). Another emerging characteristic of the transition is that several non-state actors, including some international and regional organisations, several large companies, and some non-governmental agencies, can exert significant influence on the global system on selected issues where they have a substantial capacity or competency. These changes at the global systems level have implications for the UN and for peace operations, and it is these implications that we set out to study in this edited volume.

Main Findings

In the Introduction we identified four developments at the global system level that are influencing the transformation of the global order, and we set out to study their implications for United Nations peace operations. The four transformational questions we asked, were:

- How is the *rebalancing of relations between states of the global North and the global South* impacting the UN's decision-making, financing and ability to design operations that go beyond the minimum common denominator;
- How is *the rise of regional organisations* as providers of peace impacting the primacy of UN peace operations and how and whether the UN can remain relevant in this era of partnership and competition;
- How have *violent extremism and fundamentalist non-state actors* changed the nature of international responses and what does this mean for previously advanced longer-term approaches to conflict resolution; and
- How are *demands from non-state actors for greater emphasis on human security* impacting UN's credibility and whether in light of the first three transformations the UN is even able to prioritise people-centred approaches over state-centred ones?

The various contributors to this volume have analysed each of these trends in depth, and in the following section we will briefly consider some of their key observations and findings, and the implications for the future directions that UN peace operations may evolve towards.

Relations Between the Global North and the Global South

As Mateja Peter and Adam Day explored in their chapters, previous phase-shifts in the global order, such as from a bipolar to a unipolar world order at the end of the Cold War, have had a significant impact on UN approaches to peace. As Peter details, during the Cold War, UN peace operations were mostly limited to unarmed or lightly armed peacekeeping operations observing and monitoring cease-fires in the Middle-East, Cyprus, and Kashmir. The UN operation in the Congo (ONUC), deployed from 1960 to 1964, was an exception, but it resulted in a further consolidation of the dominant trend of the period. Between 1948 and 1988, the UN deployed only 13 peacekeeping operations. During this period, peacekeeping was a military affair, and troops were mostly from countries that had no strategic interest in these conflict, such as Canada, India, Ghana, the Nordics, and Ireland. UN peacekeeping was clearly defined by its three principles—consent, impartiality, and the use of force only in self-defence—and enjoyed the support of the West, the Soviet-bloc and the Non-Aligned countries (see Mats Berdal in this volume).

The end of the Cold War saw a dramatic increase in the number of peacekeeping operations. Since 1988, the UN has deployed 57 peacekeeping operations, and the number of military and police peacekeepers increased from 11,000 in 1988 to a high point of 107,805 in 2015. By 2018, this has decreased slightly, to 92,511 (Rappa 2018). The number of troop contributing countries also increased and changed significantly. Traditional peacekeeping contributors like Canada and the Nordics have reduced their defence budgets and they have shifted their contributions to NATO, to the extent that there are no longer any Western countries among the top 10 troop contributors. Africa and South East Asia now contribute the bulk of the peacekeepers. At the beginning of 2018, Ethiopia, Bangladesh, India, Pakistan, and Rwanda made up the top five contributors, and China was the largest contributor among the permanent members of the Security Council.

One of the significant changes that occurred since the end of the Cold War is the transformation of peacekeeping from being mostly engaged in cease-fire monitoring in inter-state conflicts, to being mostly involved in supporting the implementation of comprehensive peace agreements in intra-state conflicts in the 1990s. The emergence of a unipolar world order resulted in the UN becoming an important instrument in assisting state formation and state-building according to the dominant neo-liberal ideology of the time (Richmond 2004).

As a result of the dominance of this Western-led liberal consensus approach to international conflict management, the task of UN peacekeeping operations expanded significantly from cease-fire monitoring to the managing political transitions, which included disarming, demobilising and reintegrating ex-combatants, supporting constitutional writing processes, organising elections, supporting reconciliation processes, and helping to establish new state institutions. These new tasks resulted in another significant transformation, namely changing peacekeeping from mostly military into multidimensional operations that consisted of civilian, police, and military personnel (see Kari M. Osland in this volume).

Over time, notions of state security gave way to the concept of human security and in the 2000s this resulted in a change in the core role of UN peace operations, namely a new focus on containing and mitigating the effects of intra-state conflicts on individuals, through new policy approaches to protection of civilians and stabilisation operations (Hilde F. Johnson in this volume and de Coning et al. 2017).

The current shift in the global order from a unipolar to a multipolar world order is thus likely to, once again, have significant effects on how UN peace operations evolve. It is still unclear what form these changes may take, but we can identify three drivers that are likely to inform the future direction of UN peace operations.

Firstly, it seems that some of the traditional North-South roles, that have been fixed into a predictable pattern since the end of the Cold War, may now start to change. Some of the countries that are likely to have a significant impact on the new global order, such as China and India, have been significant contributors of military and police personnel to UN peacekeeping operations, and they are likely to continue to support UN peacekeeping as an important instrument for managing global peace and security (see He Yin in this volume). China is now also the 2nd largest financial contributor to UN peacekeeping operations, and India's financial contribution will likely increase over time in proportion to its economic growth. The other major powers in the new multi-polar world order, such as the United States, Japan, the European Union, and Russia are all significant financial contributors to UN peacekeeping, but with the exception of a few European countries like Italy, they do not contribute significant number of troops. This is unlikely to change.

The US and the European countries have dominated the research and knowledge management dimensions and have played the leading role in determining the policy directions that UN peace operations have taken during the unipolar era. China and the other rising powers and emerging economies are increasingly signalling their intent to play a more prominent role in the policy and decision-making domain when it comes to UN peace operations (He Yin in this volume and de Coning and Prakash 2016). These countries are thus likely to contribute more financially, and are likely to become more assertive in influencing the future policy direction of UN peace operations.

Secondly, in light of the uncertainty that the turbulence of a changing global order generates, and the lack of global trust that other security regimes like NATO suffer from, the UN Security Council and UN peace operations, despite their shortcomings, are likely to remain the most credible and reliable international instruments for maintaining international peace and security. As such, peace operations are likely to remain in high demand, and they are likely to remain under pressure to provide stability in conflicts characterised by violent extremism, organised crime and other forms of instability and conflict.

Thirdly, as the influence of the rising powers and the countries from the Global South more generally grow, the dominant neo-liberal ideology of the unipolar era will be increasingly challenged. As it is unlikely in a multipolar global order that agreement on an alternative globally endorsed common normative approach will emerge, one result is likely to be that UN peace operations would become less normative and less intrusive.[2] In other words, UN peace operations are likely to stop prescribing the neo-liberal peace- and state-building models that were the norm during the unipolar era. In its place, peace operations are more likely to encourage home-grown or self-determined models for peace- and state-building, and are likely to concentrate on the more technical

[2]de Coning et al. (2015) argue that the Rising Powers are seeking to bring about an alternative global order that is based on a new pluralistic normative framework, which they refer to as coexistence, where different normative approaches are allowed to coexist and where the global order is designed to prevent the hegemony of any one ideology or normative approach over others.

aspects of state-building (Call and de Coning 2017). Such technical solutions have not provided desired outcomes, and as Adam Day points out in his chapter, the UN would often achieve more with a light and nimble presence on the ground. This, according to Day, starts with the conflict prevention work.

It is also likely that UN peace operations will be tasked to concentrate more on physical security, law and order and the political dimensions of conflict management. However, this does not necessarily imply that peace operations are likely to become more robust or that the trend towards limited enforcement mandates will continue. The rising powers that are also major troop contributing countries, including China and India, are firm believers in the core principles of peacekeeping and the peaceful settlement of disputes (de Coning and Prakash 2016). Future UN peace operations are also likely to shift away from expansive mandates that include a broad range of capacity-building, peacebuilding, and state-building tasks (see Mateja Peter in this volume). The UN may still remain active in some of these areas, but more so via its development instruments, and more in support of nationally driven initiatives, rather than as an internationally driven normative agenda. Non-state actors are likely to play a greater role in this process (see Jonathan C. Agensky in this volume).

The Rise of Regional Organisations

One of the paradoxes of increasing globalisation is that it simultaneously seems to have stimulated the need for people to invest more in local and regional identities. In this volume, Thierry Tardy has addressed the impact of these developments in Europe, and I have addressed some of the developments in Africa. In my chapter, I describe how this trend manifested in a significant effort over the last two decades to develop Africa's peace and security architecture. Both the African Union and the European Union have invested in strengthening their early warning and prevention capacities, their ability to deploy mediators and special envoys, their ability to support countries emerging from conflict, and their ability to deploy peace support or crisis-management operations. The African Union has invested in establishing a peace operations standby capacity, the African Standby Force, and it has deployed and supported a dozen Africa-led operations over the past decade and a half. The EU has similarly invested in the EU Battle Group model and has deployed several missions of its own. In the process, both African-led peace operations and EU crisis-management missions have evolved beyond the UN peacekeeping model.

Over the last five years another type of security arrangement has emerged in Africa, what the AU now refers to as ad hoc security arrangements. In response to the threat posed by Boko Haram, a violent extremist group operating in northern Nigeria and neighbouring territories, the countries that make up the Lake Chad Basin Commission established the Multinational Joint Task Force (MNJTF). Following this model and faced with international terrorism and transnational organised crime in the Sahel region, Burkina Faso, Chad, Mali, Mauritania, and Niger formed the Group of Five (G5) Sahel joint force in 2017. The MNJTF and the G5 Sahel forces represent the latest generation of regional security arrangements that started with the AU's regional arrangement against the Lord's Resistance Army. It also drew inspiration from the early successes of the Force Intervention Brigade in the Democratic Republic of Congo, where countries from the SADC region (Southern African Development Community) came together to establish a robust brigade capable of containing and neutralising rebel groups such as the M23.

The trends that seem to be emerging from these experiences, at least in Africa, seem to be that where there is a need to counter a determined insurgency with force, the most effective response that can be mustered is to mobilise countries from the region that have a national security interest in the stability of the region, and whom are thus more willing to use force to counter terrorist or other violent threats, than forces organised via the UN peacekeeping model. And secondly, that by mobilising national forces to operate in their own border regions, and as necessary beyond their own borders in hot pursuit operations or in joint operations, these arrangements solve many of the force generation and use of force type challenges the UN faced elsewhere (see Mats Berdal in this volume).

As I argue in my chapter about Africa's role in peace operations, these adaptations of the UN peacekeeping model in Africa may contribute to an evolution of the international peace and security architecture. In the past, the UN was the sole internationally recognised actor when it came to maintaining international peace and security. In the future, regional organisations like the African Union and European Union are likely to take primary responsibility for maintaining peace and security in their own regions and immediate neighbourhood. The implication is that a new global peace and security architecture is emerging, where the UN, together with regional organisations, where they exist and are capable, are co-managing international peace and security. Thierry Tardy, in his chapter about the role of the European Union, argues that the European Union has embraced a conception of crisis management that is close to the UN's, and is willing to support such a global-regional peace and security partnership. Likewise, the Africa Union has signalled its willingness to increasingly take responsibility for peace and security in Africa. A new global peace and security architecture, based on the principle of regional subsidiarity, may thus be emerging. In the mean-time the AU, EU and UN are cooperating closely in what the HIPPO has referred to as a new era of peacekeeping partnership (UN 2015).

Violent Extremism and Fundamentalist Non-state Actors

The previous Secretary-General of the United Nations, Ban Ki Moon, referred to peacekeeping as the flagship enterprise of the UN (2016a, b). However, he also recognised that UN peacekeeping is under severe pressure. UN peacekeepers are operating in very complex and dangerous environments (van der Lijn and Smit 2015; Karlsrud 2018). The UN mission in Mali (MINUSMA) is a good example of the kind of challenges UN peace operations face today, and by early 2018, it has suffered the highest number of casualties in a UN operation in 20 years. The high number of fatalities and injuries is largely due to asymmetric terrorist attacks on the UN, including the use of improvised explosive devices.

As John Karlsrud argues in this volume, the threats the UN is facing are closely linked to the fact that it is not viewed as an impartial actor by the militant opposition groups, because its mandate involves helping the government in Bamako to extend its authority and control over the North of Mali. This puts the UN in direct confrontation with those armed groups and political factions campaigning for more autonomy for the North, and increasingly now also in the central region of Mali.

Scholars of armed conflict have long noted structural changes in the nature of conflicts, such as the proliferation of so-called new or hybrid war. In the post-Cold War period there is increasingly a blurring of war and crime. Arthur Boutellis and Stephanie Tiélès, in this volume, conclude that despite the recognition by the UN system and Member States that organised crime is a threat to peace and stability, particularly when in conjunction with terrorism and violent extremism, there is still much uncertainty about what the role of a multilateral organisation like the UN should be. In particular, the UN is uncertain about what UN peace operations could and should do about it. The issue has, however, become front and centre with almost three quarter of UN peace operations now operating in environments considered significantly affected by organised crime, particularly in the West Africa and Sahel contexts.

John Karlsrud in his chapter argues that the UN is neither principally nor operationally set up to fight terrorist groups by force. The HIPPO report drew a red line against a role for UN peace operations in counter-terrorism operations, saying that "UN peacekeeping missions, due to their composition and character, are not suited to engage in military counter-terrorism operations. They lack the specific equipment, intelligence, logistics, capabilities and specialized military preparation required, among other aspects" (UN 2015, p. 31). Karlsrud also points out that the Secretary-General has warned against a securitised approach to countering violent extremism, and has outlined a prevention agenda where the main goals must be to better understand the motivations for joining groups such as the IS; avoid using 'terrorism' as a label to eliminate political opposition; and deal with root causes through strengthening governance, the respect for human rights, more accountable institutions, service delivery and political participation. Kari Osland also points out in her chapter that the UN may be better served with a greater emphasis on trust-building in the local police rather than continued focus on the security aspects of their task.

Karlsrud, de Coning and others in this volume point out that coalitions of the willing, and in some instances regional organisations, seem to be the only mechanisms with the requisite political will, capabilities and staying power to conduct counter-terrorism operations. They point out however, that defeating violent extremism is not ultimately about military strength. Rather, it needs a holistic approach that addresses the root causes and drivers of the conflict. The comparative advantage of the UN lies in its convening power and impartiality, and its ability to provide and coordinate comprehensive support across the spectrum from its peace and security, development, and human rights pillars.

The implications for the future of UN peace operations are that UN peace operations are likely to be deployed in countries and regions where violent extremism and transnational organised crimes are dominant features of the security landscape (Williams 2016). However, it is unlikely that UN peace operations will be mandated to undertake counter-terror operations. It is more likely that they will accompany, or coexist alongside, other forces that do have such a role. In such contexts UN peace operations are likely to focus on seeking political solutions while using its development and peacebuilding pillars to support state and social institutions and civil society.

Greater Emphasis on People-Centred Peace Operations

UN peace operations have long been criticised for being too state-centric. They are deployed by a multilateral body of states, their military and police officers and units are contributed by states, and they are reliant on an international legal framework that enable their presence through formal status of forces and status of mission agreements between the UN and the host state. Since especially the end of the Cold War, many individual Special Representative of the Secretary-General and other mission leaders have taken steps to reach out to civil society and community leaders, and since the late 1990s UN peace operations have a civilian component—Civil Affairs—dedicated to sub-national outreach. However, these efforts were not enough to counter the many other drivers and incentives that ensured that UN peace operations were more sensitive to the needs of the host state, and other states in the international system, than to the people they were ultimately there to protect and serve.

As Youssef Mahmoud points out in his chapter in this volume, reaching out to people and engaging with local communities and ordinary citizens are common practices in many peace operations. However, these practices tended to take the form of ad hoc activities, without sufficient strategic focus or intent. Many community engagement activities remain mission-centric (e.g. winning hearts and minds of local populations) or as appendices to various state-centric goals such as restoring and extending state authority.

As emphasised in the HIPPO, the peacebuilding review, and the twin sustaining peace resolutions, for peace to be self-sustainable, it has to emerge from local social processes and it has to build on the social resilience that is already present in societies and communities (see also Jonathan Agensky in this volume). The implications for UN peace operations are that they should find new ways to contribute to broader international and local efforts that facilitate the re-emergence of the informal norms of behaviour and shared beliefs of societies and communities that are essential for institutions to be locally owned and embedded.

To sustain peace, UN peace operations thus have to develop new tools and capacities to engage not only with the state, but also with societies, communities and individual people. These need to include strong principled leadership, supported by the capacity to monitor the missions' actions and the effect they have on local communities and the everyday lives of the people they are meant to assist (Autesserre 2014). Missions should involve representatives of the societies they are working with when undertaking assessments, analysis, planning, programming, and evaluation. The nature of the involvement will depend on the context, but the principle of giving society maximum agency to influence the work of the mission, should be a general principle that guide people-centred peace operations. Missions should identify people that are generally perceived to be credible voices for their communities, such as traditional, civil society, religious and academic leaders, and involve them in the mission's engagement with its host society in a variety of ways.

Two groups that require special attention are women and youth. The HIPPO, the peacebuilding review, the Women, Peace and Security review, and the twin sustaining peace resolutions, all reaffirm the indispensable role of women in peacekeeping and peacebuilding. In particular they recognize the substantial link between women's full and meaningful involvement in efforts to prevent and resolve conflict, and those efforts' effectiveness and long-term sustainability. The larger the gender gap between the treatment of men and women in a society, the more likely it is that a country will experience conflict (United Nations and World Bank 2018, p. 30).

In recognition of the critical role that women play in all peace and security efforts, including in the UN, the new Secretary-General, António Guterres, has launched an initiative to encourage troop and police contributing countries to increase the number of women deployed in military and police contingents. At the same time, he recognizes that it is not just about the number of women in peacekeeping but also the role they play. He has set the example by, for the first time, achieving gender parity in all his senior appointments. The Secretariat has launched a senior women talent pipeline initiative to increase the number of women in senior peacekeeping positions.

The HIPPO and other reviews also recognizes the important role youth can play in the prevention and resolution of conflicts and as key driver of sustainability and inclusiveness. The Independent Progress Study on Youth and Peace and Security (United Nations 2018) provides a framework for partnering with and investing in young people to prevent violence, to promote their inclusion and to translate the demographic dividend into a peace dividend. The report recommends three mutually reinforcing strategies: First, it is critical to invest in young people's capacities, agency and leadership through substantial funding support, network-building and capacity-strengthening, recognizing the full diversity of youth and the ways young people organise. Second, systems that reinforce exclusion must be transformed in order to address the structural barriers limiting youth participation in peace and security. Third, partnerships and collaborative action where young people are viewed as equal and essential partners for peace must be prioritised.

The literature on the "local turn"' in peace operations has highlighted the importance of local voices, but it has also presented a powerful critique of the potential challenges of focusing on the local (Mac Ginty and Richmond 2013; Mahmoud and Agensky in this volume). Peace operations should not be naïve about the potentially challenging features of traditional forms of authority that can represent persistent structures of inequality. Local culture is important, but can also be a limiting factor or an element used to perpetuate systems of domination: "local actors and contexts can be partisan, discriminatory, exclusive and violent (as can international actors)" (Mac Ginty and Richmond 2013, p. 770).

There is still disagreement among some member states whether peace operations should be engaging directly with societies and people, grounded in concerns about how this could potentially undermine the authority of the host government. Few member states disagree that UN peace operations should continue to have the government as its principal partner. However, as the HIPPO pointed out, if sustainable and durable peace remains the main goal of peace operations, then enhancing state-society relations must be front and centre among the tasks that peace operations are supposed to carry out (UN 2015, p. 66). While, as pointed out above, many of the rising powers and emerging economies are likely to favour state-centric peace operations that do not prescribe a specific set of internationally agreed norms, most will likely agree that the ultimate aim of the UN should be to foster and support resilient societies.

At the same time, global civil society is also increasing in influence, and taken together with the spread of mobile phones and access to social media, the implications of the picture that is emerging is that UN peace operations will also increasingly be under pressure to be relevant and accountable to ordinary people, both in the countries where they are deployed, and in the rest of the world.

The pressure on UN peace operations to become more people-centred are thus likely to be irreversible and relentless. There are many ways in which UN peace operations can become more people-centred, including by involving representative advisory groups from civil society and local communities in assessments, analysis, planning, implementation, and evaluation, so as to ensure continuous direct input and feedback from the society on the work of the peace operation.

Conclusion: Evolution, Adaptation, and Resilience

Our core finding is that the increasing influence of China and several other new actors from the global South in the global governance system, has already started too, and is likely to continue to, generate *a more pragmatic era of UN peace operations*. This implies a shift away from using peace operations to help countries adopt neo-liberal-style institutions. In its place, peace operations are likely to become less intrusive and to become more supportive of locally-led and bottom-up solutions. At the same time, UN peace operations as an institution and a form of international conflict resolution is under increasing pressure. It needs to adapt its operations to a rise in violent conflict characterised by violent extremism and transnational organised crime. It must also reduce expenditures, improve effectiveness, and find new ways to improve internal accountability, in order to prevent scandals such as some of its peacekeepers sexually abusing the very people the UN is meant to protect. These internal or technical pressures, together with turbulence introduced by the transitions underway in the global order, has introduced a period of flux during which significant innovation and experimentation, including with new forms of peace operations, is possible.

In the various contributions to this edited volume, three main themes stand out. These—strategic political coherence, the employment of force, and the limits of peace operations—will drive the evolution of UN peace operations in the coming decades.

First, strategic political coherence relates to the HIPPO's emphasis on the primacy of politics, that is the recognition that peace operations always serve a political purpose, and that there is rarely a sustainable solution that does not boil down ultimately to a negotiated political agreement (see Adam Day in this volume). However, strategic coherence also refers to the new reality that the UN, and UN peace operations, will rarely, if ever, operate on its own in the future. In every theatre it will operate alongside other international and regional actors, each with its own mandate, responsibility, and comparative advantages. The HIPPO framed it as a new era of networked peace operations. The UN system, and UN peace operations, now need to adapt to this new reality and develop the capacity to play its role, which may often include the convening role, in a network of national and international efforts.

In this new system-of-systems reality, several international actors, including the World Bank and other regional development banks, bilateral donors, the EU, and other regional organisations each play an important role alongside national and local actors. It is the combined and cumulative role of all of these national and international actors together that constitute the larger political project. UN peace operations need to understand its role in this larger political project, and it needs to have the capacity to support the effort necessary to coordinate, track and take stock of this larger political project. The complexity of maintaining overall strategic political coherence among these various systems-within-systems should not be underestimated. Nor can it be avoided as it is the organising feature of global governance in the twenty-first century. The performance of UN peace operations will thus not be judged only on the ability of the mission to carry out its own civilian, police, and military tasks. Nor will it be enough to be integrated with the rest of the UN system. In future, effectiveness will also depend on the degree to which a UN peace operation contributes to the strategic political coherence of the larger national and international effort to sustain the peace in a given country or region.

Second, the employment of force seems to remain one of the key defining challenges of UN peace operations. How force is employed in UN peace operations is one of the key features that distinguishes it from AU, EU and NATO peace support operations. As Mateja Peter points out in this volume, the principled approach to the use of force in UN peace operations has been one of its most resilient features. Whenever the UN has deviated from this norm, for instance in the 1960s during the ONUC mission in the Congo, or more recently in the Central African Republic, the Democratic Republic of the Congo, and Mali, the norm seems to be validated and reinforced. This does not mean that the

Security Council is unlikely to continue to task UN peace operations, as a last resort, with enforcement or stabilisation operations (de Coning et al. 2017). It does imply, however, that the principled approach to UN peace operations, including the minimum use of force principle, is likely to remain one of the defining features of UN peace operations (Mats Berdal in this volume and Karlsrud 2018). As discussed earlier in this concluding chapter, not only are rising powers like China and India in favour of maintaining this principled approach, but the HIPPO has also argued against utilising peace operations in counter-terrorism and other enforcement roles, on the basis that the inherent features of UN peace operations, including its globally diverse force generation structure, its civilian logistics chain, its multilateral financing system and its political command and control mechanism, make it unfit for combat operations.

Third, debates about what the outer limits of UN peace operations should be, seems to be one of the features of UN peace operations that is constantly adapting to changing requirements. When peacekeeping started it was mostly unarmed or lightly armed military observers or units that implemented and monitored cease-fire agreements. More complex tasks were added over time, including supporting the implementation of comprehensive peace agreements, facilitating the birth of new states, and the protection of civilians. Police and civilian experts were added and peacekeeping became multi-dimensional. During the unipolar era, UN peace operations became a key facilitator for the adoption of neo-liberal state institutions. UN peace operations organised elections, oversaw the writing of new constitutions, helped to develop rule of law and promoted western-style multiparty democratic models. While several peacekeeping missions ended successfully during this period in places like Angola, Cambodia, Guatemala, Mozambique and Namibia, criticism started mounting in the 2000s against the seeming inability of mission like the UN mission in the Democratic Republic of the Congo and the joint AU and UN mission in Darfur to reach a fitting end.

Together with increasing pressure on the funding of peace operations questions are increasingly being raised about the scope of peace operations. Why do some contemporary peacekeeping missions have responsibility for justice, police and corrections and other governance functions? Should they have human rights mandates? Why is the support for elections part of UN peace operation missions, why should it not be the role of, for instance, the UN Development Programme (UNDP)? Thus far the reasons why many of these functions were included in UN peace operations seem to have more to do with the assessed contribution funding model of UN peace operations than with any theory of change model. Many of these efforts are simultaneously also supported by UN agencies, funds, and programmes, as well as other bilateral donors, regional organisations, and international and national NGOs. This debate seems to be leaning towards the side that argues for a new era of limited UN peace operations, where these operations should be focused on fewer priority areas, mainly protection, stability, and politics, organised around functions unique to UN peace operations, or at least functions that UN peace operations have a comparative advantage in. This debate will be one of the most important debates for UN peace operations in the years to come. It is also likely to be one of the most contentious, because it has financial implications, it involves the roles of other UN agencies, and also because member states have widely divergent opinions about what the role of UN peace operations should be.

While one of the characteristics of UN peace operations has been the resilience of the idea, defined by its three core principles, another has been the continuous evolution of the specific manifestations of that idea into practice. UN peace operations have shown a proven capacity to continuously adapt to new challenges. If there is one thing we can predict with a fair amount of certainty, then it is that UN peace operations will continue to adapt and evolve in response to changes in the global order, to the way the nature of conflict develops, and to the internal reforms in the UN system, and yet it will also remain resiliently identifiable as UN peace operations.

References

Autesserre, Séverine. 2014. *Peaceland: Conflict Resolution and the Everyday Politics of International Intervention.* Cambridge: Cambridge University Press.

Boutellis, Arthur, and Lesley Connolly. 2016. *The State of UN Peace Operations Reform: An Implementation Scorecard.* New York: International Peace Institute.

Call, Charles T., and Cedric de Coning (eds.). 2017. *Rising Powers and Peacebuilding.* London: Palgrave.

de Coning, Cedric, and Chander Prakash. 2016. *Peace Capacities Network Synthesis Report: Rising Powers and Peace Operations.* Oslo: Norwegian Institute of International Affairs.

de Coning, Cedric, and Eli Stamnes (eds.). 2016. *UN Peacebuilding Architecture: The First Ten Years.* Abingdon: Routledge.

de Coning, Cedric, Chiyuki Aoi, and John Karlsrud (eds.). 2017. *UN Peacekeeping Doctrine in a New Era: Adapting to Stabilisation, Protection and New Threats.* New York: Routledge.

de Coning, Cedric, Thomas Mandrup, and Liselotte Odgaard (eds.). 2015. *The BRICS and Coexistence: An Alternative Vision of World Order.* Abingdon: Routledge.

Karlsrud, John. 2018. *The UN at War: Peace Operations in a New Era.* London: Palgrave.

Mac Ginty, Roger, and Oliver P. Richmond. 2013. The Local Turn in Peace Building: Acritical Agenda for Peace. *Third World Quarterly* 34 (5): 763–783.

Peter, Mateja. 2015. Between Doctrine and Practice: The United Nations Peacekeeping Dilemma. *Global Governance: A Review of Multilateralism and International Organizations* 21 (3): 351–370.

Rappa, Ryan. 2018. Reversing the Trend: UN Peacekeeping in 2017. *Global Peace Operations Review.* In Focus, March 27.

Richmond, Oliver P. 2004. UN Peace Operations and the Dilemmas of the Peacebuilding Consensus. *International Peacekeeping* 11 (1): 83–101.

Stamnes, Eli, and Kari Osland. 2016. *Synthesis Report: Reviewing UN Peace Operations, the UN Peacebuilding Architecture and the Implementation of UNSC 1325.* Oslo: NUPI.

United Nations. 2015. *Uniting Our Strengths for Peace—Politics, Partnerships and People, Report of the High-Level Independent Panel on United Nations Peace Operations.* New York: United Nations.

United Nations. 2016a. *United Nations General Assembly Resolution 70/262.* New York: United Nations.

United Nations. 2016b. *United Nations Security Council Resolution 2282.* New York: United Nations.

United Nations. 2018. *The Missing Peace: Independent Progress Study on Youth and Peace and Security.* New York: United Nations.

United Nations, and World Bank. 2018. *Pathways for Peace: Inclusive Approaches to Preventing Violent Conflict.* Washington, DC: World Bank.

van der Lijn, Jaïr, and Timo Smit. 2015. *Peacekeepers Under Threat? Fatality Trends in UN Peace Operations.* Stockholm: Stockholm International Peace Research Institute.

Williams, Paul. 2016. *The Peace Operations Challenge for the Next Secretary-General.* New York: International Peace Institute Global Observatory.

Open Access This chapter is licensed under the terms of the Creative Commons Attribution 4.0 International License (http://creativecommons.org/licenses/by/4.0/), which permits use, sharing, adaptation, distribution and reproduction in any medium or format, as long as you give appropriate credit to the original author(s) and the source, provide a link to the Creative Commons license and indicate if changes were made.

The images or other third party material in this chapter are included in the chapter's Creative Commons license, unless indicated otherwise in a credit line to the material. If material is not included in the chapter's Creative Commons license and your intended use is not permitted by statutory regulation or exceeds the permitted use, you will need to obtain permission directly from the copyright holder.

Index

© The Editor(s) (if applicable) and The Author(s) 2019

C. de Coning and M. Peter (eds.), *United Nations Peace Operations in a Changing Global Order*, https://doi.org/10.1007/978-3-319-99106-1

www.ingramcontent.com/pod-product-compliance
Lightning Source LLC
LaVergne TN
LVHW080022210926
848481LV00011B/3082
* 9 7 8 1 0 1 3 2 7 5 9 2 0 *